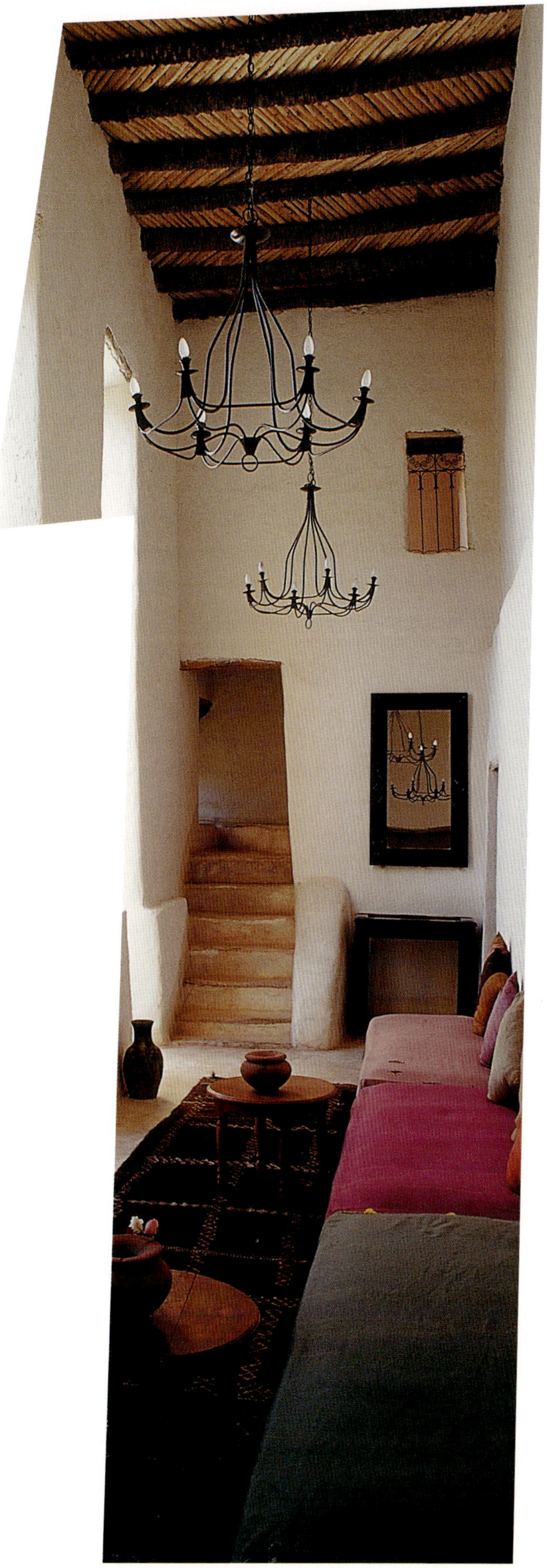

2

3

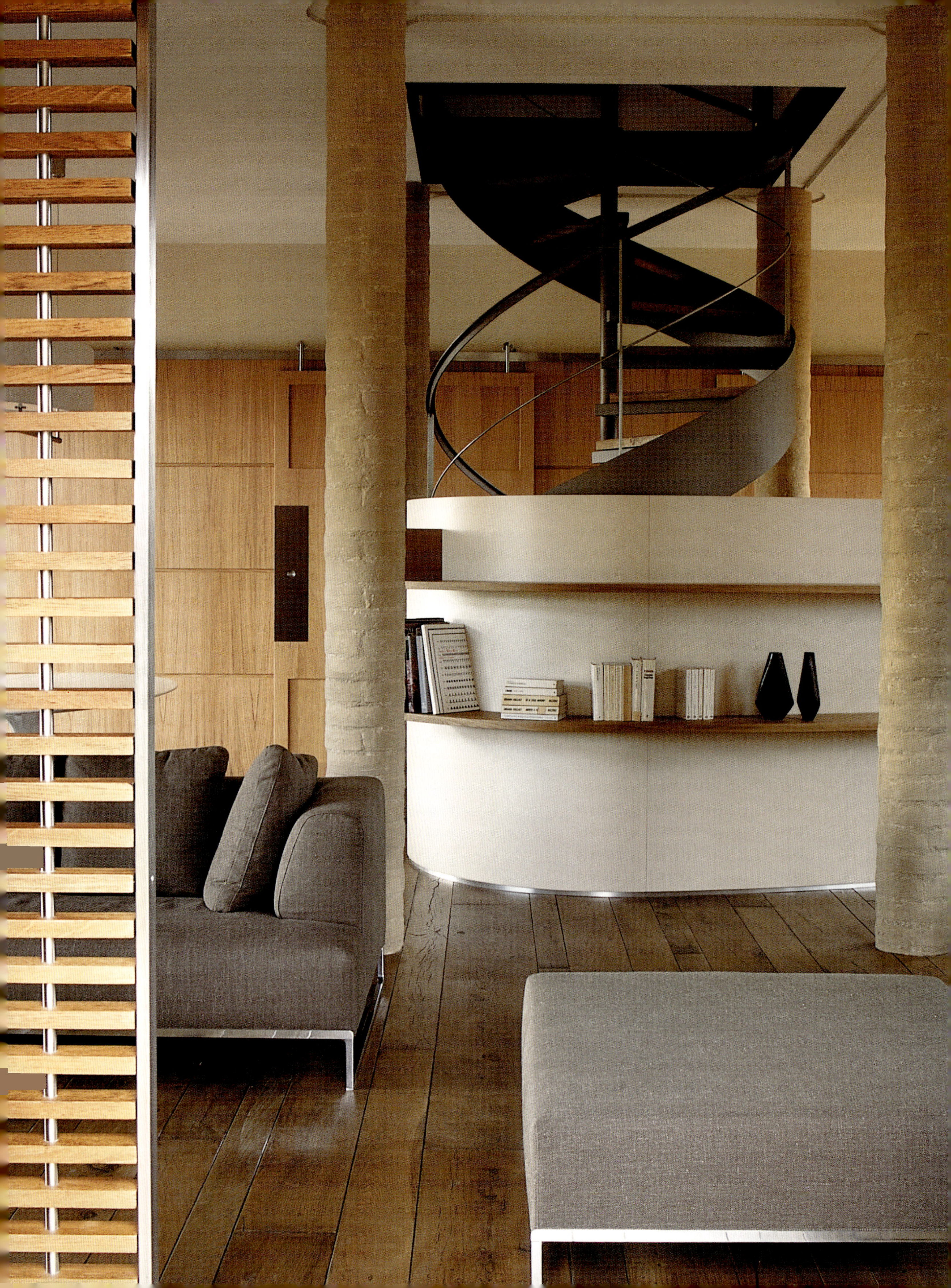

STAFFORD CLIFF
1000
ホームデザイン BOOK

スタッフォード・クリフ　著

クリスチャン・サラモン　写真

今井 由美子　翻訳

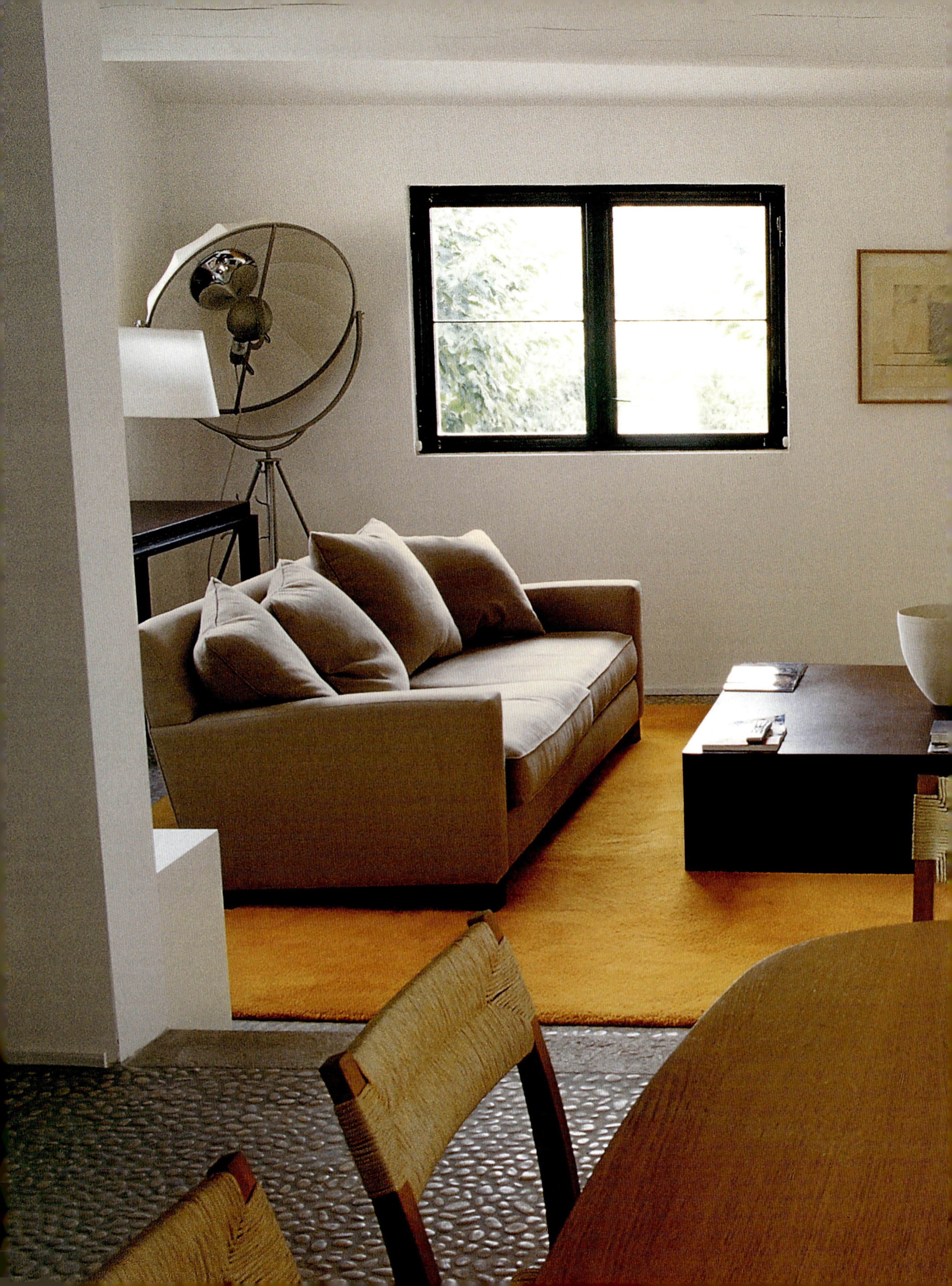

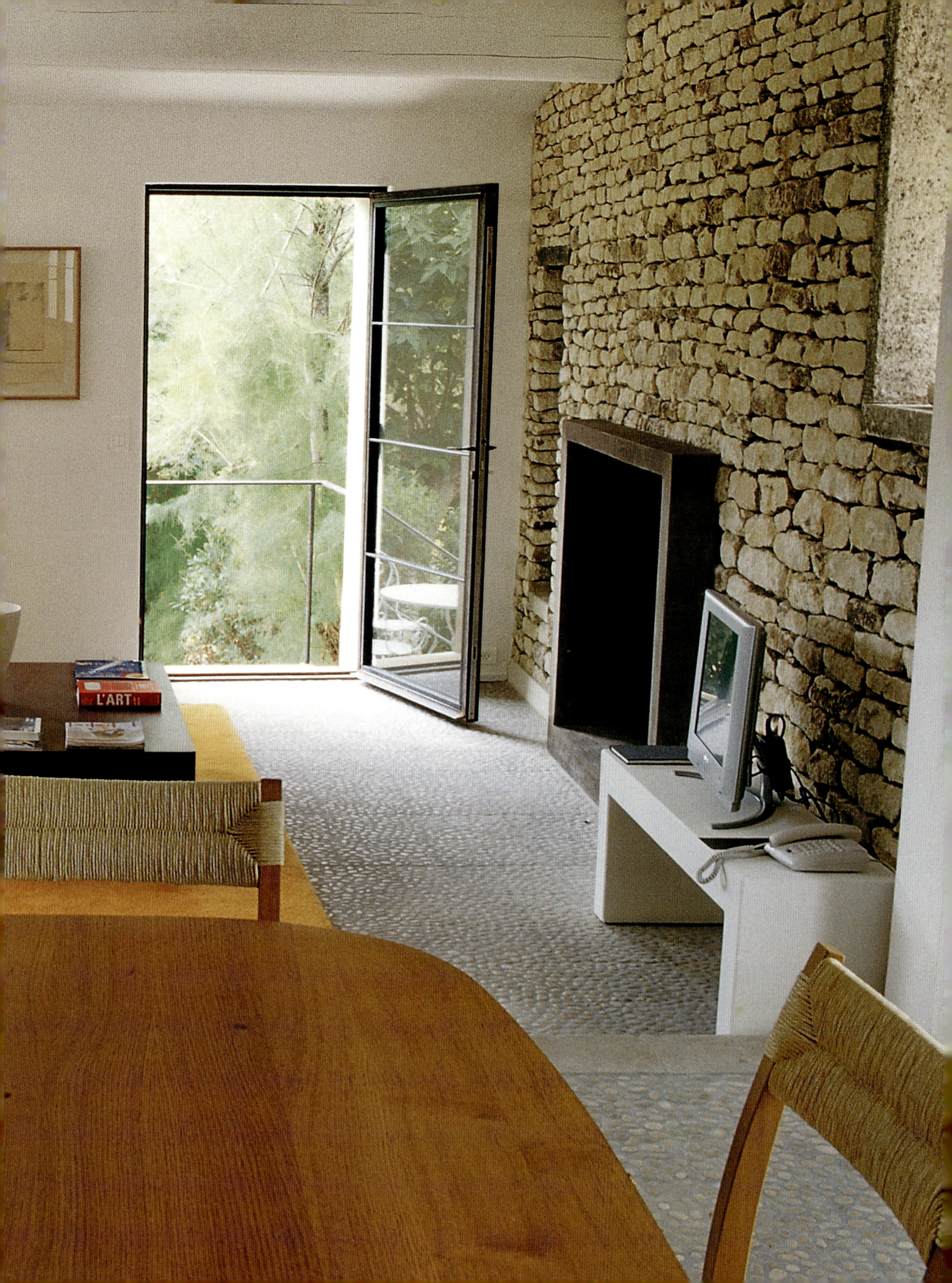
L'ART

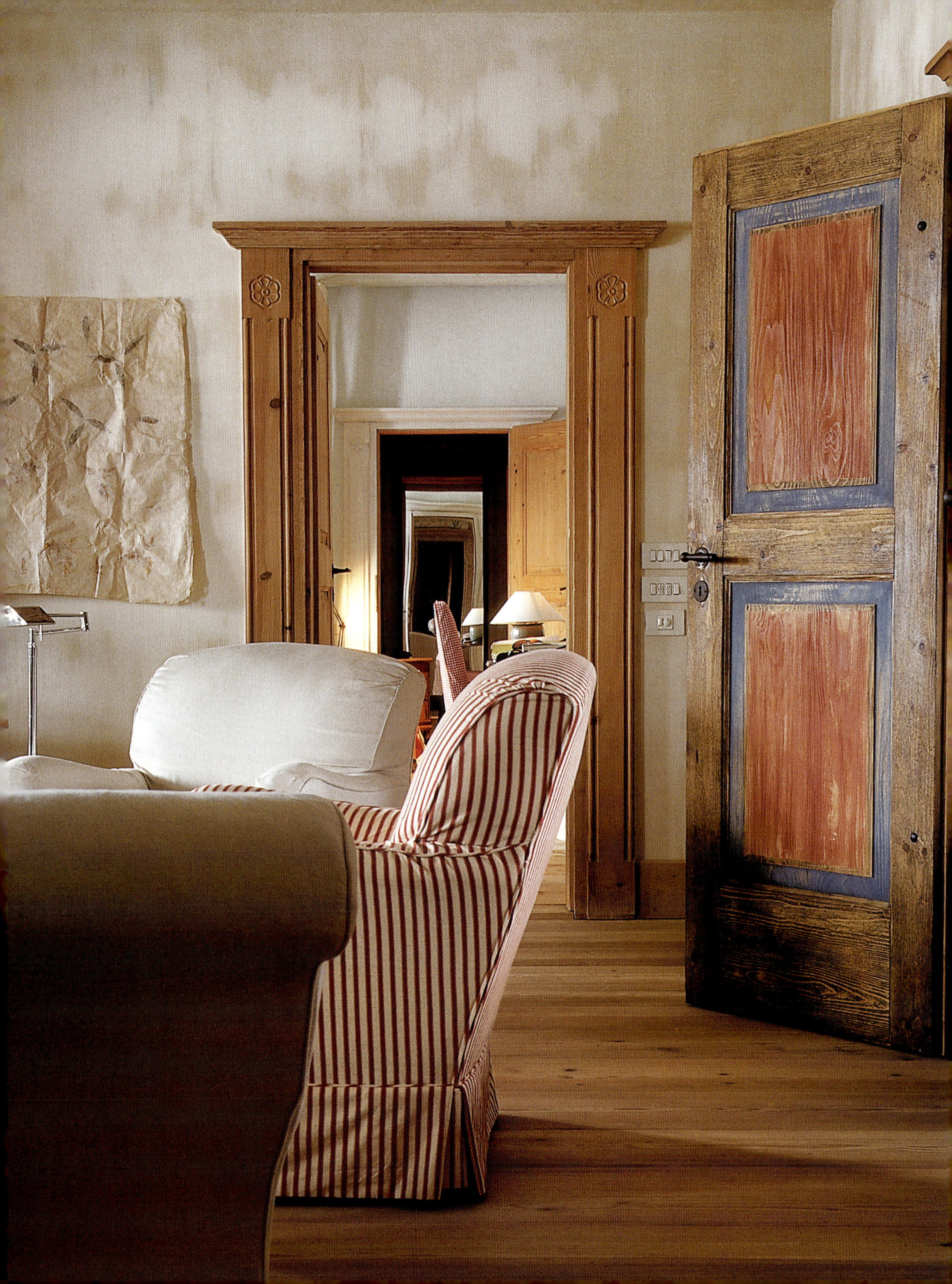

はじめに　10

ドアと窓　12

床　34

階段と手すり　52

調理と食事　68

書棚・オープン棚　88

戸棚・食器棚　104

プライベートコーナー　118

壁の装飾　134

暖炉　144

色と素材感　162

開放感　192

はじめに

誰しも自分の家について考えをめぐらせます。子どもの頃に個室を与えられると、その部屋が自分の世界になります。すぐに、自分なりに部屋を飾り始め、自分の城にしてしまったことでしょう。家を出る時は、新たな住まい作りの出発点です。これからの生活に必要な物は何か、すべて自分自身で決断を下さねばなりません。怖じ気づく人もいるでしょうし、ワクワクして、買い物に飛んで行く人もいるでしょう。しかし、店で手に入れられないものもあります。それは、アイデアです。新しい家は、どんな床でしょうか？ カーペット、マット、それともフローリング？ 石や、レンガかもしれませんね。床は元のまま引き続き使うことになるでしょうし、空間の広さや、以前の家主の好みに関しては、変えようもありません。たとえ自分好みに直したいと思っても、床、壁、天井、階段を取り替えることは不可能かもしれません。けれども、一部を塗り直したり、交換したり、移動させたりする必要は、きっと出てきます。たとえばドアや窓を替えたり、ホームオフィスを作ったり、バスルームを広げることはできそうです。それが、自分の手に余るほどの大仕事だったとしても、あきらめないでください。改装の目的がはっきりしているなら、地元の工務店や職人に仕事を頼むのはたやすいことです。どんな内装にするか、それはすべて選択の問題であり、選択せねばならないことは山ほどあります。自分たちの選んだ物ひとつひとつが、自分や、パートナーまたは両親の個性を語り始めるでしょう。新しい家に住み始めた時だけでなく、引っ越したり、リフォームしたりと、住まい作りをする間ずっと、覚悟しておかねばならないことがあります。自分を取り巻く状況や、収入は変わるということです。どんな家でどう暮らすか──この自らへの問いは、いつまでも続くものですが、答えは必ずあります。1000以上のインテリアの実例が本書に掲載されています。どれも、フランスのすばらしい写真家、クリスチャン・サラモンの作品です。彼はアイデアにあふれた世界中の住宅を、30年にわたってカメラに収め続けています。

Everybody thinks about their home. When you're young, if you have your own room, it becomes your world, and you soon set about personalising it, making it your private domain. When you leave home, you start to create another one – and you wonder how you're going to manage with all the decisions you'll need to make. Some folk dread it, and others just can't wait to go shopping. But not everything is available from a shop. You'll need ideas, too. What type of floor will you have: carpets, mats, rugs or floorboards? Stone or brick, maybe? You will inherit some of the elements, and certain decisions will be made for you – by the space or the previous owners. No matter, you'll want to tailor it to your needs. Maybe you can't change the floors, the walls, the ceilings or the staircase, but you'll almost certainly need to repaint or replace some things, move them about – doors, perhaps, or even windows; an extension, a home office, a bigger bathroom. Even if the task is too big for you to undertake yourself, don't be put off. If you know the effect you want, you can easily find a local builder or craftsman to do it for you. It's all a matter of choices, and there will be dozens of them; each one you make will say something about you, or your partner – or your parents. A terrifying prospect, and one you'll need to be prepared for – not only at the start of your homemaking life, but throughout it; when you move, or when you refurnish – as your circumstances, your influences, or your income changes. The questions go on and on – but so do the answers – over 1000 of them, all collected here in the work of the brilliant French photographer Christian Sarramon – who has spent 30 years photographing some of the most extraordinary, ideas-filled homes in the world.

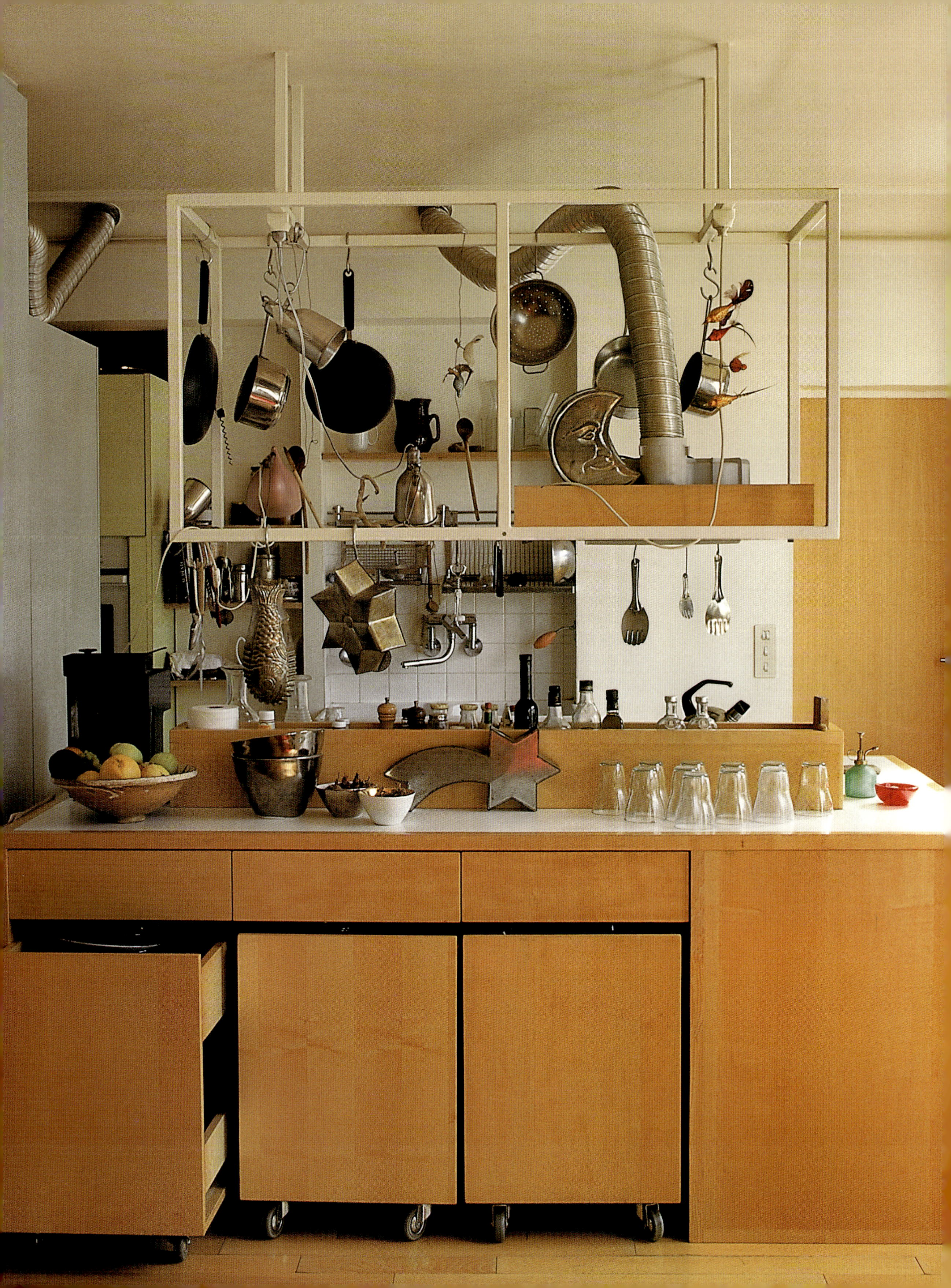

ドアと窓

Openings & Closings

引越しや、家の購入を考えている時、その家の少し癖のあるディテールが、引っ越し計画を進めるか、それとも止めるかの決め手になり得ることを、皆さんご存じだと思います。一風変わった窓があったり、天井を縁取るモールディングがかわいらしかったり、珍しいデザインだったり、見映えの良いドアが付いていたりすれば、住まいはより個性的になり、結果的に、手に入れたい物になるのです。もし空間を広げるために、造作を取り外そうとしているのなら、初めてその家を目にした時に、心惹かれたその家の個性まで、なくしてしまわないよう、気をつけてください。その家のドアが気に入らない場合は、折りたたむタイプか、スライドタイプのガラスドアに、替えてみてはいかがでしょう。フレームのあるガラスドアでも、良いかもしれません。伝統的な家に、モダンな玄関ドアを組み合わせると、ダイナミックな効果が得られます。窓に関しては、あまり必要ないと思われる場所にあると、人の興味をそそります。珍しい形の窓枠や付属品も同様です。たとえば円形の窓は、常に特別な印象があり、カラーガラスや、模様入りガラスの窓も、とても人目を引きます。もし、これと言った特徴のある窓が付いていなくても、がっかりしなくていいのです。ほんの少し想像力を働かせれば、自然光を採り入れたい場所に、窓を作ることができます。古い窓枠すら、簡単に手に入れることができます。もしそれが難しければ、窓の装飾を工夫してみてください。たとえば、羽根板のブラインド、ビーズのカーテン、美しいアンティークのレース、木製のシャッターなどは、既成のカーテンの代わりとして、窓を個性的に演出します。また、曇りガラスを取り入れるのもいいでしょう。曇りガラスなら、貴重な自然光を遮ることなく、プライバシーを守ることができます。

When we're looking to move or buy a new property, we all know that the quirky little details in a house can be the difference between a 'yes' and a 'no'. An interesting window, pretty or unusual ceiling mouldings or nice-looking doors will make a place more individual and, therefore, more desirable – and, if you're ripping everything out to give yourself extra space, take care not to remove those features that attracted you in the first place. If your doors are not great, consider replacing them with folding, sliding or even framed glass doors. A modern front door on a traditional house can create a dynamic effect. Windows where you don't expect them are intriguing, as are unusually shaped frames or fittings. Round windows, for instance, always look special, as do those with coloured or patterned glass. If you don't have a feature window, don't let that stop you. With a bit of inspiration, you can add one where you would most like some extra light, and it's easy to pick up a reclaimed window frame. Failing that, think 'outside the box' about window treatments: slatted blinds, beaded curtains, pretty vintage lace or even wooden shutters will make a more individual alternative to off-the-peg curtains. Or consider using frosted glass – so that you can ensure your privacy without losing your precious light.

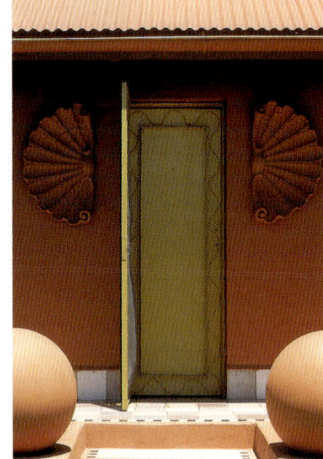

ドアと窓

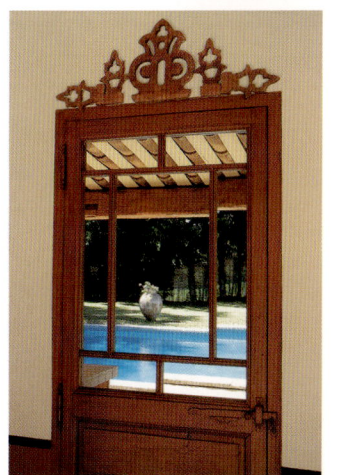

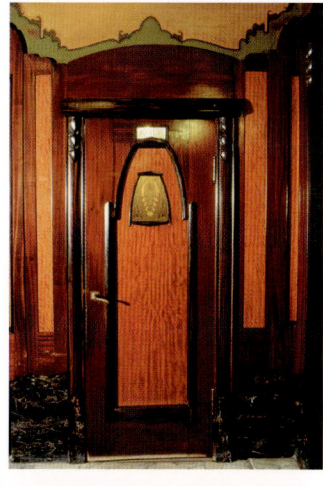

ドアと窓

ドアと窓

ドアと窓

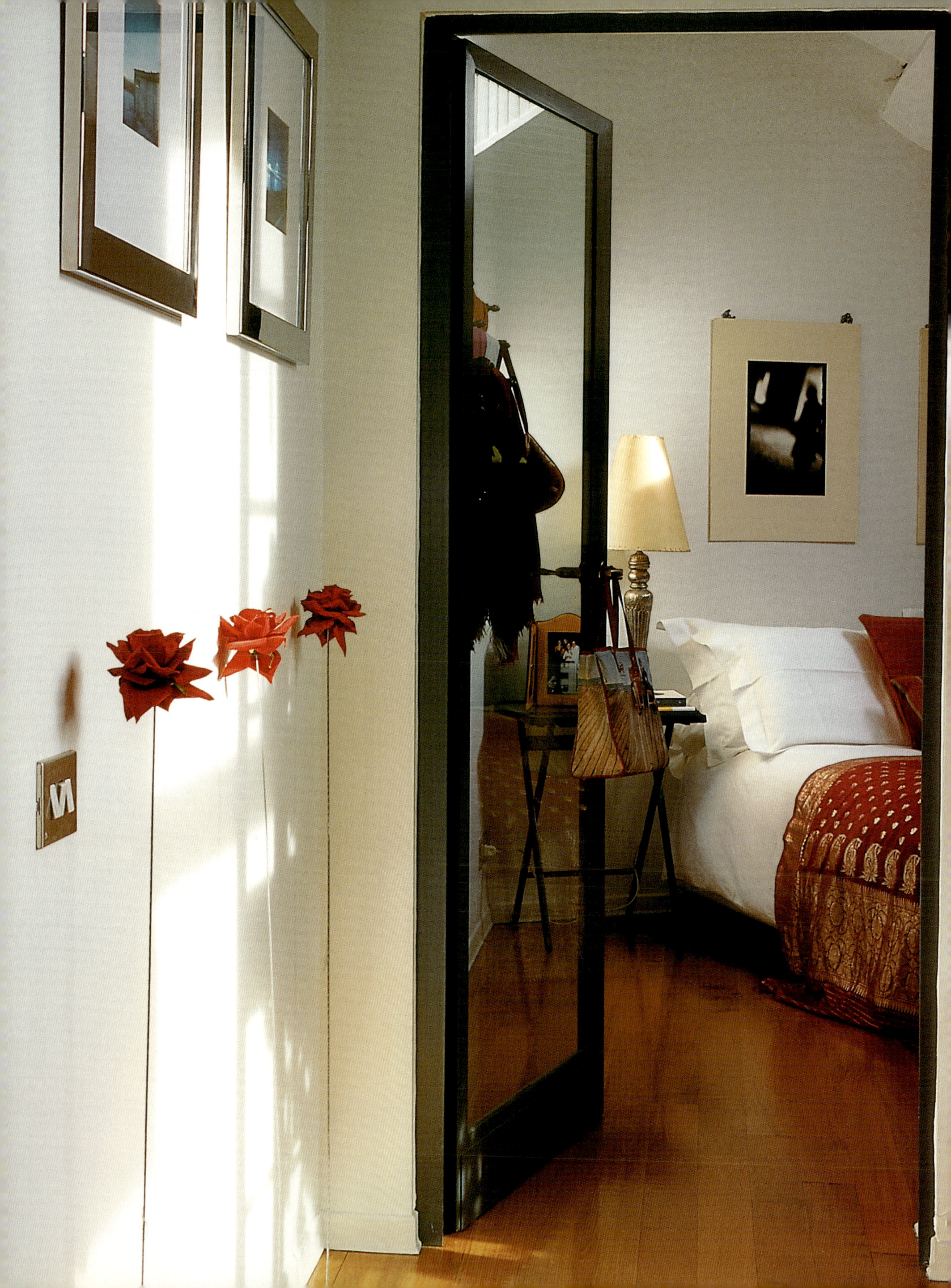

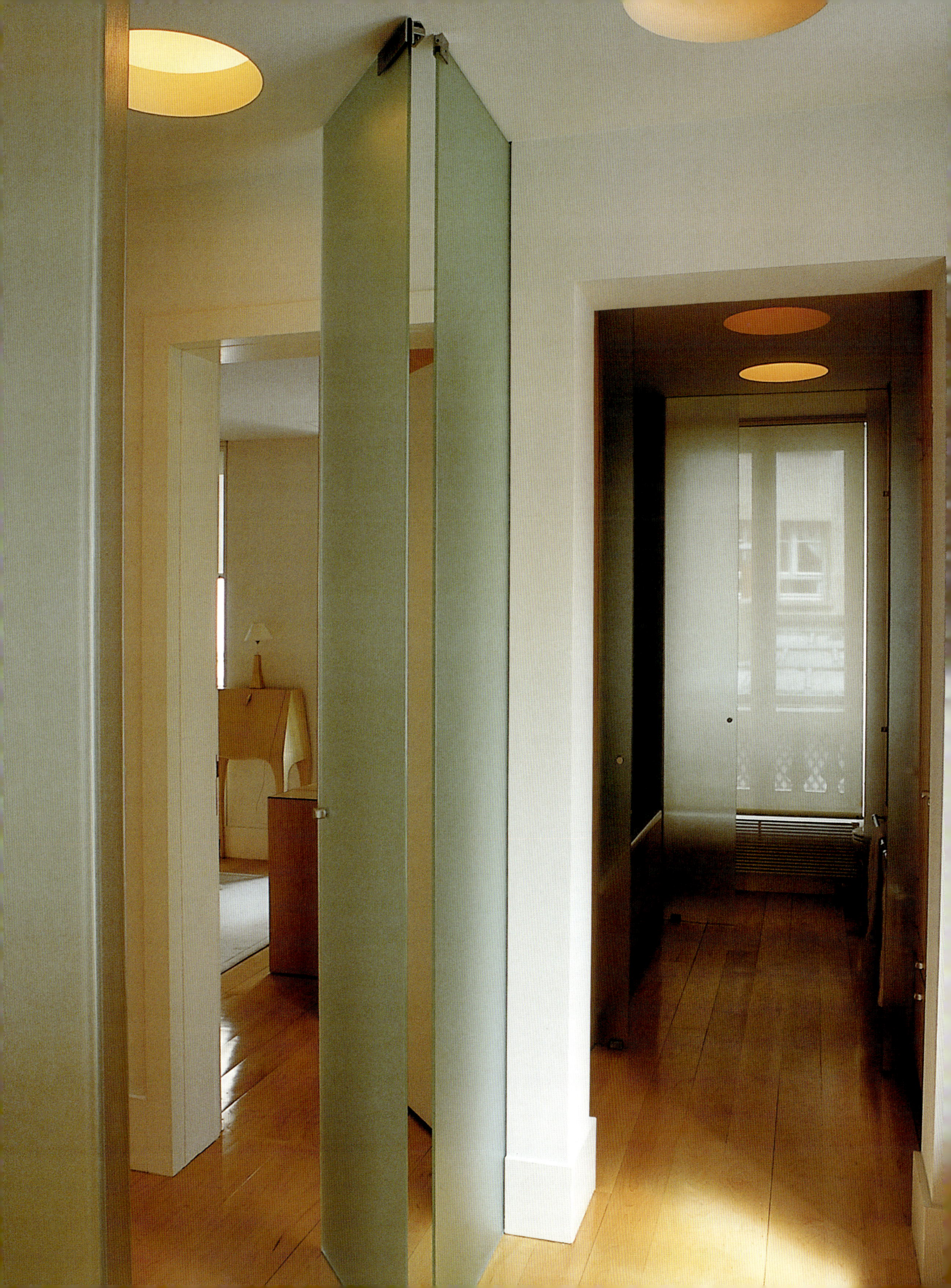

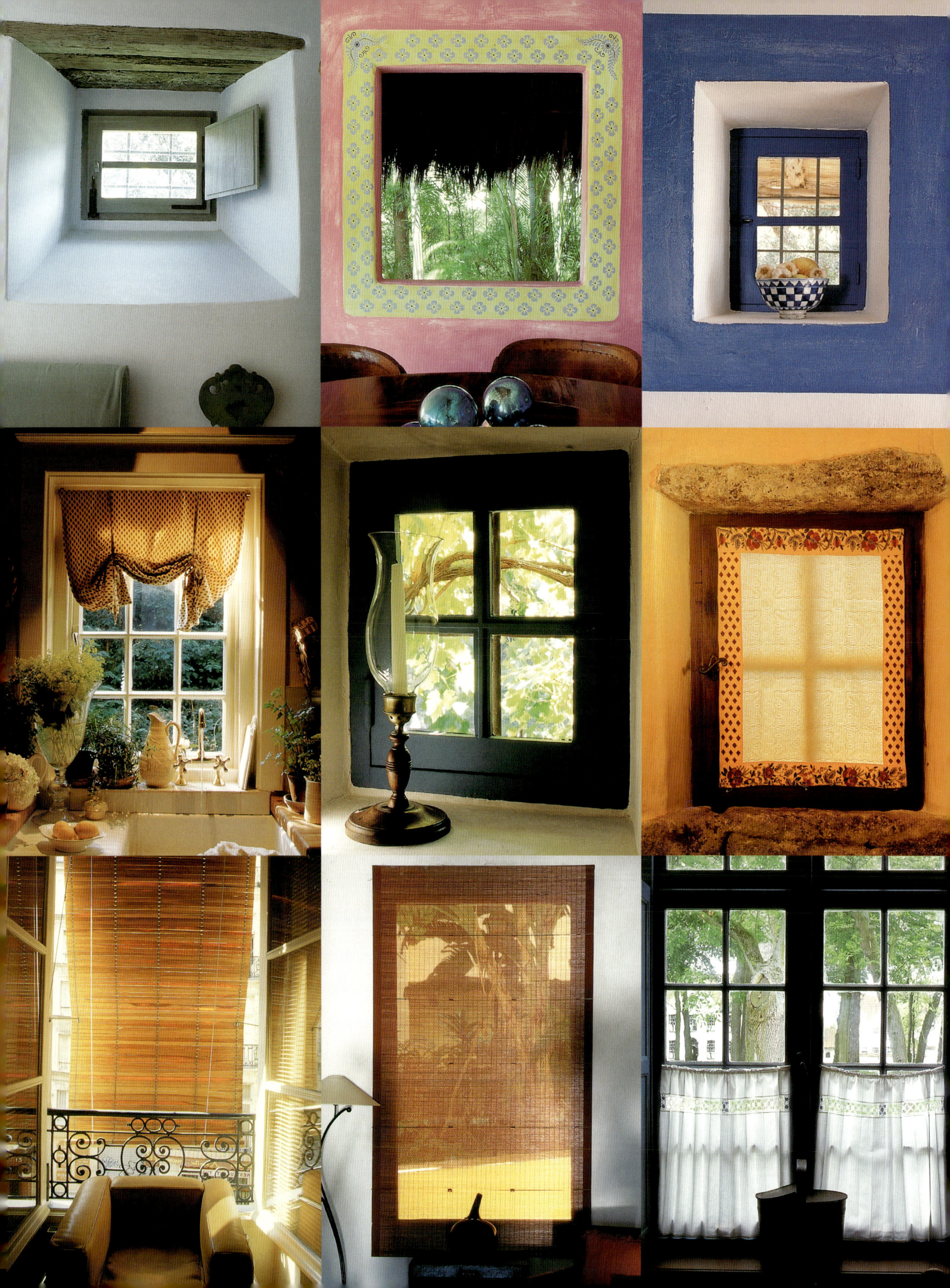

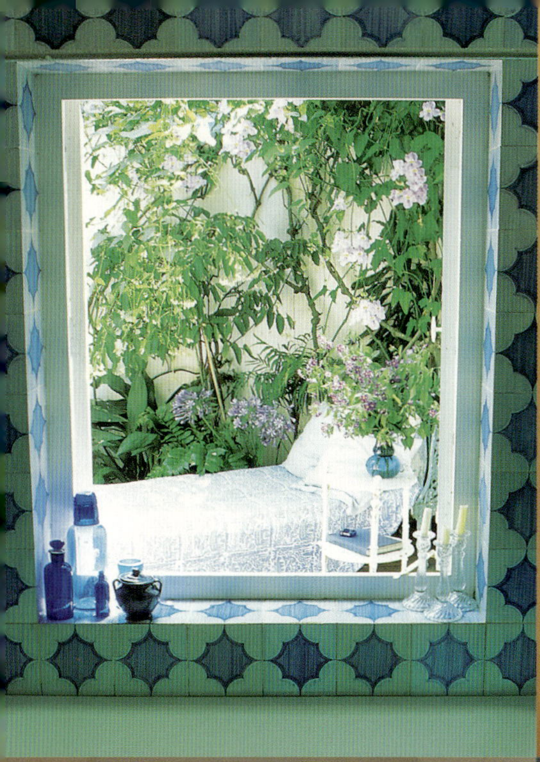
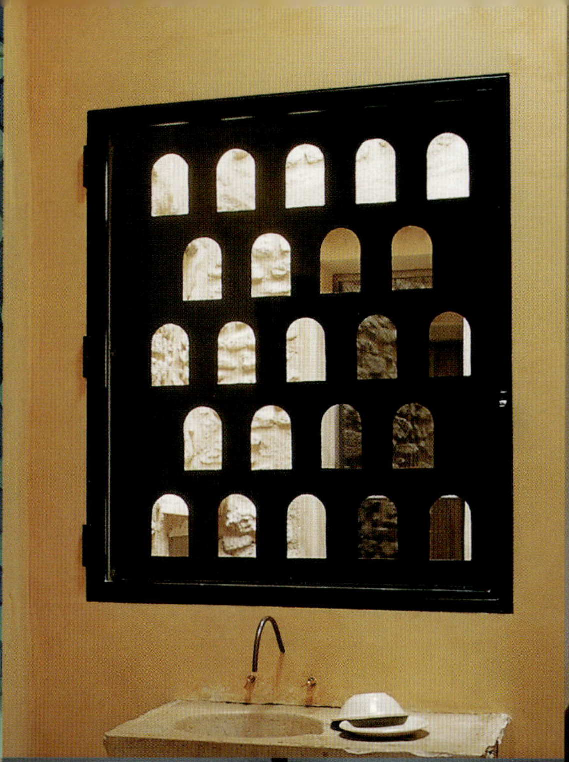
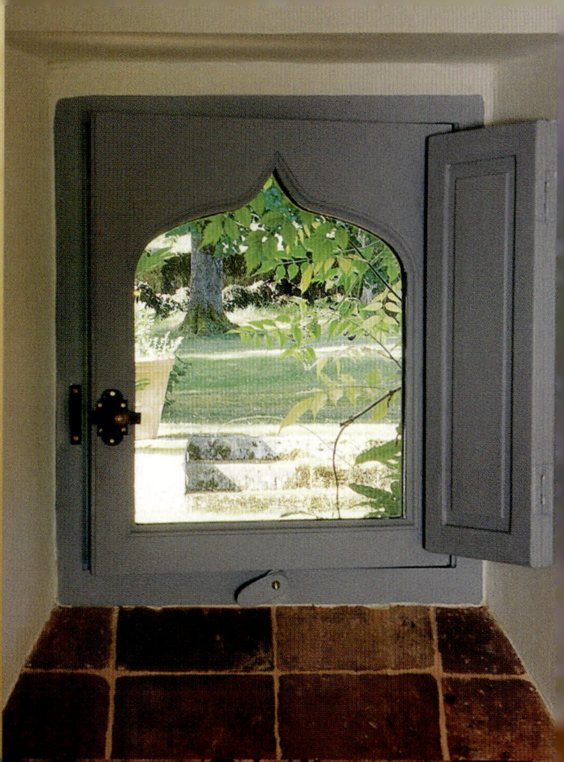
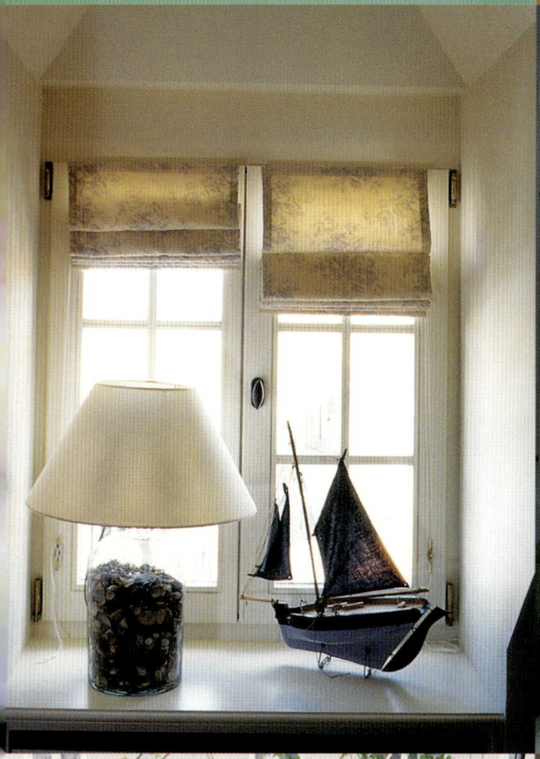
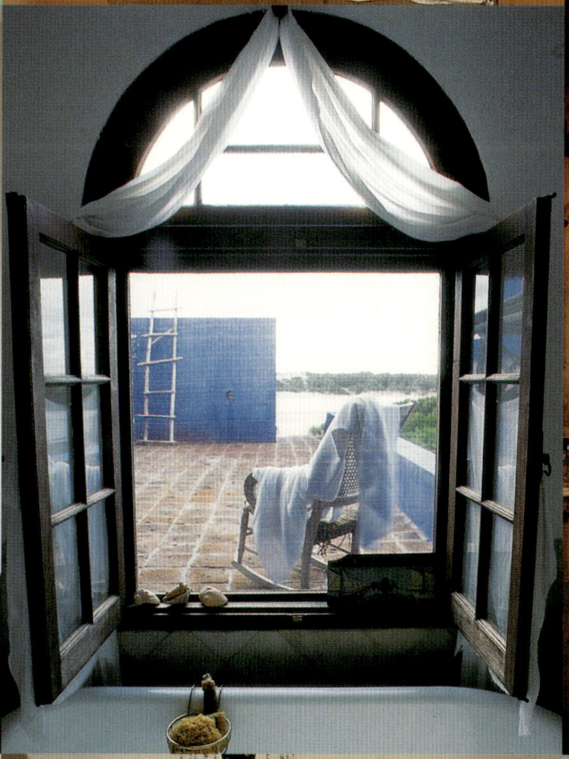
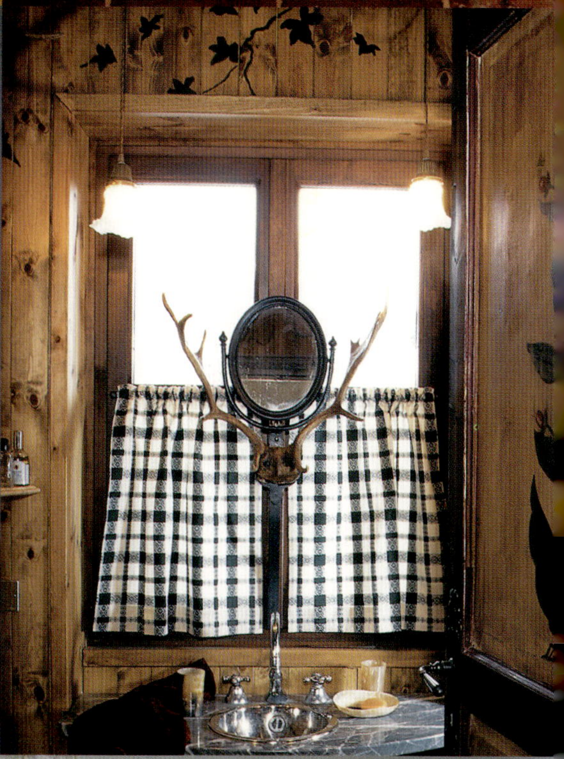
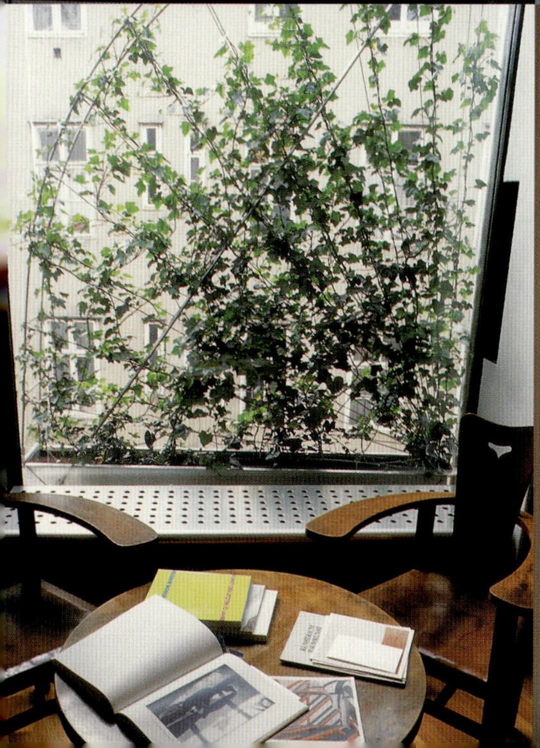
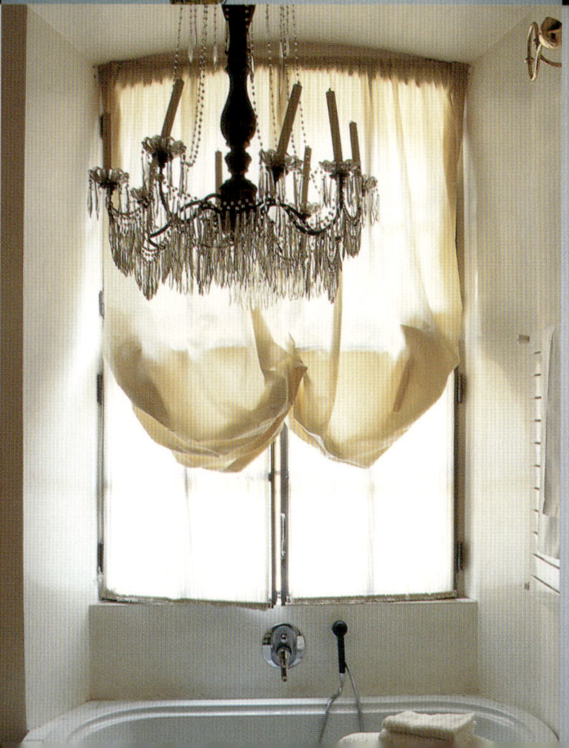
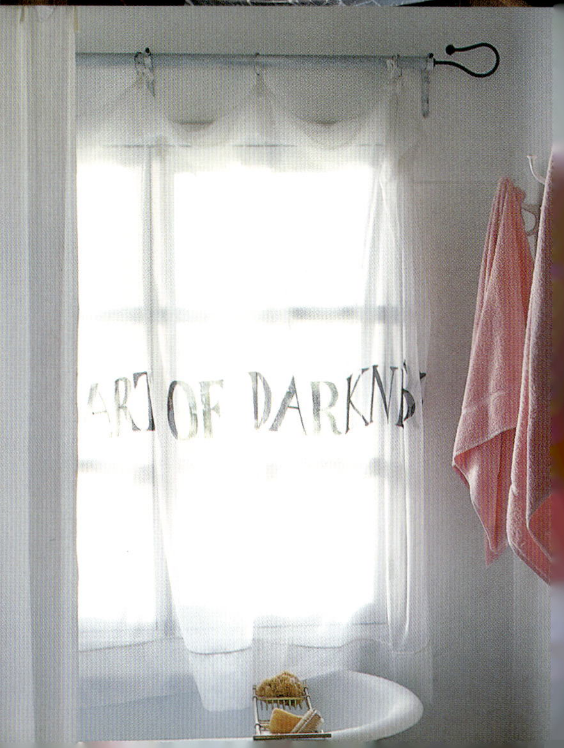
ART OF DARKN

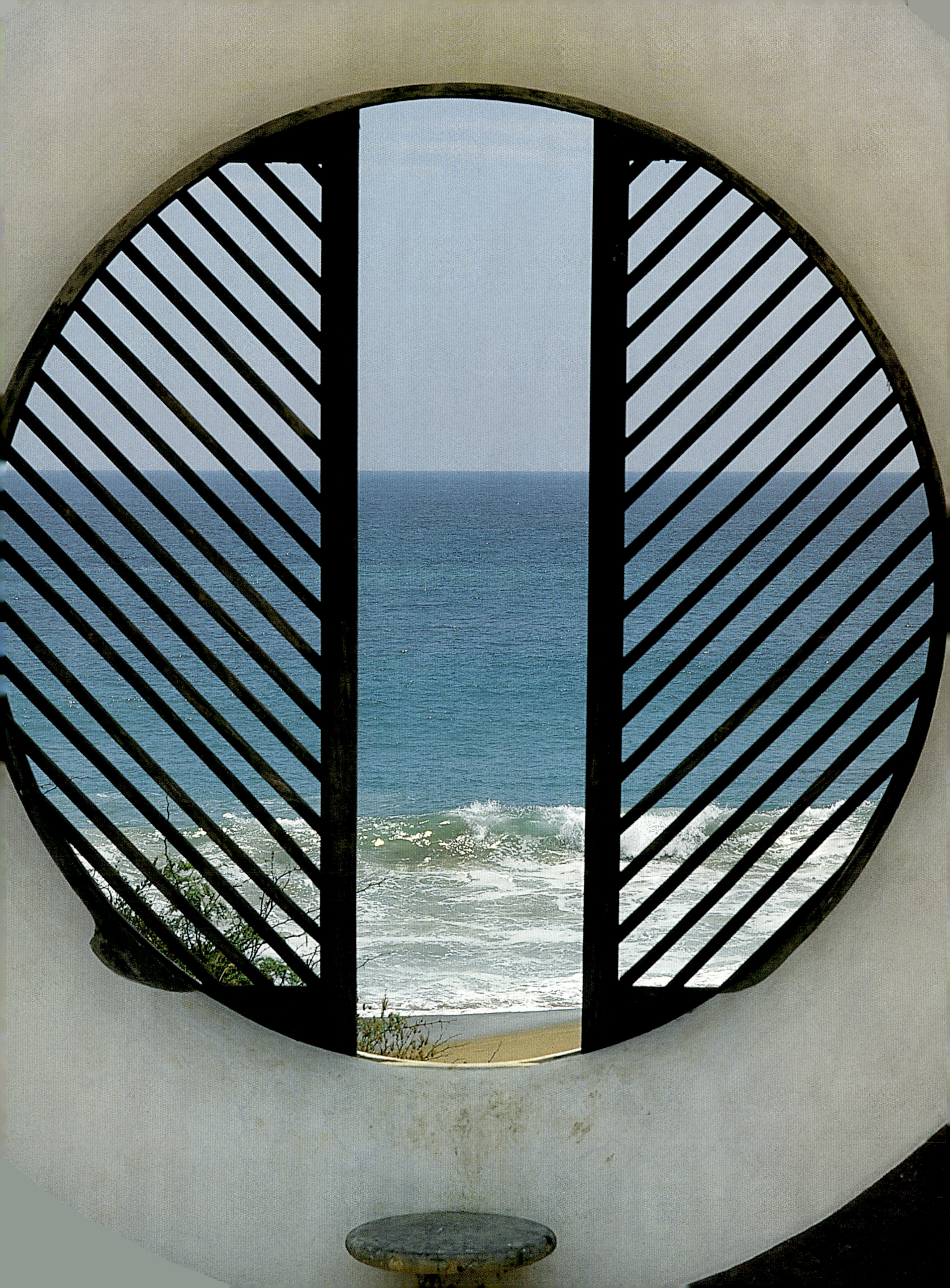

ドアと窓

ドアと窓

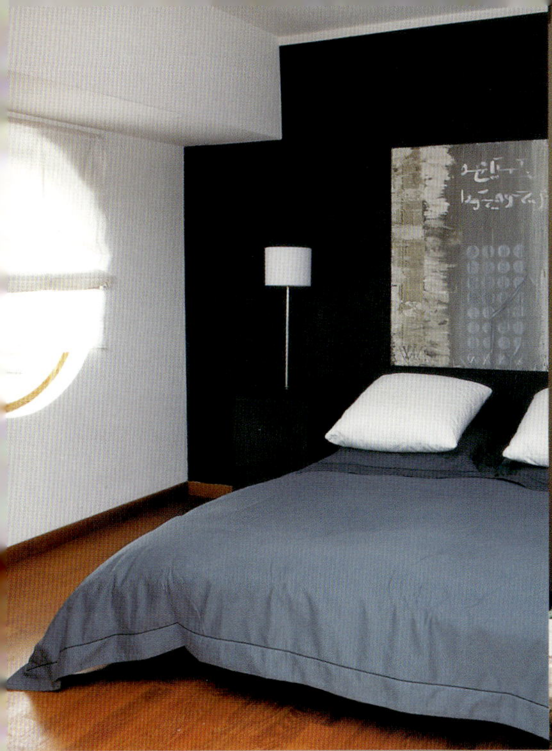
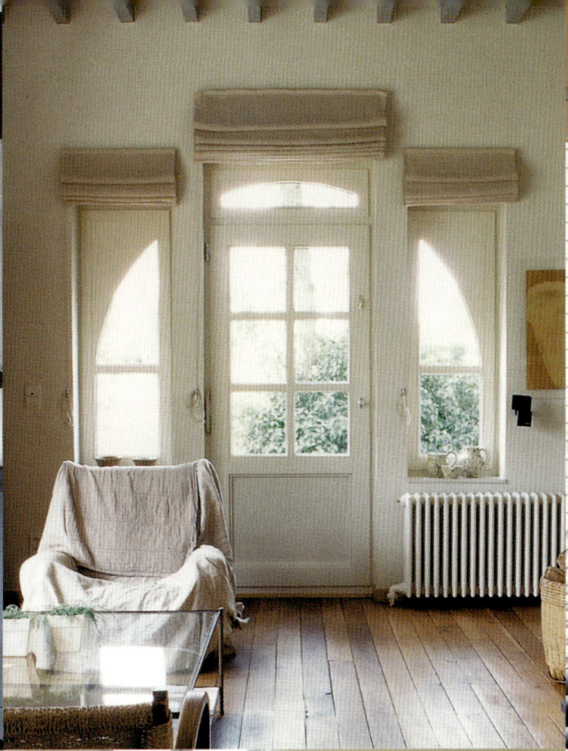
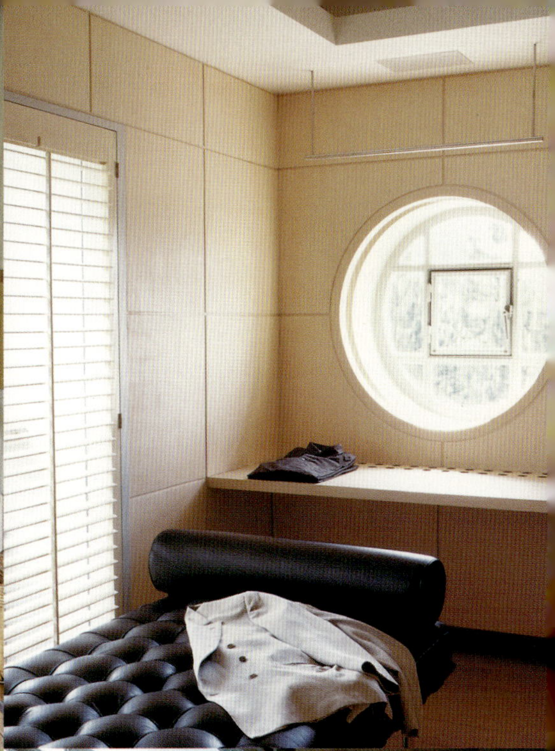
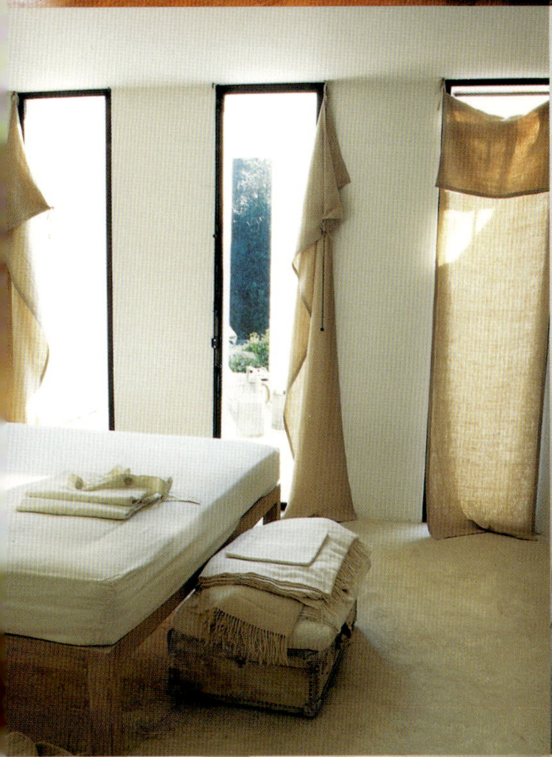
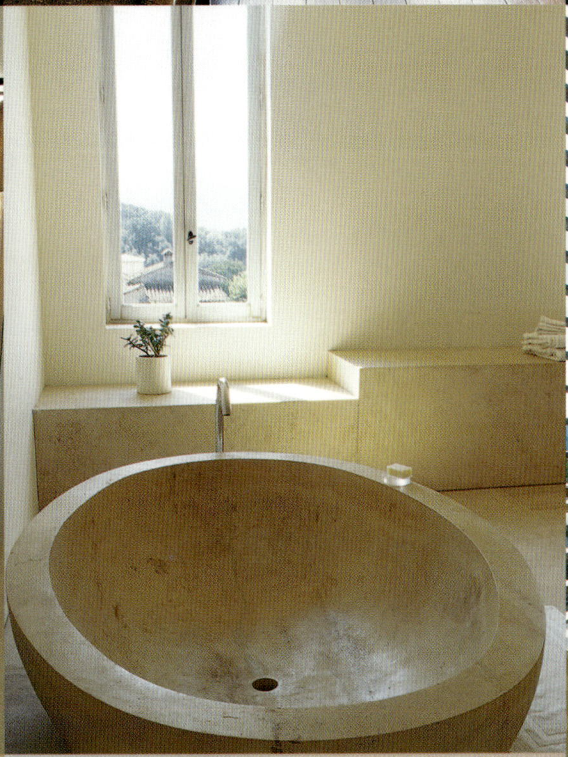
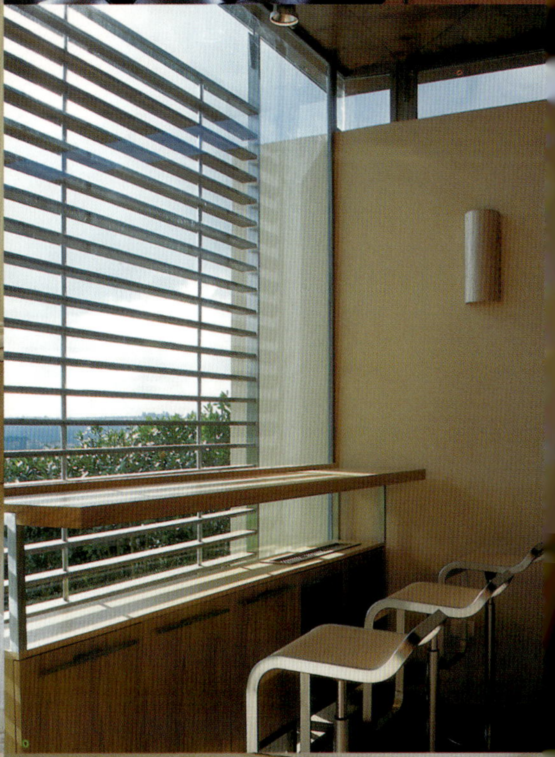
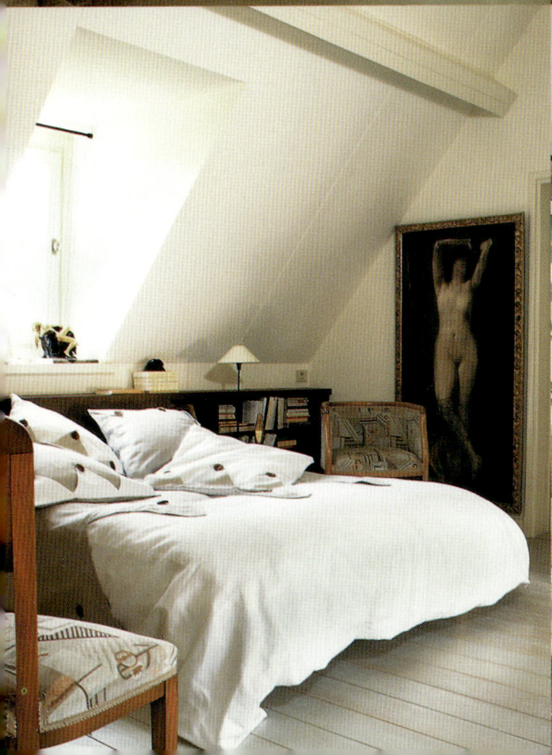
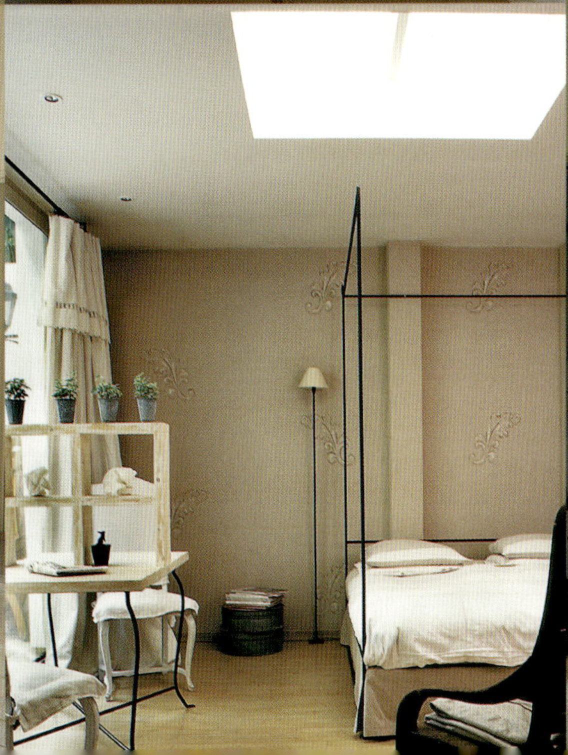
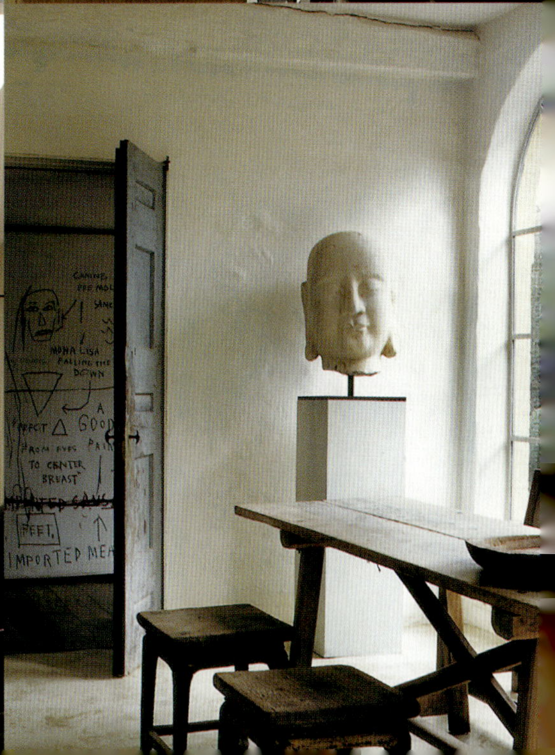

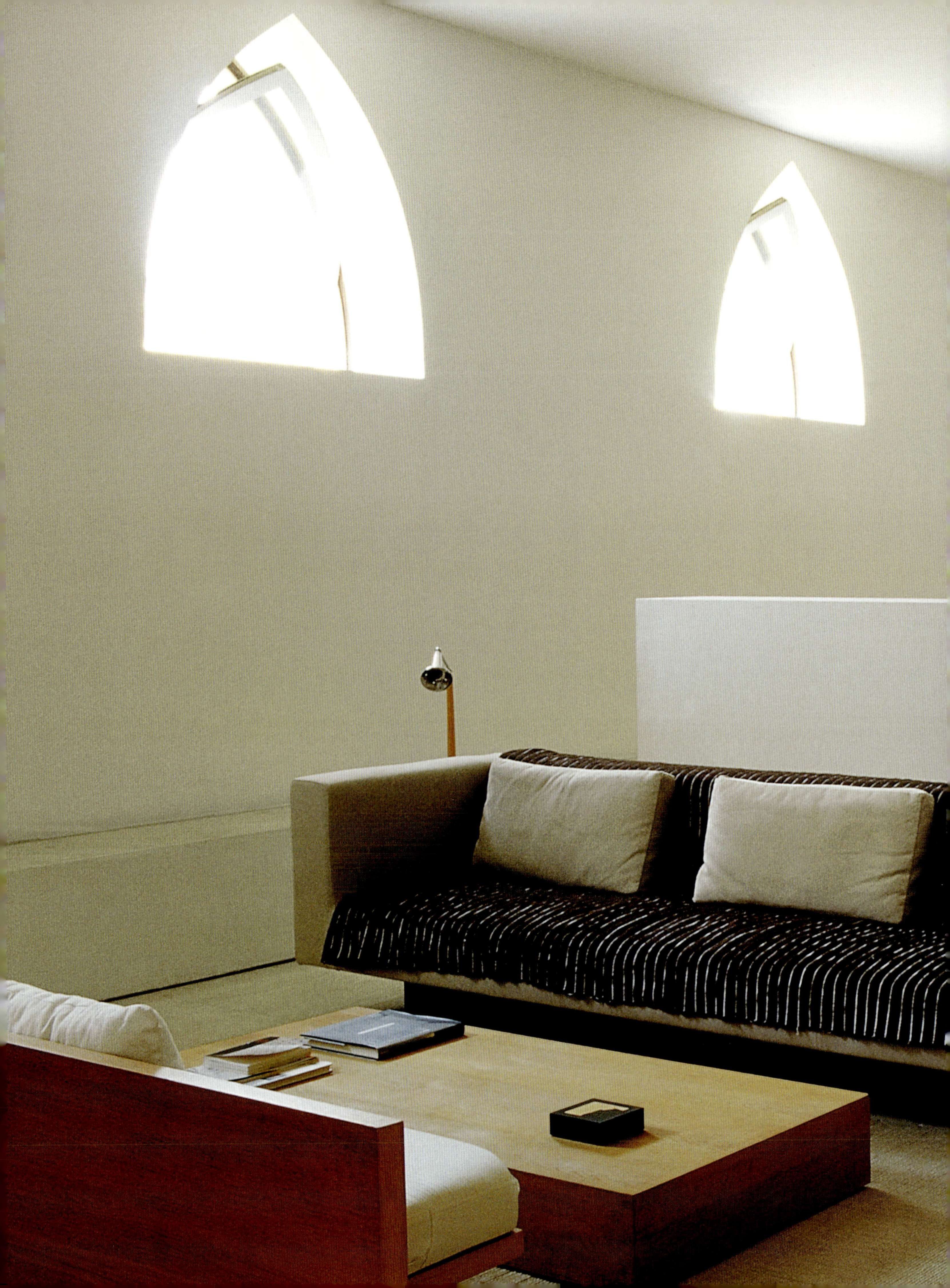

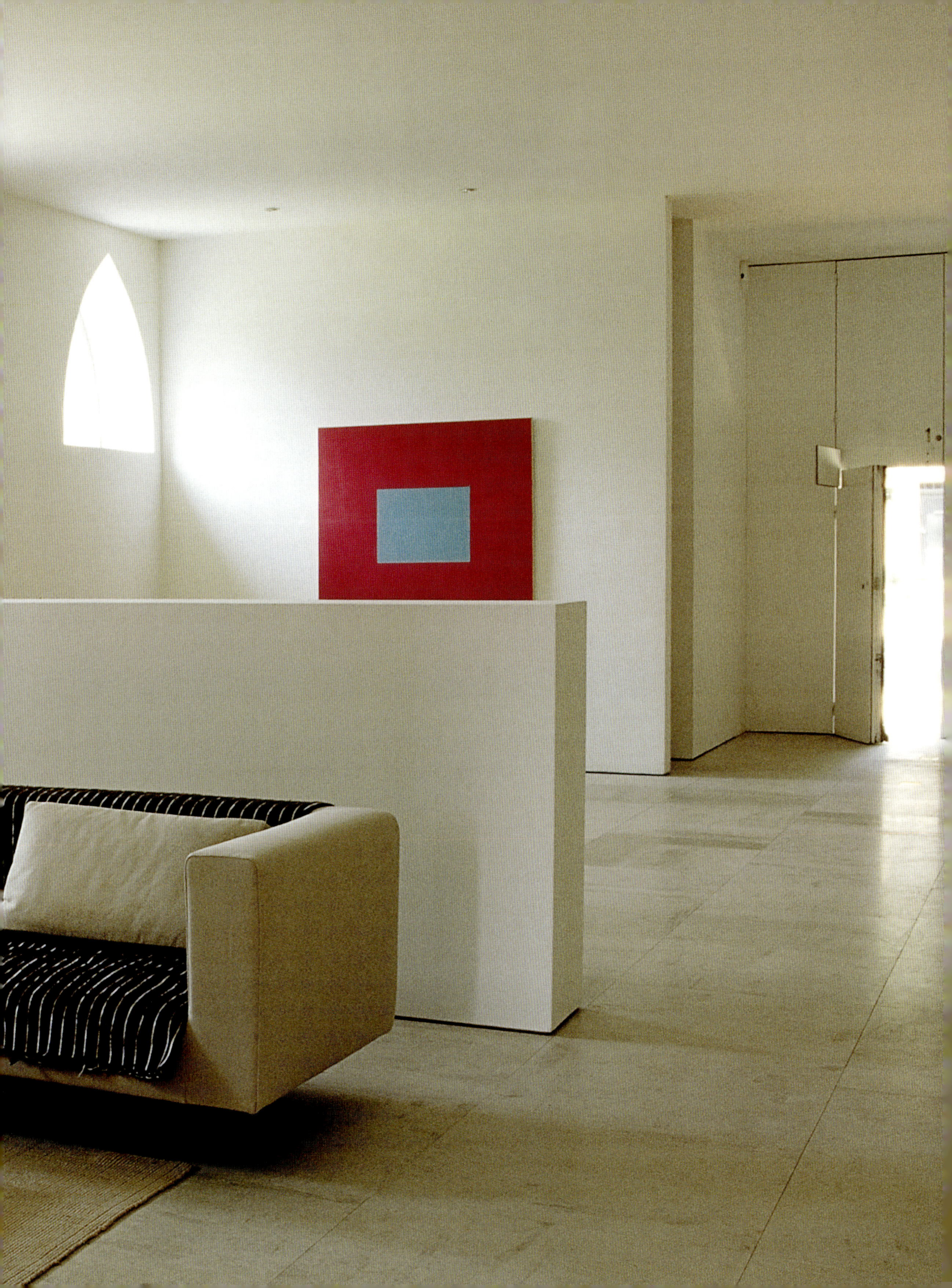

ドアと窓

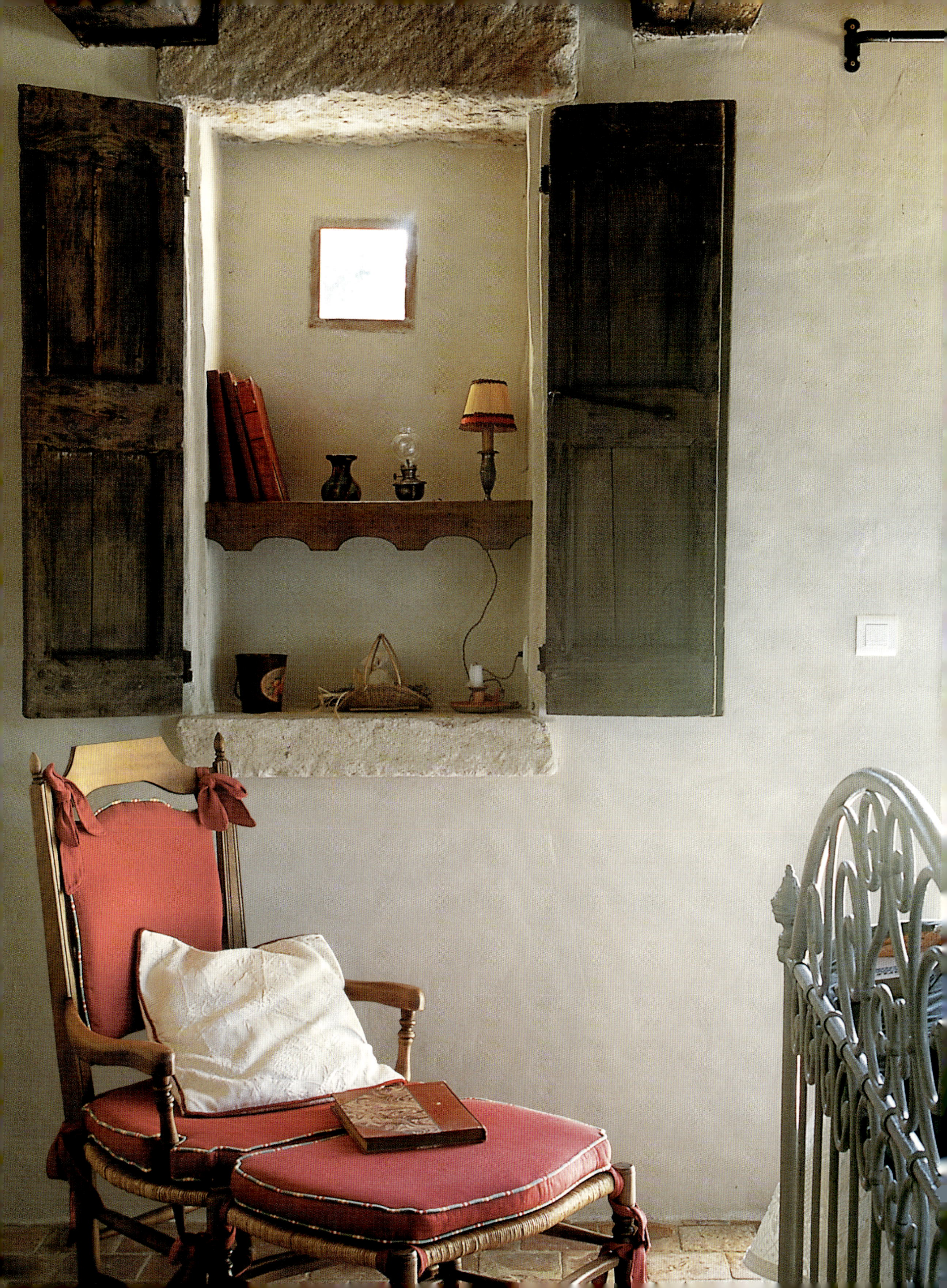

ドアと窓

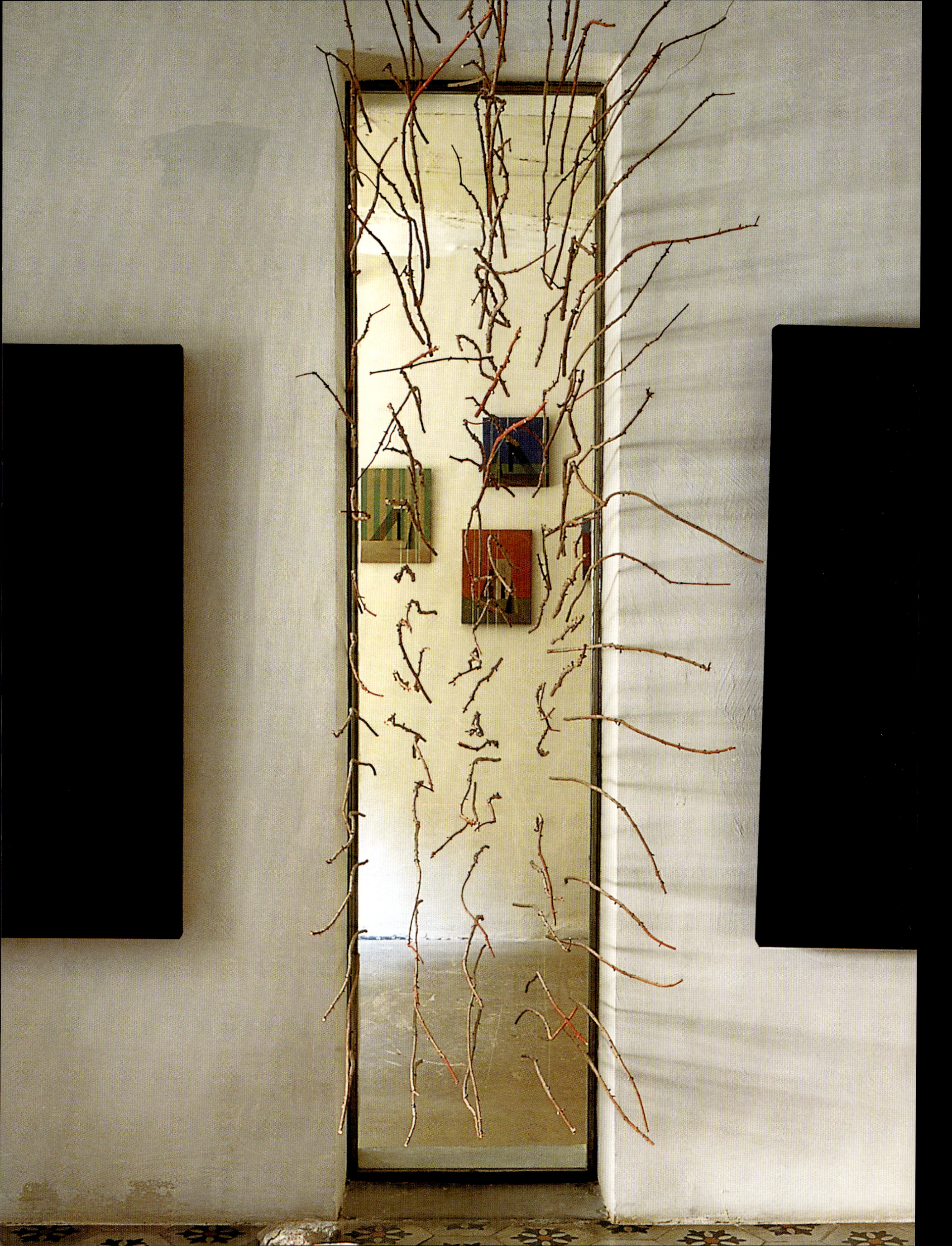

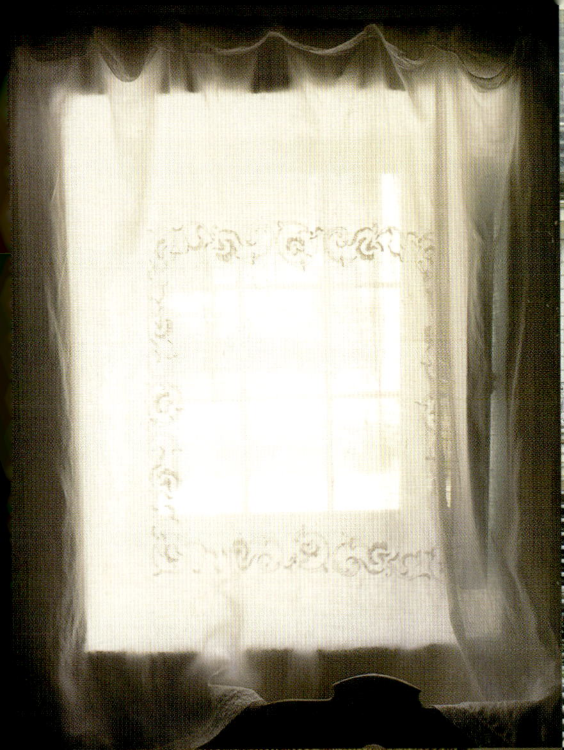
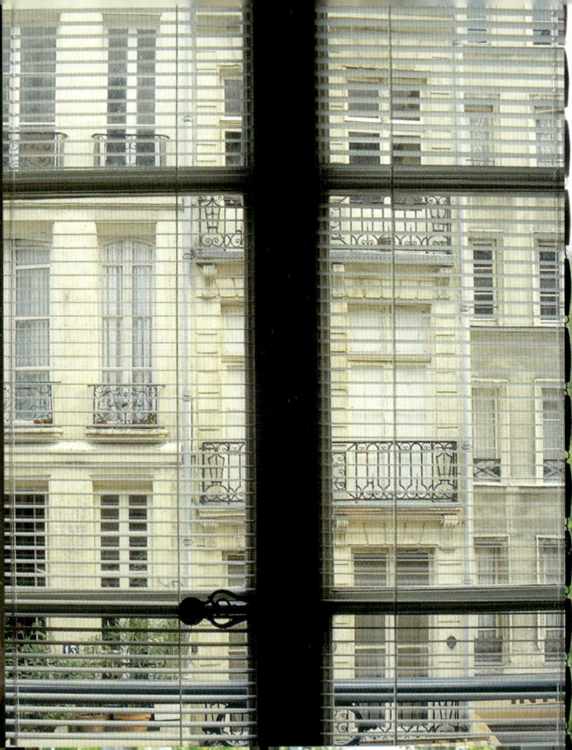
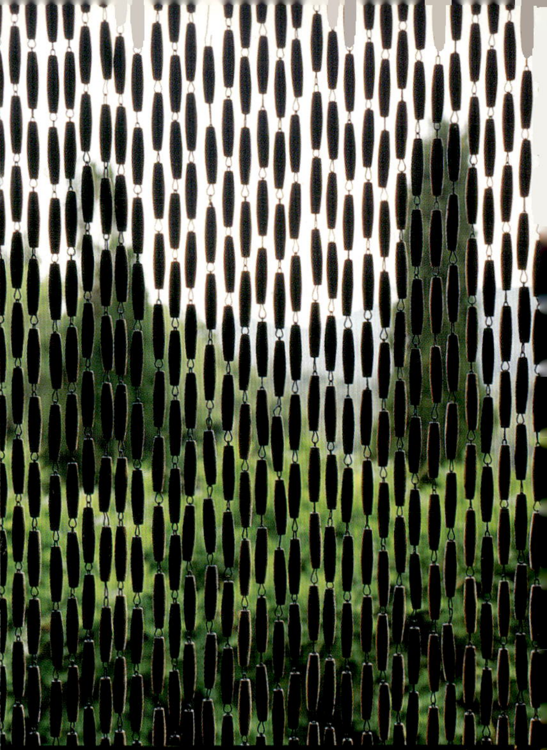
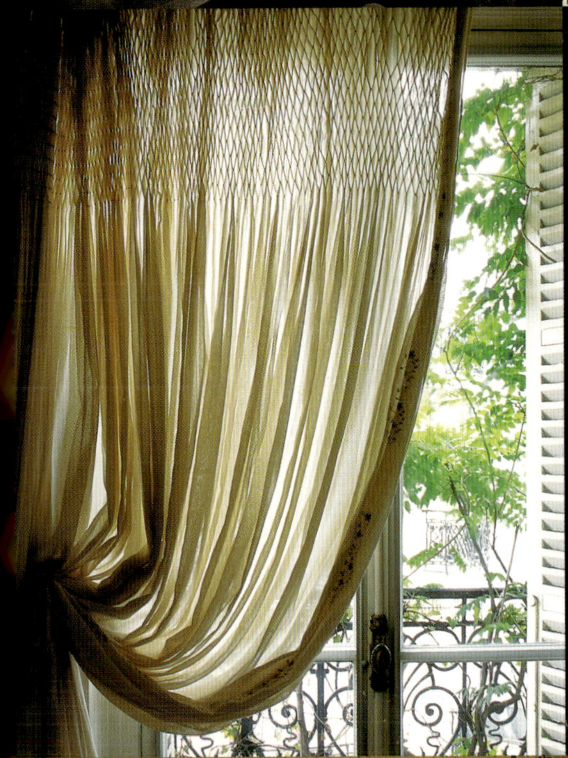
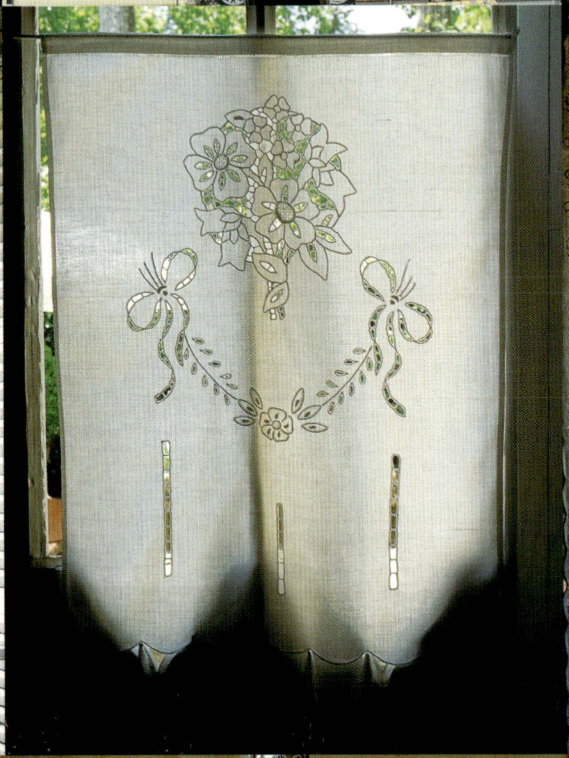
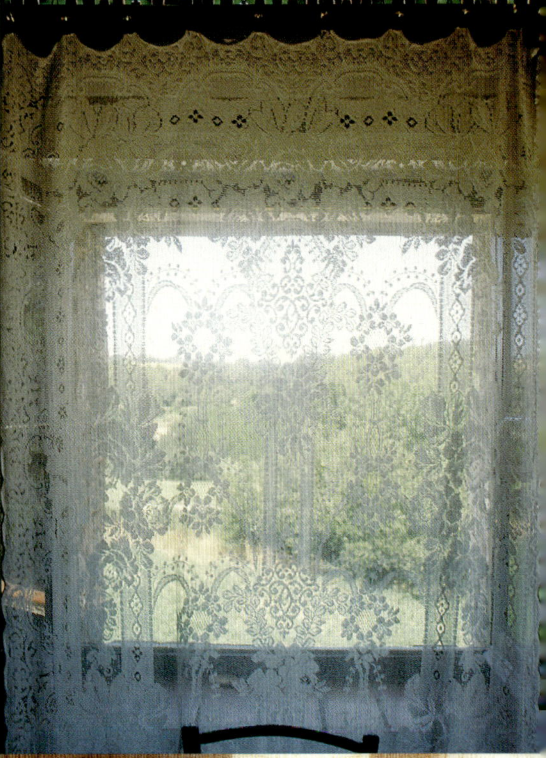
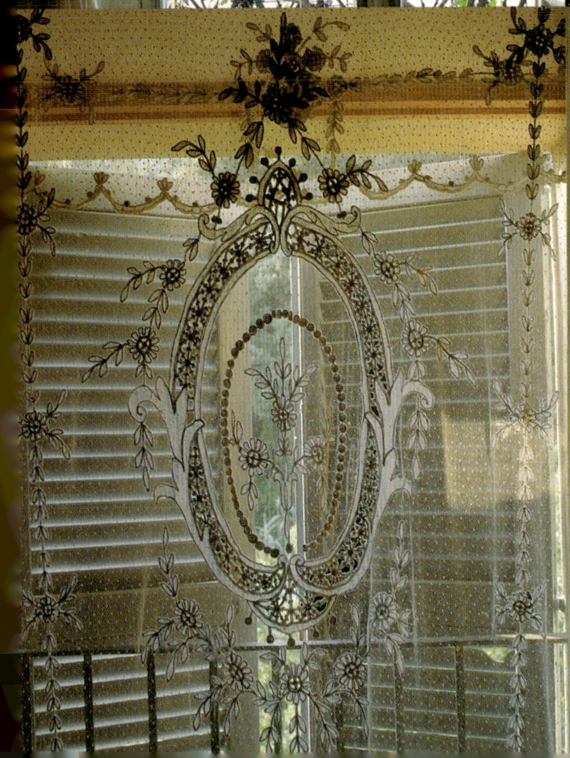
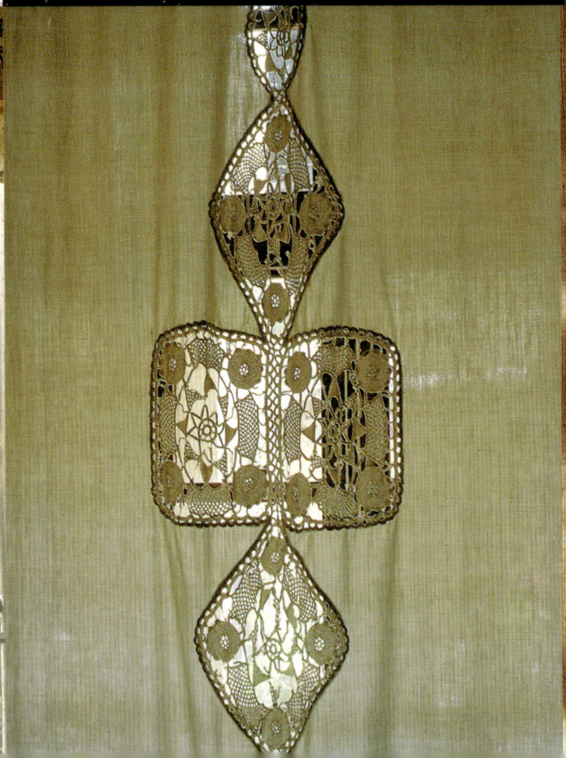
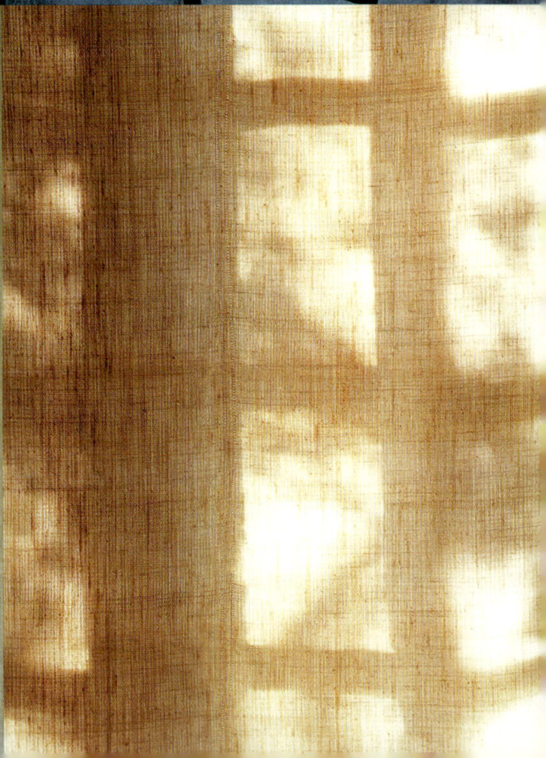

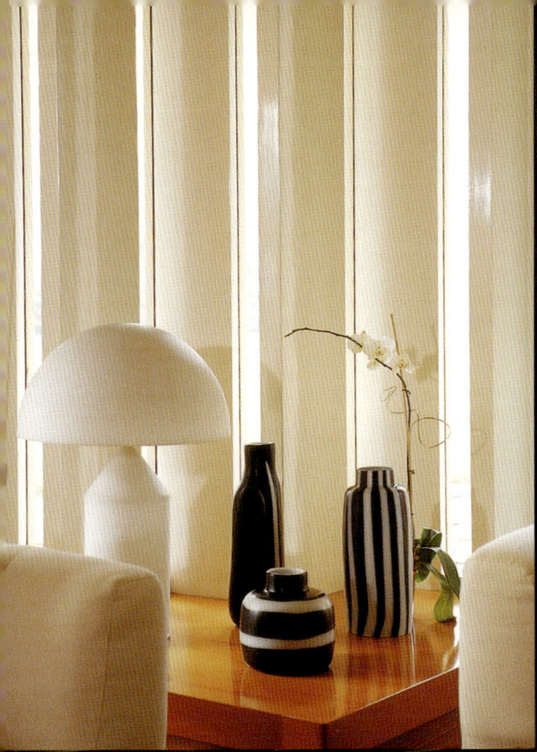
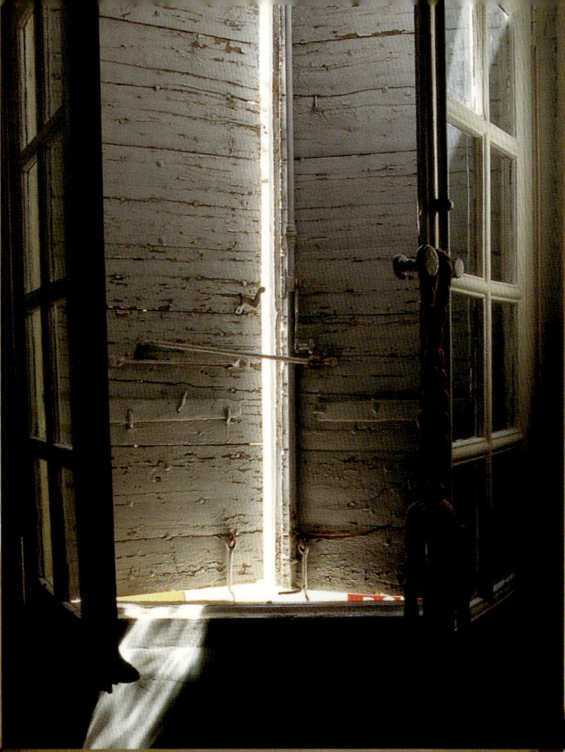
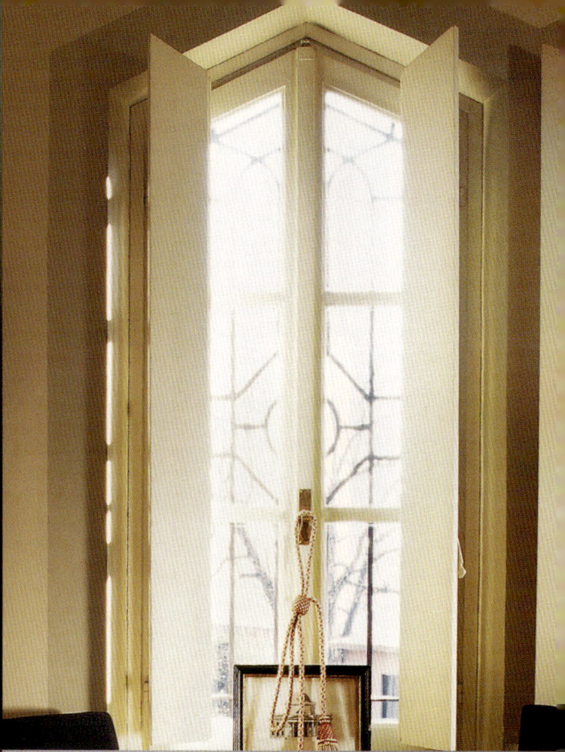
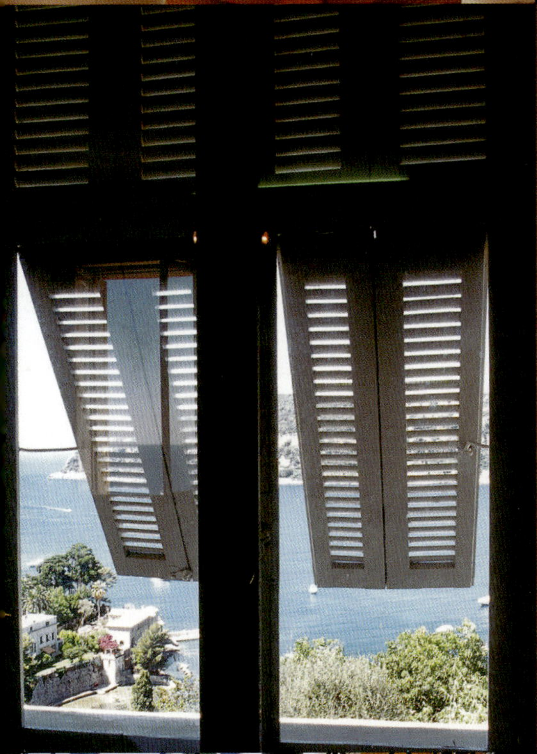
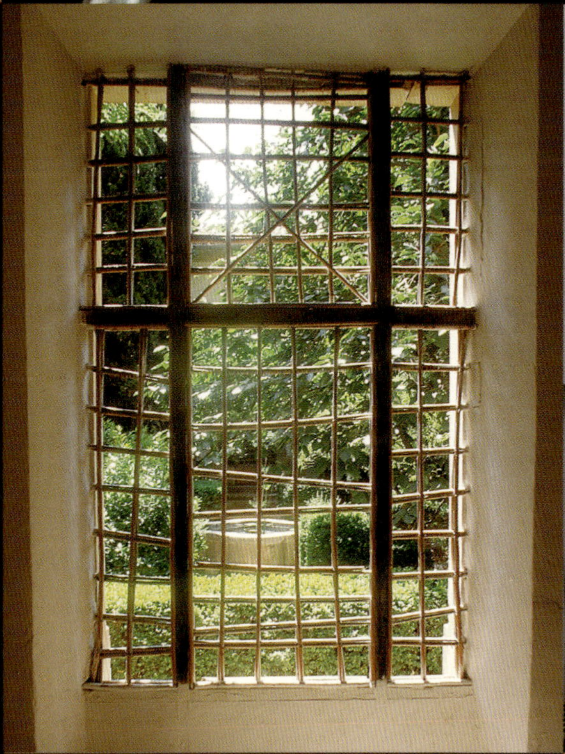
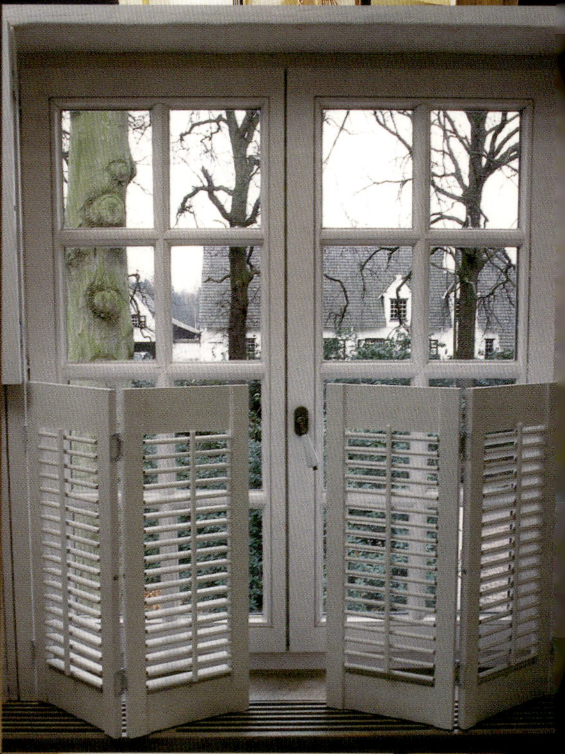
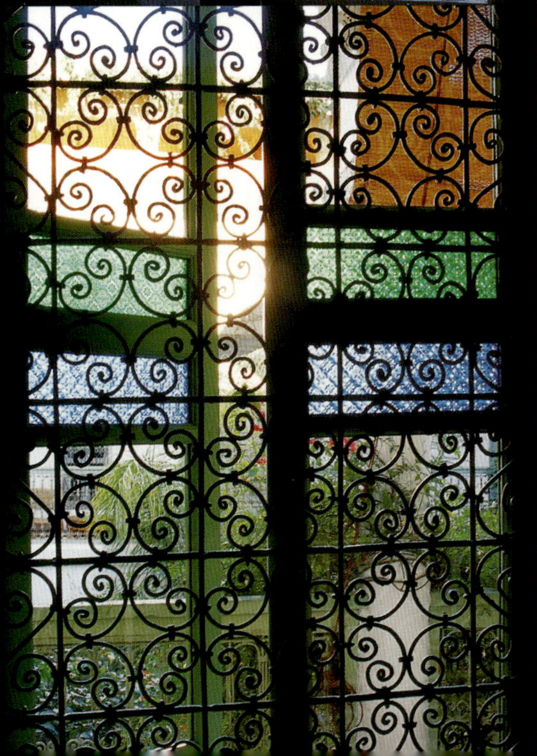
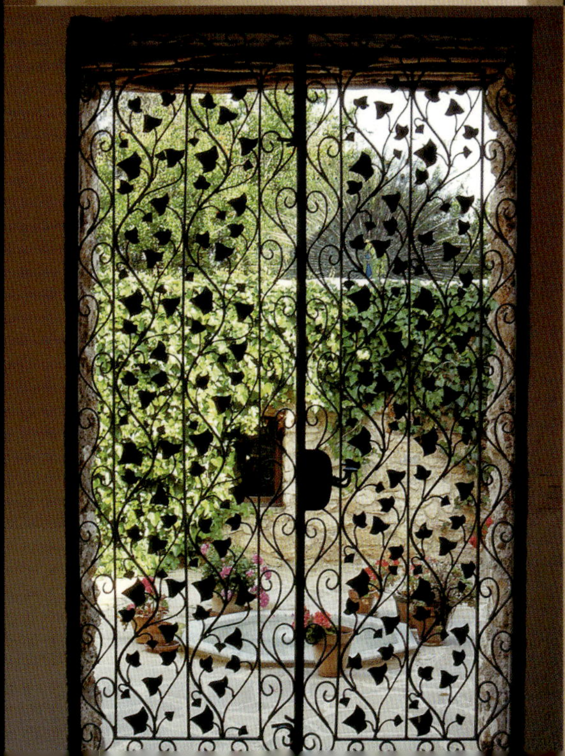
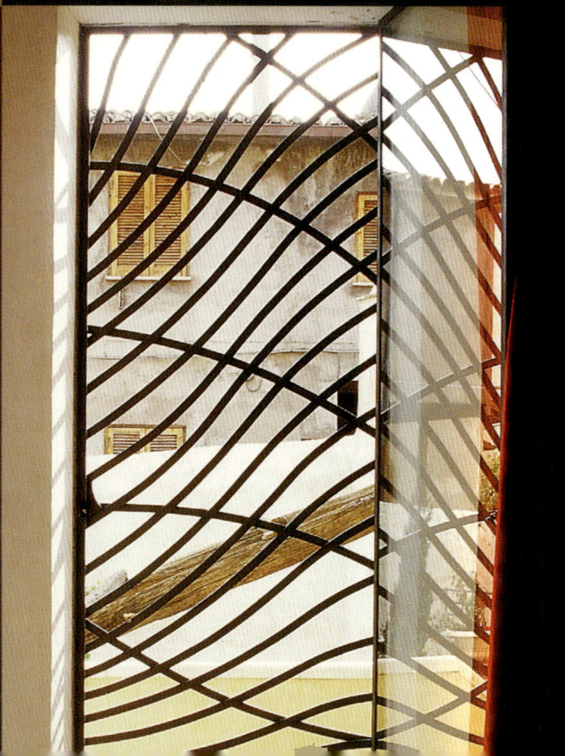

床

Interest Under Foot

以前、私が新しい家に引っ越した時の、ある人の言葉を思い出します。それは、「カーペットを敷き終えるまでは、家らしくならない」というもの。確かにその人の言うとおりでした。敷物を敷くと、物音がしにくくなり、ソファひとつと、床にいくつかクッションが置いてあるだけの状態でも、家が落ち着いた感じになったのです。それに、新しいカーペットを敷くと、独特のにおいが漂いました。新車の車内に似た、非常に官能的なにおいです。しかし、20年ほど前から、床一面にカーペットを敷き詰めることが、流行らなくなってしまいました。最近足を運んだ人気レストランを、思い浮かべてみてください。カーペットを敷き詰めている店があったでしょうか。かつては、サイザル麻のカーペットがよく使われていました。これは民族調で、独特の雰囲気を持つ素材ですが、手入れがしにくく、裸足では痛くて歩けません。また、柄物のカーペットも、完全に姿を消しました。次第に、インテリアデザイナーやデコレーターは、希少な木材を使ったフローリングや、大理石などの石材といった、硬質の床を好んで使うようになっていきました。現在では、多種類の木材やフローリング風の床材が、広く手に入ります。また、廃品回収所や解体現場で、古い床板を拾い出す人々もいます。この他にも、石、れんが、タイル、さらに表面の滑らかな小石までもが、床材として人気を集め始めています。どれも、バスルームや、床暖房のあるスペースに向く素材です。そして今日、再び流行が変化しつつあります。床に色が戻ってきたのです。壁に絵を掛ける代わりに、大胆なグラフィカル・デザインのデザイナーズ・ラグで、足元を華やかに彩る家も増えてきました。

I recall somebody saying to me years ago, when I moved into a new house, that 'it won't feel like a home until you've got the carpets down'. And in a sense it was true. The floor coverings softened the sound and somehow made everything feel finished, even with only one sofa and some cushions on the floor. Then, of course, there's the smell of new carpet – it's quite sensual, like the smell in a new car. But, over the past 20 years, wall-to-wall carpets have fallen out of fashion in modern interiors. Think of any of the trendy restaurants that you've been to recently, you very rarely see carpet these days. First, there was sisal: ethnic and satisfying, but difficult to clean and horrible on bare feet. And pattern was definitely out, as decorators and designers began using hard flooring: floorboards in rare woods, stone and marble. Now, a wide range of wood or wood-effect flooring is available to everyone, and people are even rescuing old floorboards from salvage yards and building sites. At the same time, stone, brick, tiles and even smooth pebbles began to be popular. These are ideal for bathrooms or areas with underfloor heating. Now, things are changing once again. Colour is back – on large 'designer' rugs with bold modern graphics, that are rather like putting a painting on the floor.

床

床

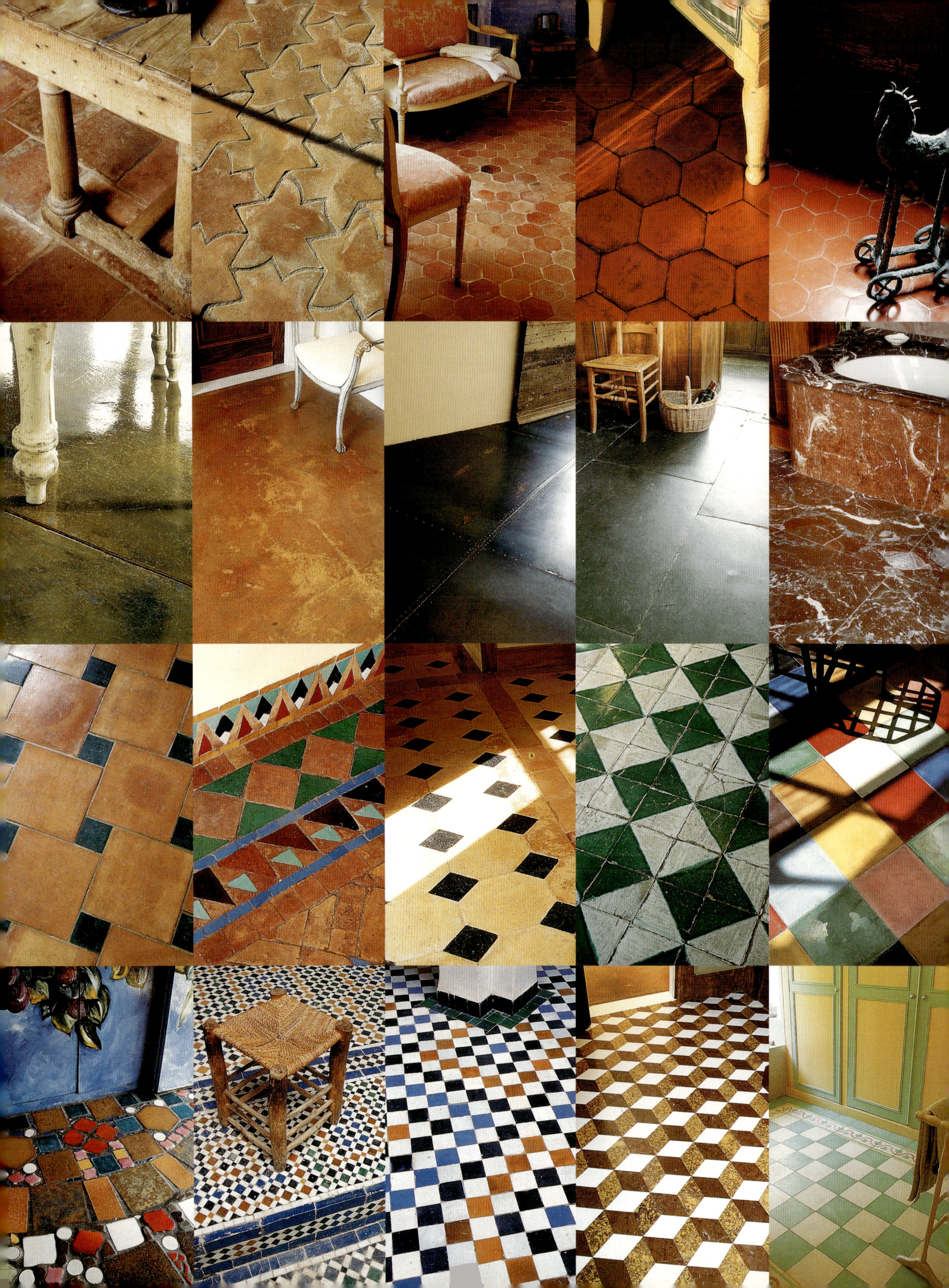

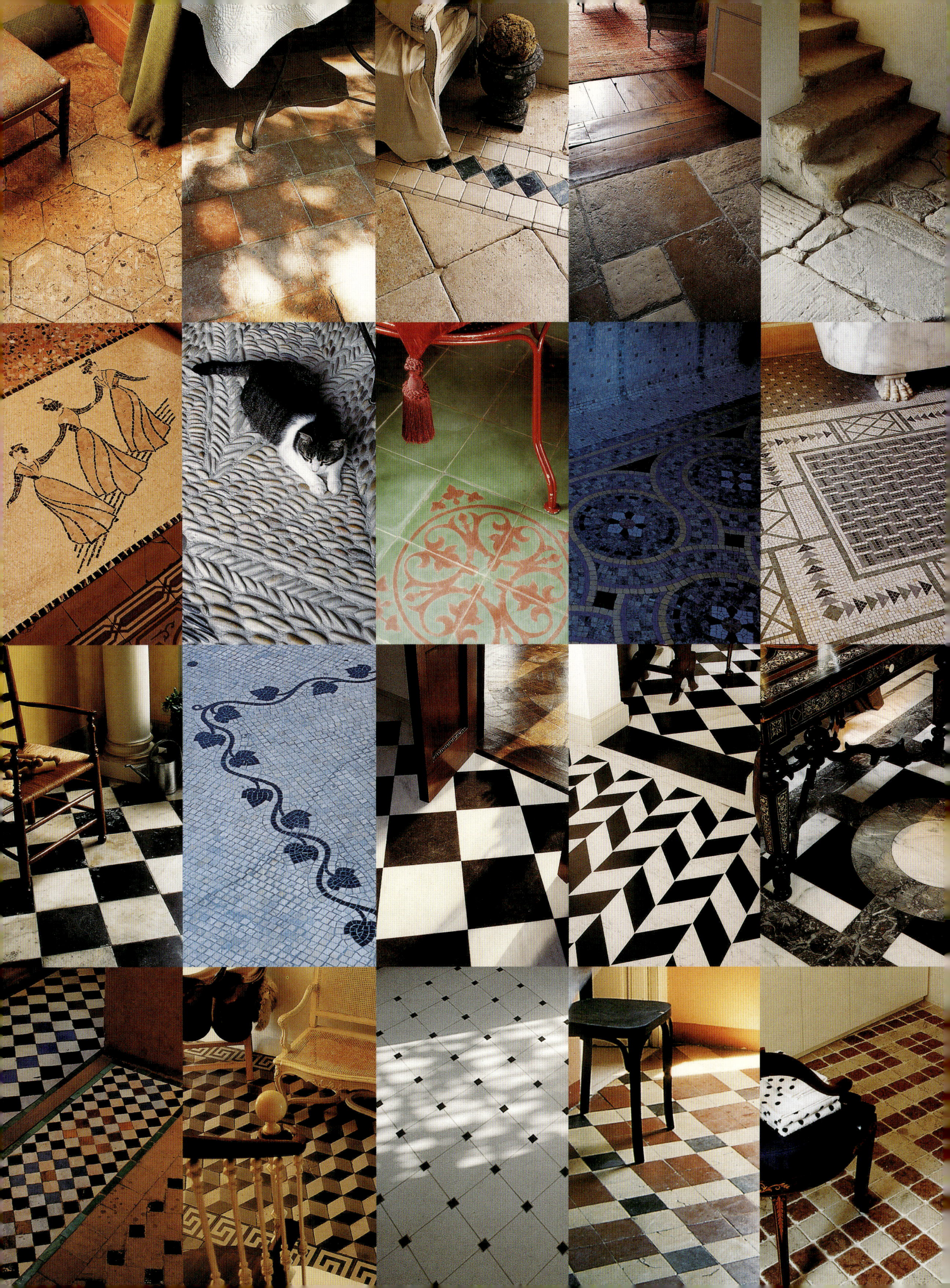

床

床

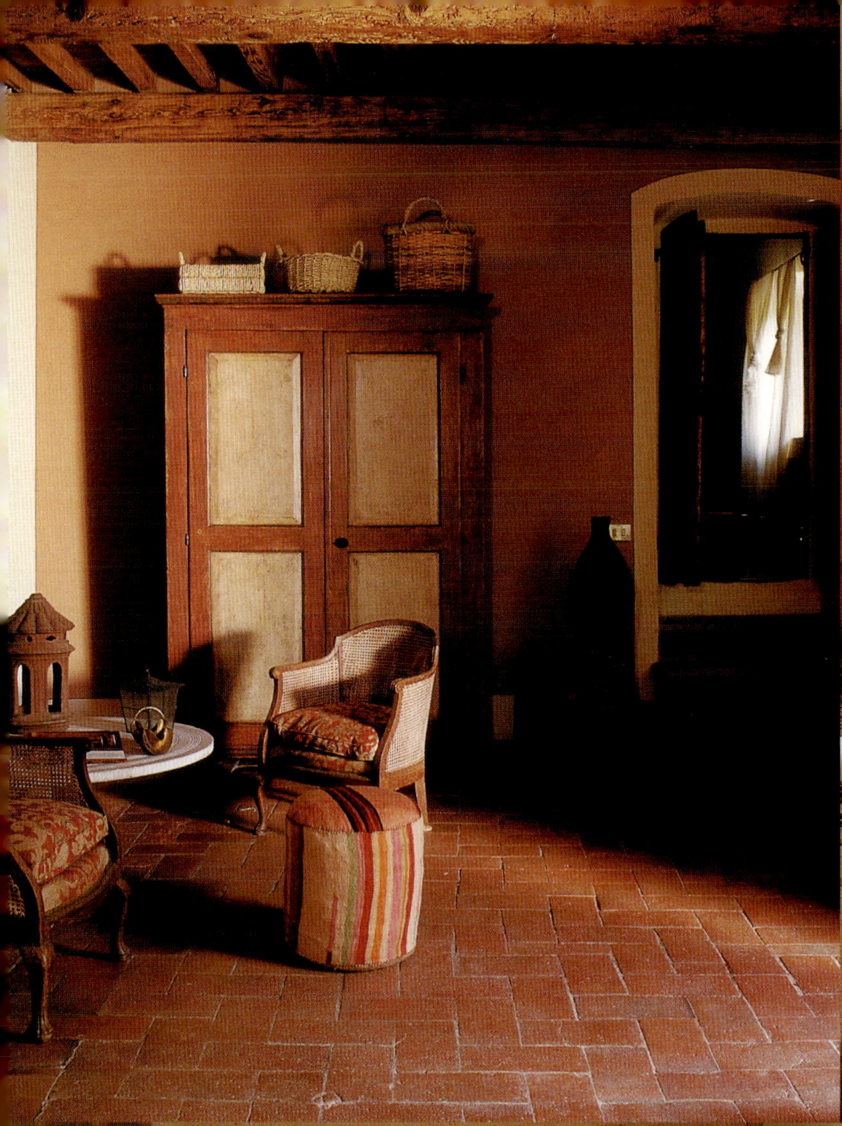
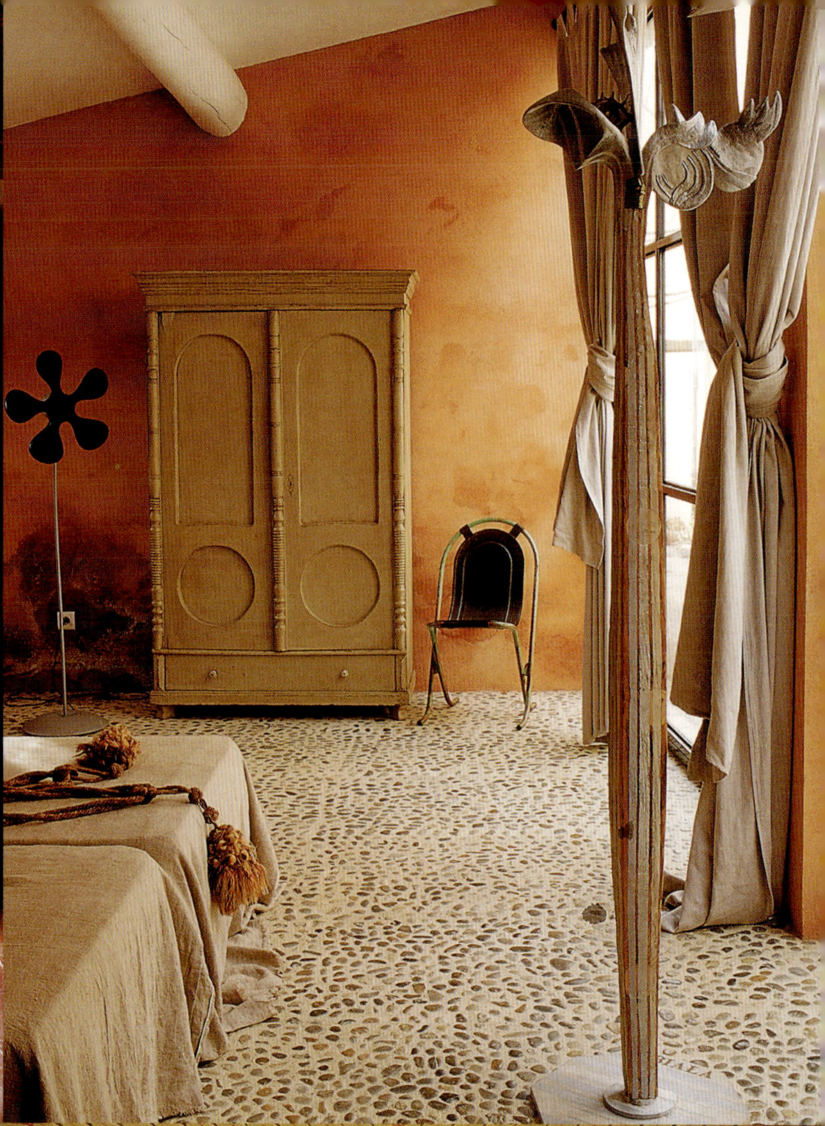
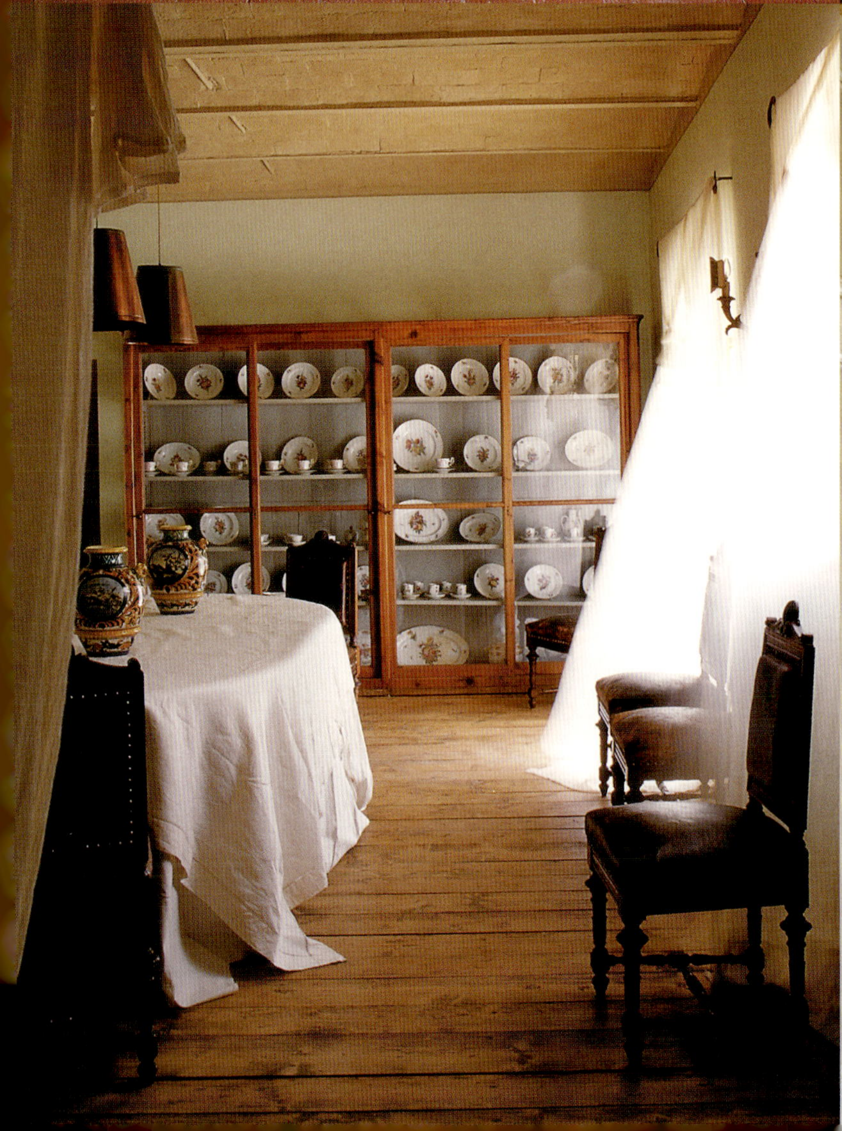
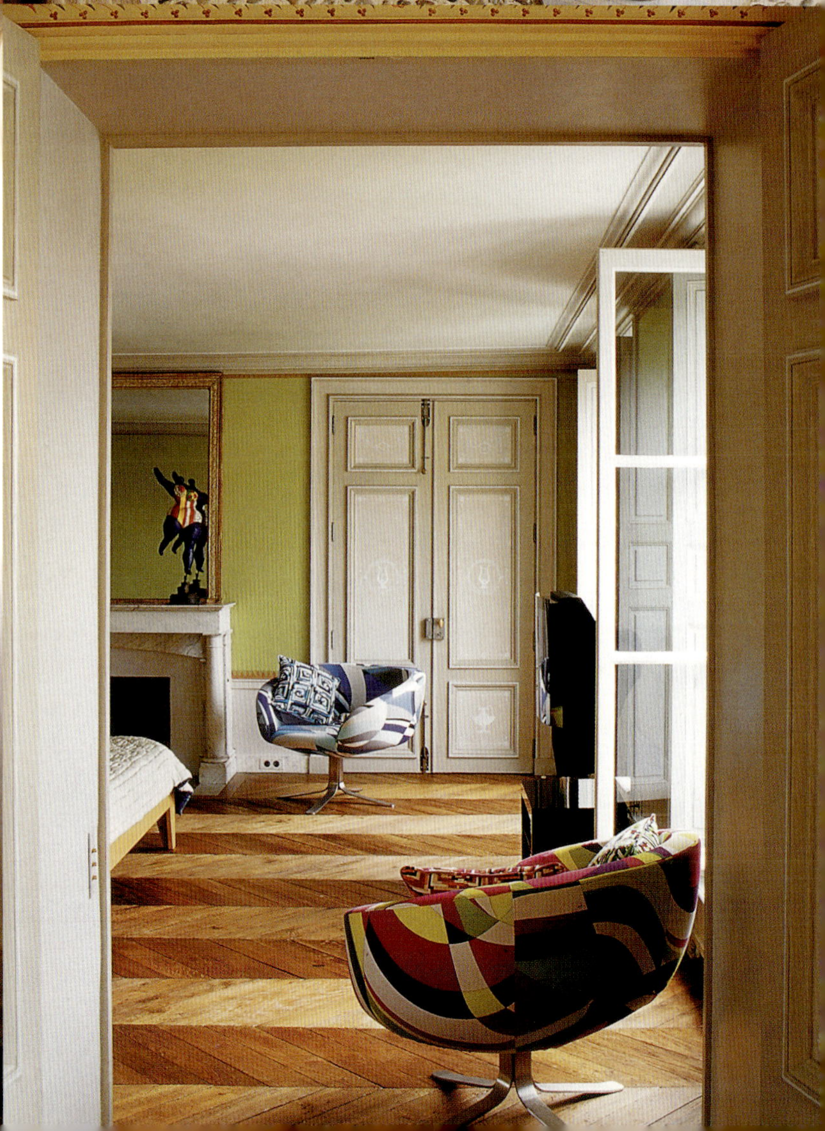

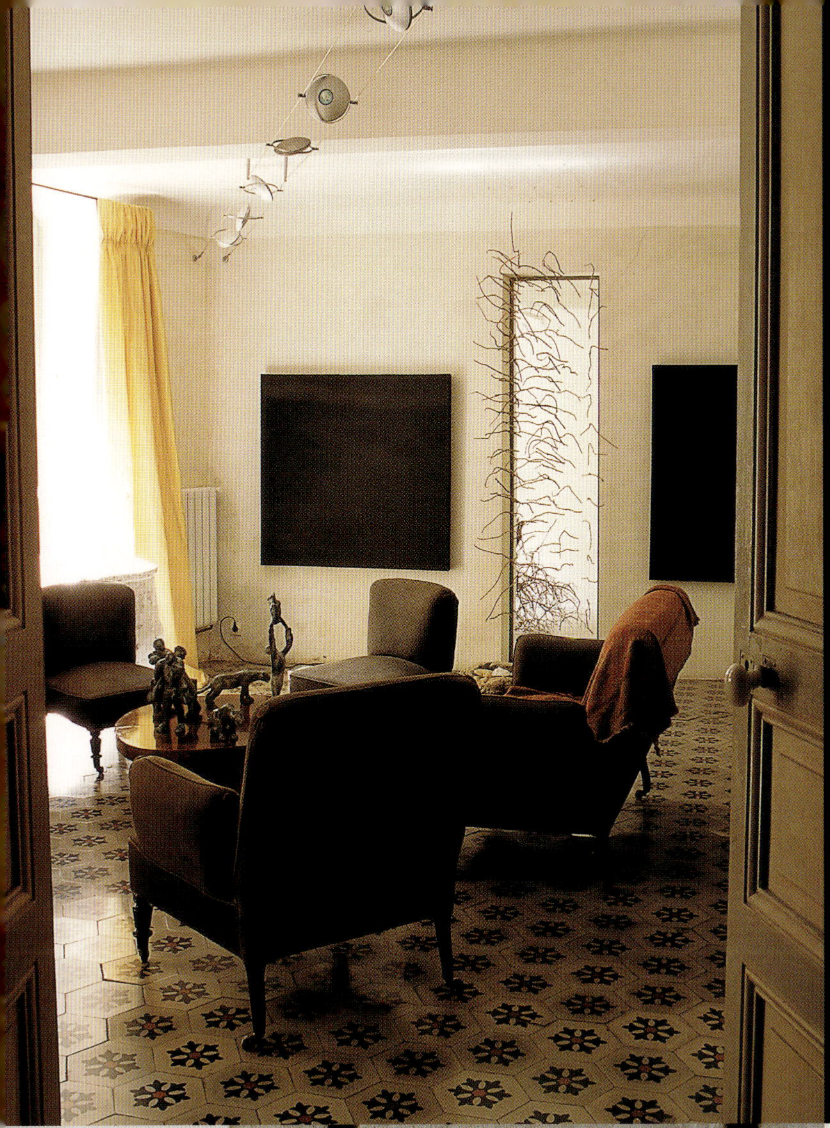
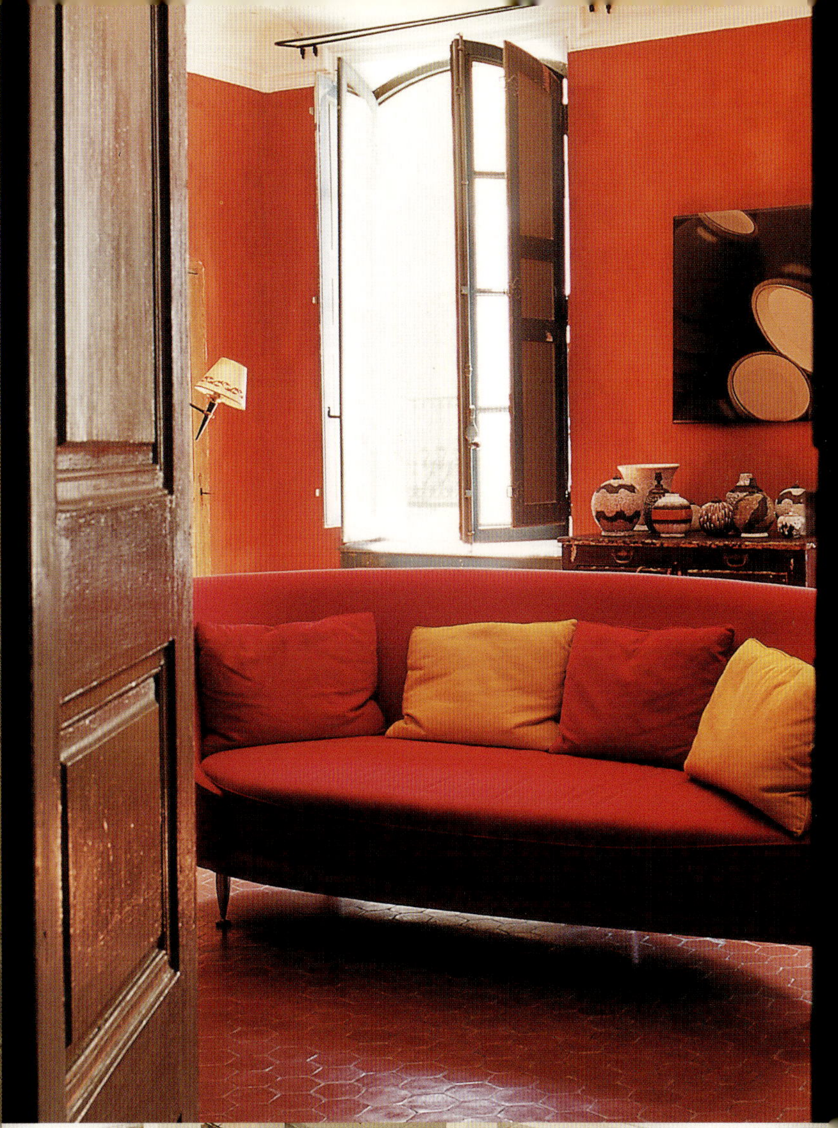
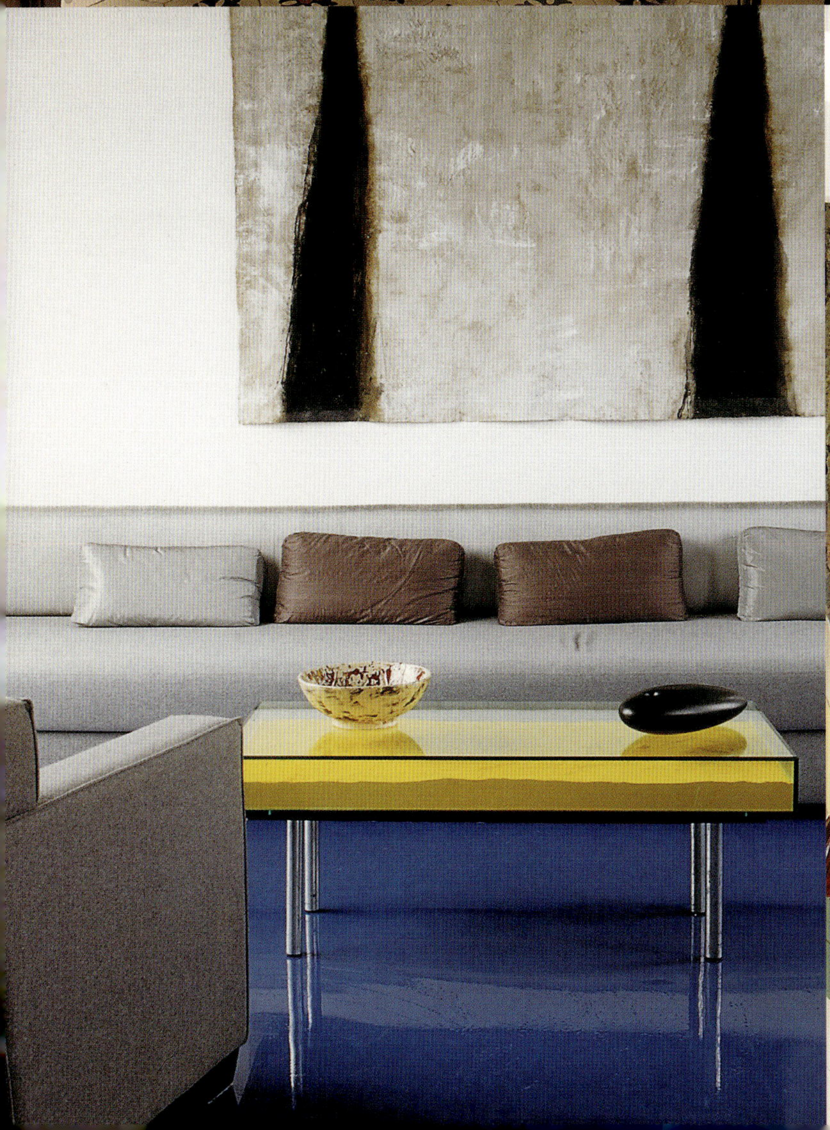
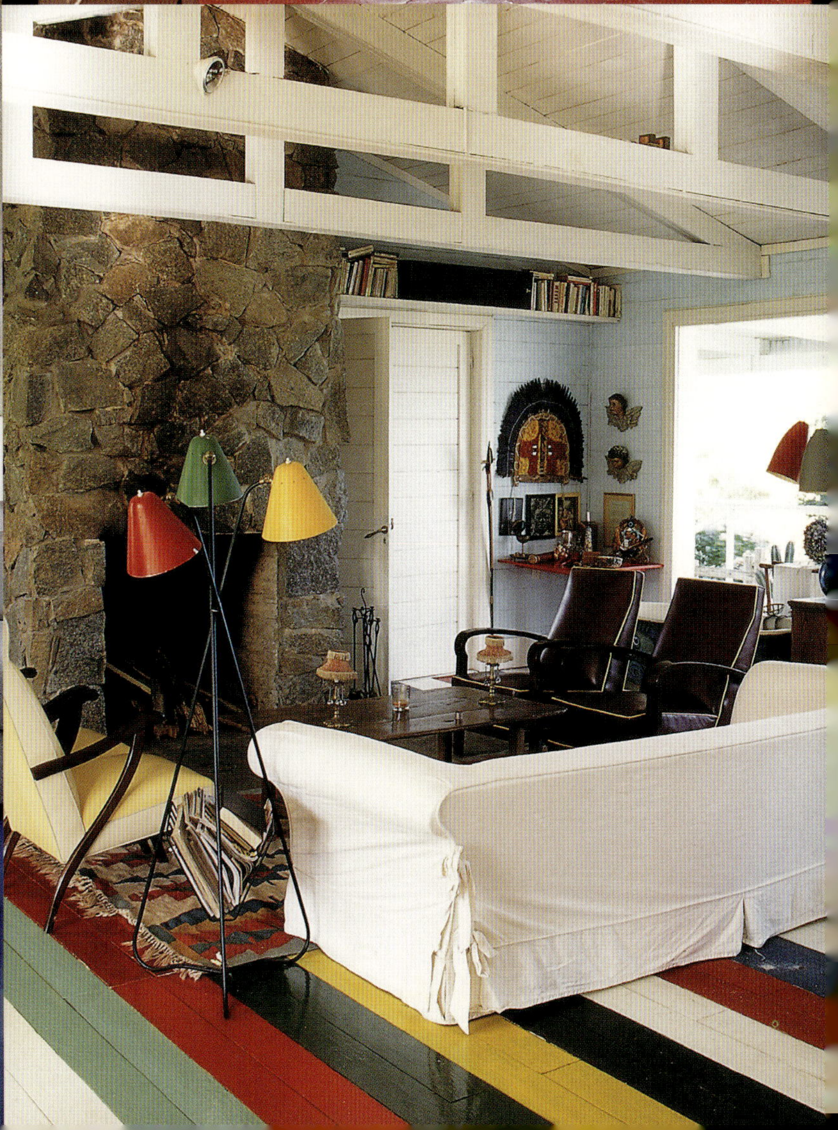

床

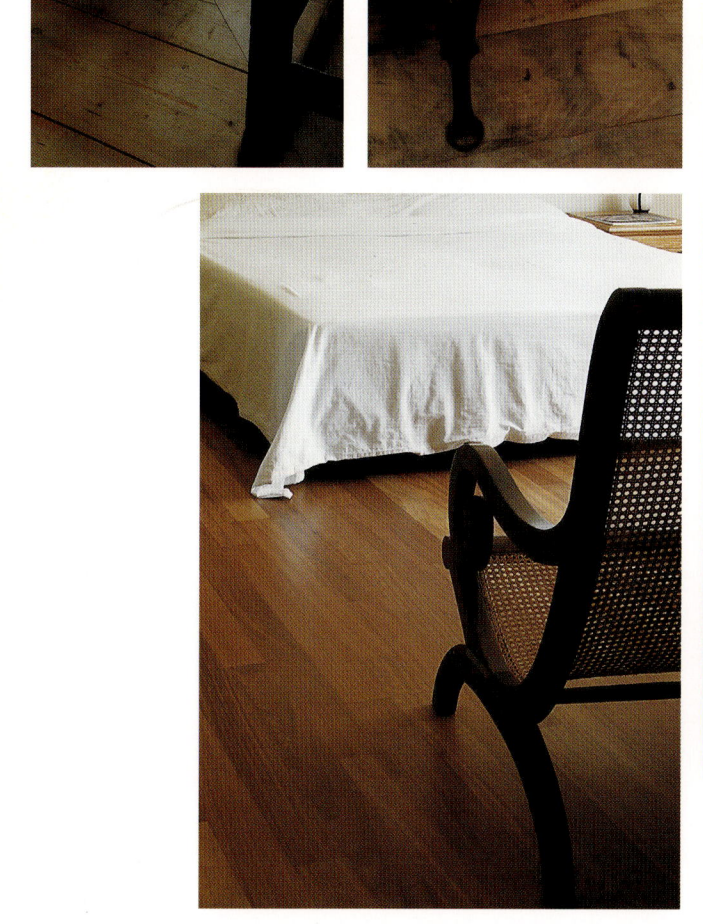

床

45

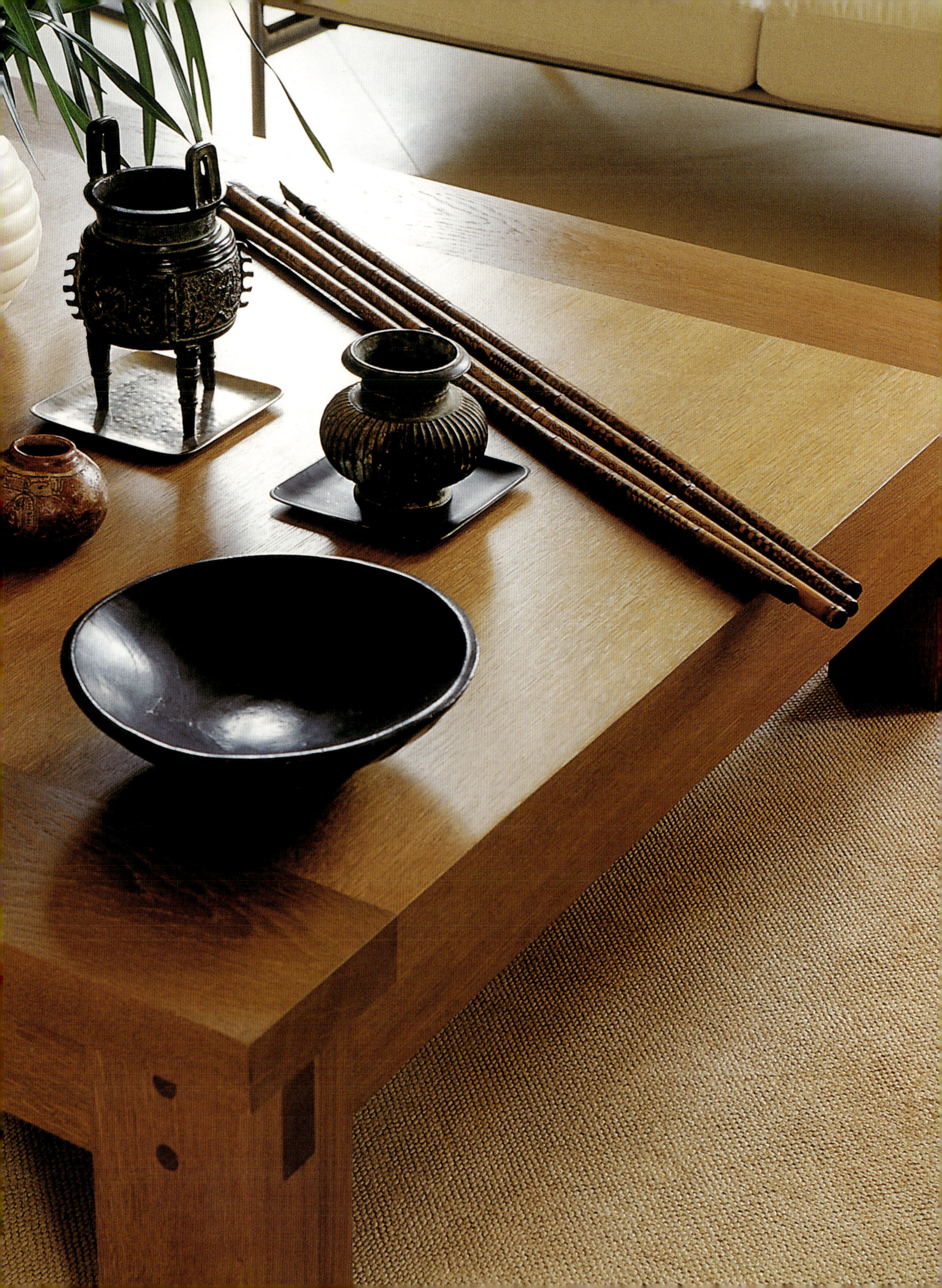

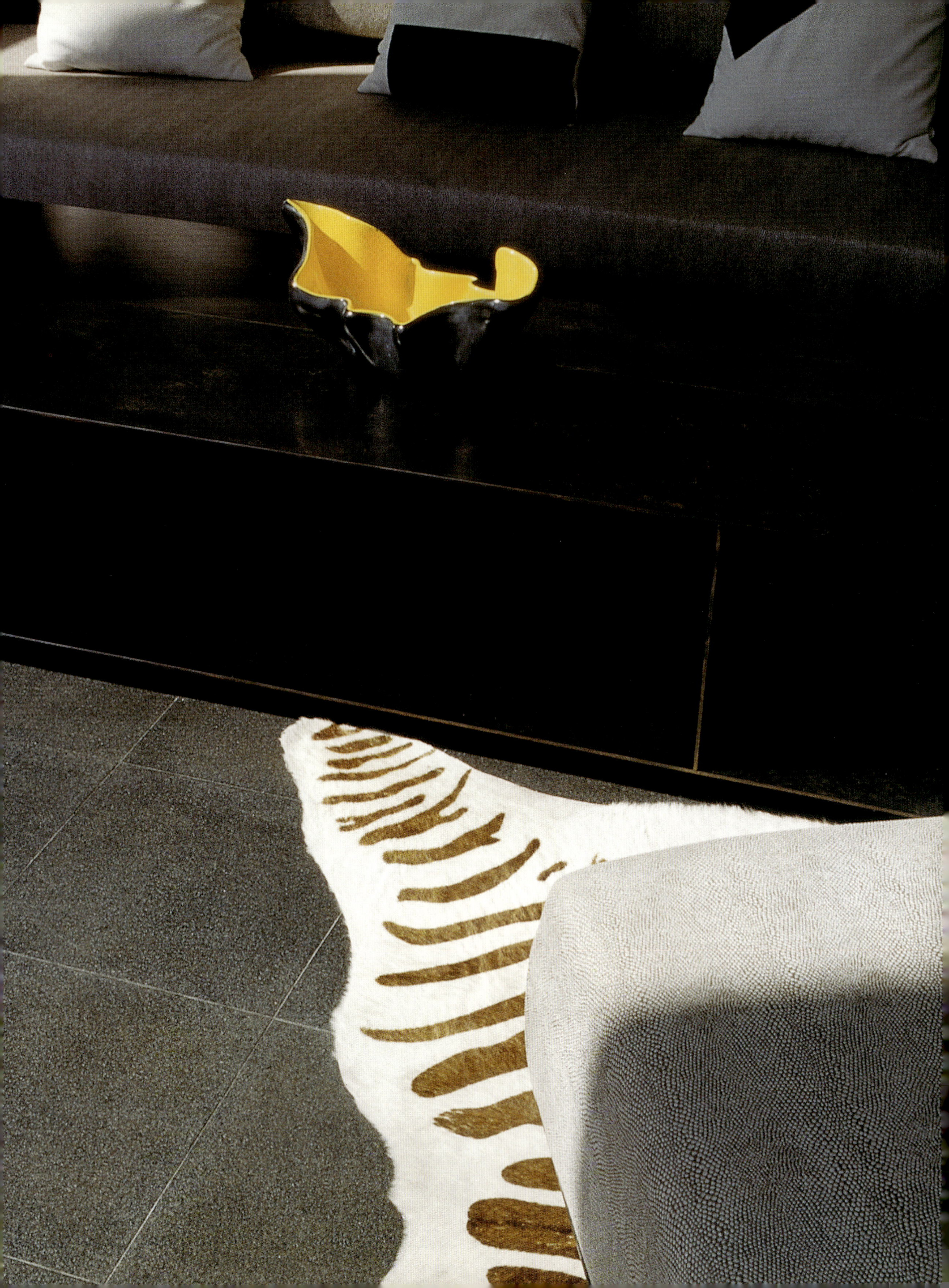

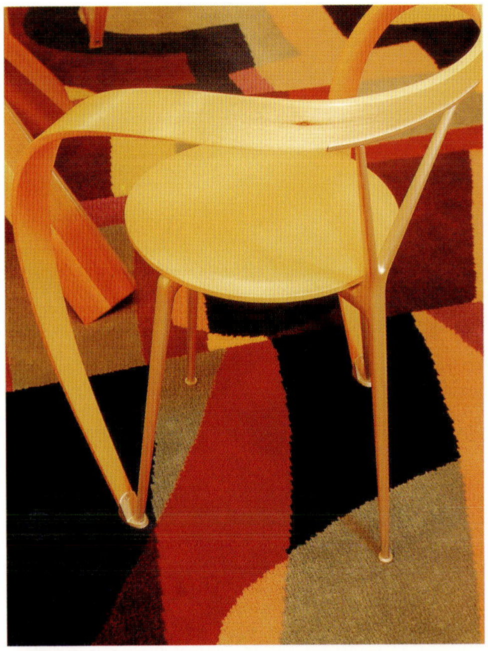
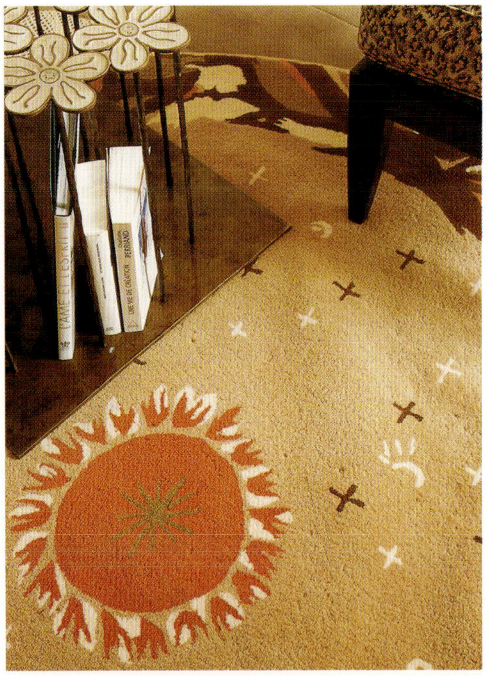
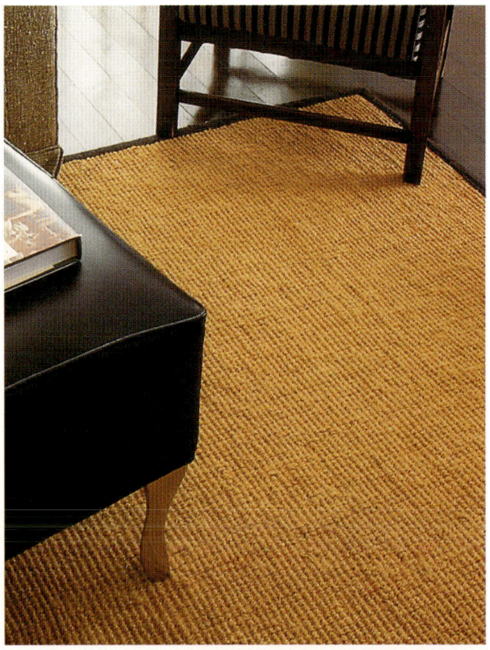
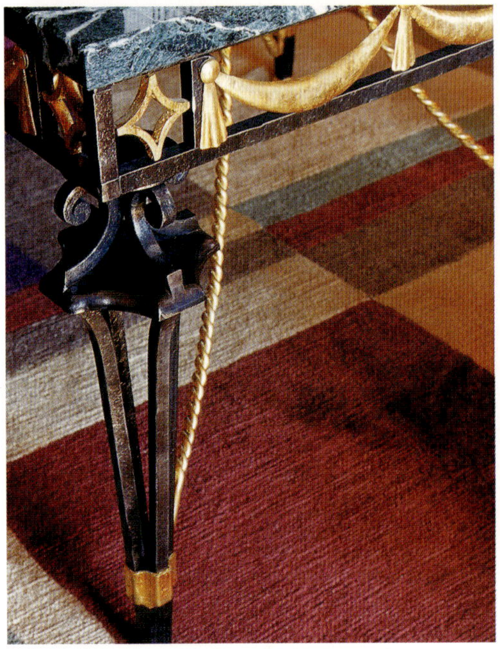
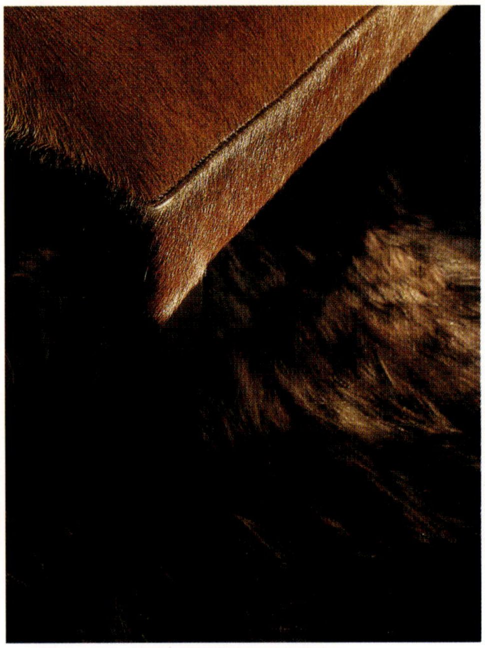
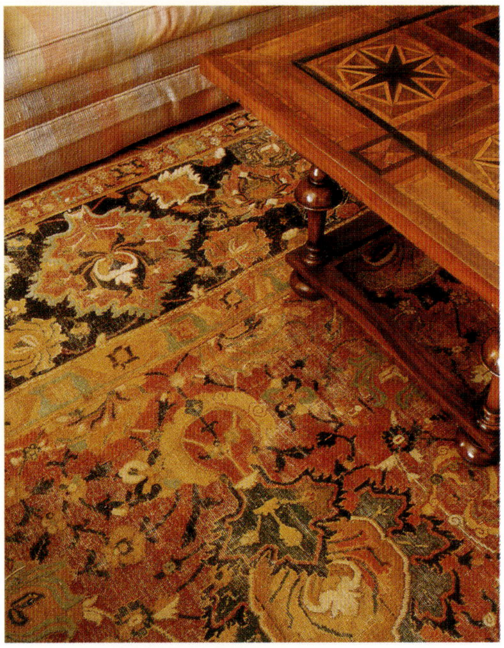
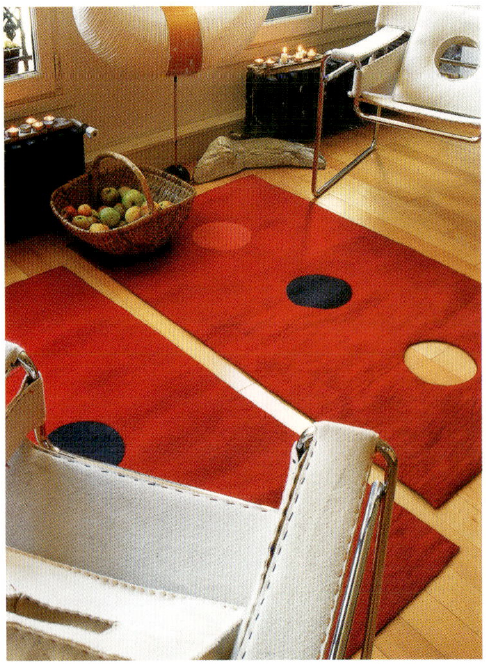
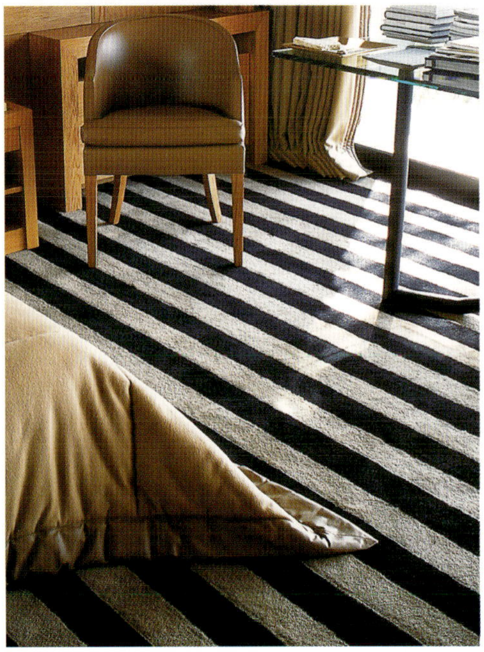
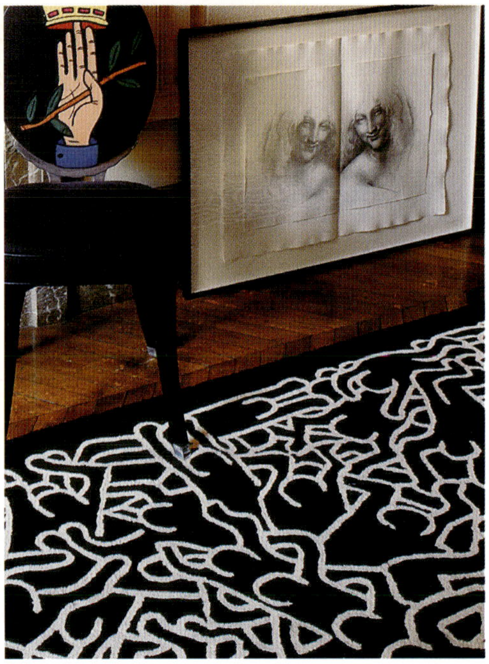

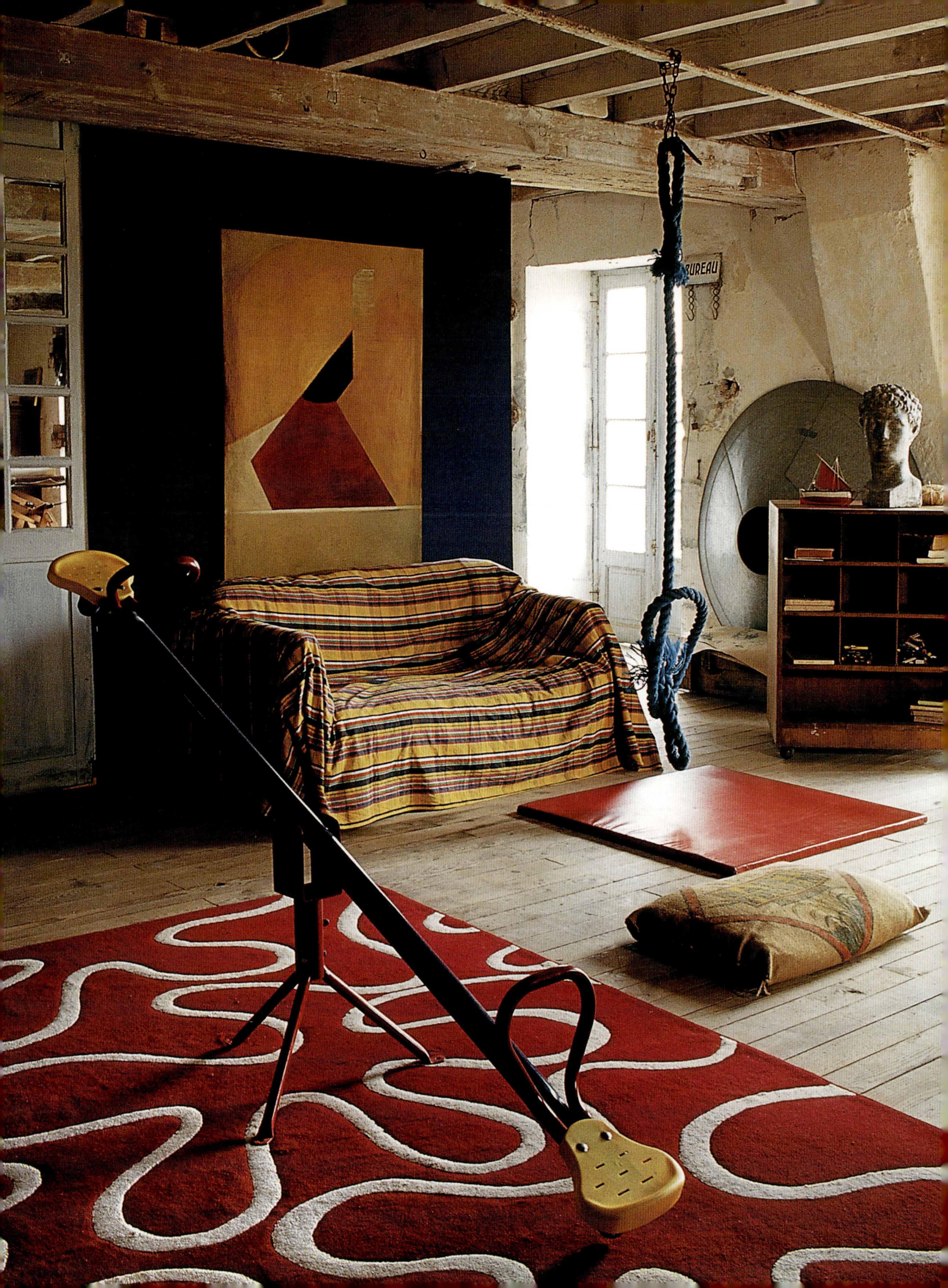

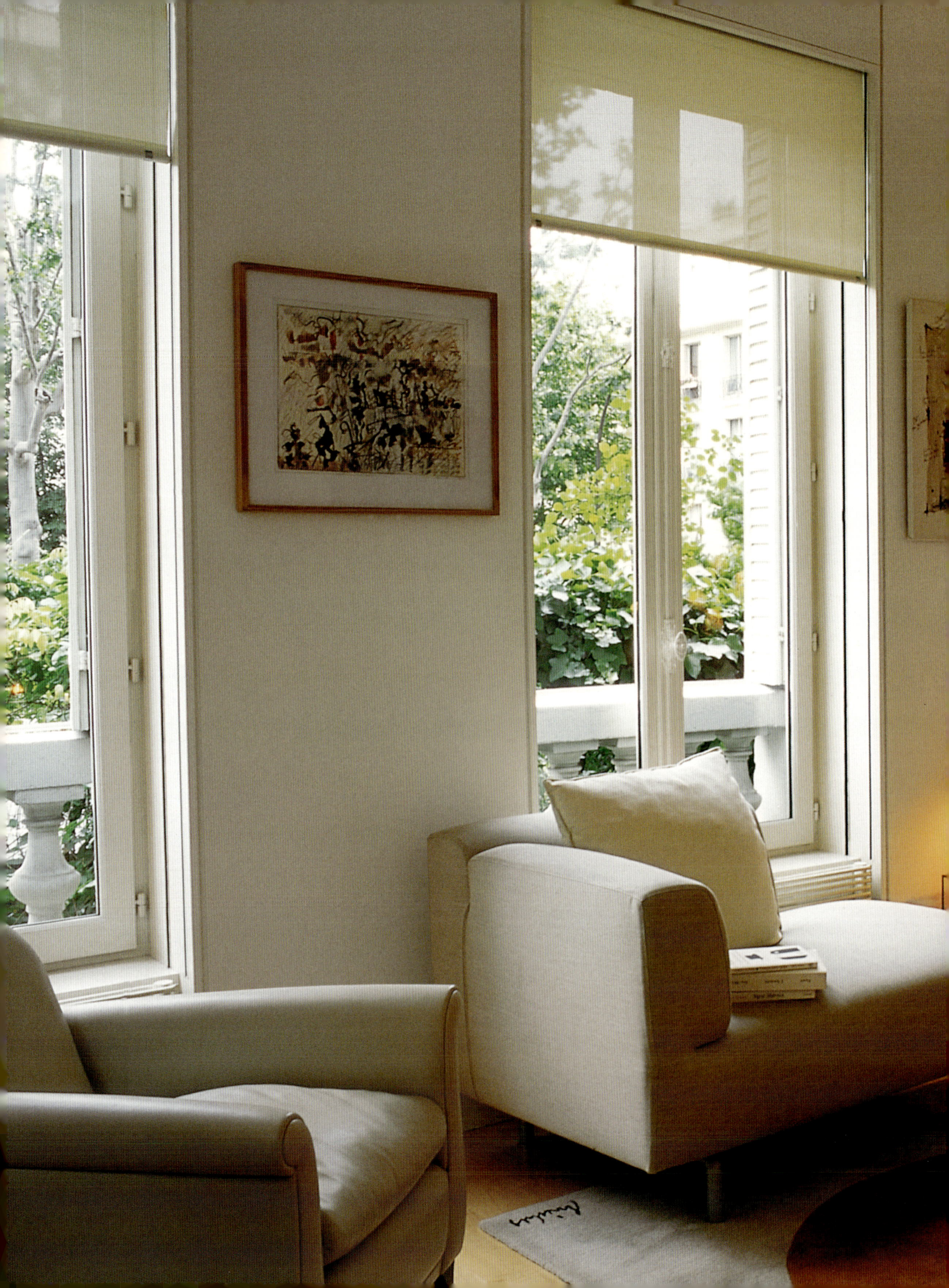

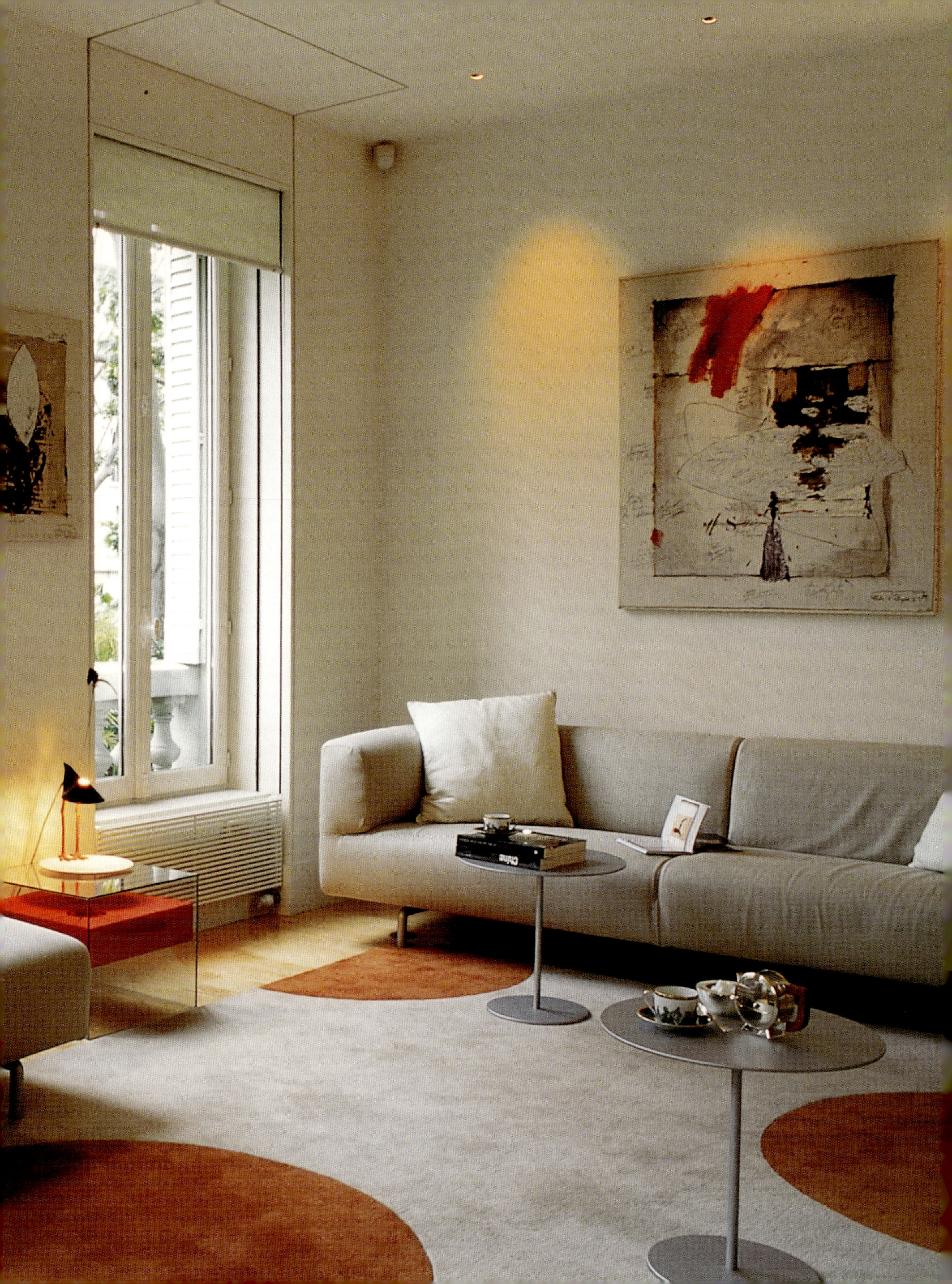

階段と手すり

Steps & Banisters

ある家の建築時の特徴は、いわば家の指紋です。どれも、建築家や施工者の手による本格的な造りであり、その家に個性を与えています。こういった内外装の特徴を見れば、その家の建築年代や様式、建築家の個性が読み取れます。もしそれが、ある時代様式を持つ家なら、その特徴は、資材業者のカタログに、きっと掲載されているはずです。一方、人々が自宅を「モダン」に見せたがった時代がありました。1970年代です。DIY好きな人は、自宅のモールディングや、幅木や、暖炉を取り外し、クラシックなパネルドアや階段の手すりを、ベニヤ板で覆うようになりました。ところが、今再び、インテリアの流れが変わりつつあります。人々は、再び住まいに伝統的な雰囲気を求め始めています。そのため、宅地開発が進む地区には、本格的な時代様式の住宅が、次々と建てられています。時代様式をもっとも感じさせる要素といえば、階段です。住まいの中心を華やかに演出する階段は、玄関ドアを開けた時に、目に飛び込んでくる位置に造られていることが多いものです。強烈な印象を与えるモダンインテリアの住宅では、金属やガラスのオープン階段や、彫刻的で、曲線的なデザインの階段をポイントにしていることが少なくありません。誰もが階段を取り替えたいと思っているわけではないでしょうが、階を増したり、屋根裏を改装したりするなら、階段を増やす必要があります。デザインで言えば、らせん階段から、折返し階段、非常階段、はしごに至るまで。材料で言えば、金属から木、石、コンクリートまで。階段は可能性の宝庫です。

The original features in a house are like its fingerprints. They are the authentic ingredients, added by the architect or the builder, to make it unique. They show the time in which it was built, its style and its creators' handwriting. If it's a period house, then those features will probably be from an amazing catalogue of builders' suppliers. But there was a time – during the 1970s – when people wanted their homes to look 'modern' and DIY enthusiasts began ripping out mouldings, skirtings and fireplaces and covering panelled doors and stair banisters with plywood. Now the tide has turned: people want a little bit of tradition, and reclamation yards are doing big business in authentic period features. Most defining of all the elements is the staircase, which can offer a spectacular flourish at the heart of the house – often in prime position when you open the front door. Some of the most impressive modern interiors often feature an open staircase in metal or glass, or a sculptural curving creation down which to glide. Not everyone wants to replace their staircase, but if you are adding an extra floor or converting the attic, you may need to add one. In which case, from spiral to dog leg to fire escape to ladder; from metal to wood to stone to concrete, there is a world of possibilities.

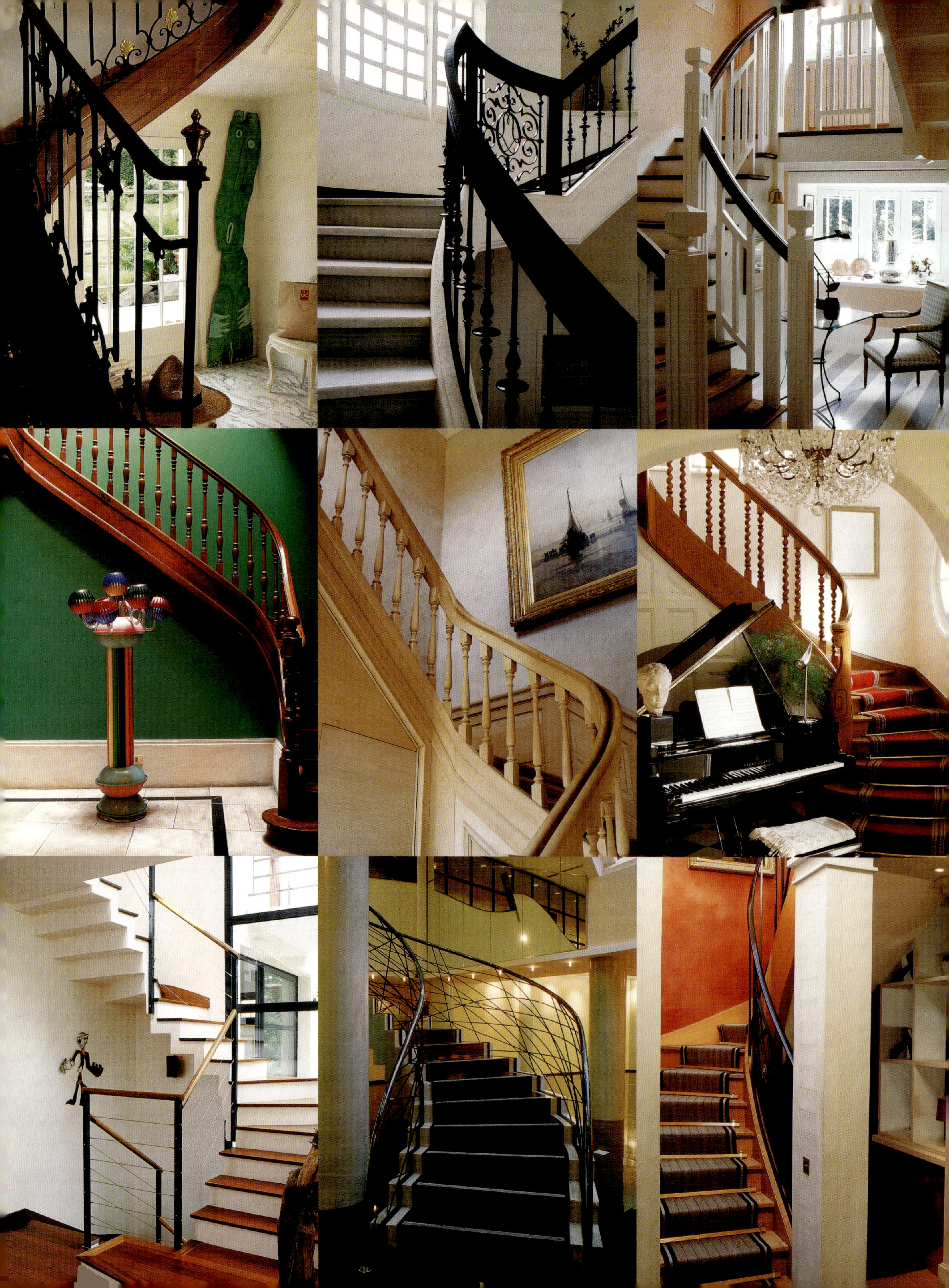

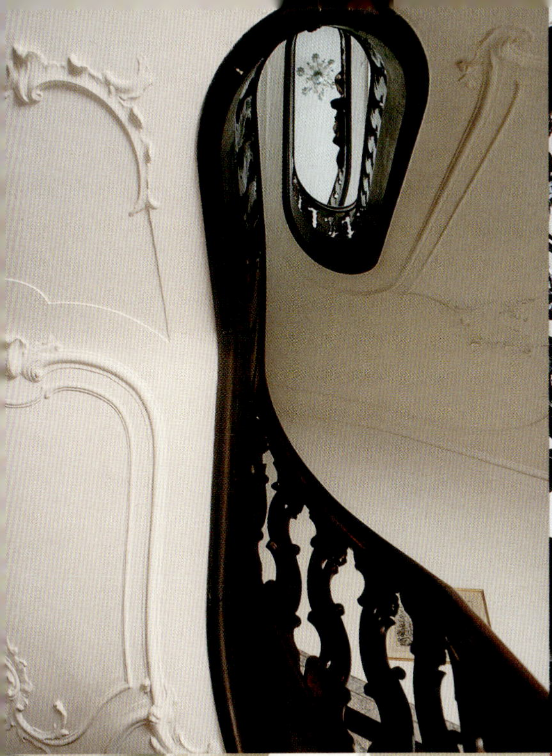
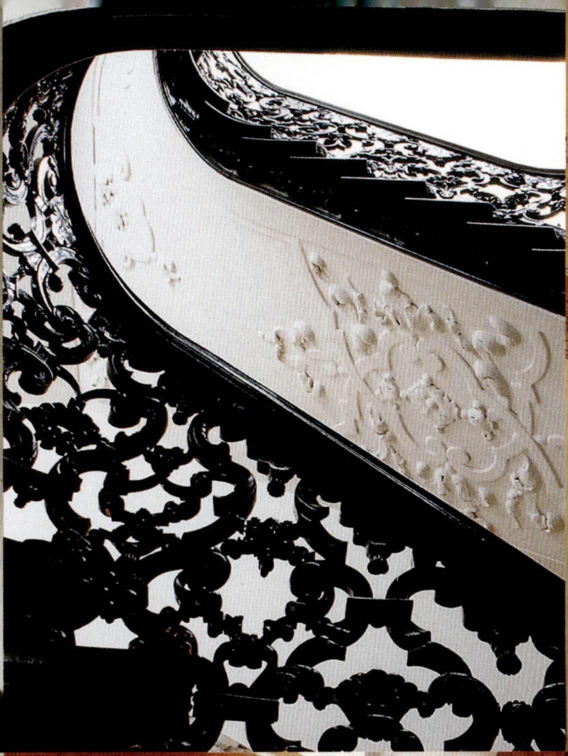
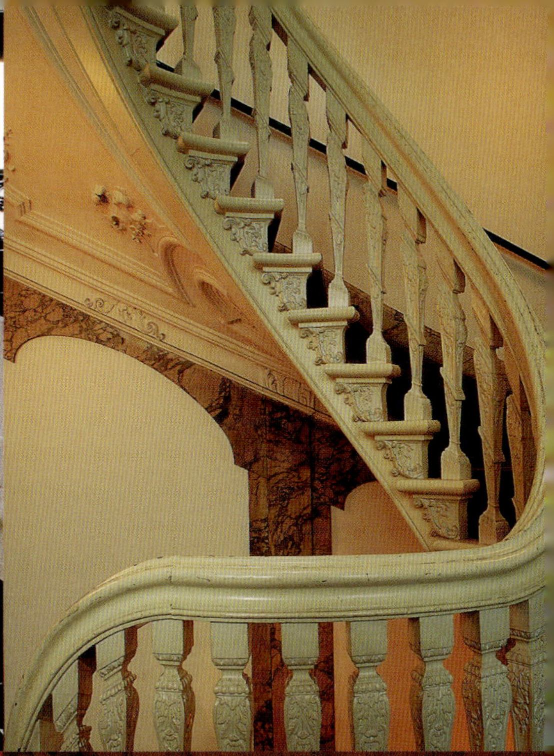
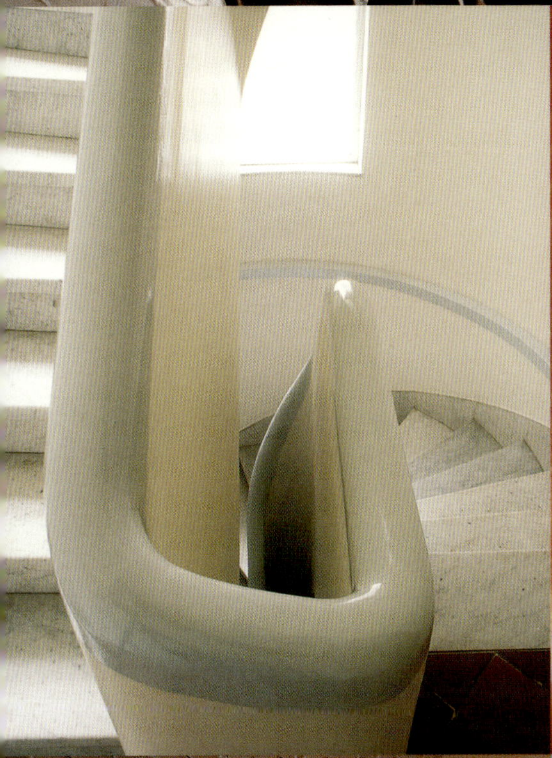
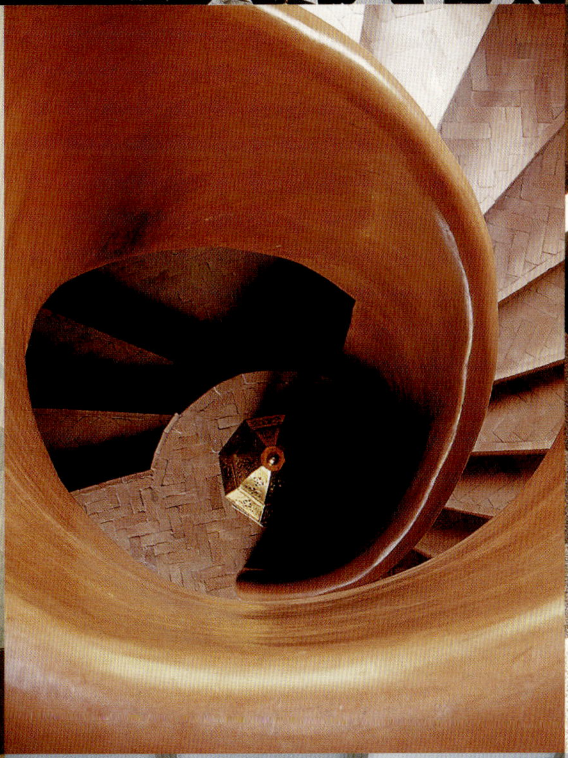
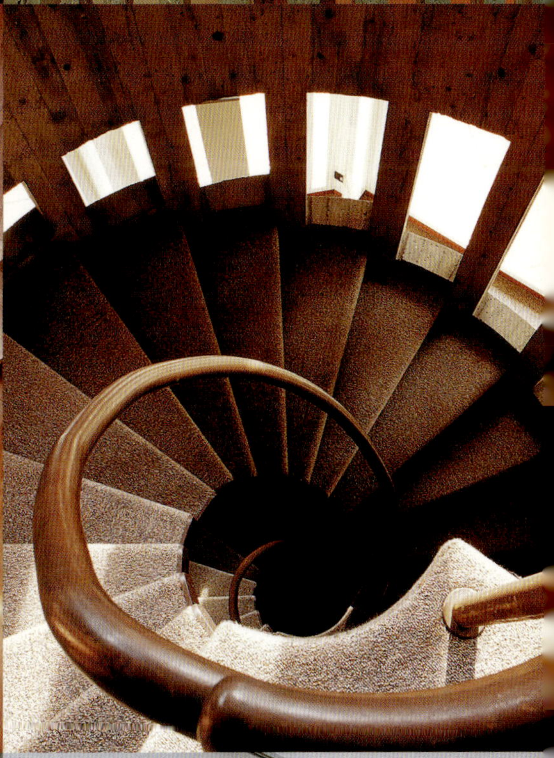
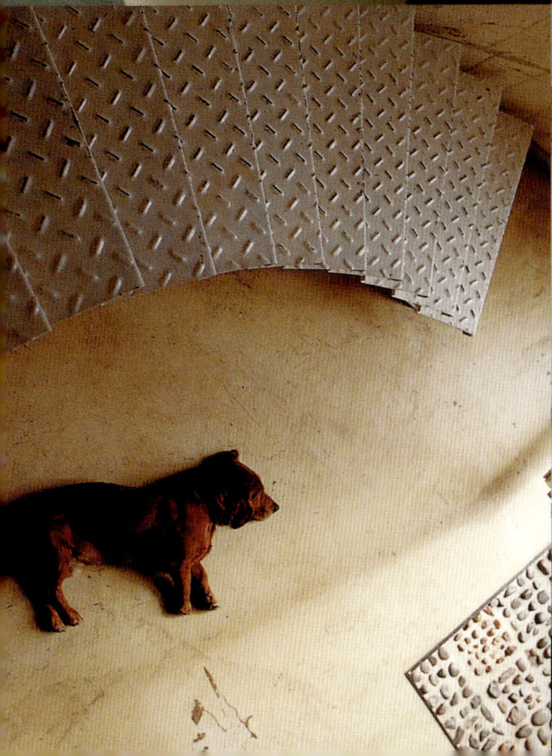
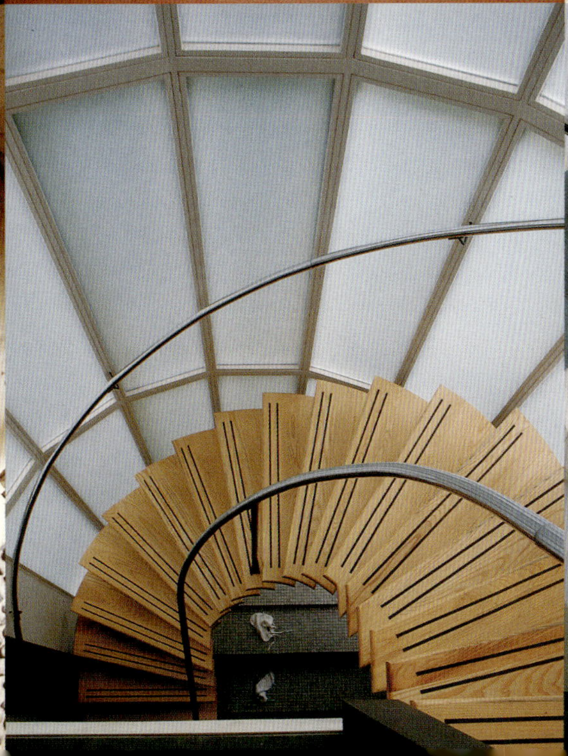
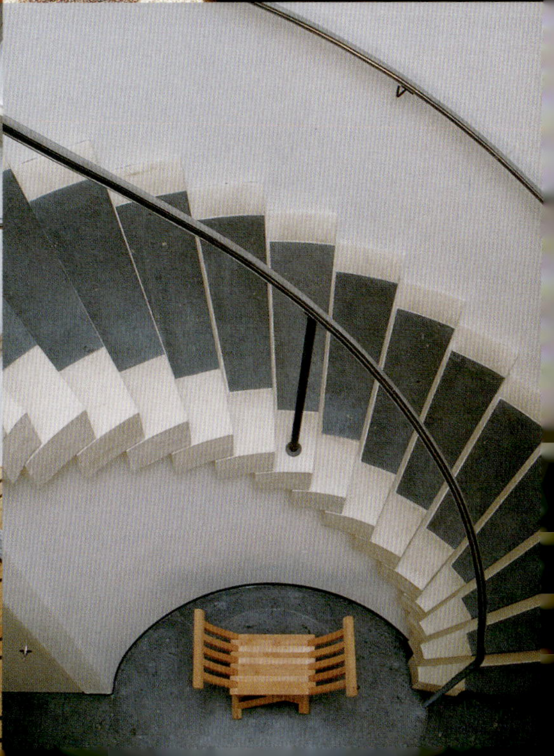

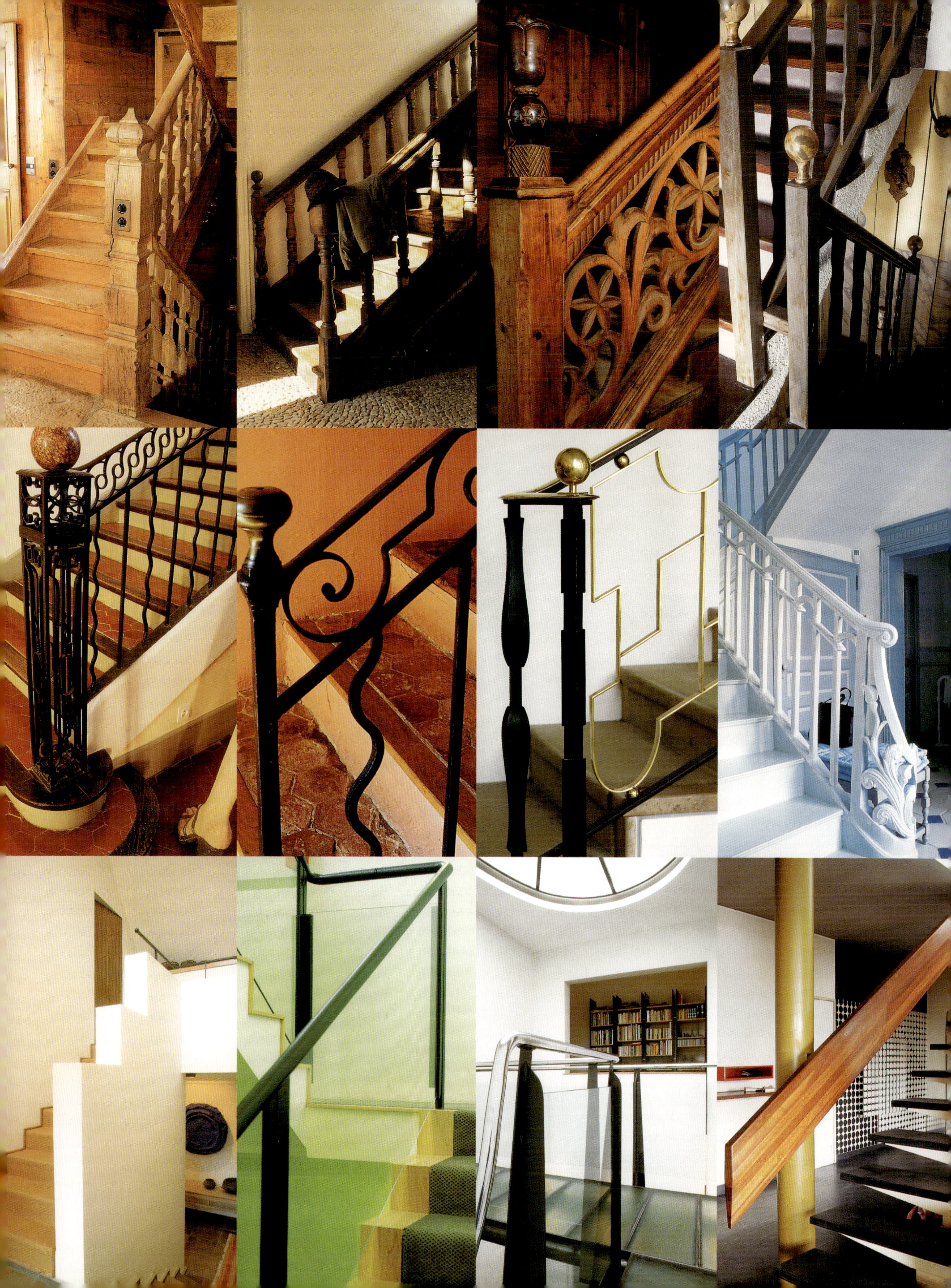

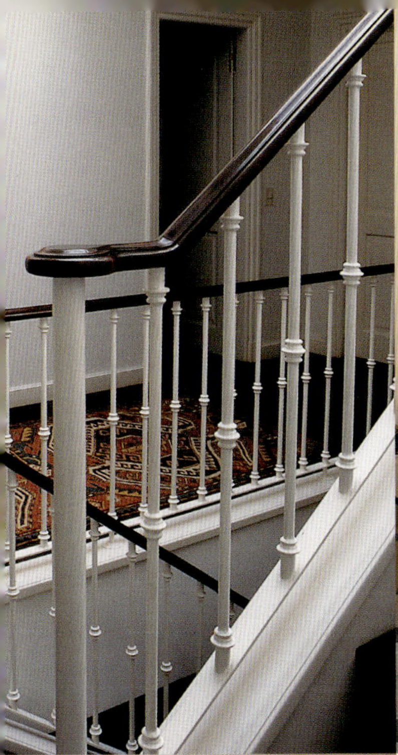
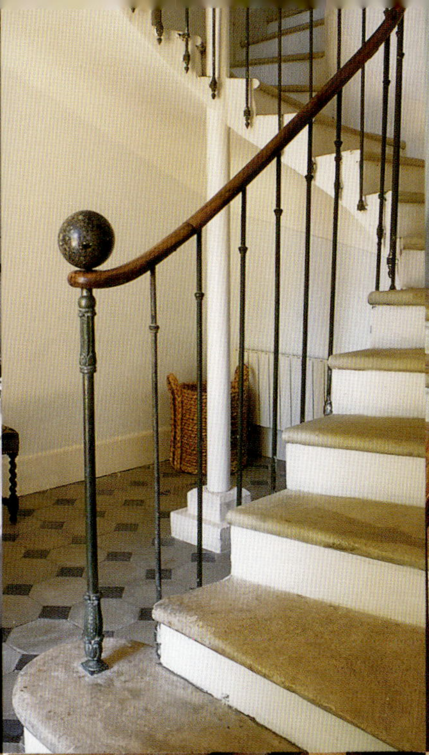
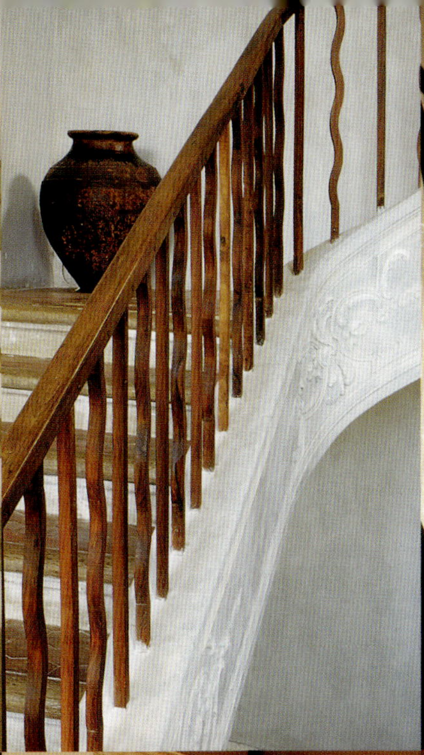
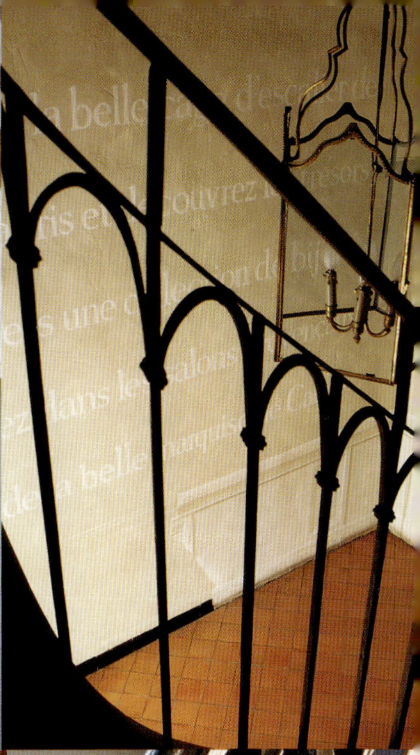
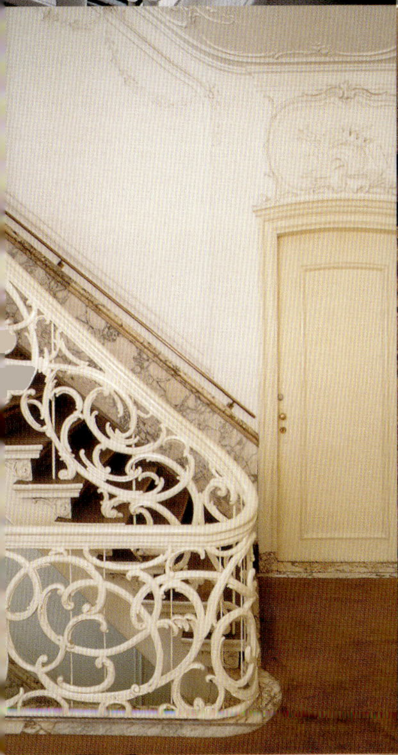
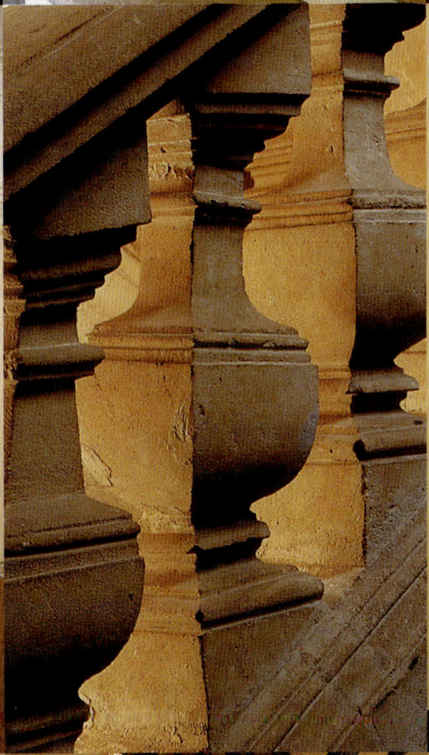
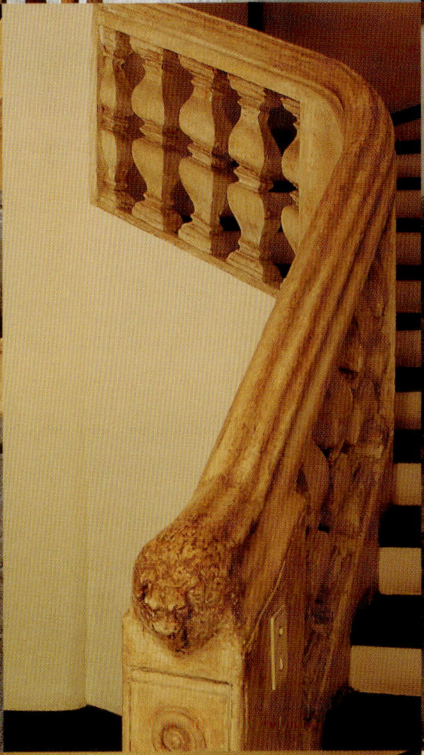
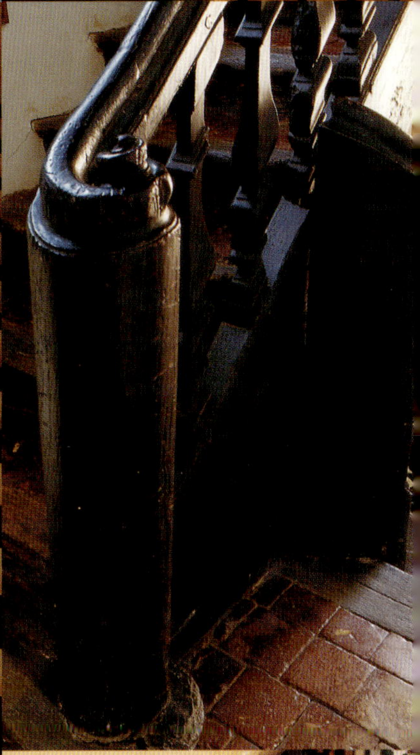
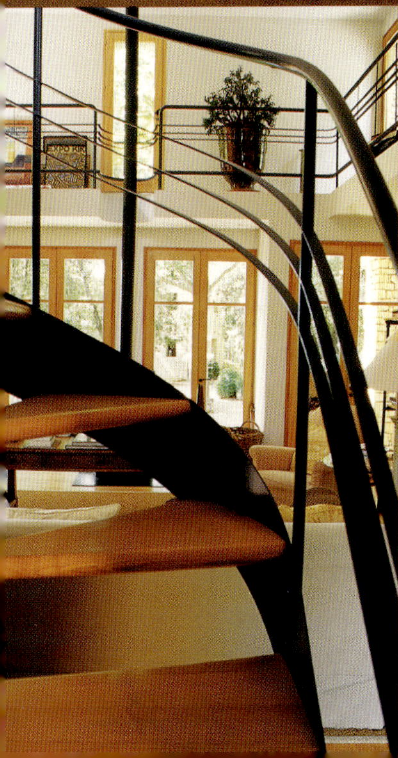
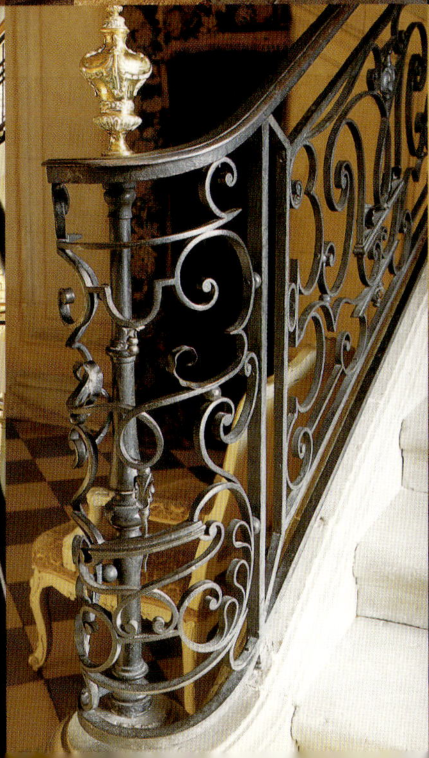
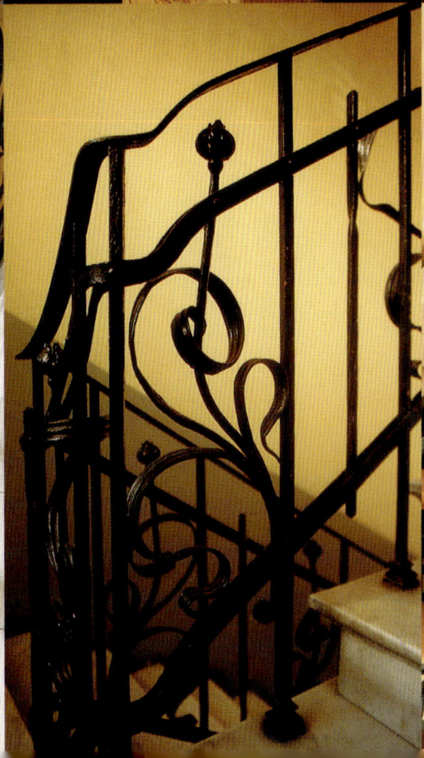
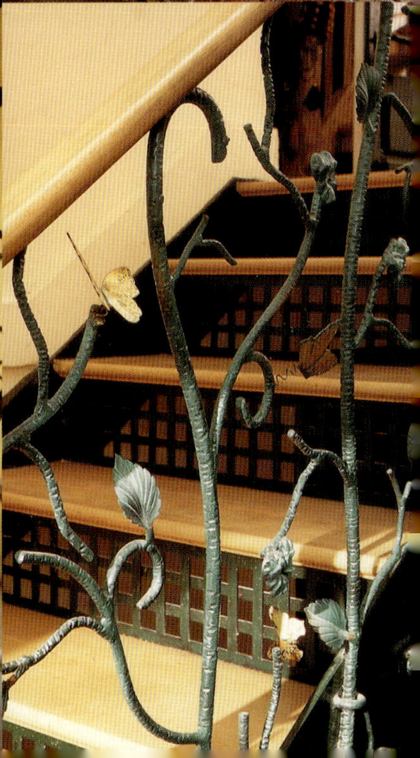

階段と手すり

階段と手すり

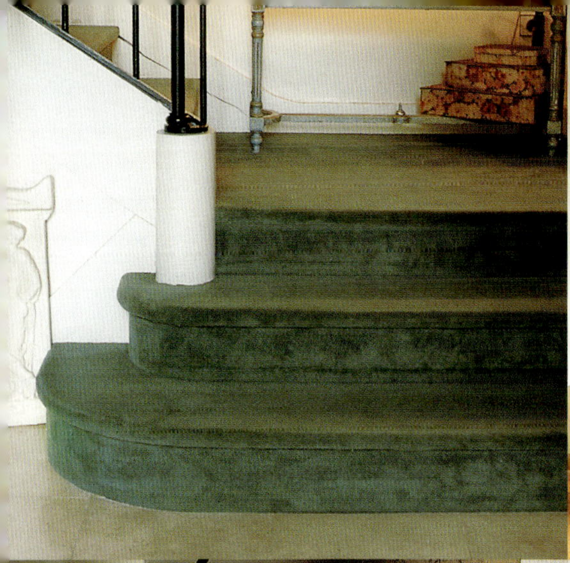
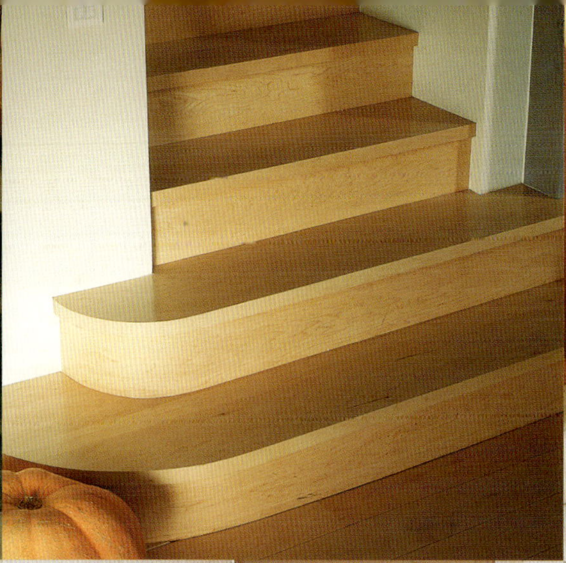
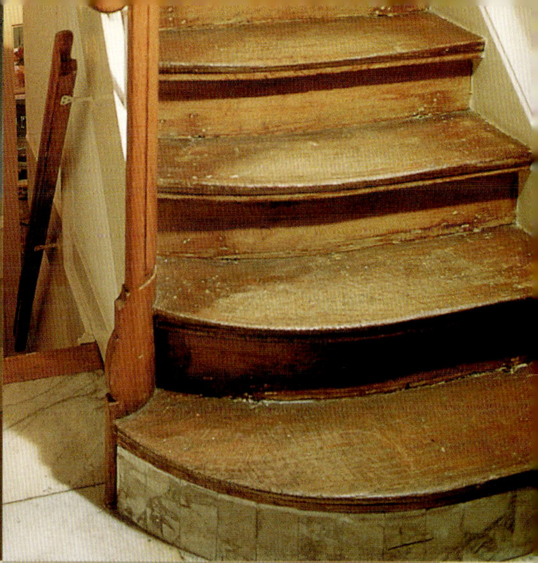
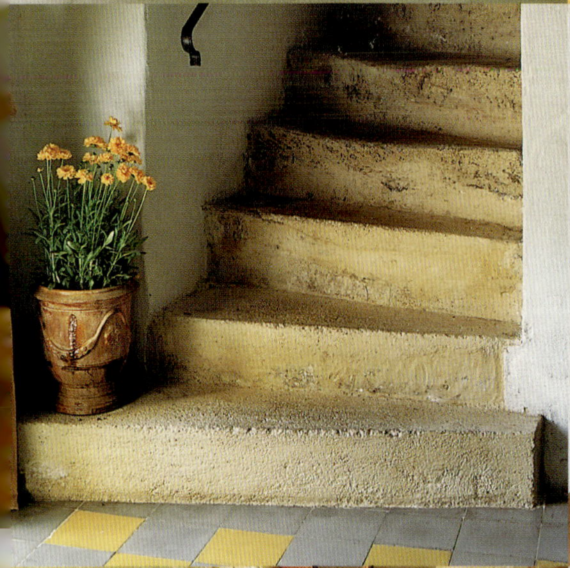
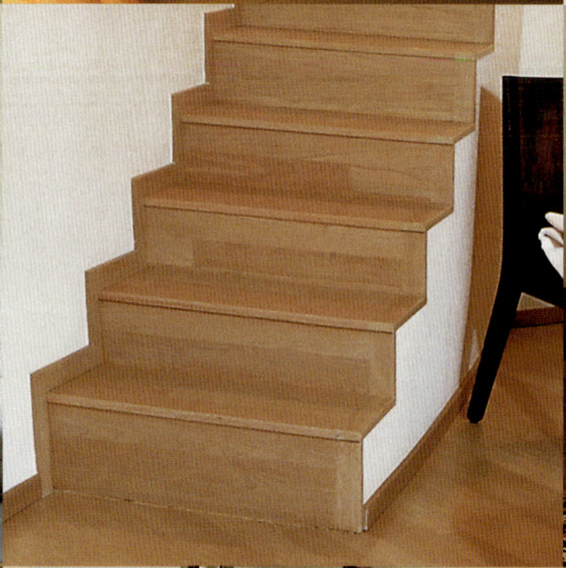
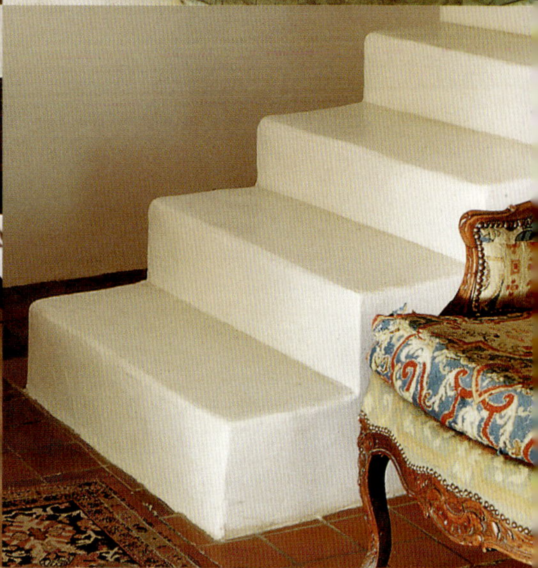
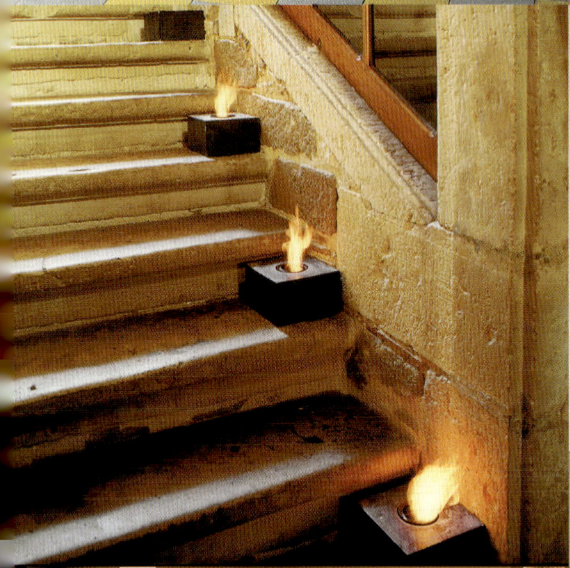
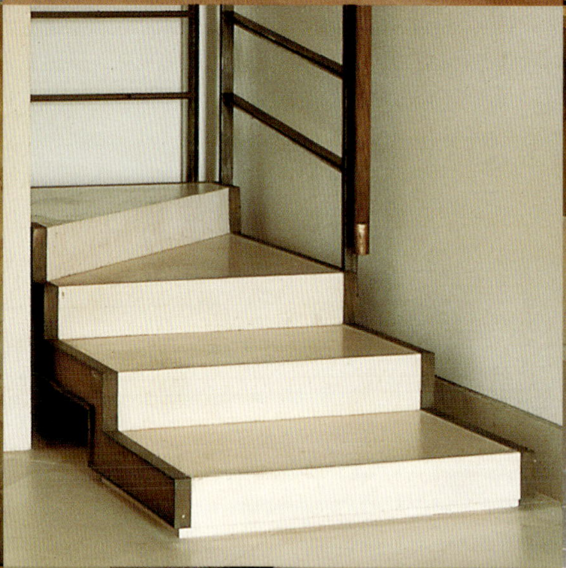
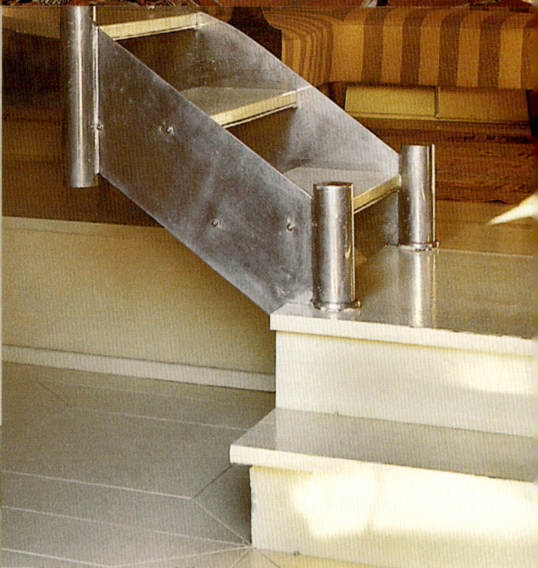
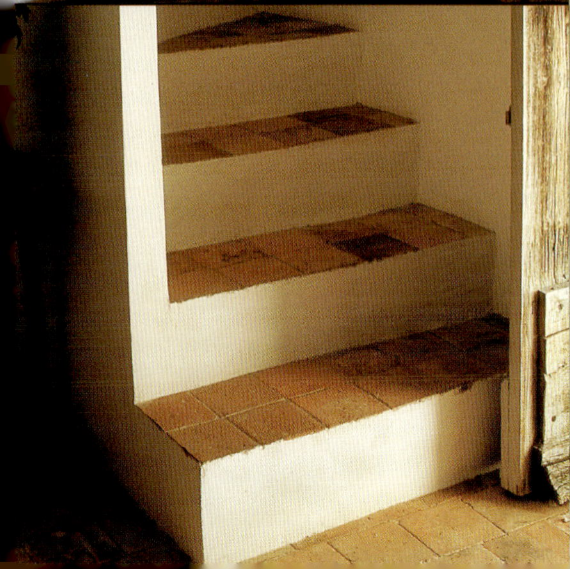
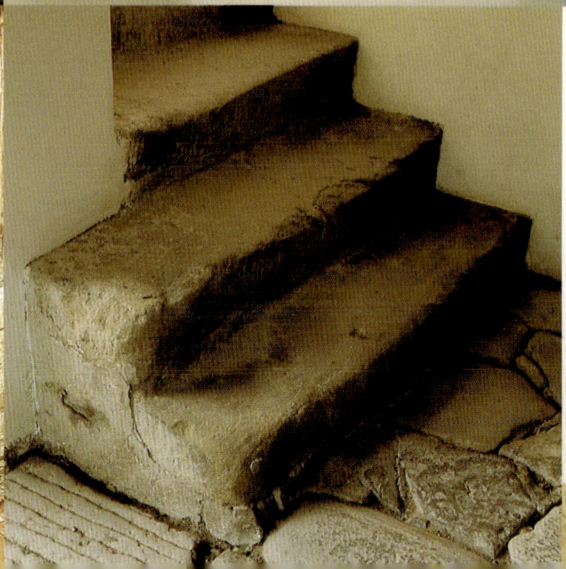
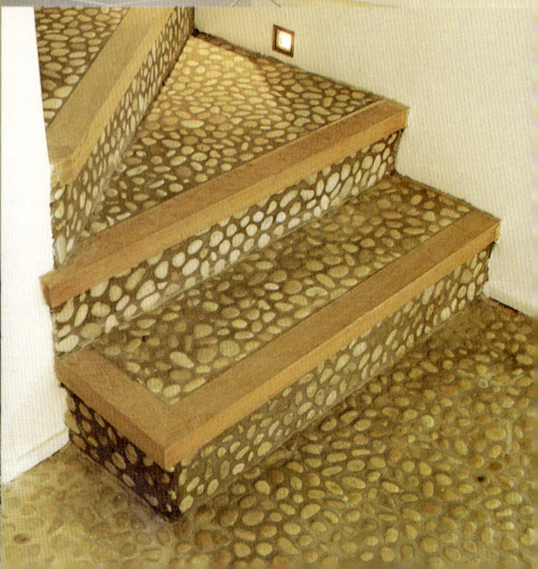

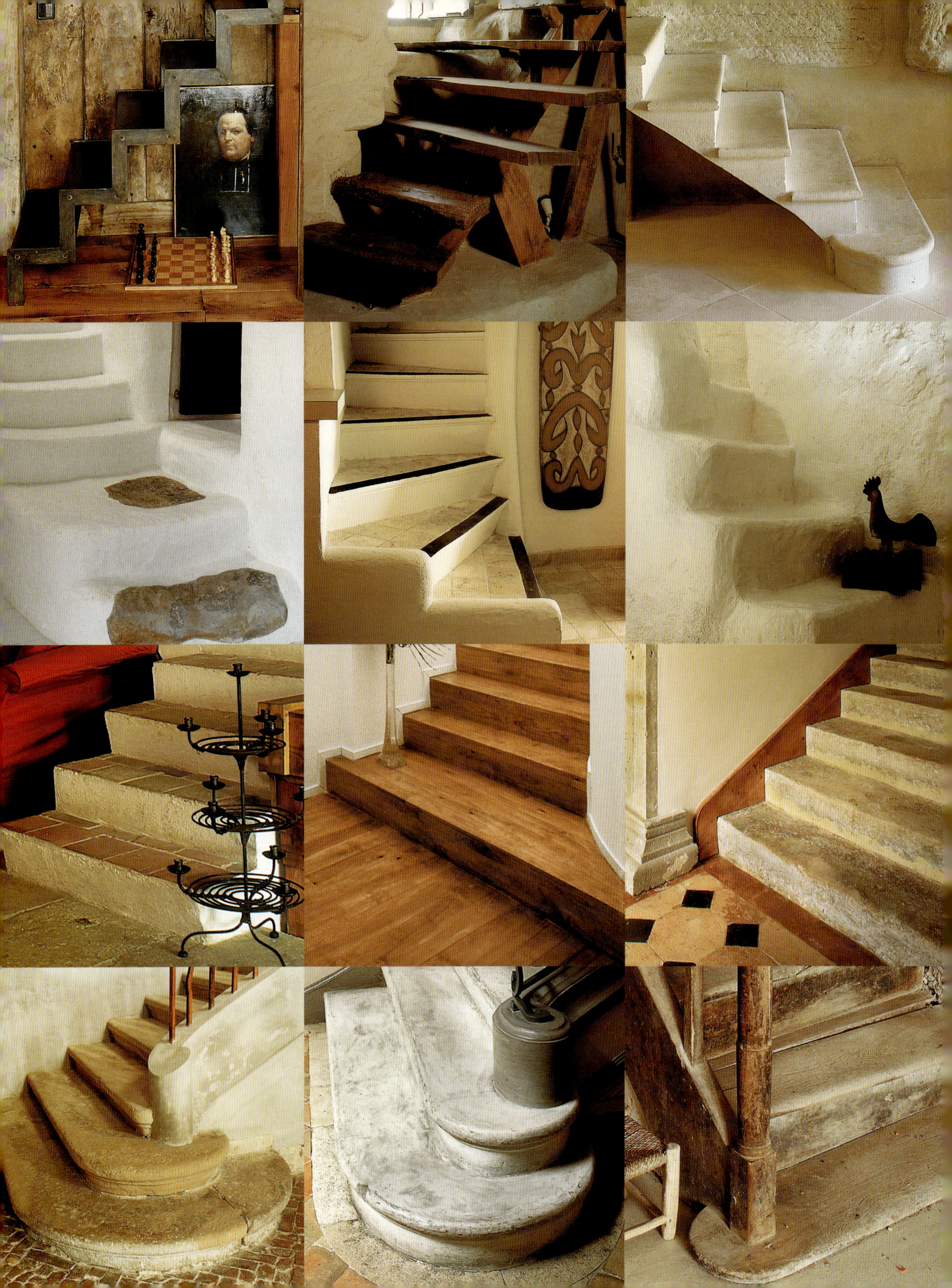

階段と手すり

階段と手すり

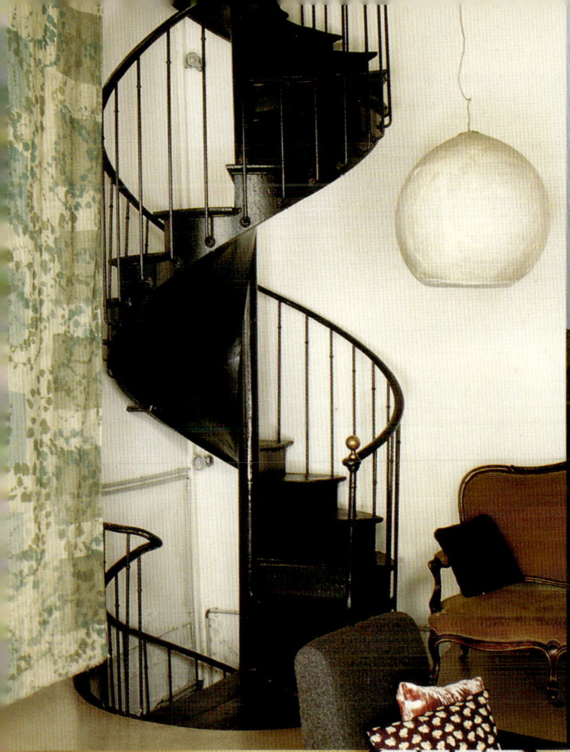
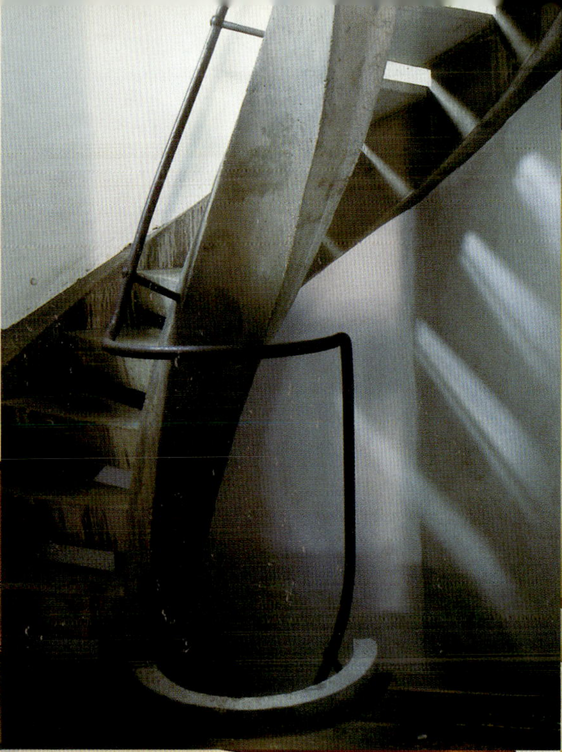
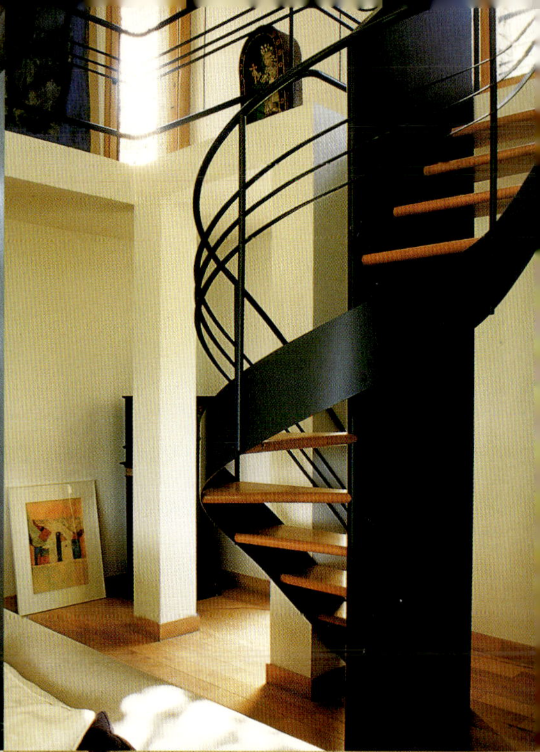
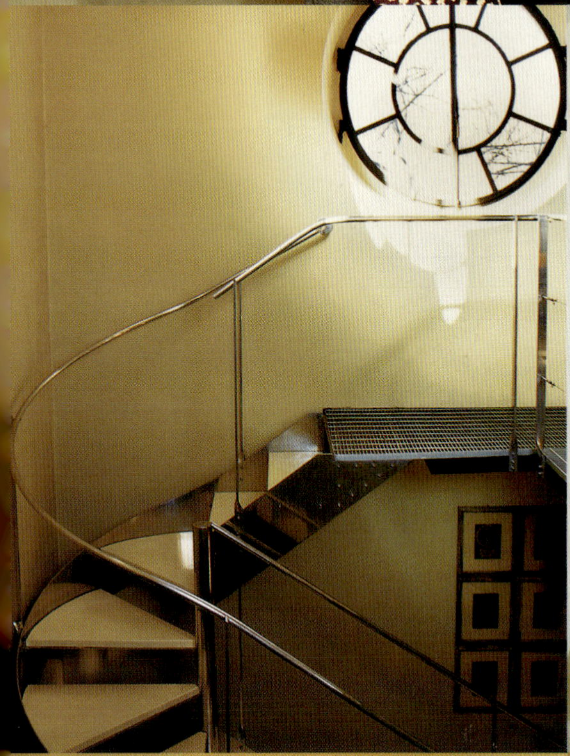
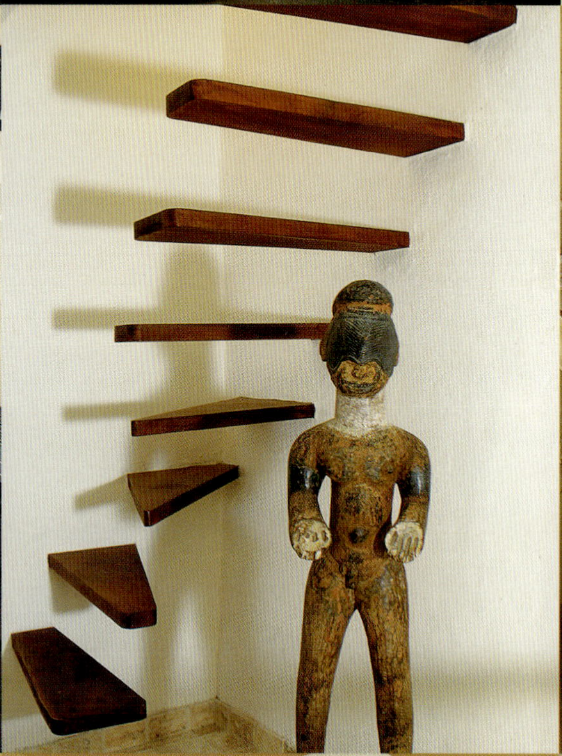
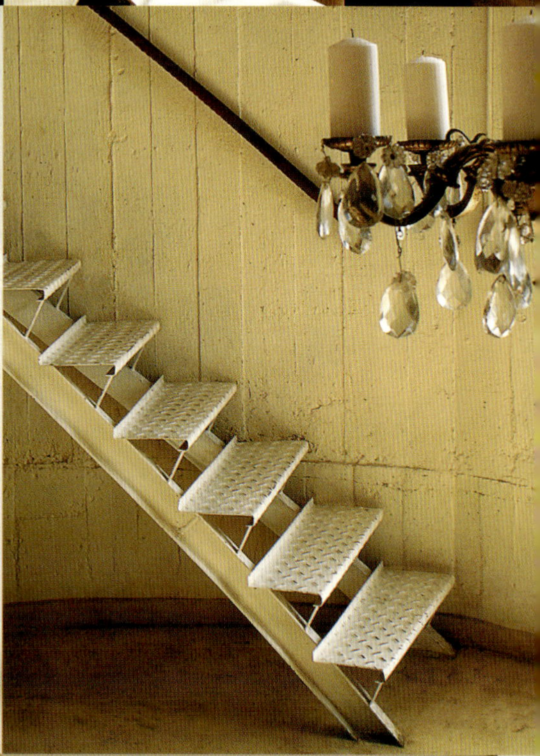
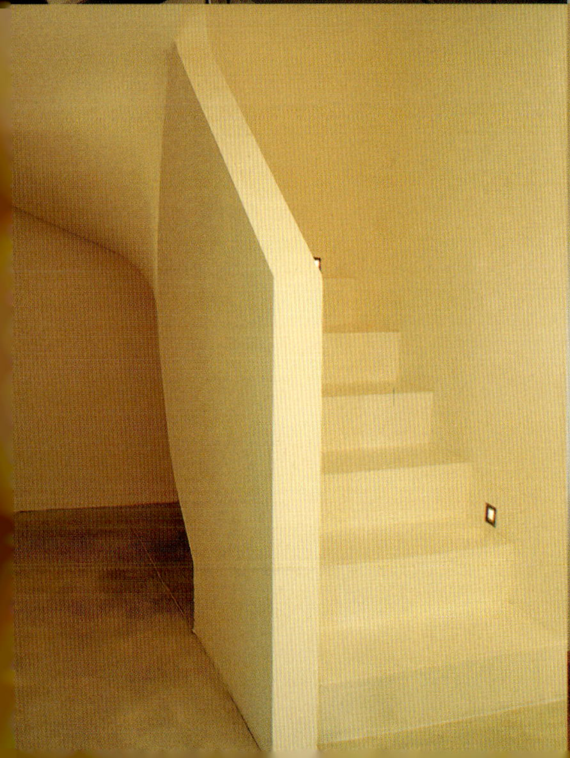
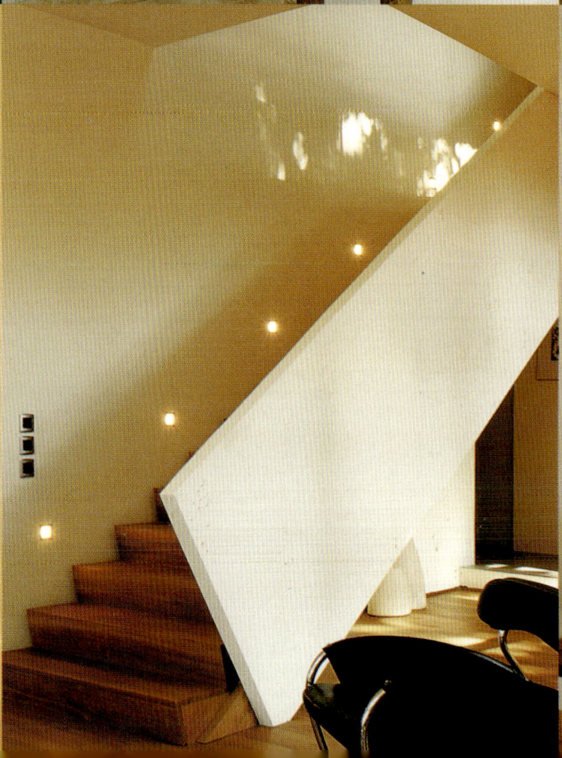
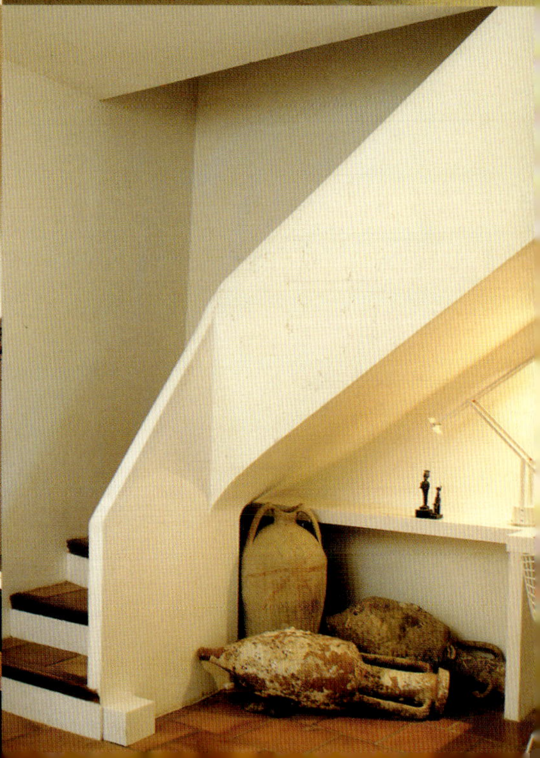

階段と手すり

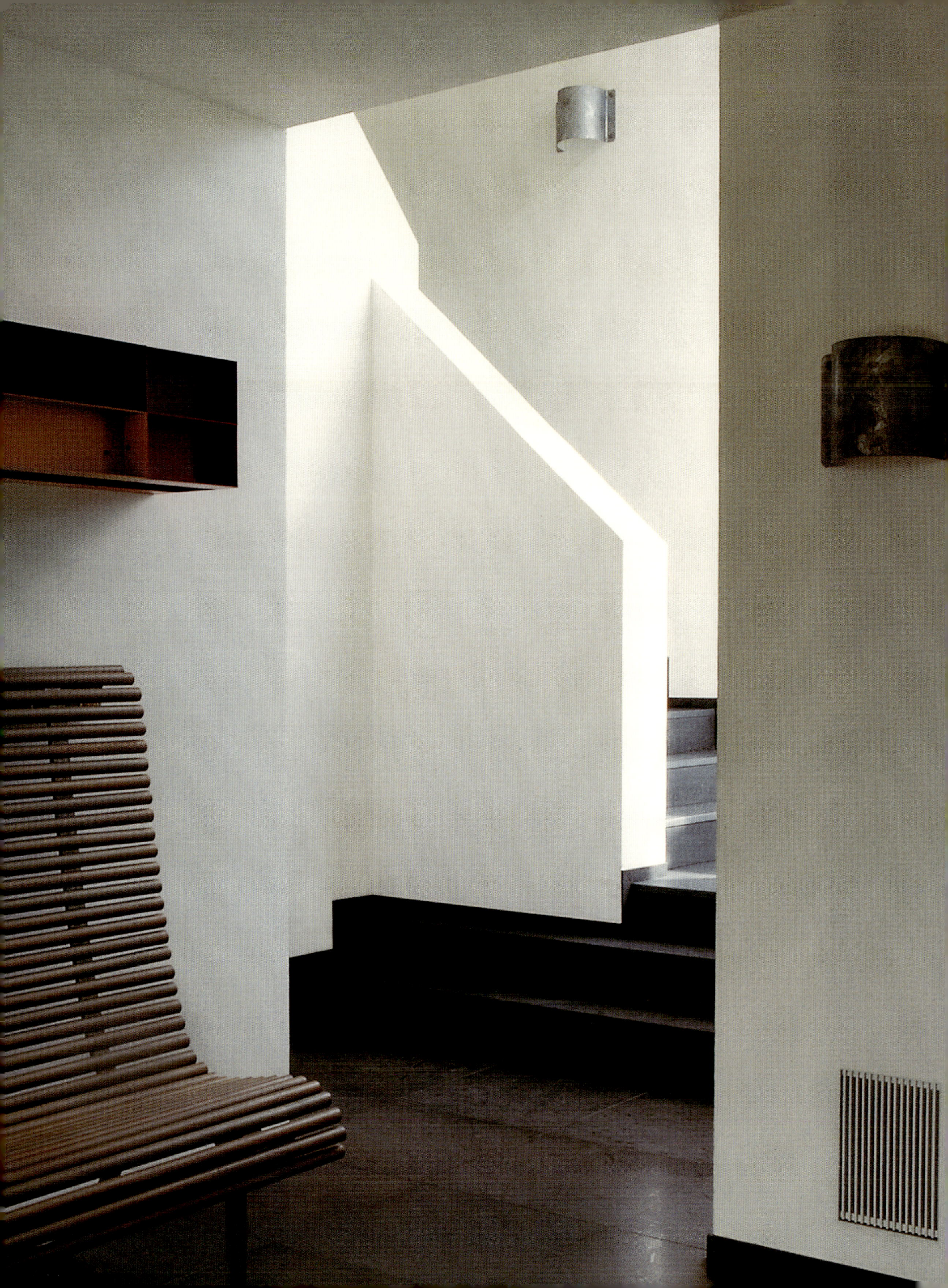

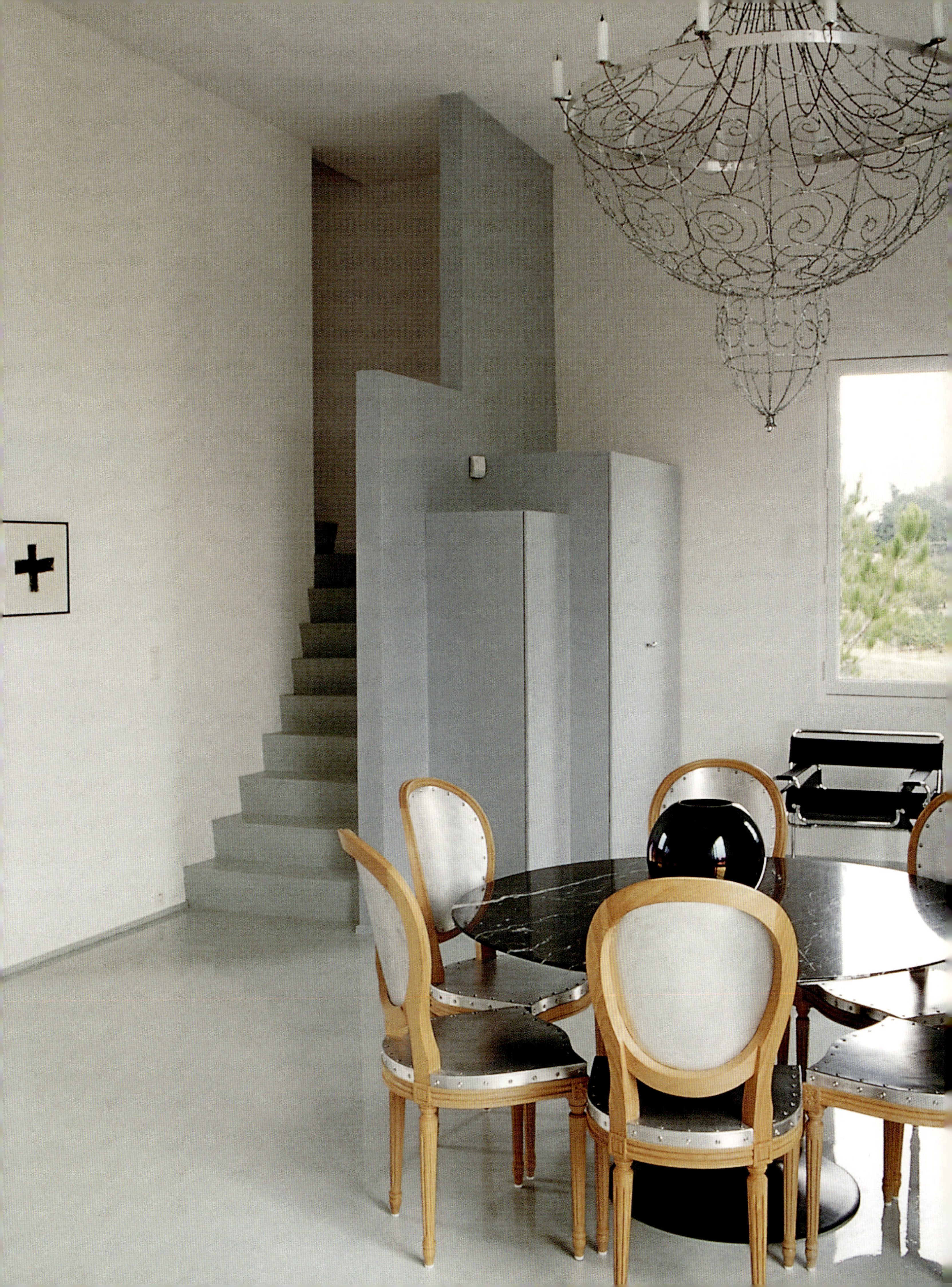

調理と食事

Cooking & Eating

家は、住む人の生活スタイル——人生のどのステージにいるか、収入はどの程度か、そして独身か、パートナーがいるか、子どもがいるか、といった家族構成の違いなど——に応えてくれます。1950年代に、「動線を三角形に」というコンセプトが生まれ、加熱調理器、冷蔵庫、シンクという3要素の、理想的な配置が確立しました。主婦が、調理のために歩く距離を、できるだけ短くするためです。調理、食事、娯楽に対する人々の姿勢は急速に変わり、技術の大きな進歩は、住まいのどの部屋よりも、キッチンに大きな影響を与えました。1920年代、都市近郊の住宅のキッチンは非常に狭く、作業スペースは建物の奥にあって、ほとんど目に付くことがありませんでした。しかし、1990年代には、キッチンのスペースが広くなり、高機能の調理器具や最先端の収納家具とワンセットになり、住まいの中心的な場所に移ったのです。現在では、都心回帰が進み、魅惑的なレストランが住まいの近隣にあるために、まったく料理をしない若者たちもいます。このような流れの中で、3タイプのキッチンが生まれました。すなわち、フォーマルなダイニングルームを備えた、洗練されたモダンキッチン、料理、食事、娯楽など、家族の生活がほぼすべてまかなえるオールインワンのファミリータイプキッチン、そして、飲食店の調理場のような加熱調理器具や、蒸し器、コーヒーメーカー、さらにガラス扉が付いた冷蔵庫などを備えたレストラン・スタイル・キッチンです。この中に、時代に合わなくなったキッチンのスタイルは、ひとつとしてありません。どれも、住む人次第、住む人の望む生活スタイル次第なのです。

Our homes respond to the way we live: the stages of our life, our income and our domestic set up – single, married or a family unit. In the 1950s, the 'work triangle' concept was formulated, establishing the ideal position for the cooker, the fridge and the sink unit, so that a housewife didn't have to walk too far – if at all. Rapid changes in attitudes towards cooking, eating and entertaining, and massive advances in technology have had a bigger impact on the kitchen than anywhere else in the home. In the 1920s, the suburban kitchen was a tiny, rarely seen work station at the back of the building, but in the 1990s it was enlarged and moved to a prime position with high-tech equipment and state-of-the-art joinery. Now, with the move towards city centre living and with the abundance of tempting neighbourhood restaurants, some young people choose not to cook at all. Along the way, we had the smart modern kitchen and formal dining room, the family room with its cooking, eating, entertaining and general family life free-for-all, and the restaurant-style kitchen with its industrial-looking cookers, steamers, coffee makers and even glass-fronted fridges. None of these solutions have become inappropriate, it's up to you, your style and how you want to live.

調理と食事

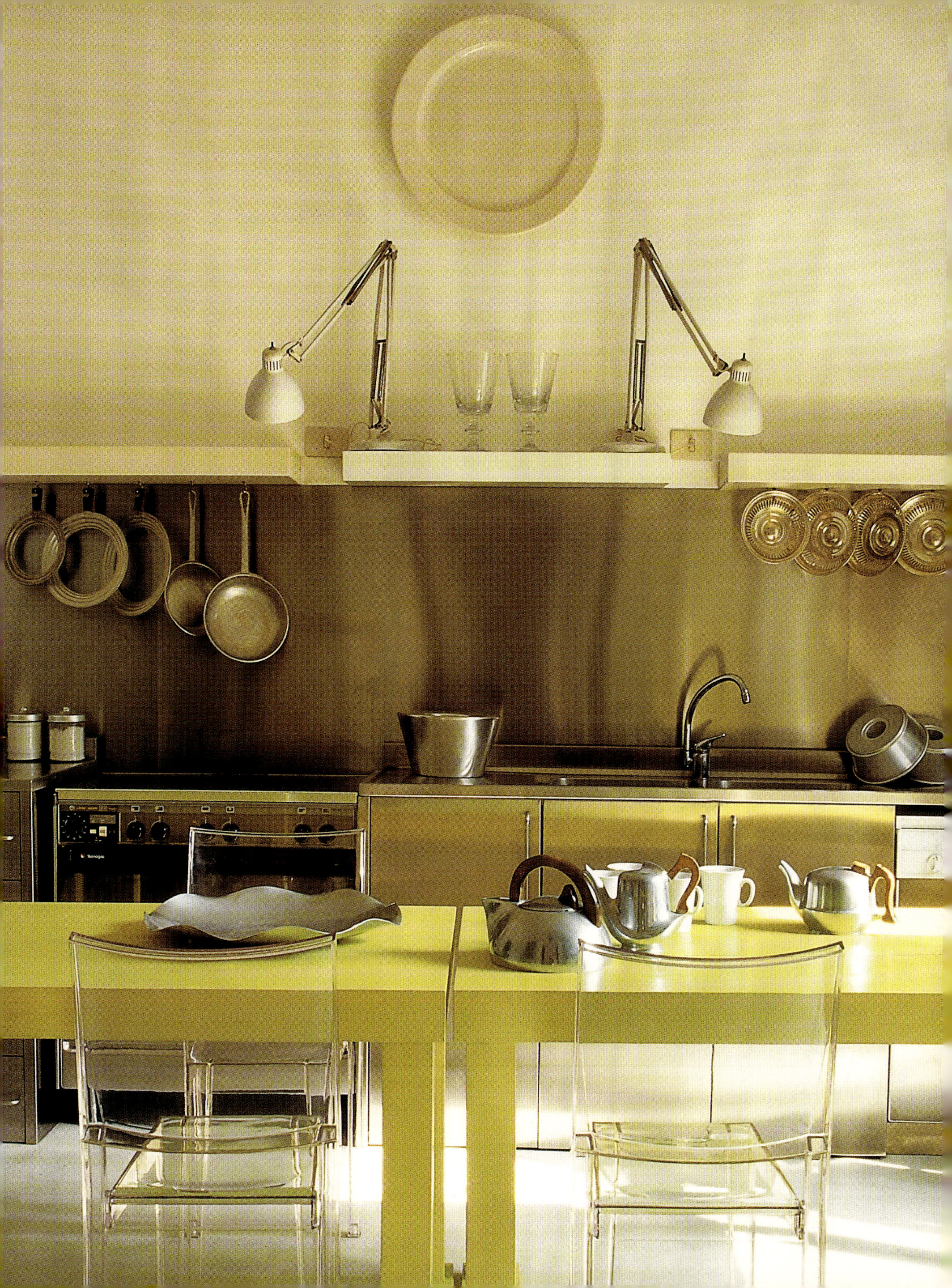

調理と食事

調理と食事

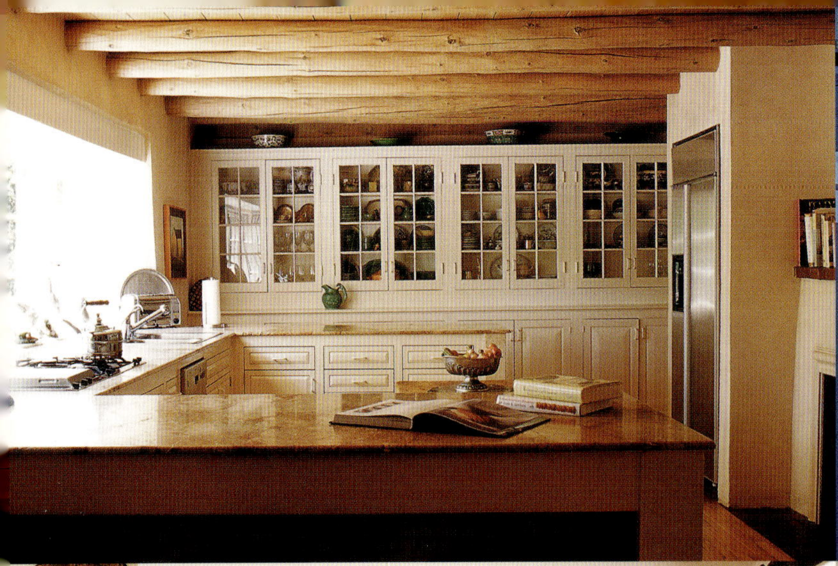
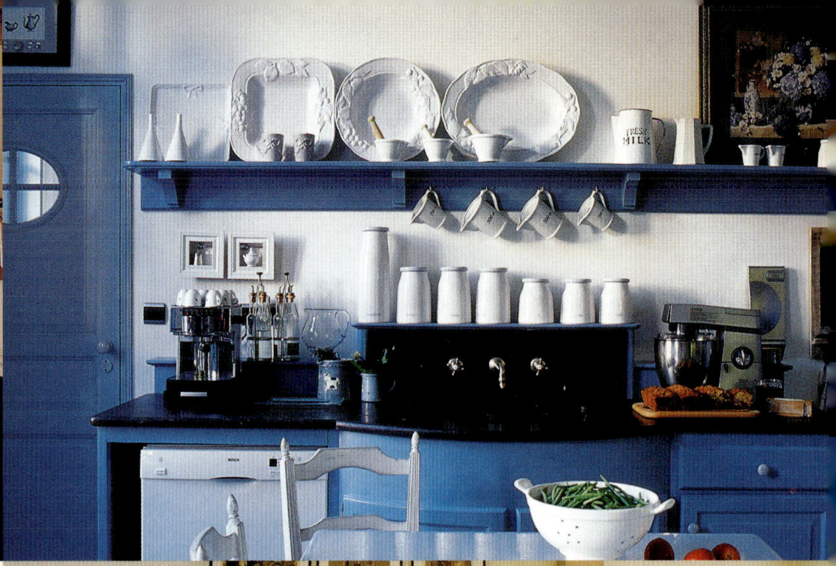
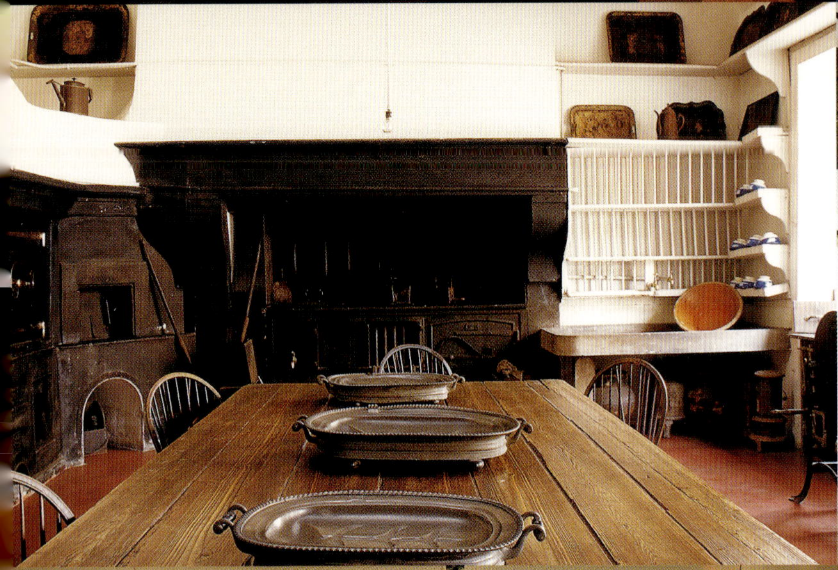
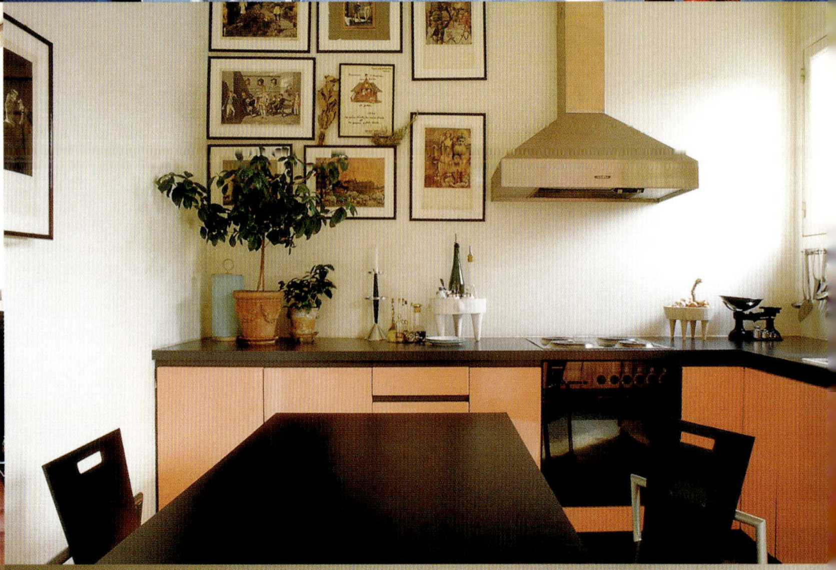
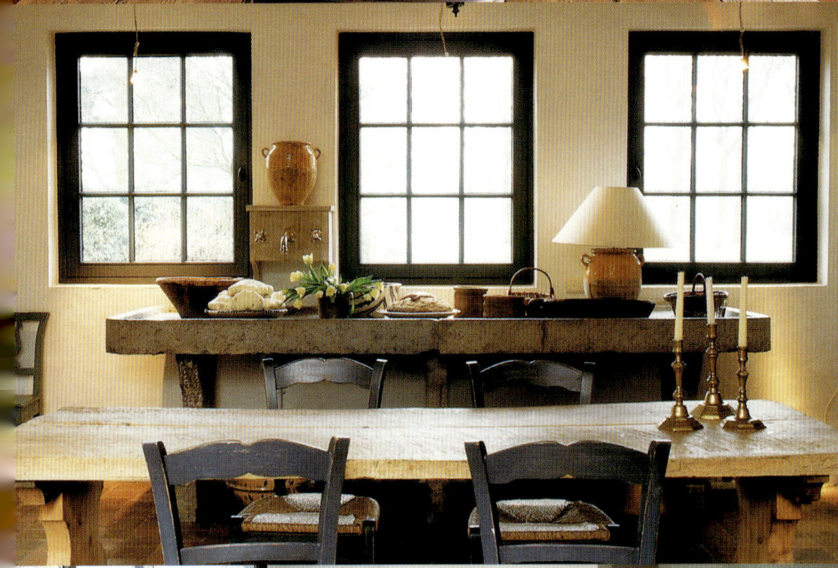
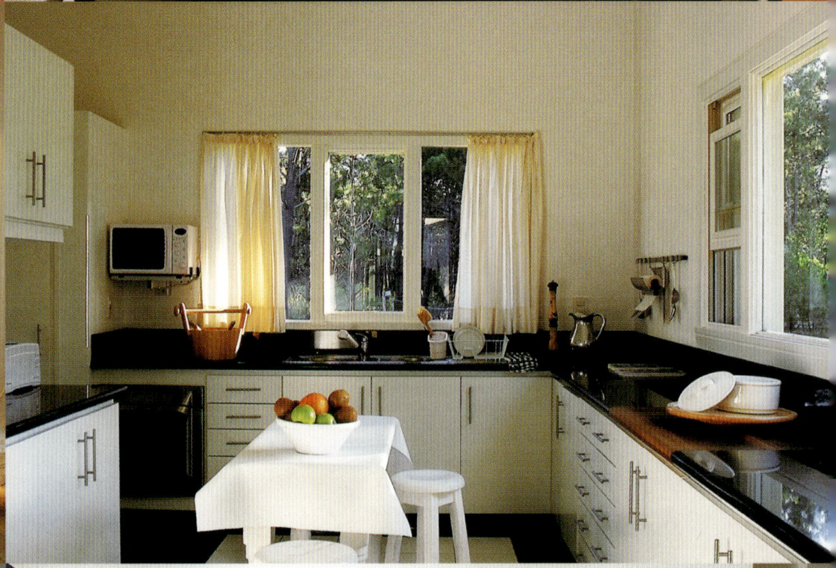
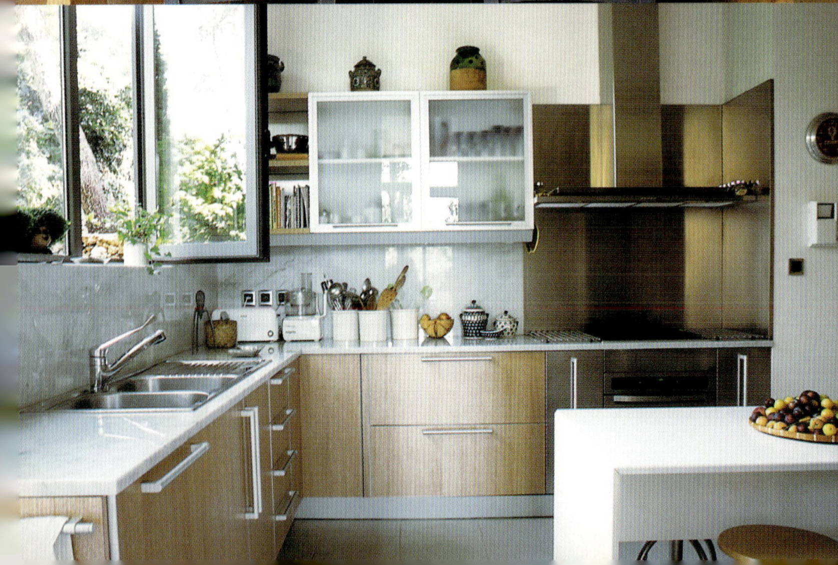
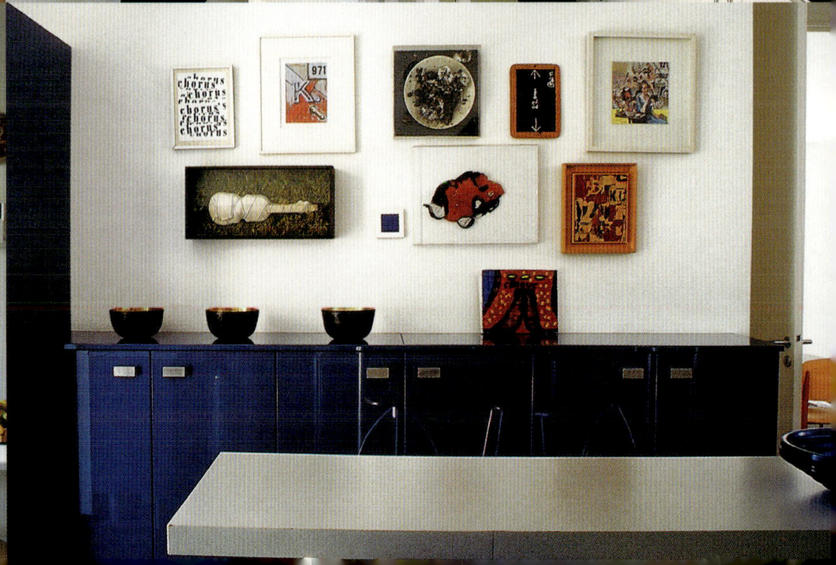

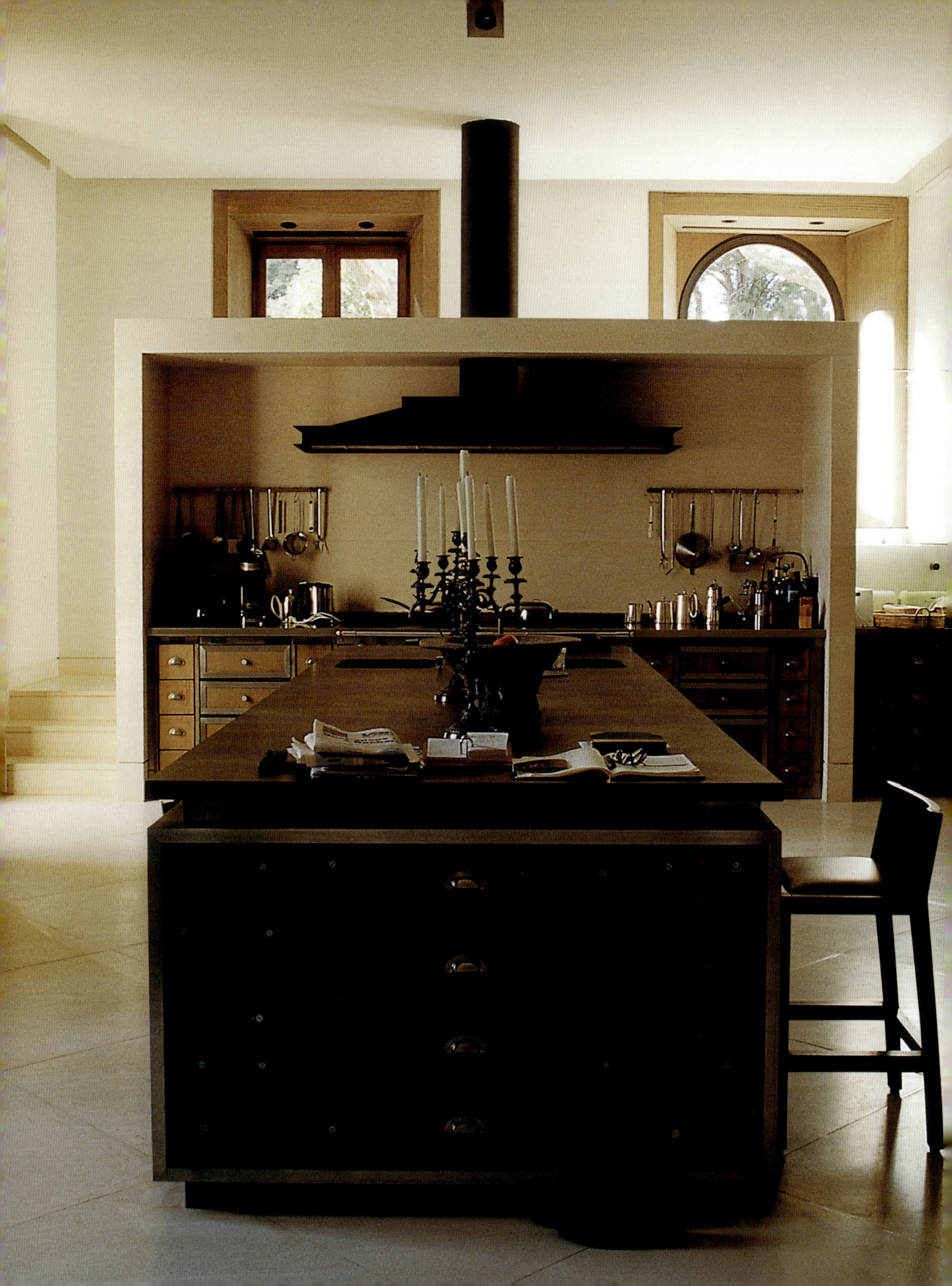

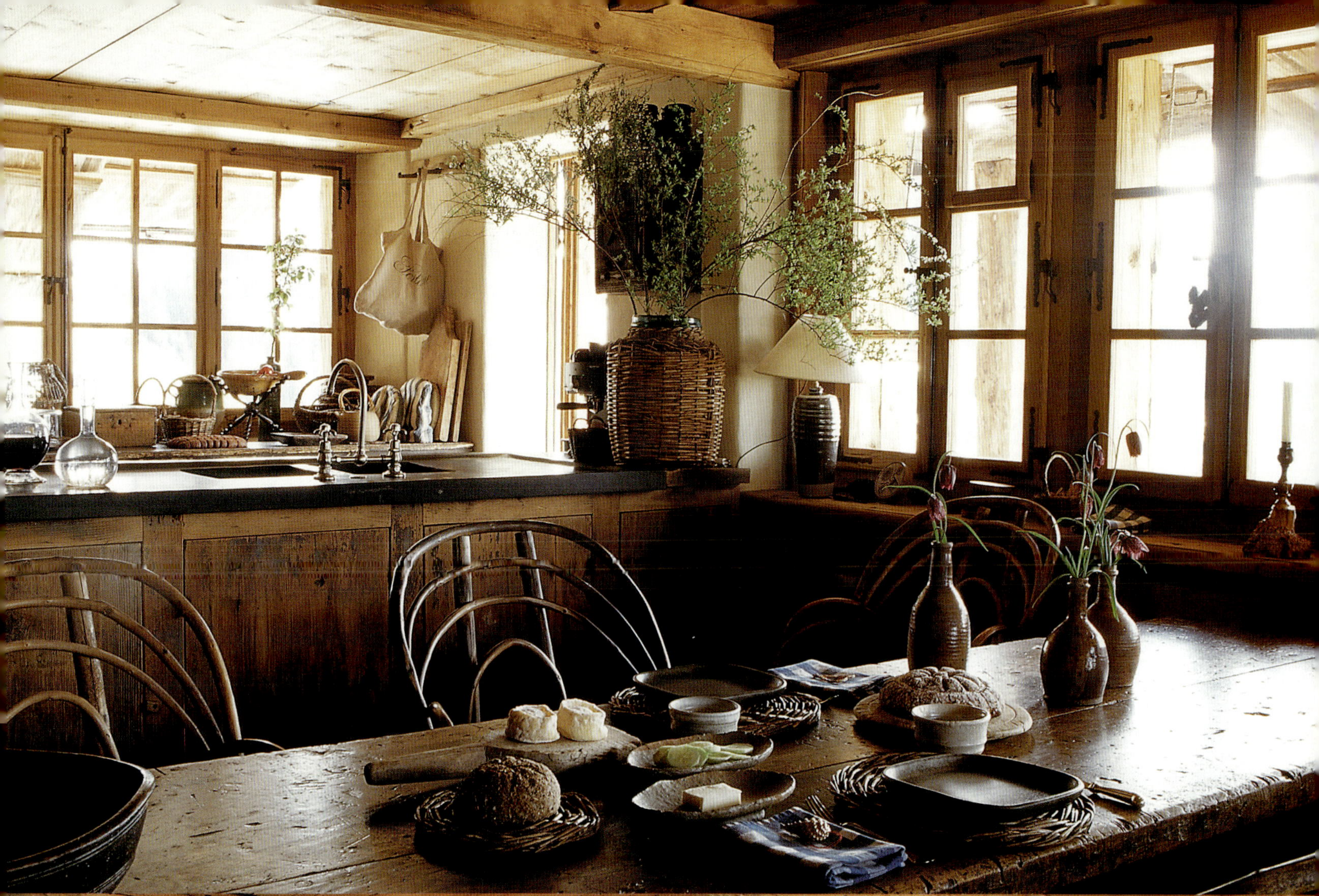

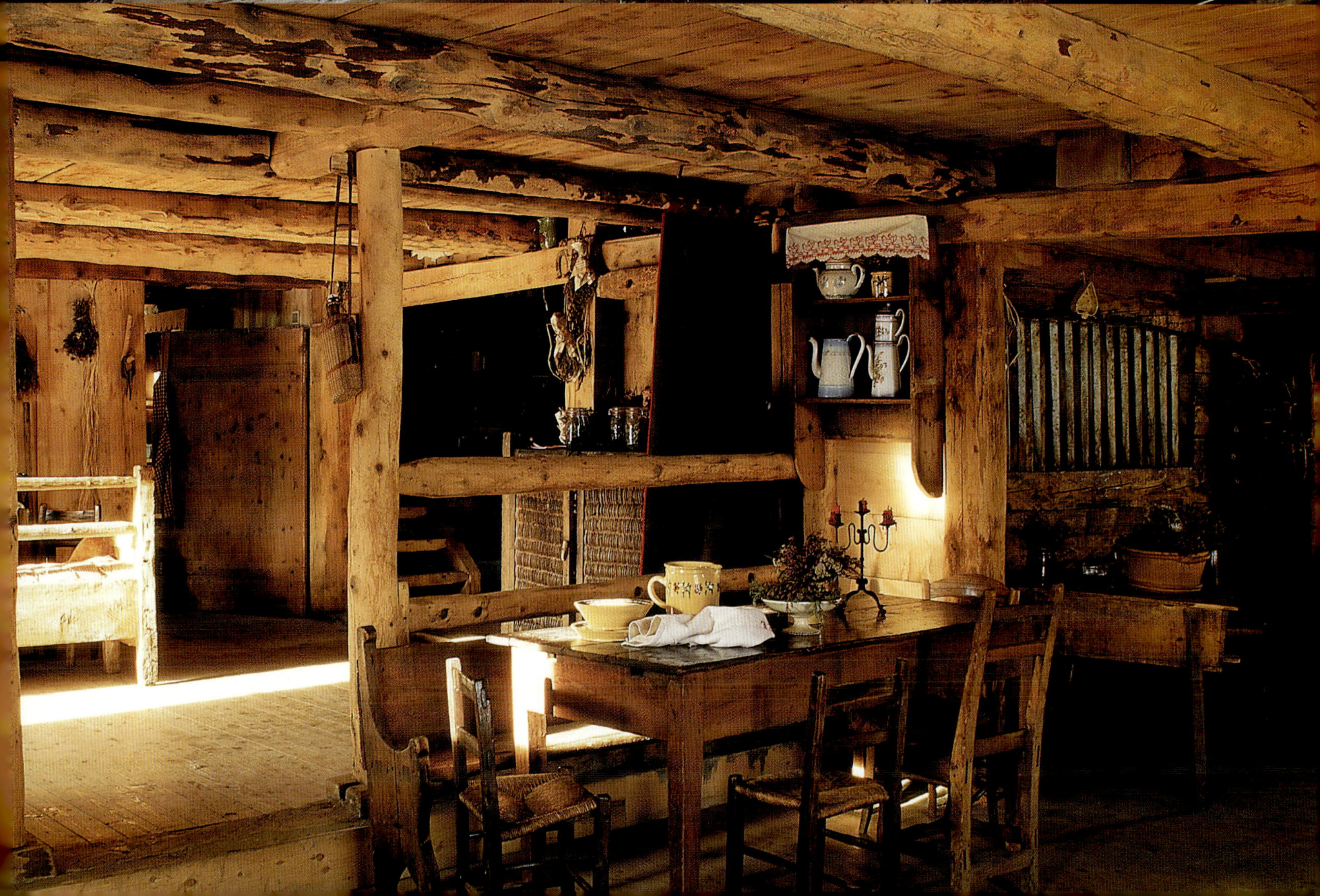

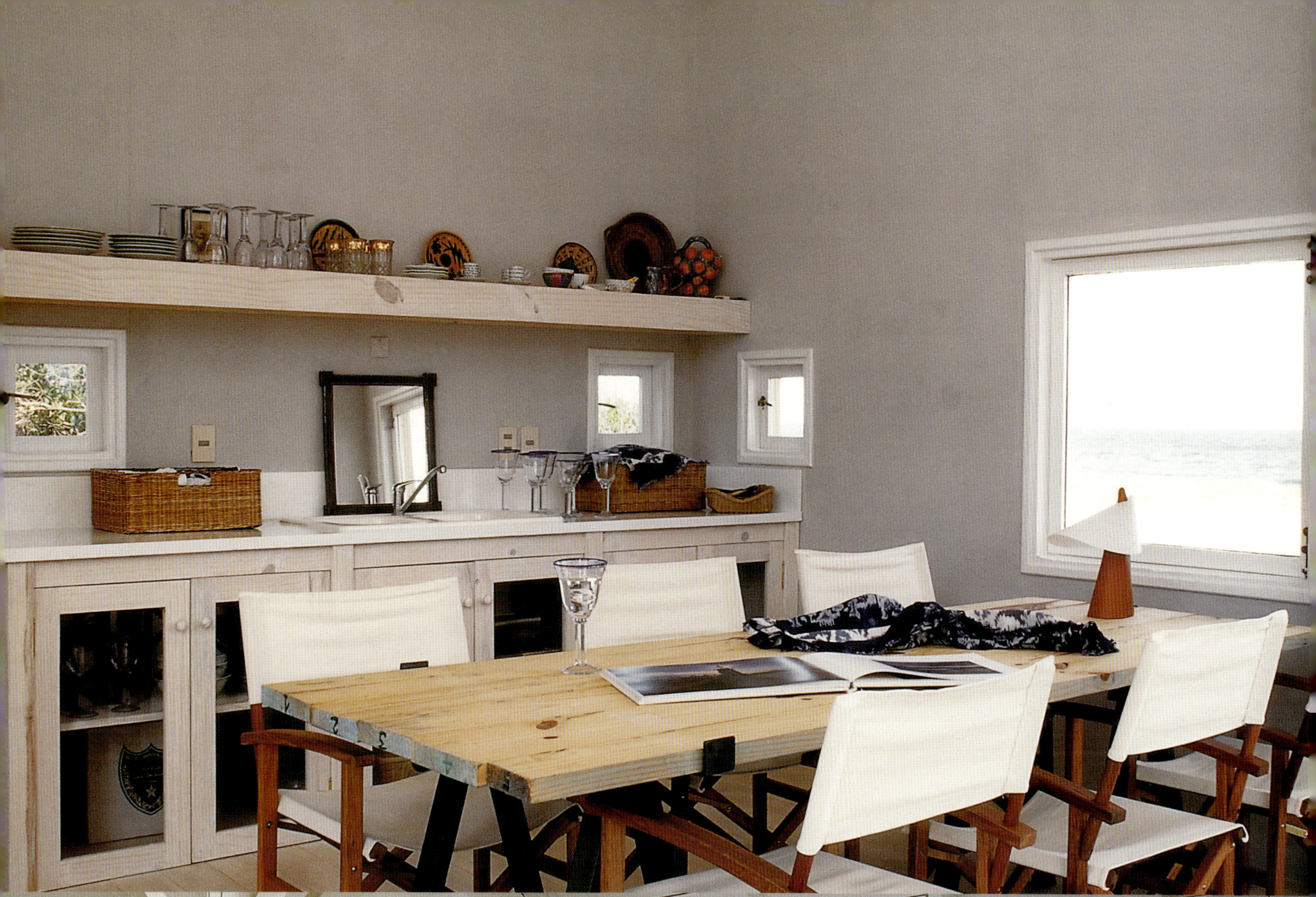

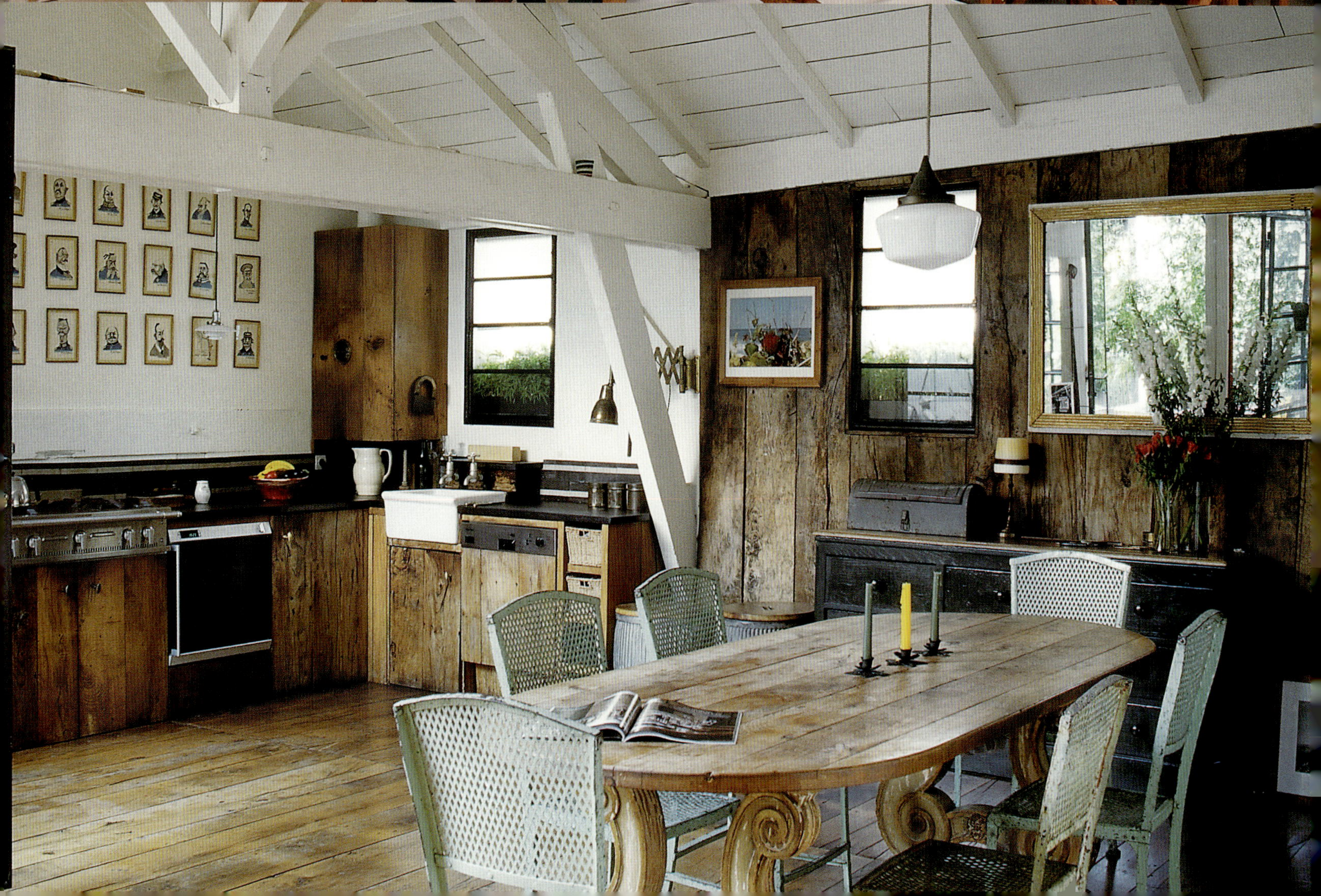

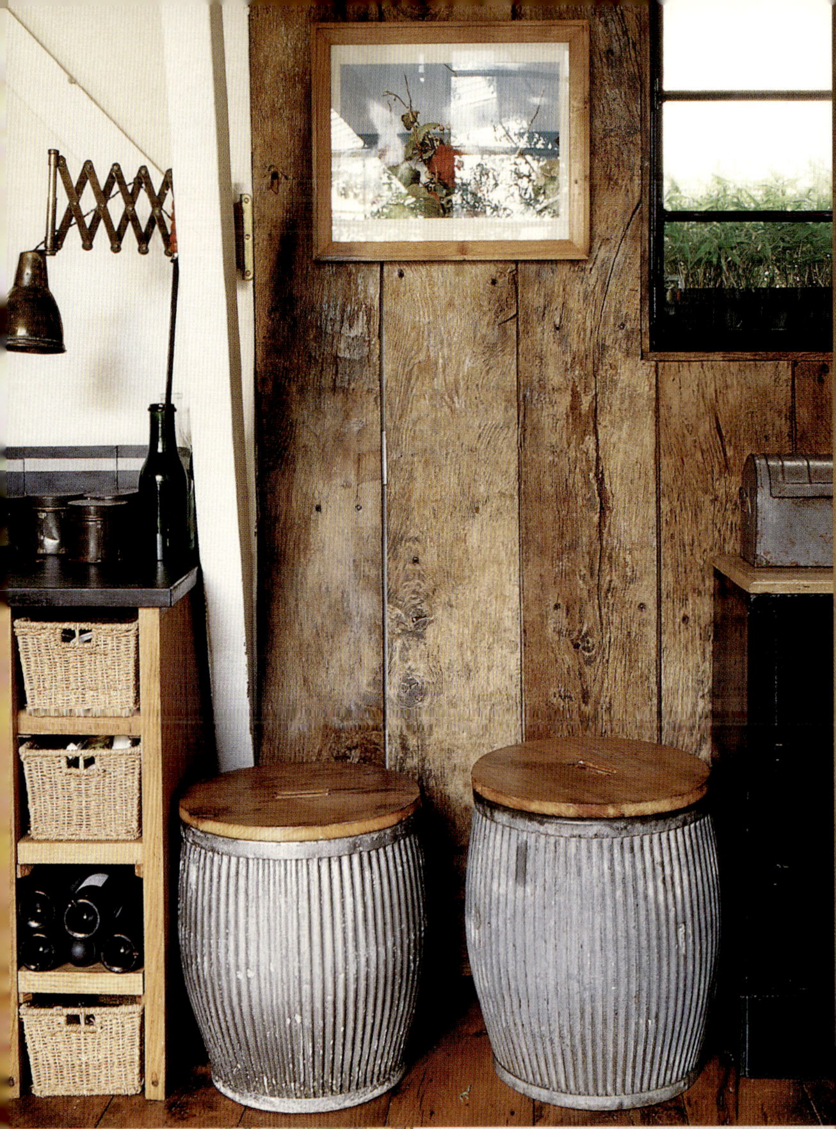

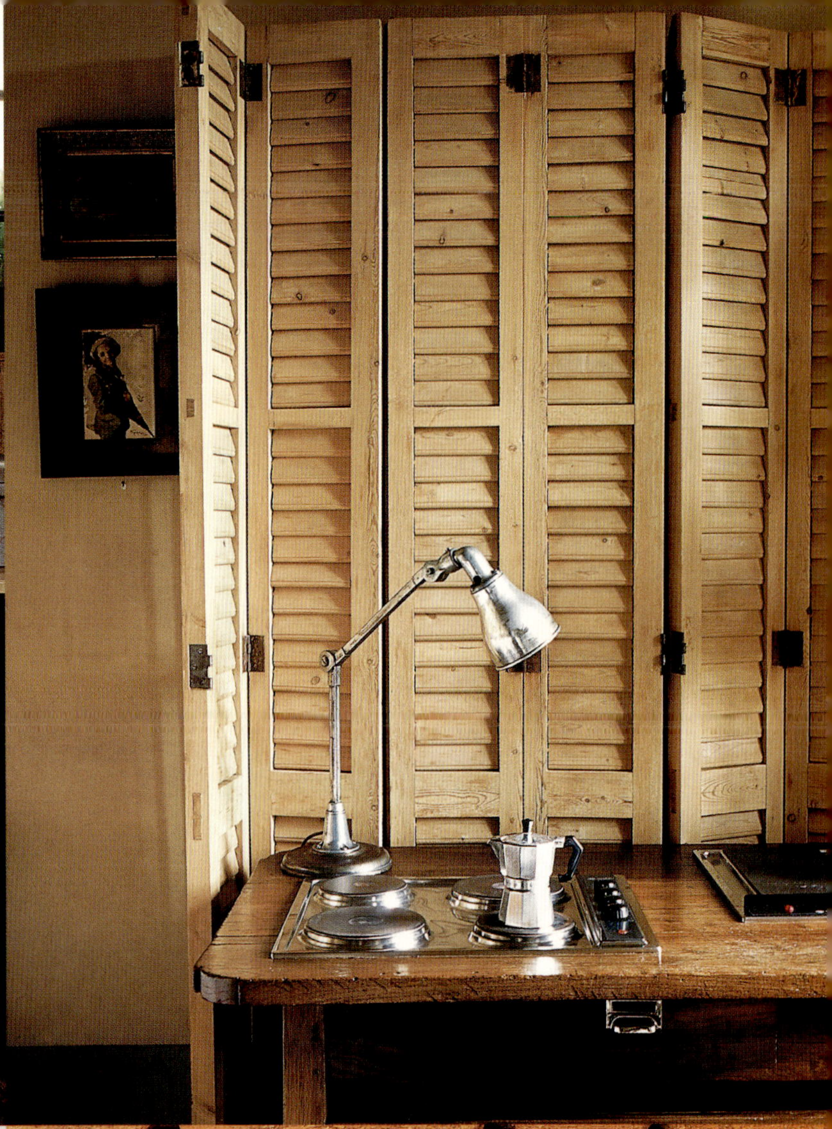

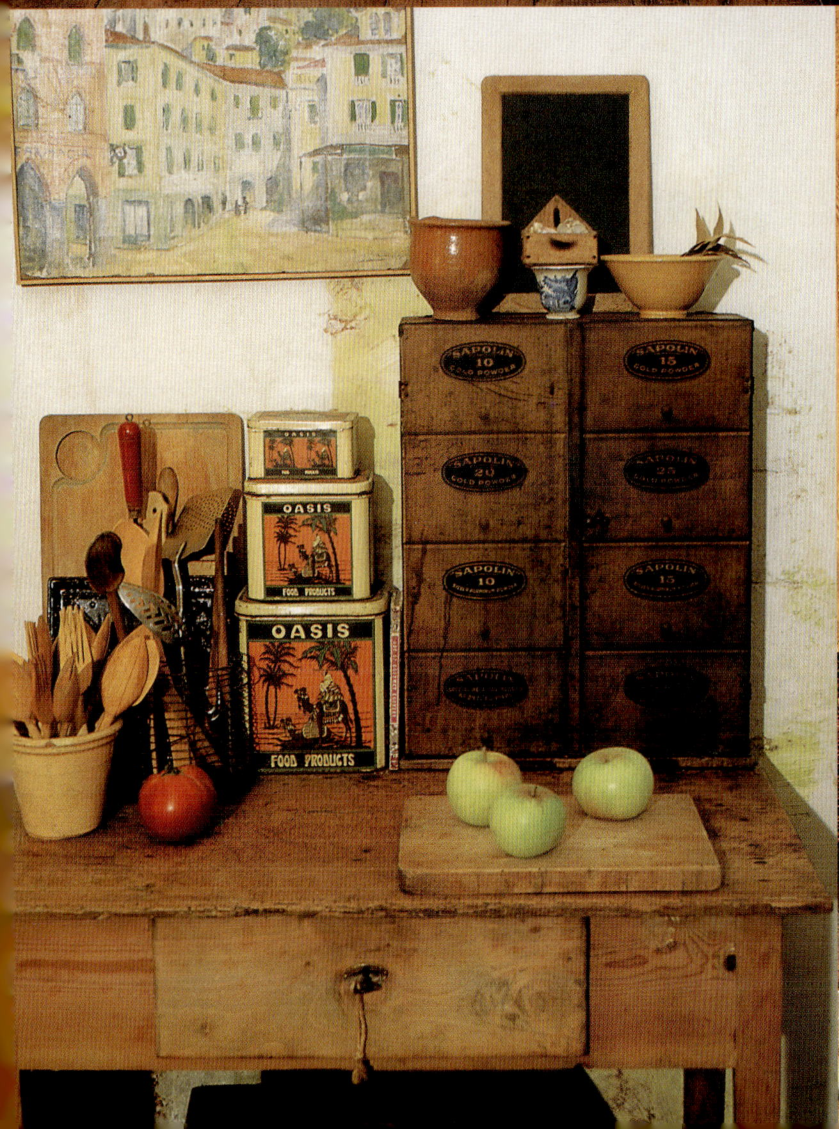
OASIS
FOOD PRODUCTS
OASIS
FOOD PRODUCTS

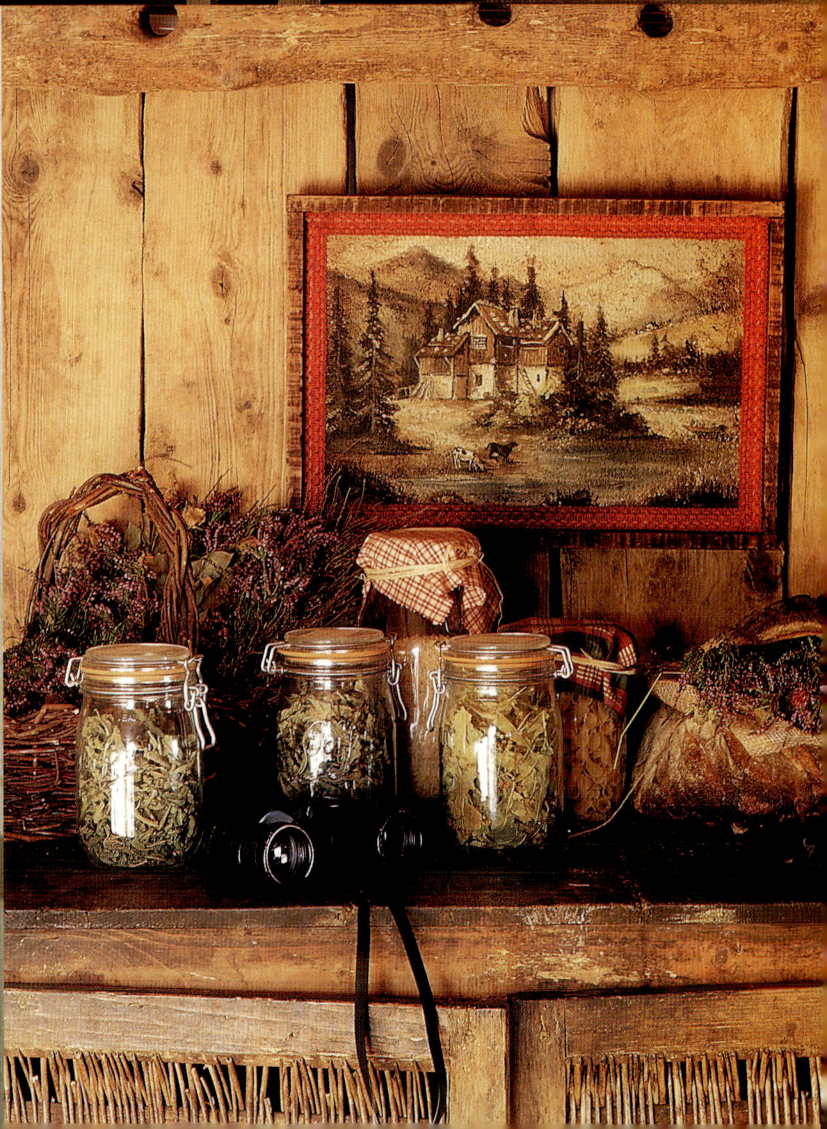

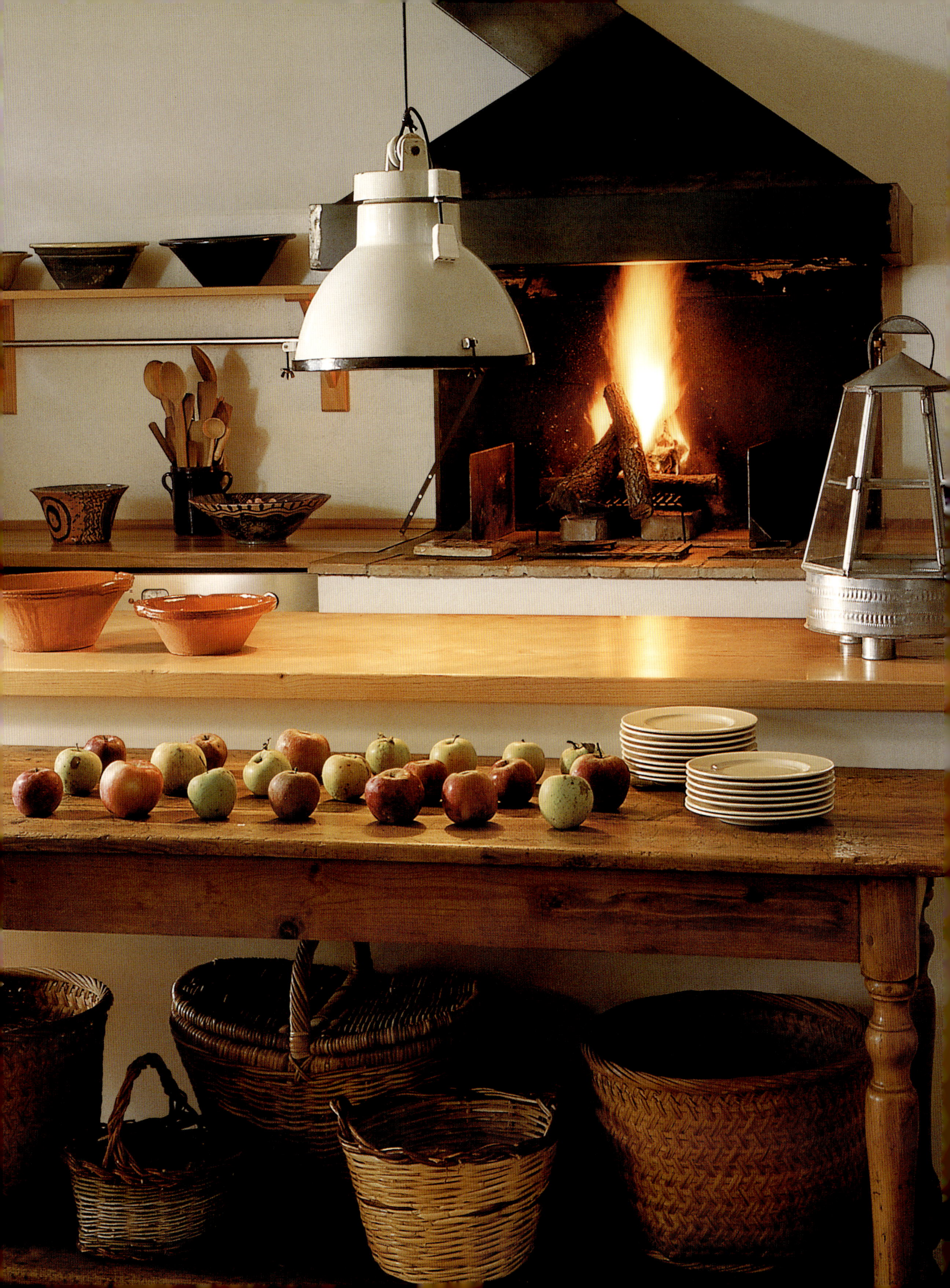

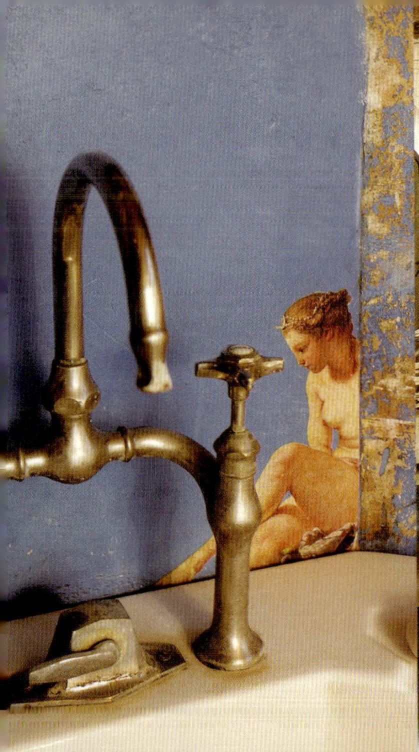
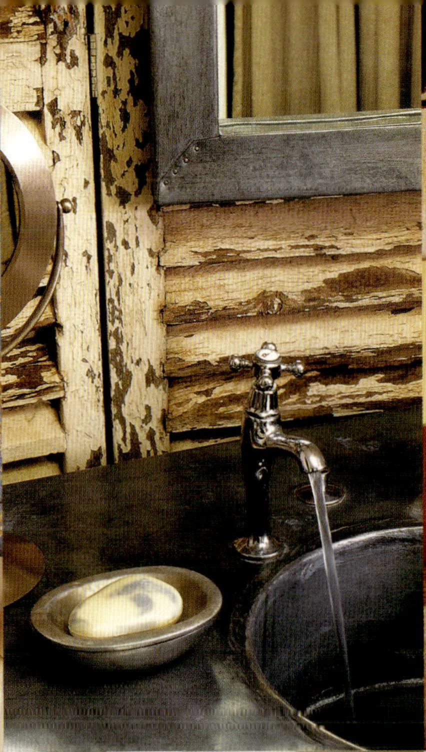
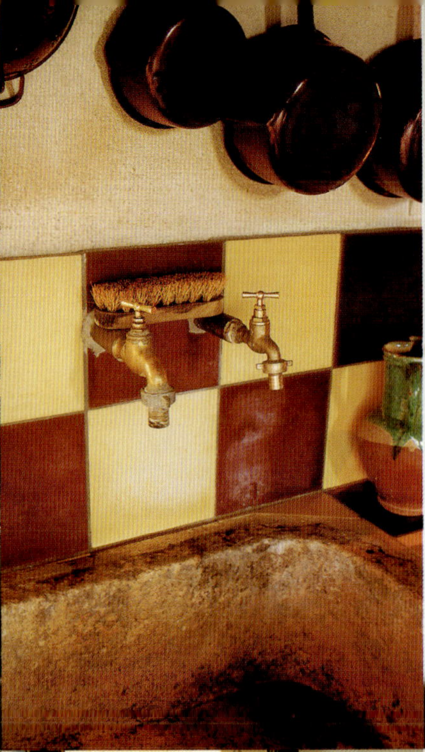
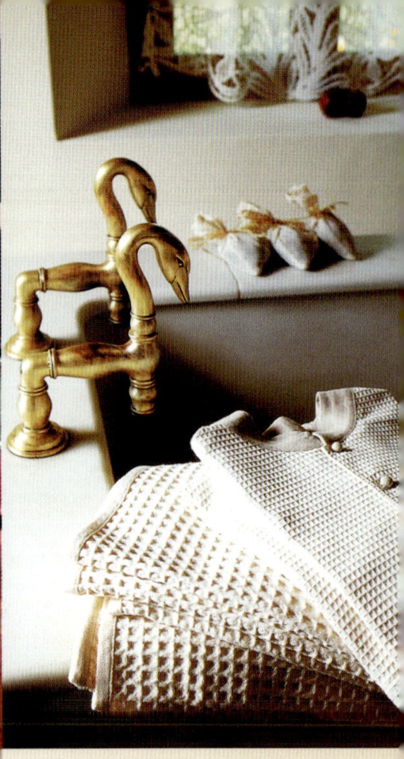
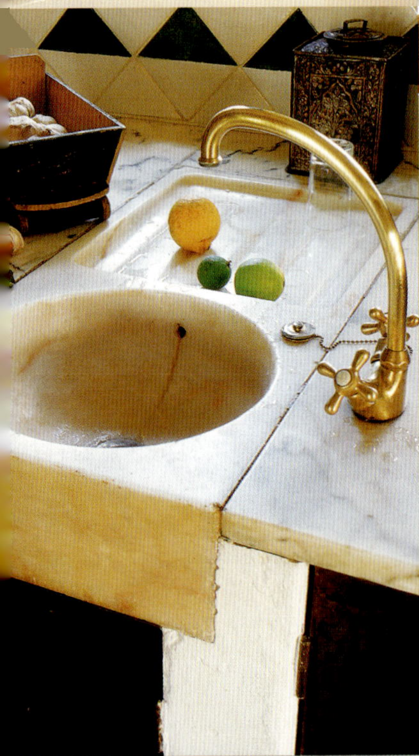
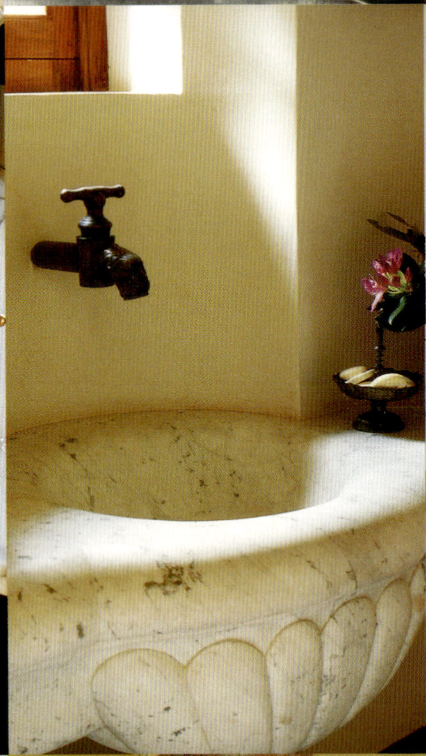
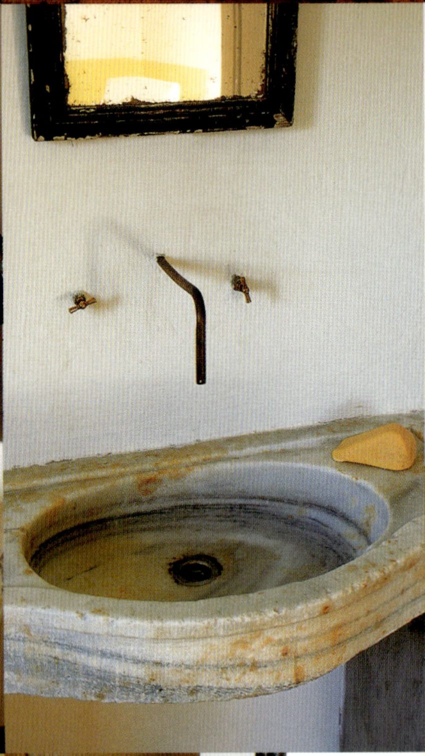
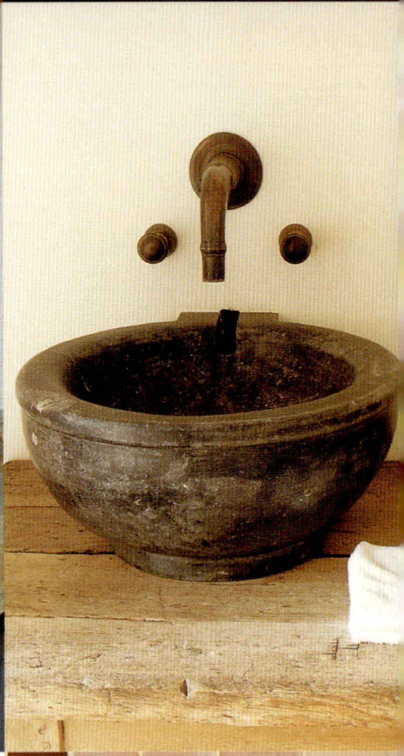
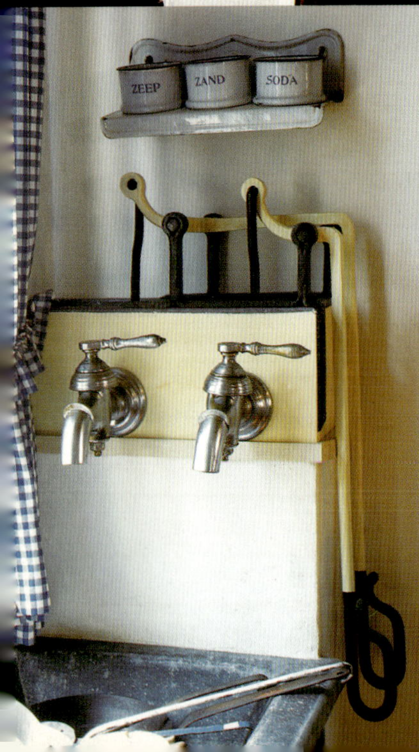
ZEEP
ZAND
SODA
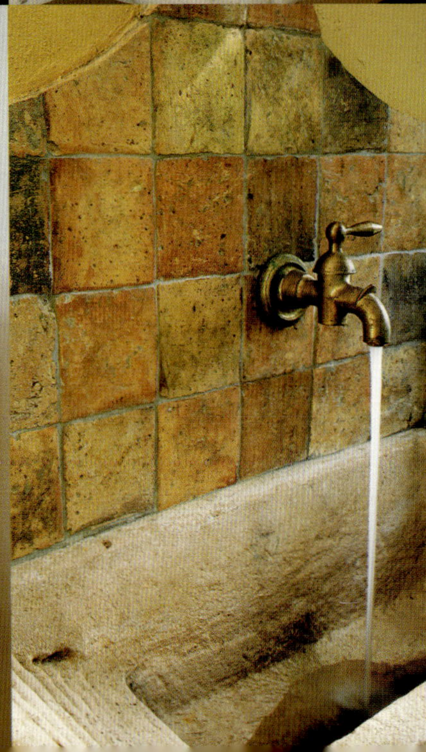
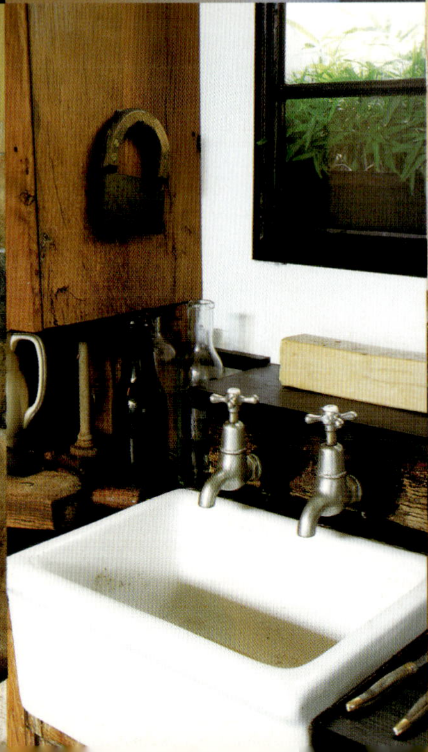
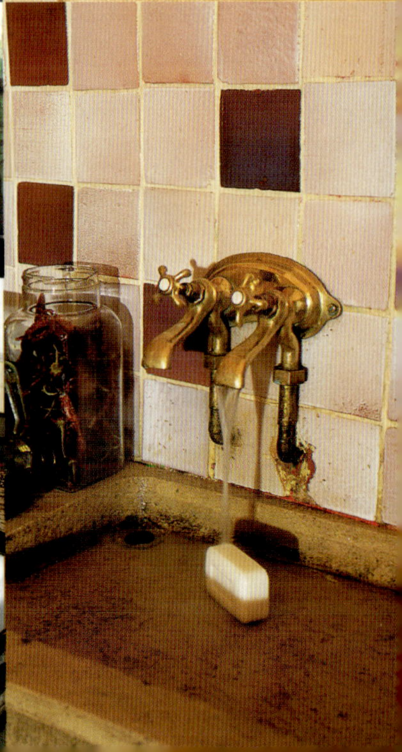

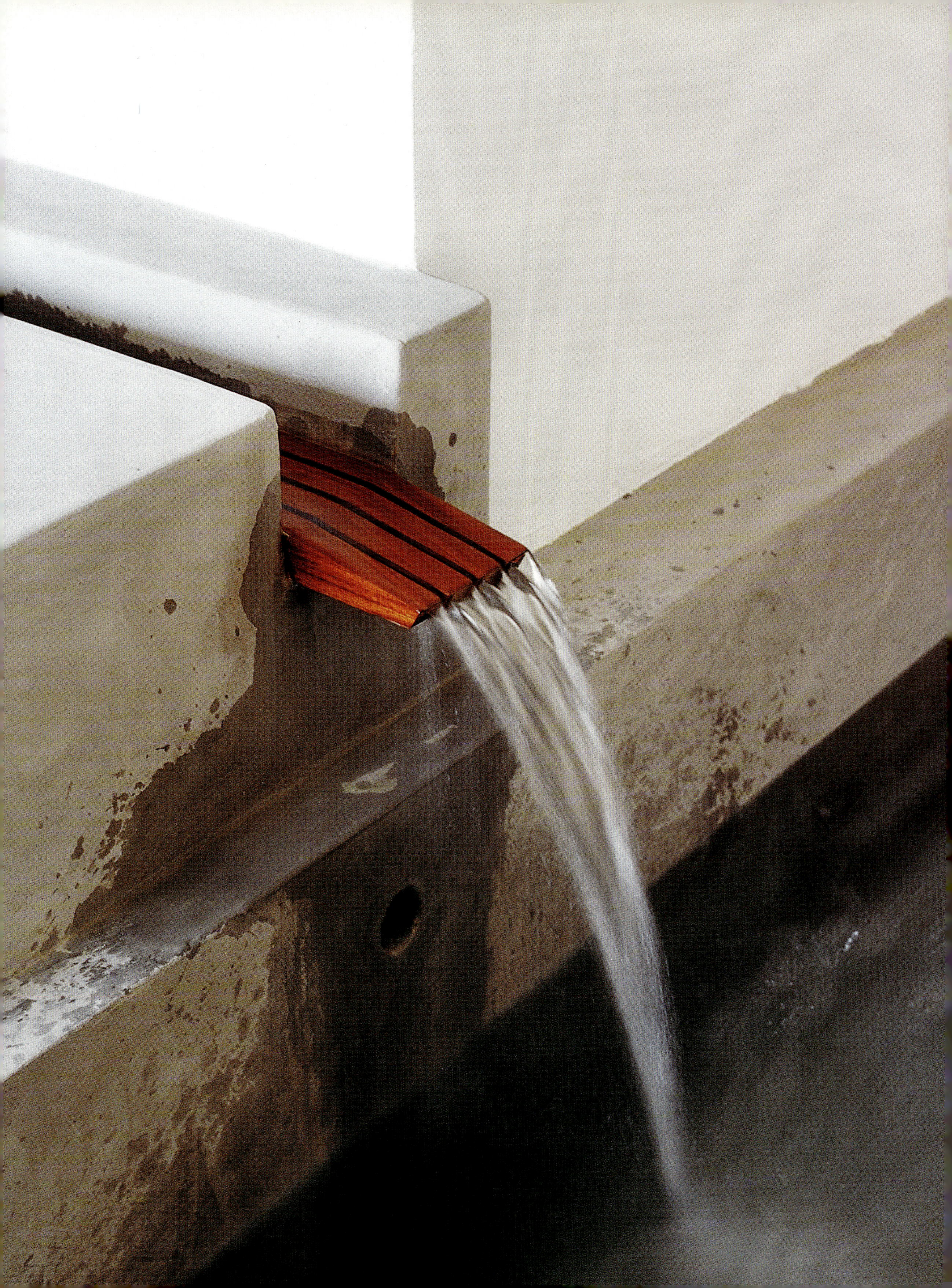

調理と食事

調理と食事

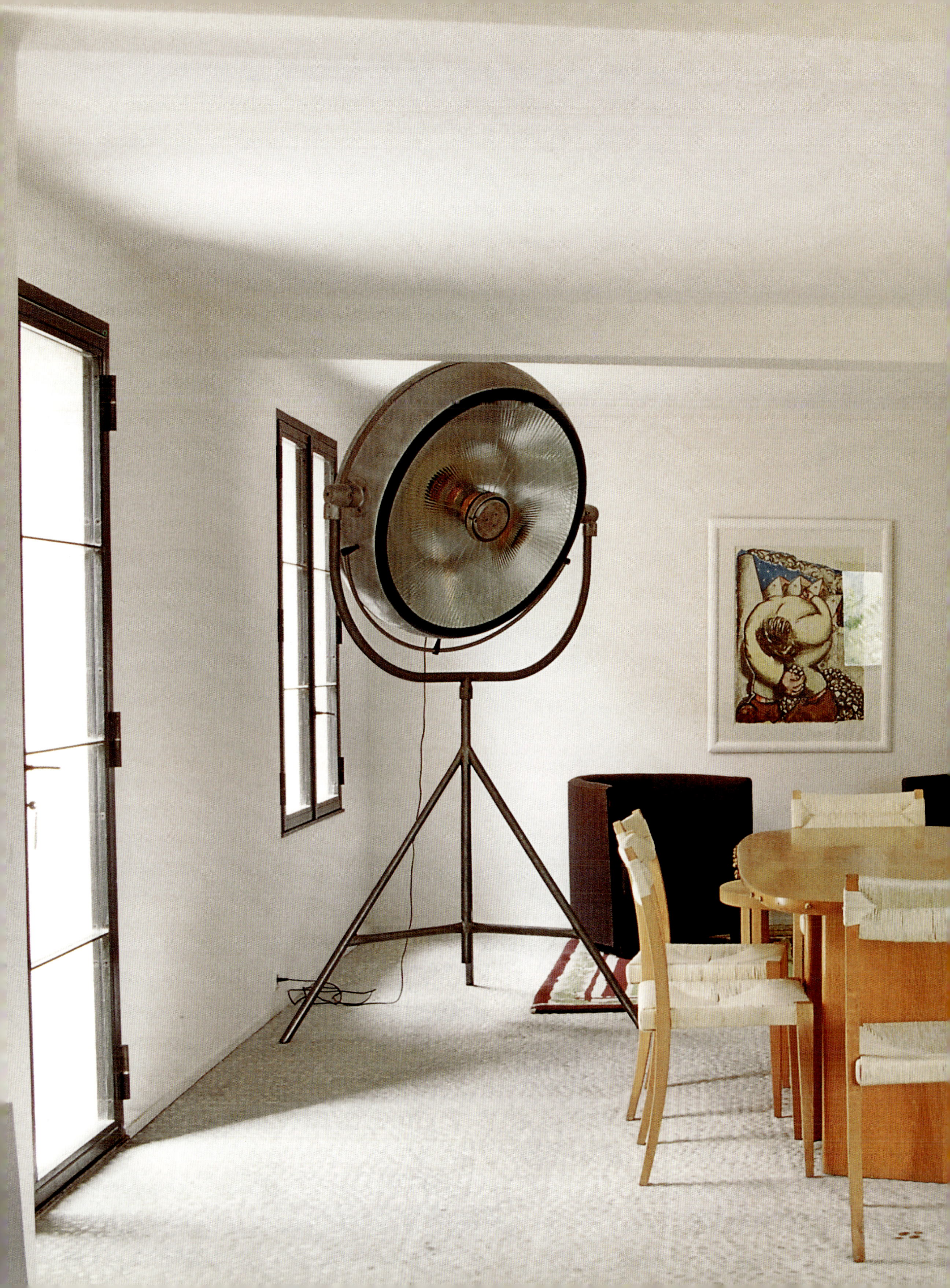

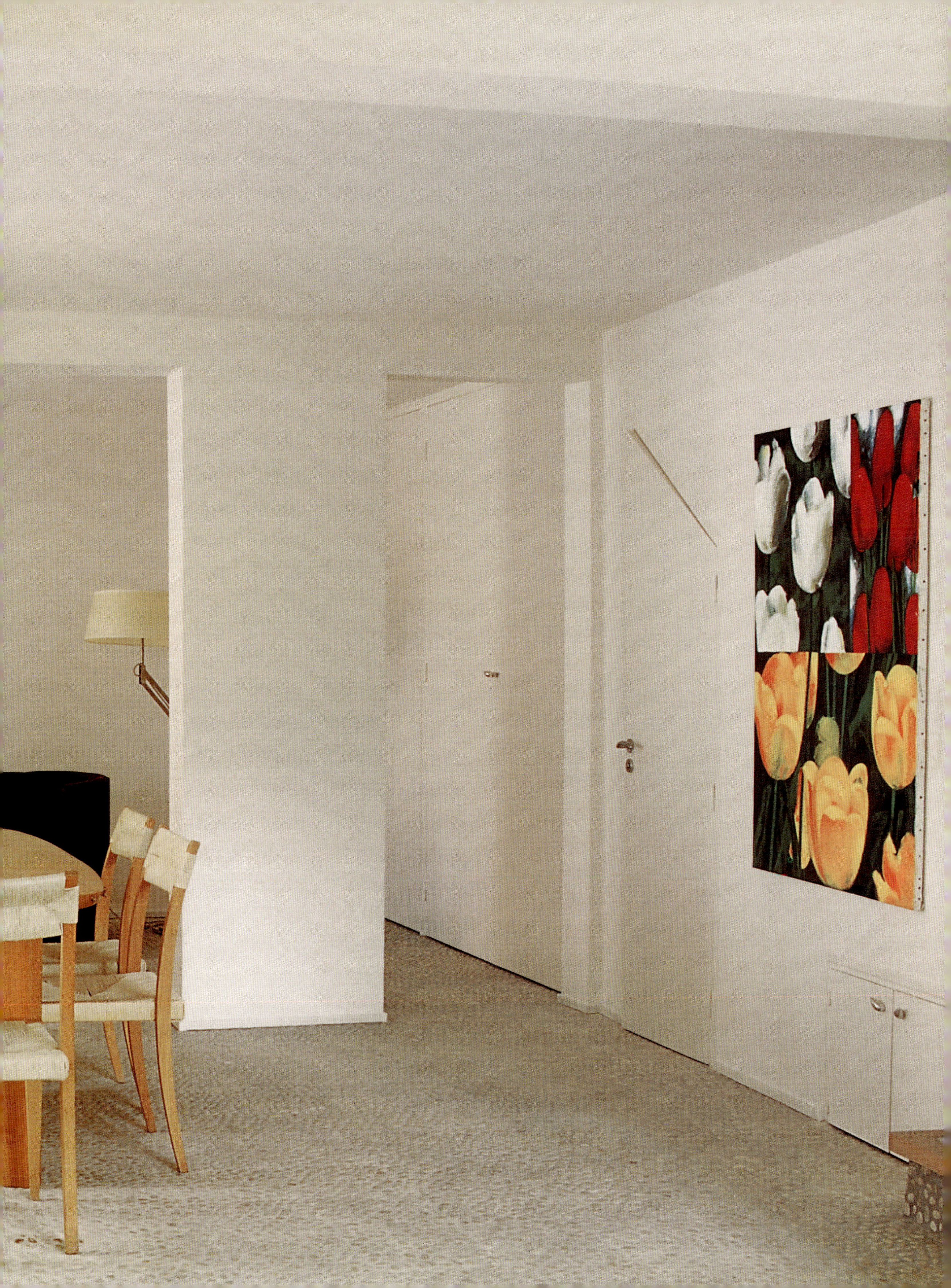

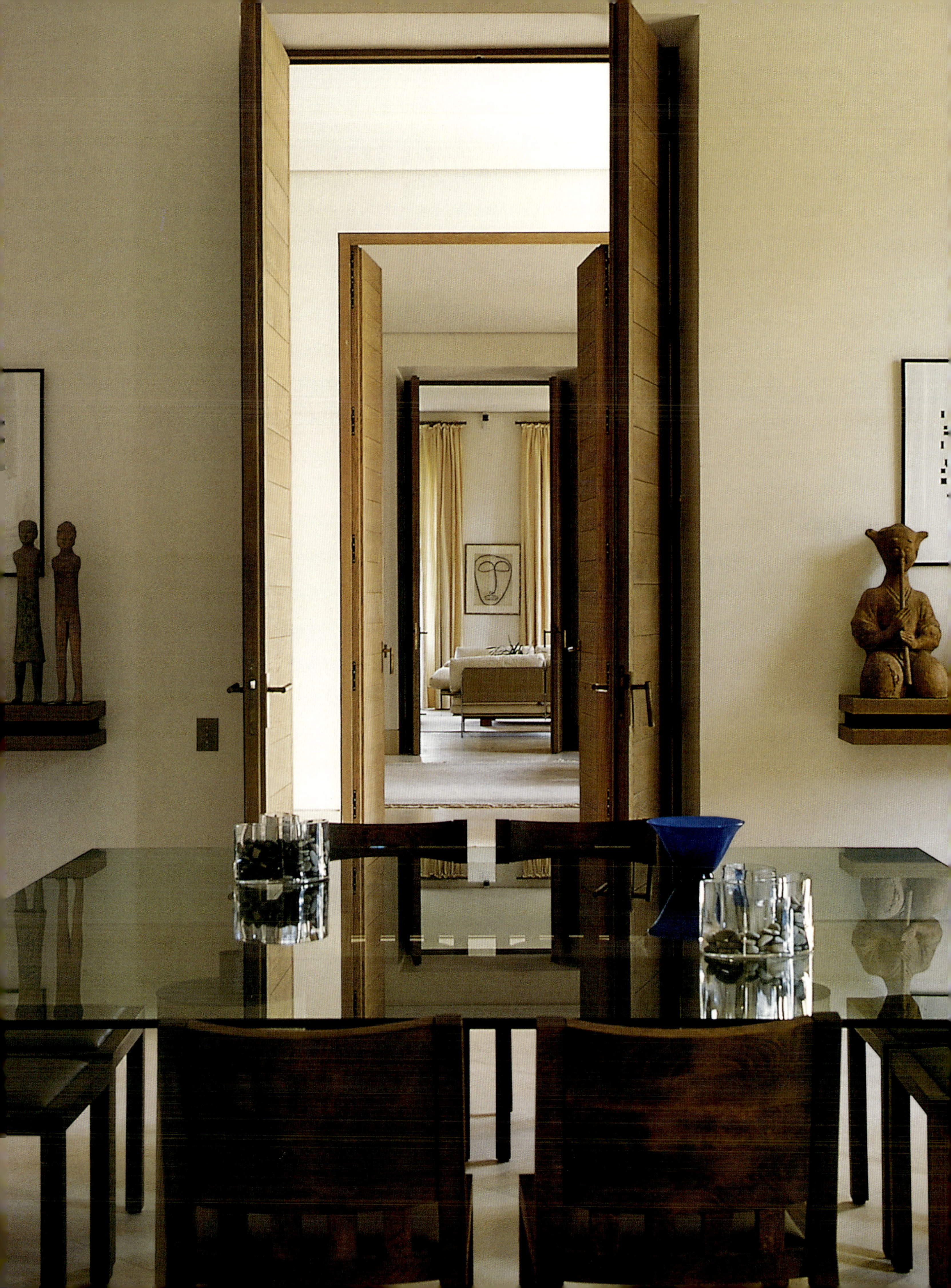

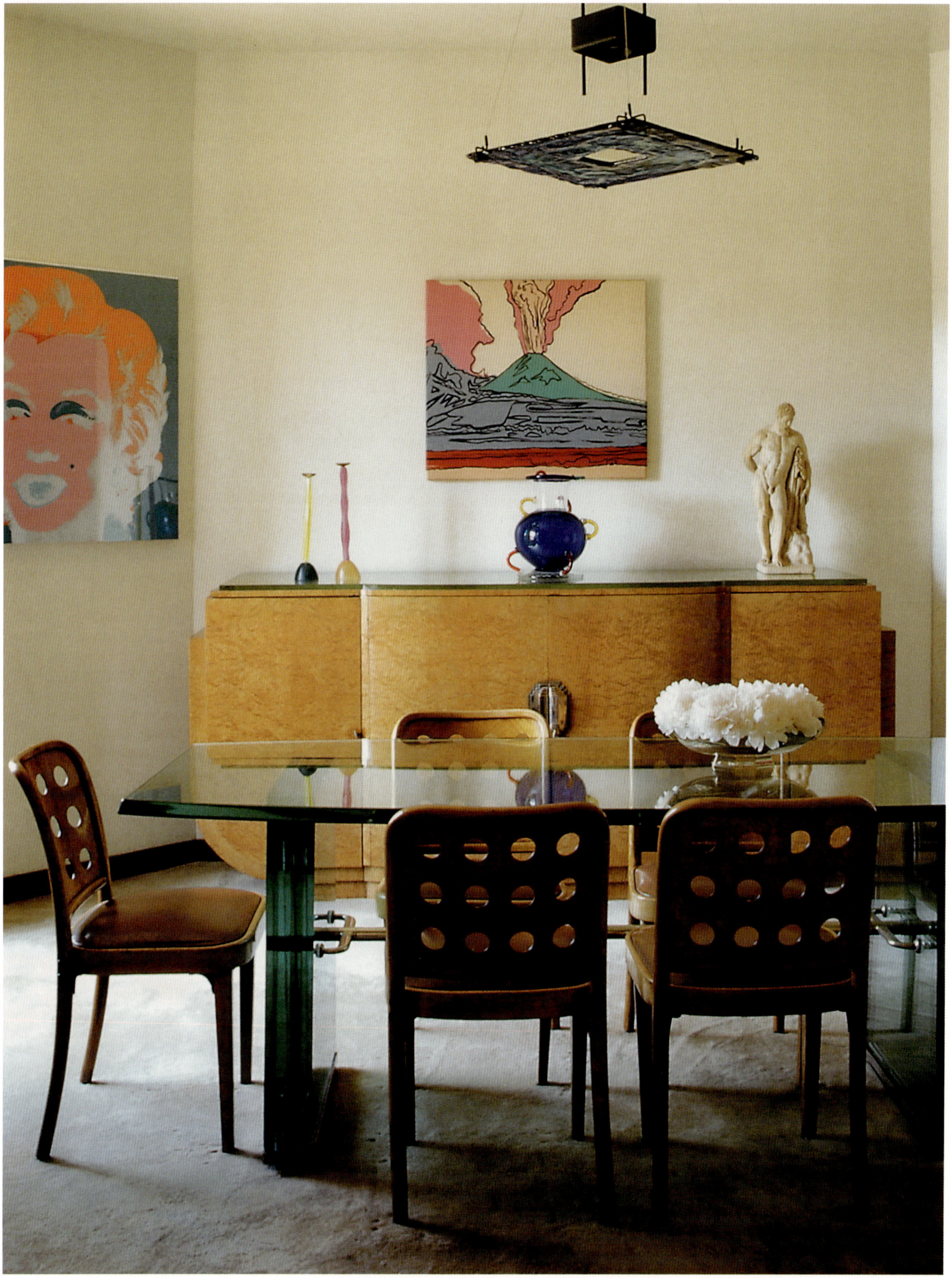

書棚・オープン棚

Shelf Life

よその家に上がった時、どこに目が行くかという私の質問に対して、もっとも多かった答えは、「本」です。「並べてある本を見れば、その家に住む人の興味や、性格が分かるから」というのがその理由。確かにそうです。私たちは本をたいてい無意識に選んでいますが、人は、自分自身に通じる本のテーマに反応するからです。ですから、本――または、本の少なさ――は、持ち主の人となりを、時に本人の望む以上に、雄弁に語ります。写真集、歴史書、美術書、児童書、ペーパーバック、様々な初版本は、その本の持ち主について述べているも同然です。ある家に、壁の端から端まで、または床から天井まで覆う巨大な書棚があれば、きっと私たちは書棚中を目で追いながら、そのリズムと、色と、本の構成を楽しむでしょう。しかし、書棚に本を詰め込みすぎるのは禁物です。図書館に住んでいるのではないのですから、いくつかの物を飾るためのスペースを書棚には空けておきましょう。ずらりと並ぶ本を視覚的に仕切る物――たとえば写真や、きれいな箱――を飾るスペースを取っておくのです。もしあまり多く本を持っていなくても、棚に飾ると輝きを放つ物を、たくさん持っているはず。それに、日頃から、物をあまり集めるタイプでなくても、収納量が豊富な棚を手に入れれば、すぐに飾りたい物を思い付くでしょう。ぜひ棚に何か所か照明を取り付けて、夜は、それらの物にいくらか輝きを与えてください。本をどのように種類分けするか決めるのも大切です。テーマか、サイズか、持ち主か、手に取る頻度か――その分け方もまた、住む人の性格を表します。背表紙の色で分ける人もいるでしょうからね。

When I've asked people what they look for when entering someone's house, the most popular answer has been: 'Their books. If I see what they read, I know their interests and what type of person they are'. Sounds obvious, but in most cases it's subconscious. We respond to things that are similar to our own, and books – or the lack of them – sometimes say more about us than we might like. Photography books, history books, art books, children's books, paperbacks or first editions tell a host of stories, and if the room has a large bookshelf, or even wall-to-wall, floor-to-ceiling shelving, our eyes dance across it, enjoying the rhythm, the colour and the intrigue. But don't overdo it; you're not living in a library. Allow space on the shelves for a few objects – pictures, perhaps, or beautiful boxes – things that make a visual break. Even if you don't have lots of books, there are plenty of other things that will shine on a shelf, and if you don't normally collect things, then having a generous set of shelves will soon inspire you to fill it. Best of all, add some concealed lighting here and there, to give a bit of sparkle at night. Finally, decide how you will group your books – by subject, by size, by ownership, by frequency of use or – and this, too, reveals something about the homeowner – by the colour of the spine.

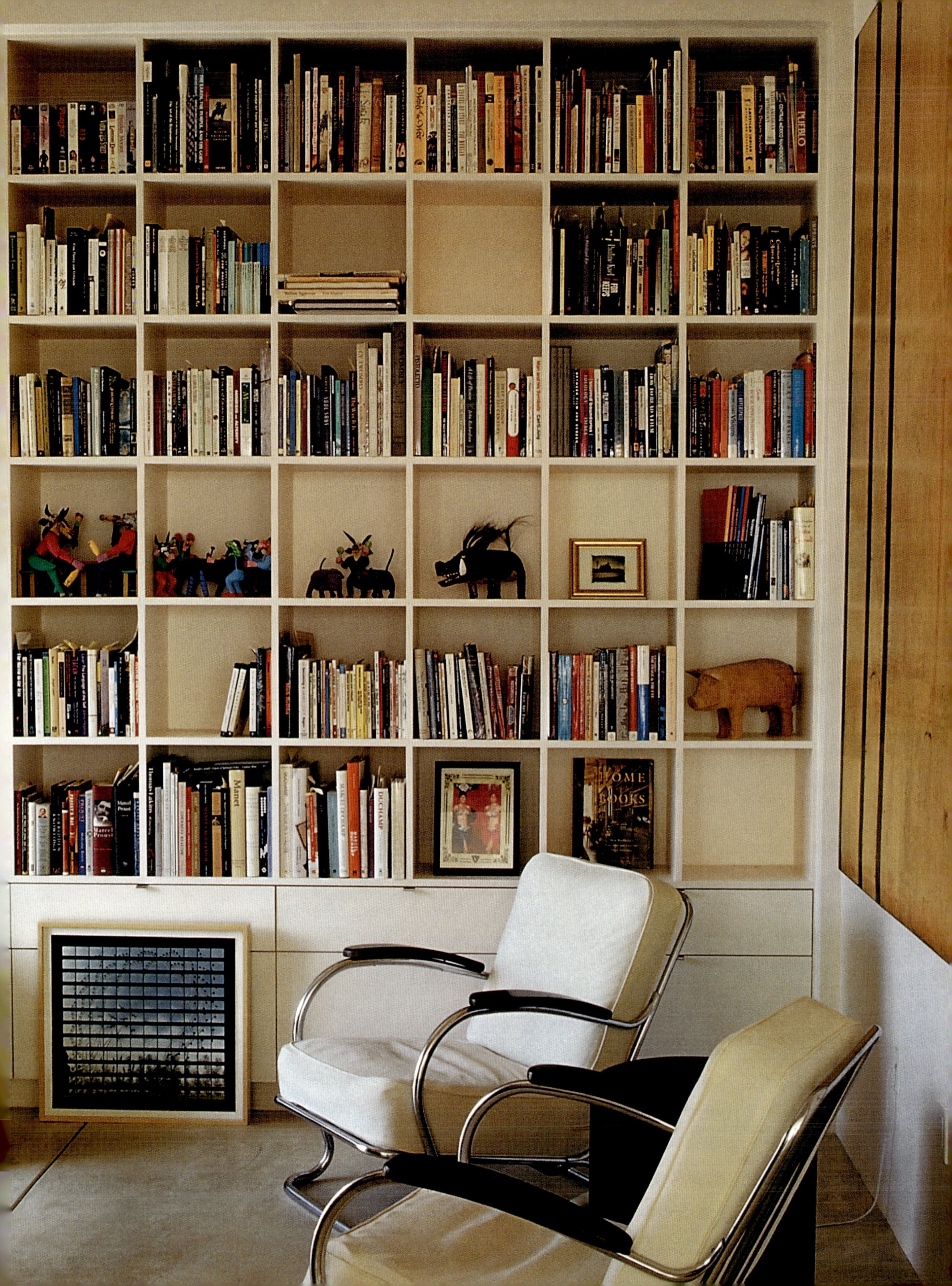

Manet
DUCHAMP

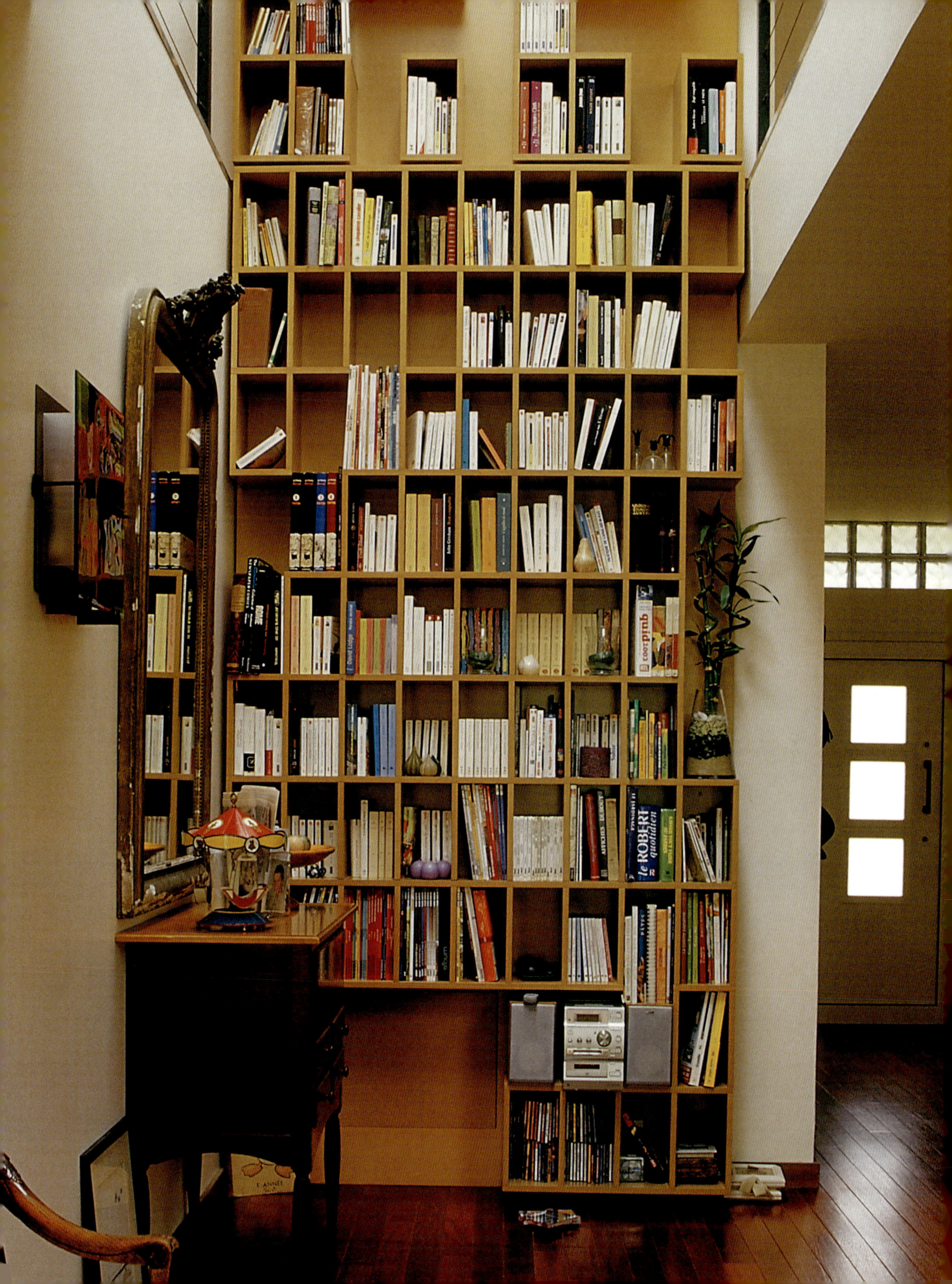
le ROBERT
quotidien

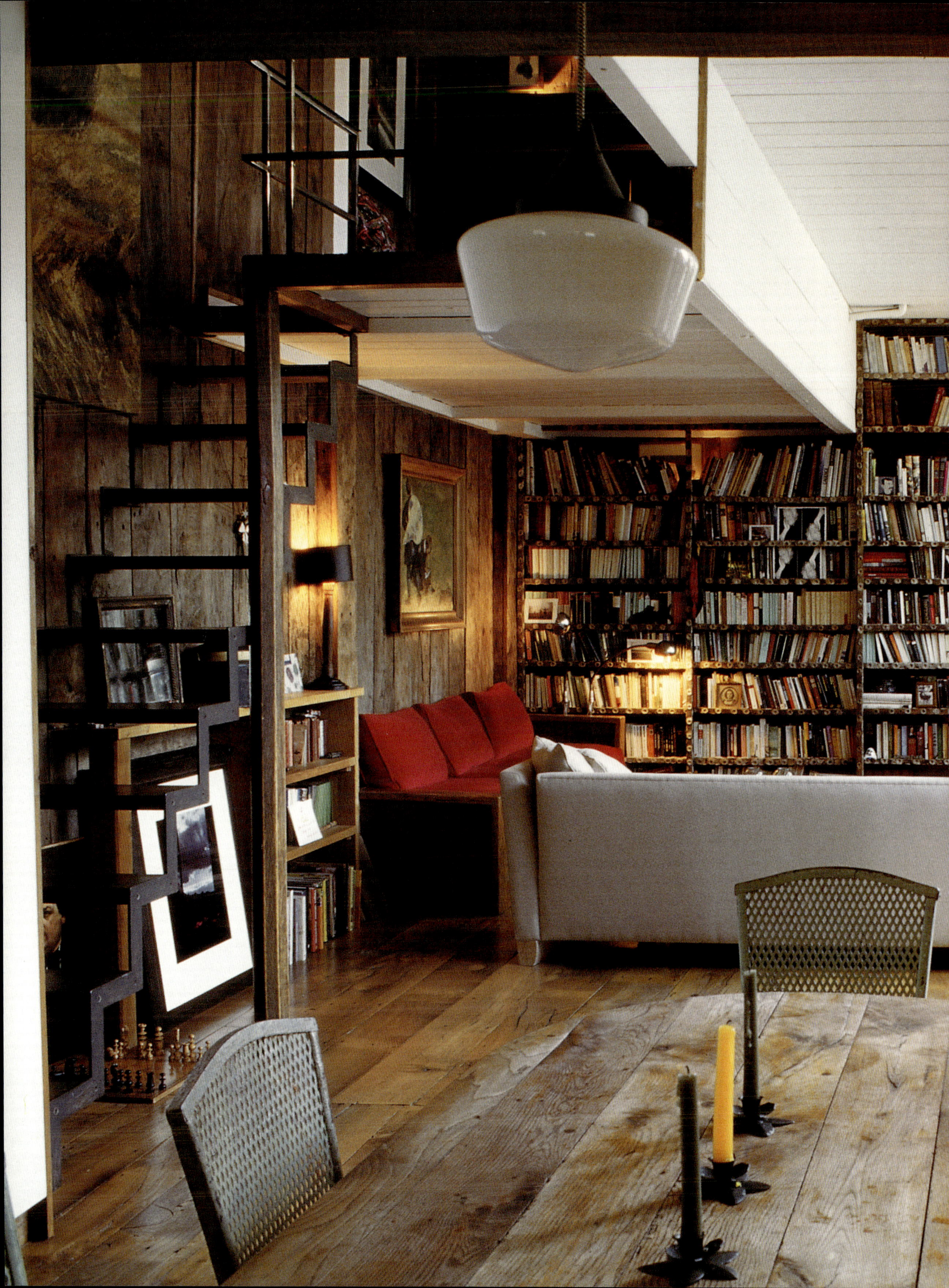

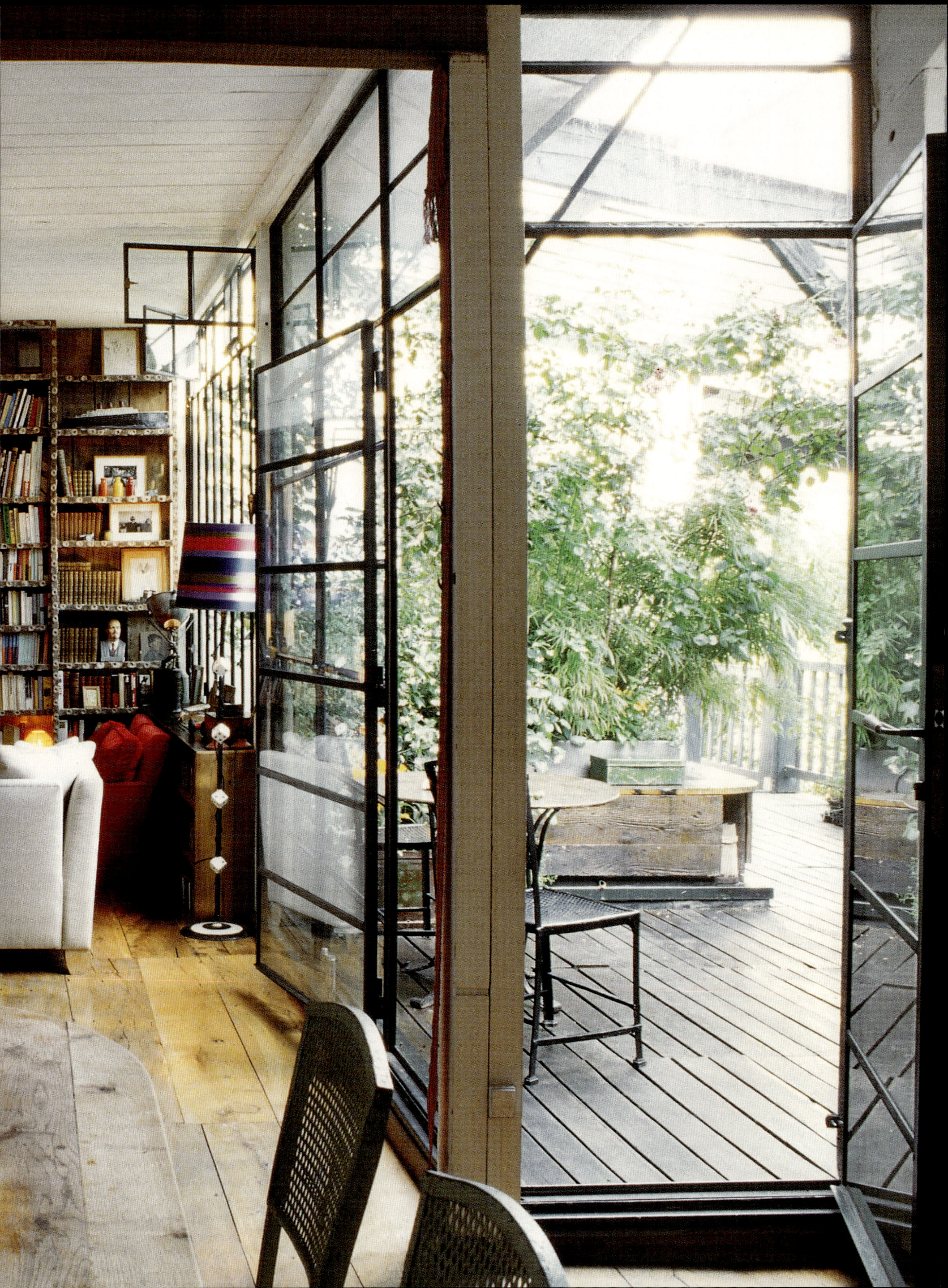

書棚・オープン棚

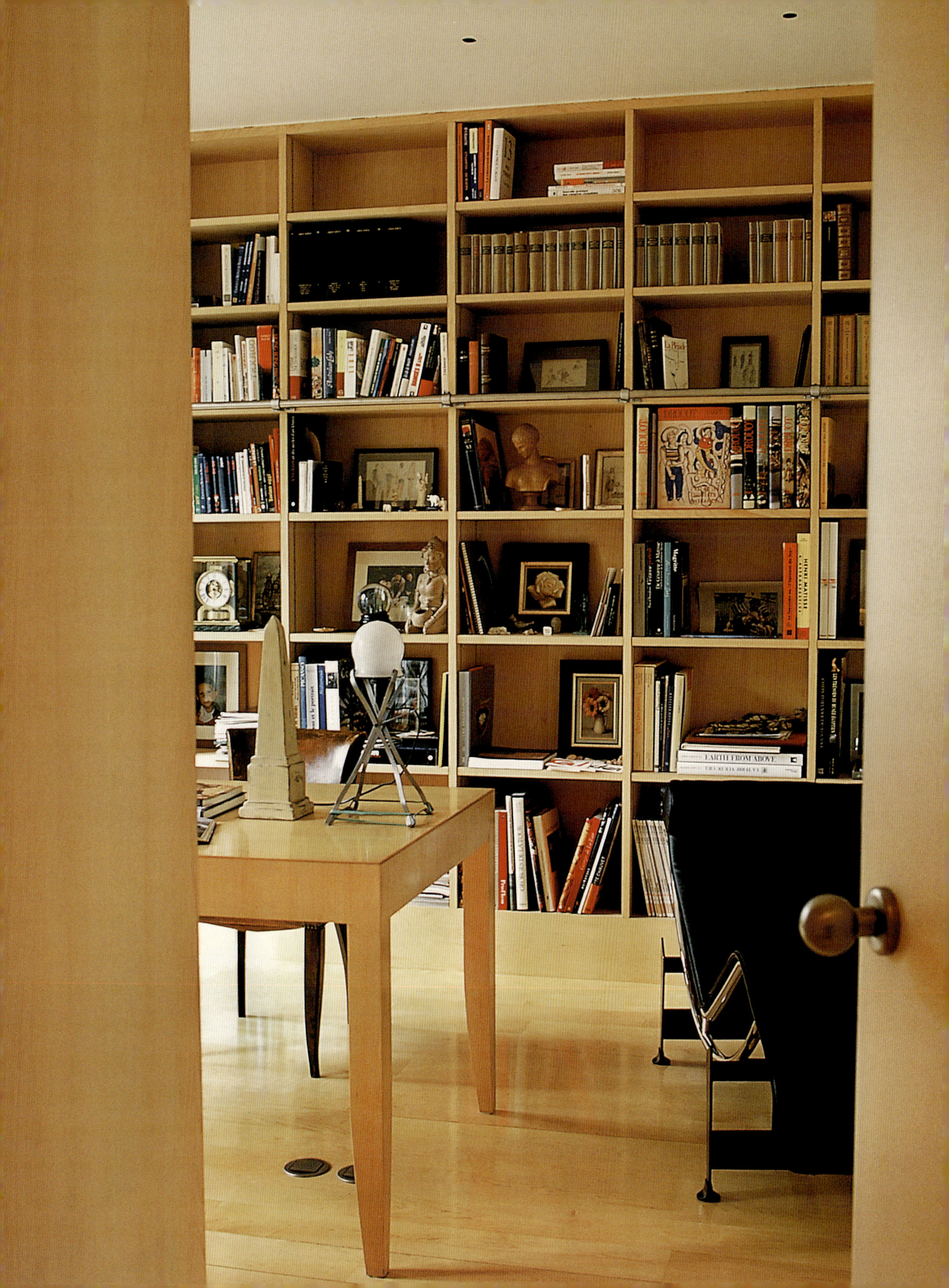
La Pléiade
DROUOT
HENRI MATISSE
EARTH FROM ABOVE

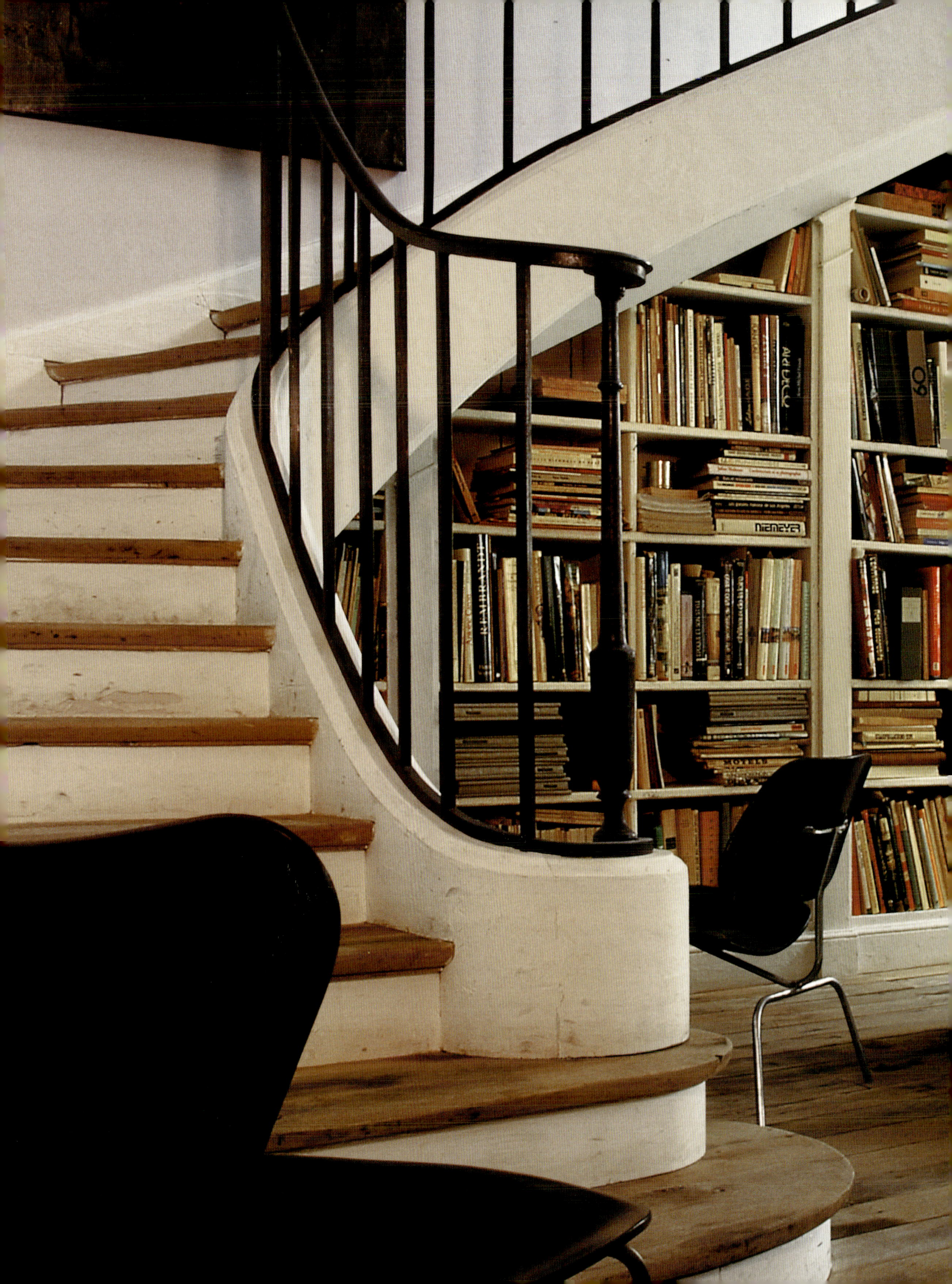
REMBRANDT
NIEMEYER
MOTELS

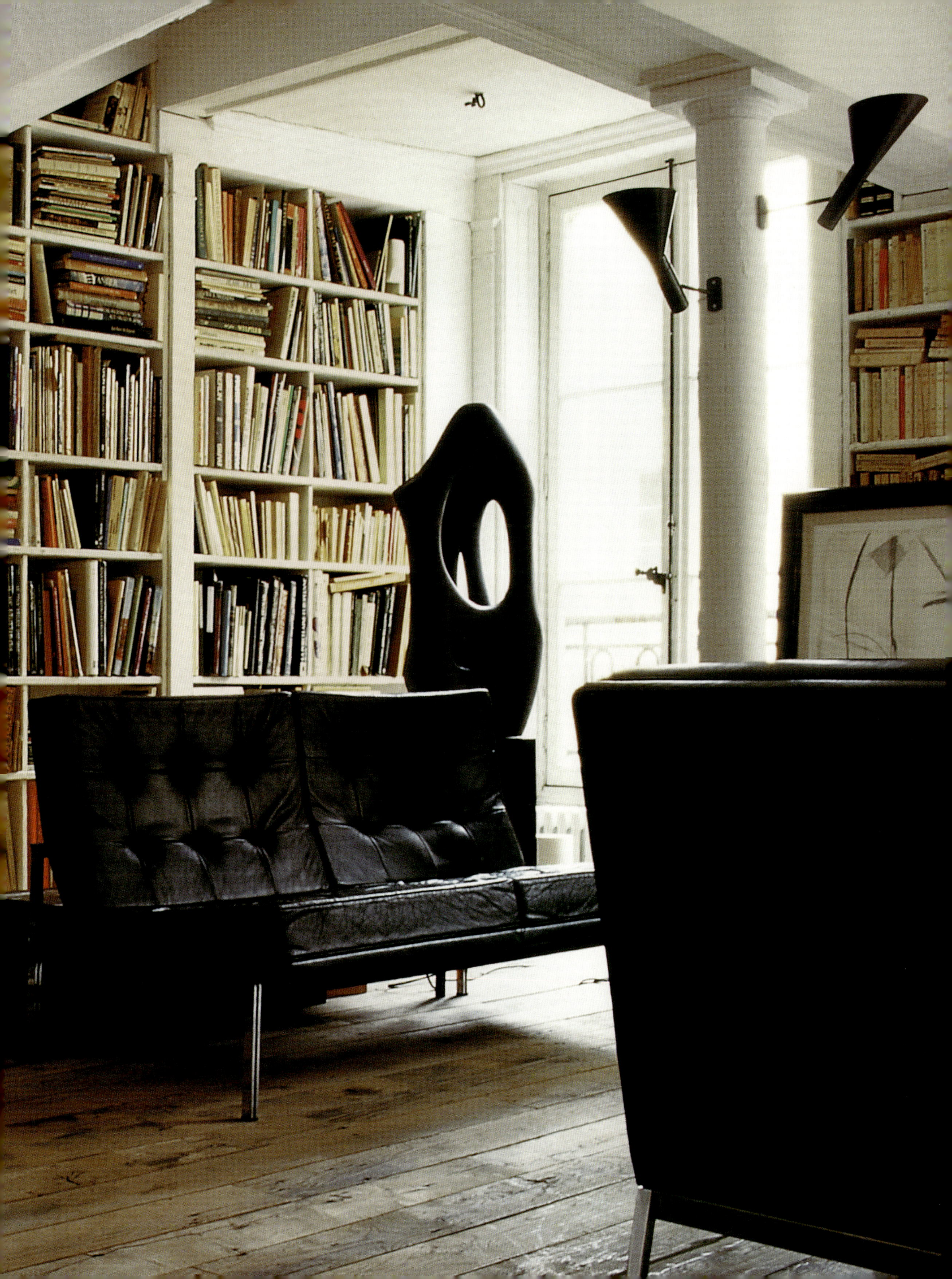

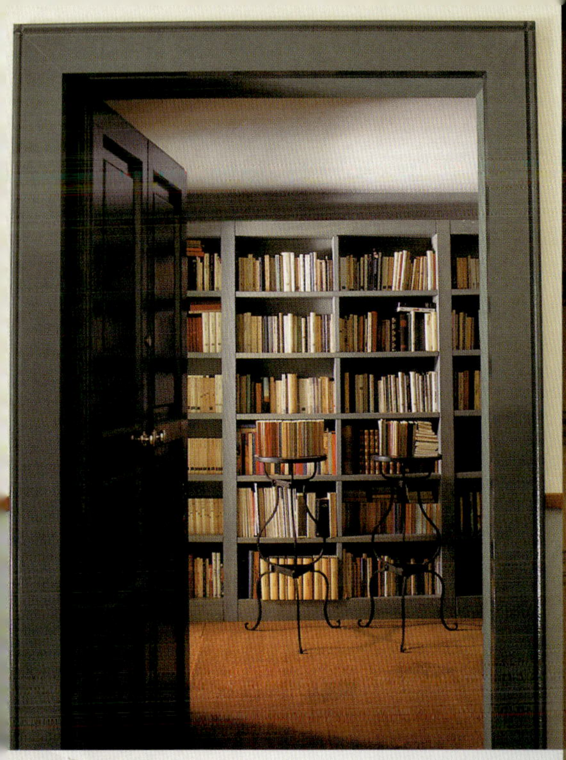
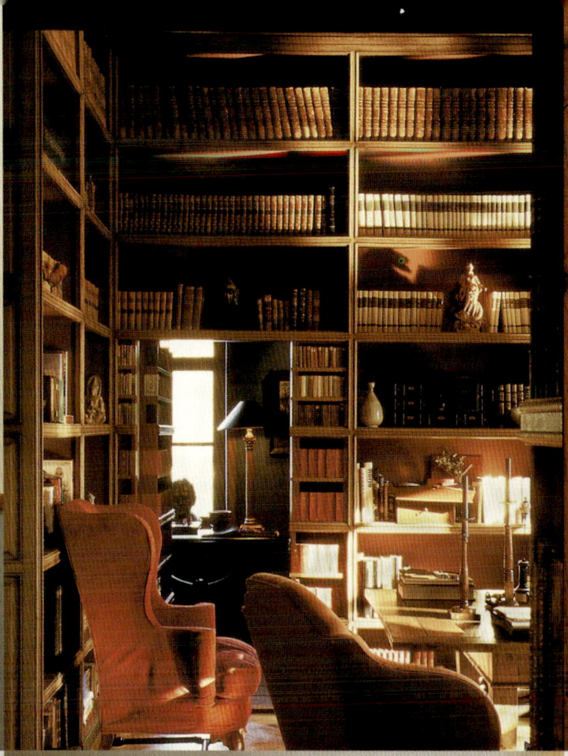
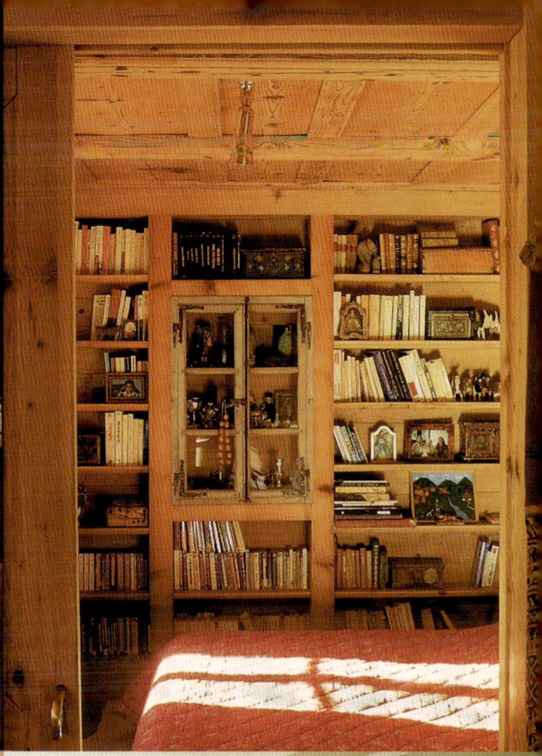
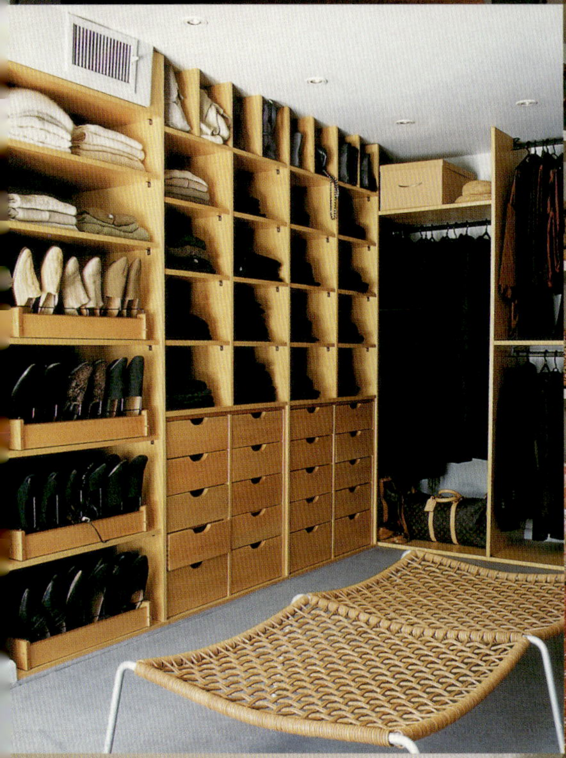
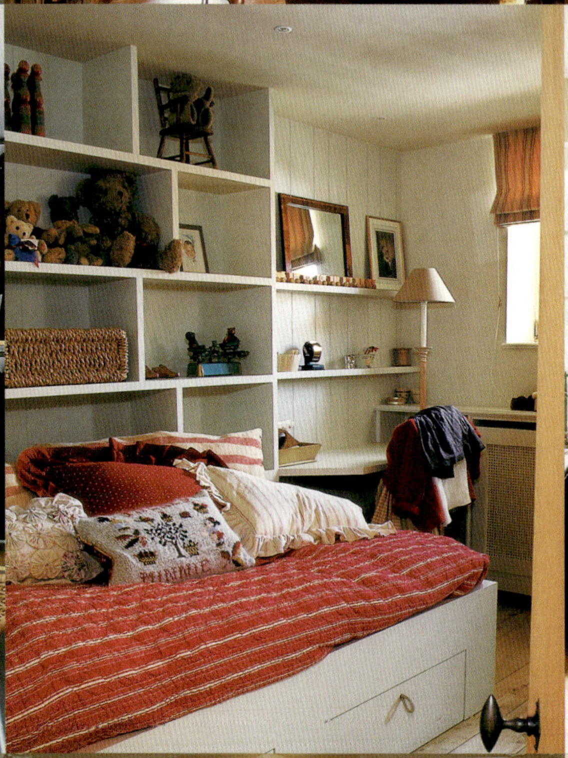
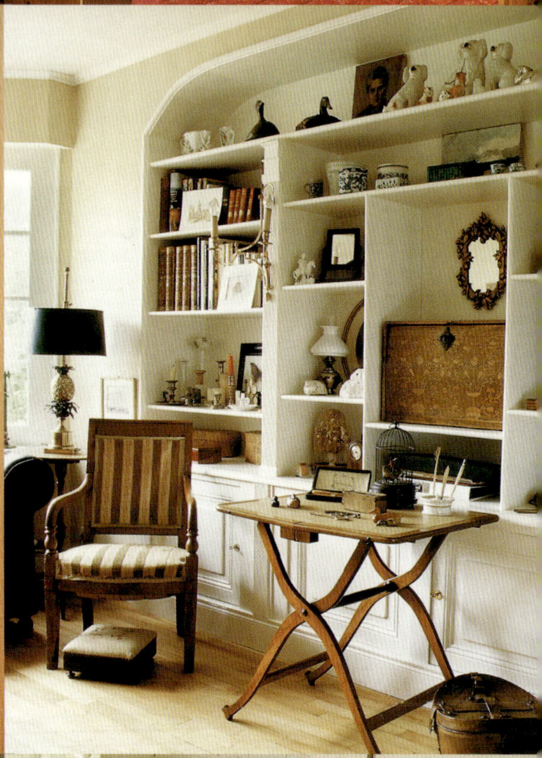
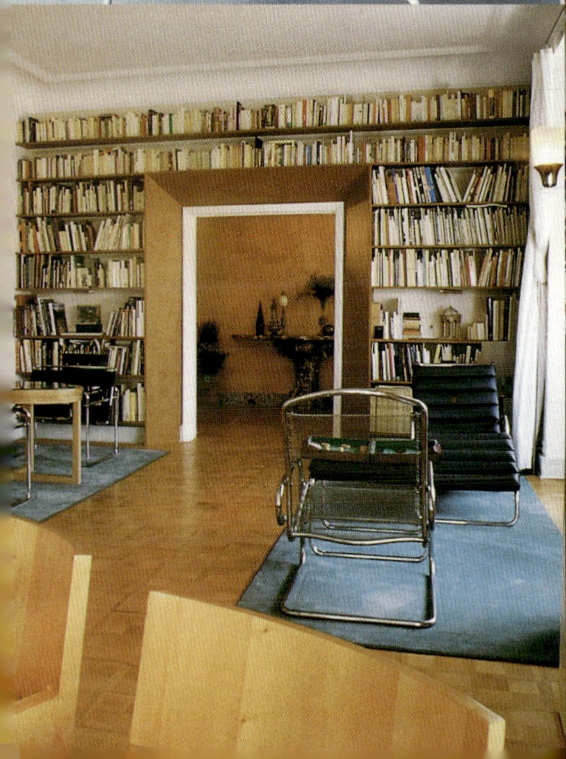
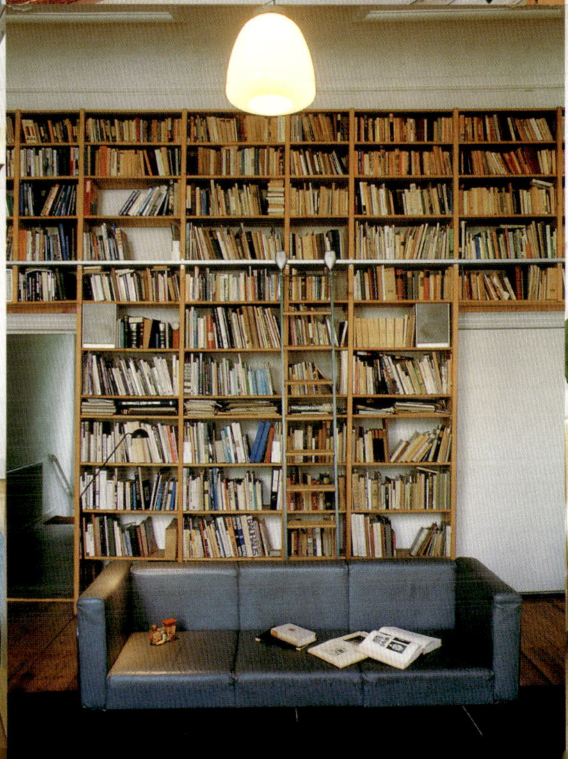
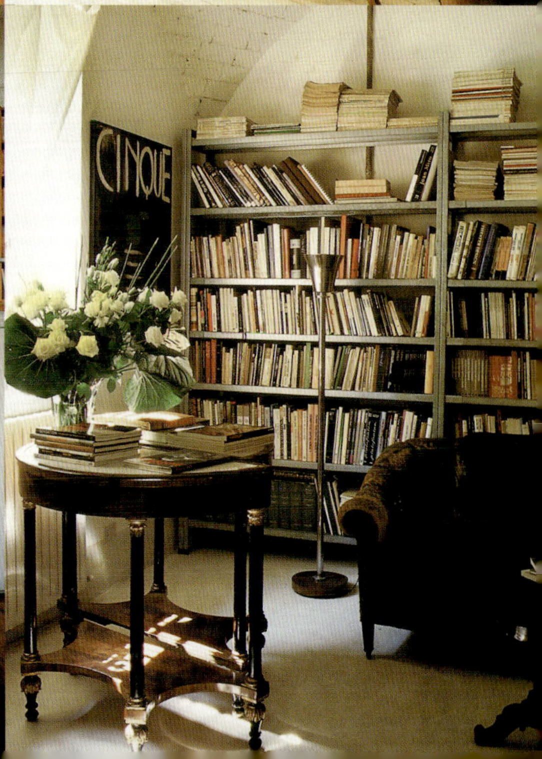
CINQUE

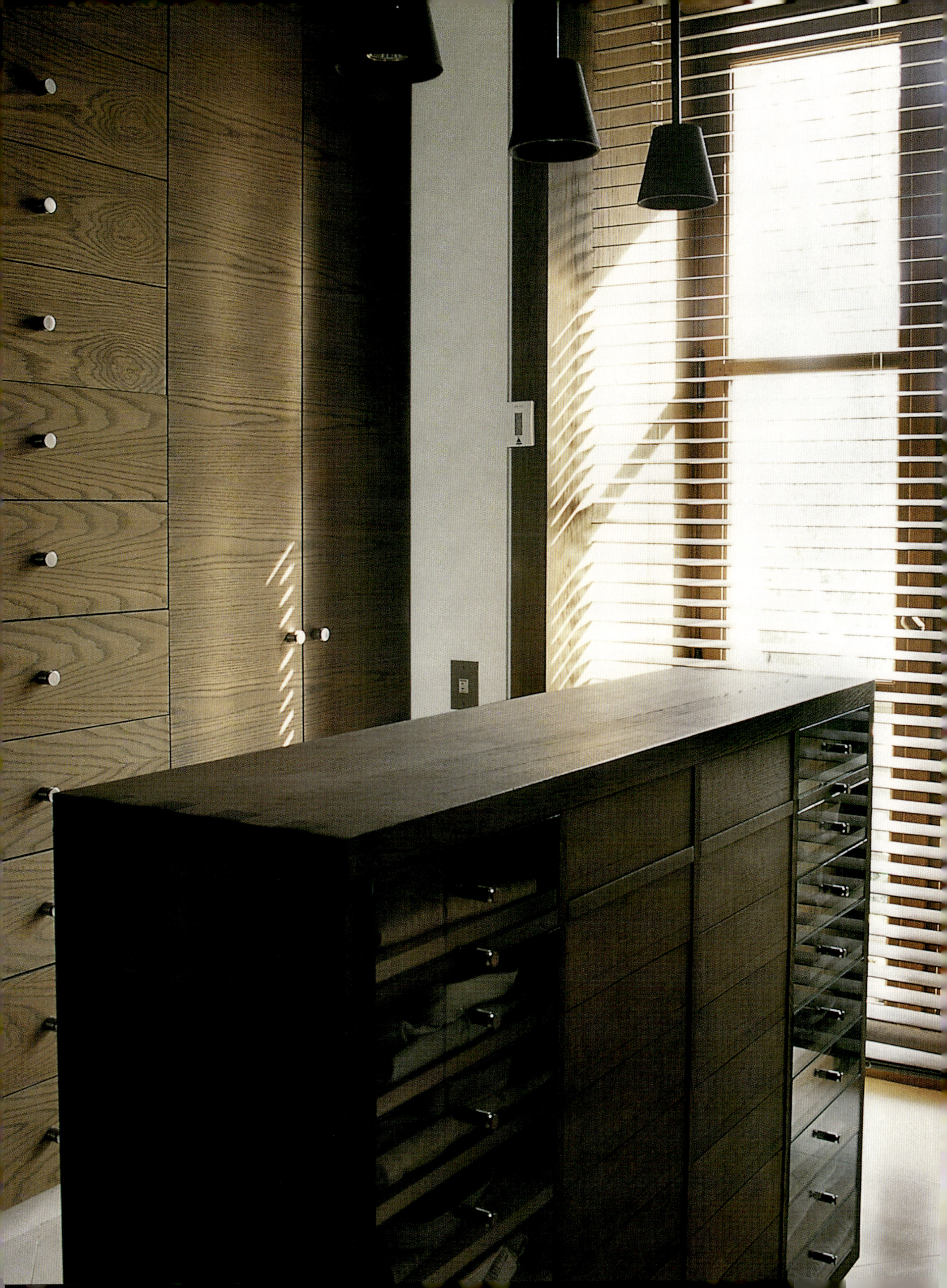

書棚・オープン棚

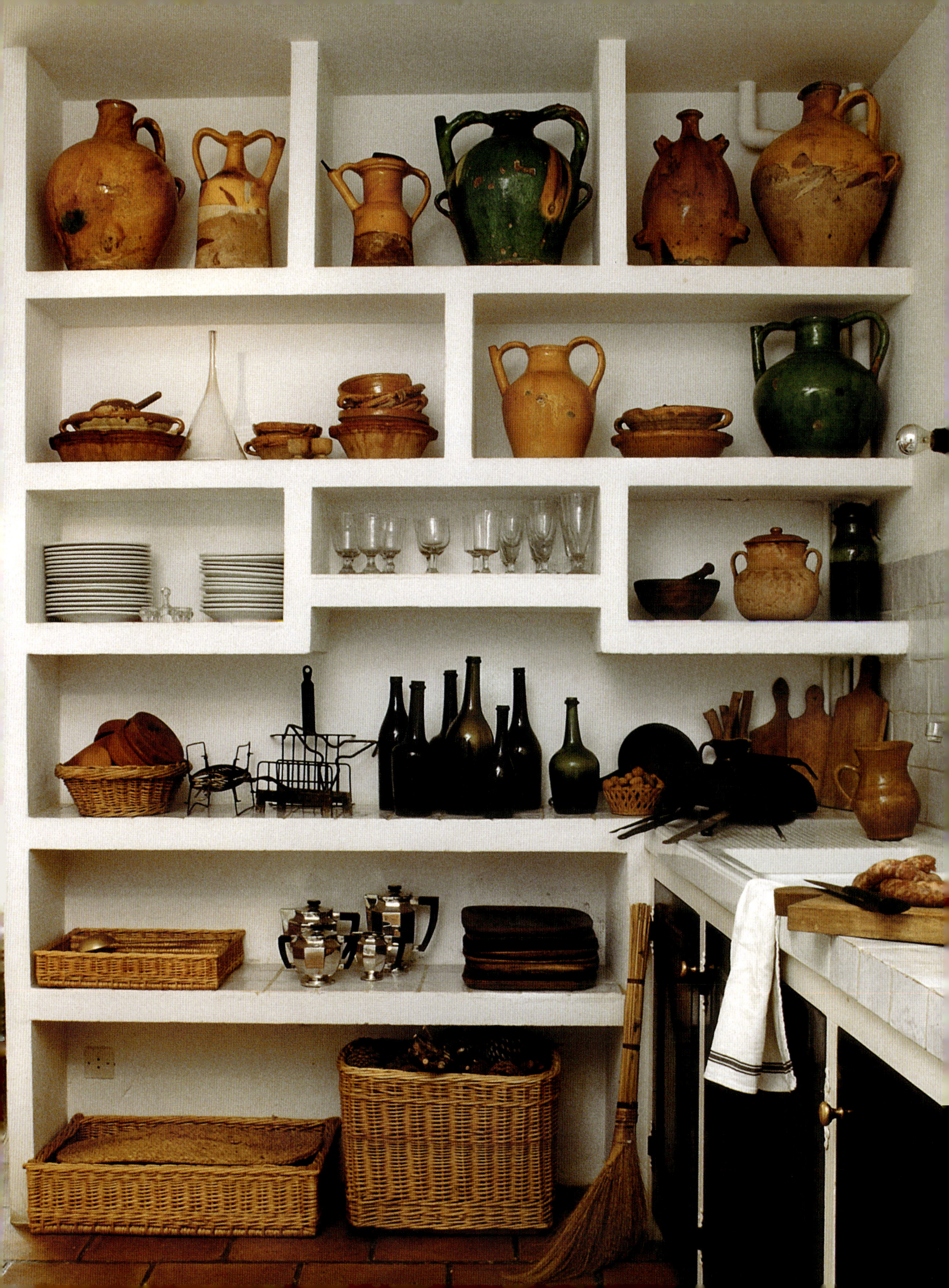

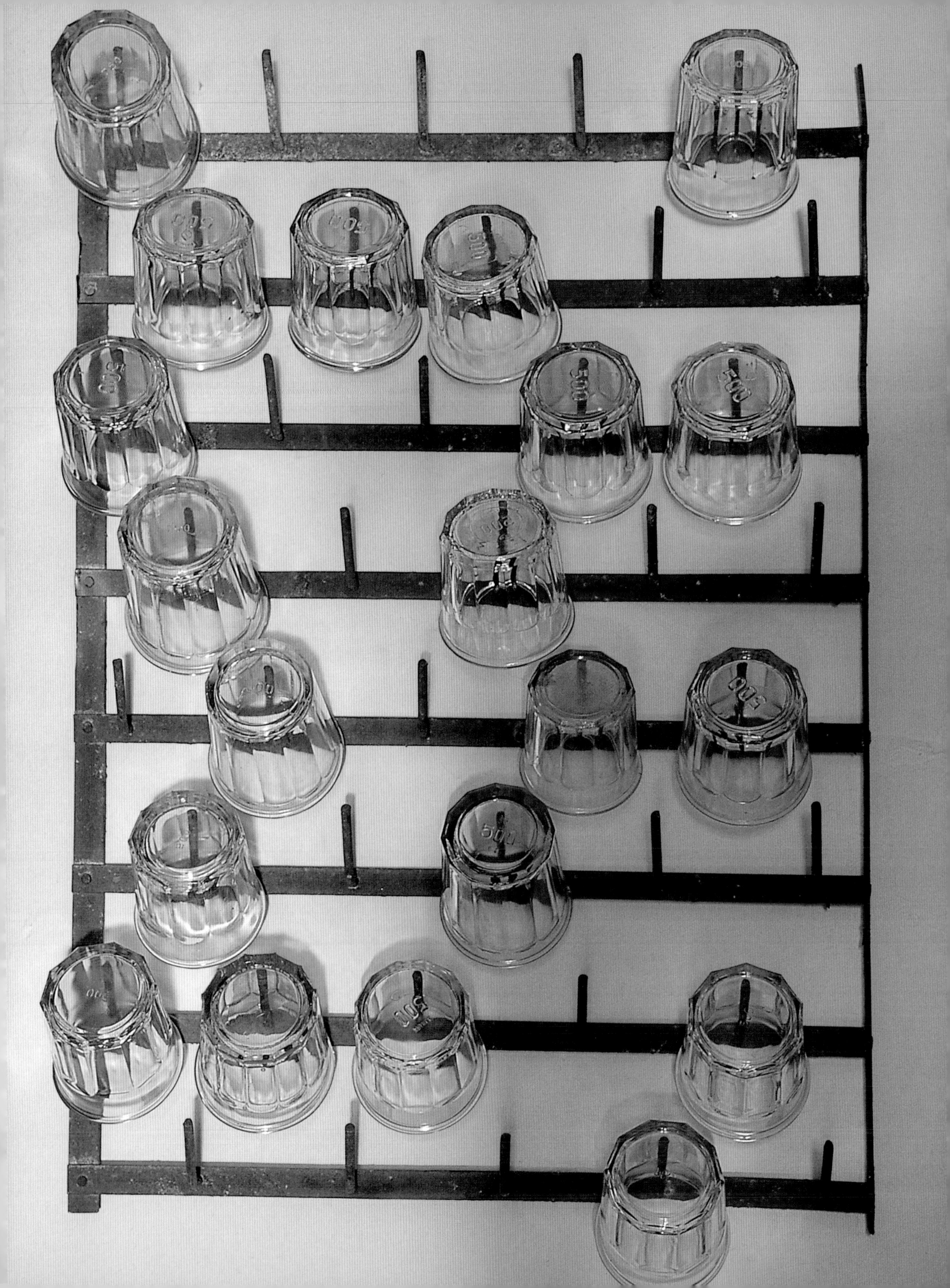
500

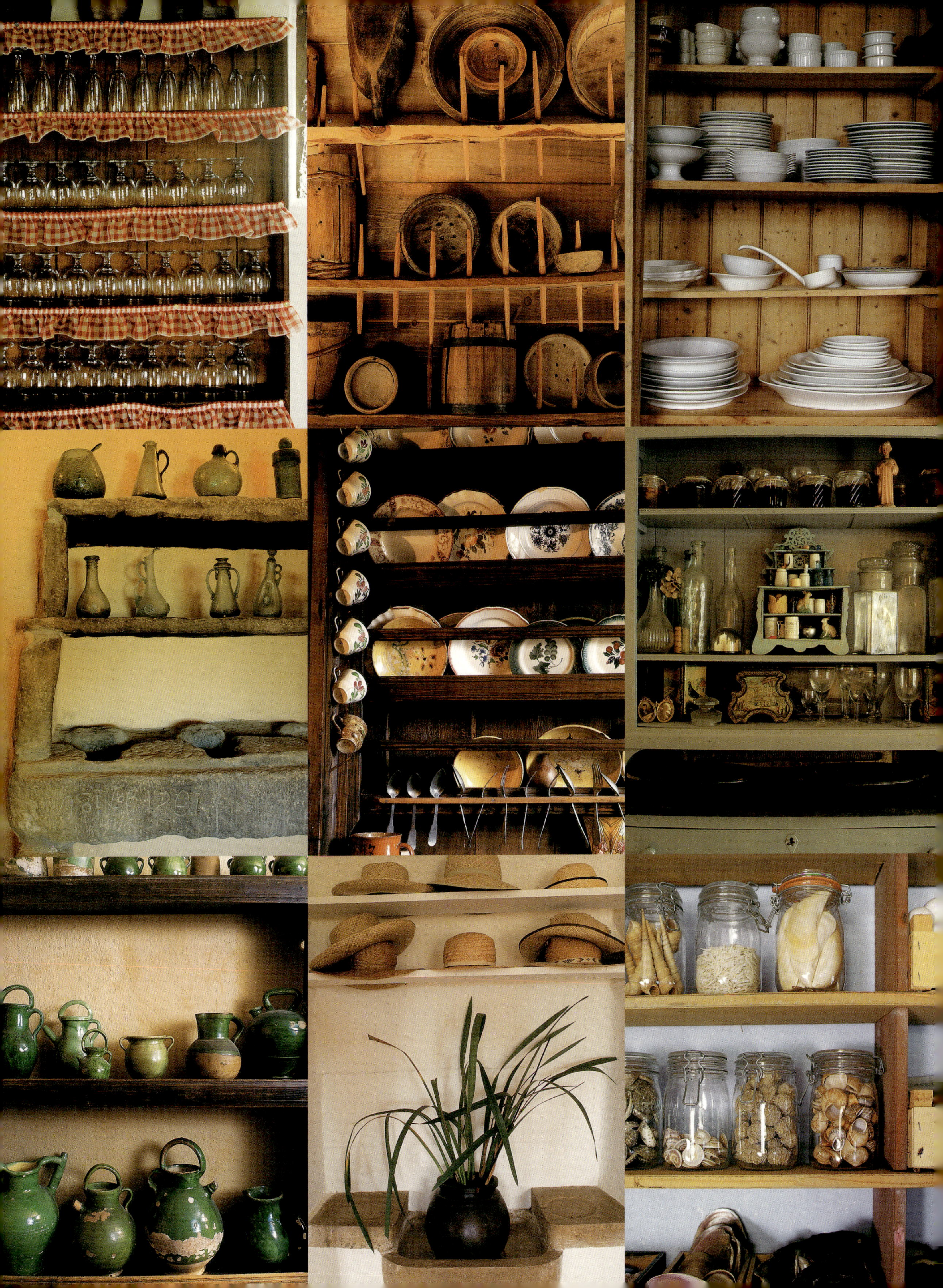

戸棚・食器棚

Coveted Cupboards

家の中の物が、すべて片付く戸棚を置くことなんて無理だと言う人もいます。また、ミニマリストは、自分の好むインテリア——平面を装飾せず、物を置かない殺風景なまでの空間——は、禁欲的に生活し、白いドアの向こうに、床から天井までの収納スペースがある場合だけ、実現するということを知っています。しかし、収納スペースがあればあるほど、物を貯め込み、捨てなくなるのも事実です。収納について質問すると、こう答えた人がいました。「何かひとつ家の中の物を処分した時にだけ、別の物を家に入れるべきなんです」。確かに良い心がけだと思いますが、続けられる人はごくわずかではないでしょうか。大多数の人には、多くの物がしまい込める、豊富な収納スペースが必要です。もちろん、どこに何がしまってあるのか、きちんと把握していなければなりませんが。ですから、大型で見映えのよい戸棚を持つことには、実用性と装飾性という2つの喜びがあります。造り付け収納とは対照的に、食器棚には、移動させられるという利点があります。素朴なカントリースタイルや、装飾の多い民族調の食器棚、もしくは1920年代や1930年代のように、デザインに特徴のある年代物の食器棚を選びましょう。こういった家具は、家具店が店舗を移る際に、驚くほど安く売り出されることがあります。こうして手に入れた家具を、いったん玄関ドアの向こうに運び入れてしまったら、手を入れずに使おうなどと思ってはいけません。まず、ニスをはがし、ペイントするか、壁紙を貼ります。もっとも大切なのは、棚板をたくさん追加することです。

Some say that a house can never have enough cupboards, and minimalists know that the look they love – bare surfaces and cool empty spaces – can only be achieved by monastic discipline and floor-to-ceiling storage behind seamless white doors. But it's also a fact that the more storage space you have, the more you hoard and the less you chuck out. I once interviewed someone who told me: 'We only allow one more thing into the house if we take something out'. It's a good intention, but one that few of us can maintain. The rest of us need plenty of space to store things away, but at the same time, to know exactly where to find everything. To that end, having a large beautiful cupboard is a two-fold joy. As opposed to built-in storage, it has the benefit of being able to be moved about. Choose a simple country style or an embellished ethnic piece, or you might prefer something from a particular design period like the 1920s or '30s. The sort of thing that gets abandoned during house clearances can often be surprisingly inexpensive. And once you've got it through the front door and – heaven forbid – up the stairs, don't stop short of customising it. Strip off the varnish, apply paint effects or cover it with bold wallpaper, and, most importantly – fit in lots of extra shelves.

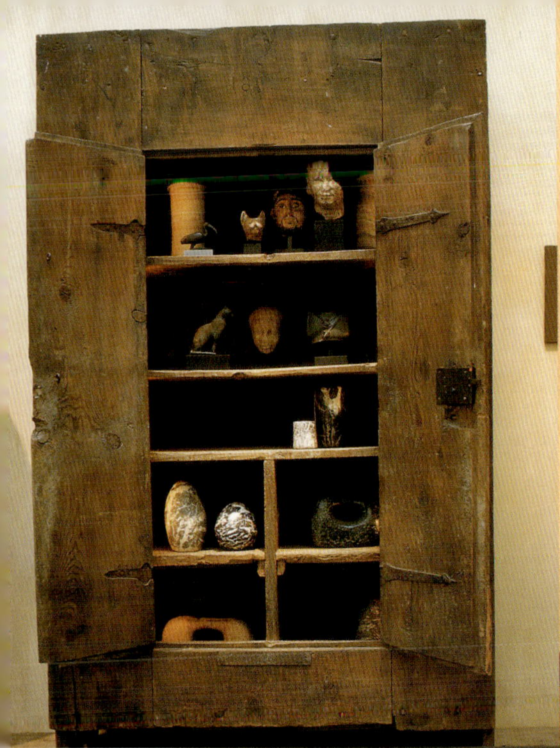
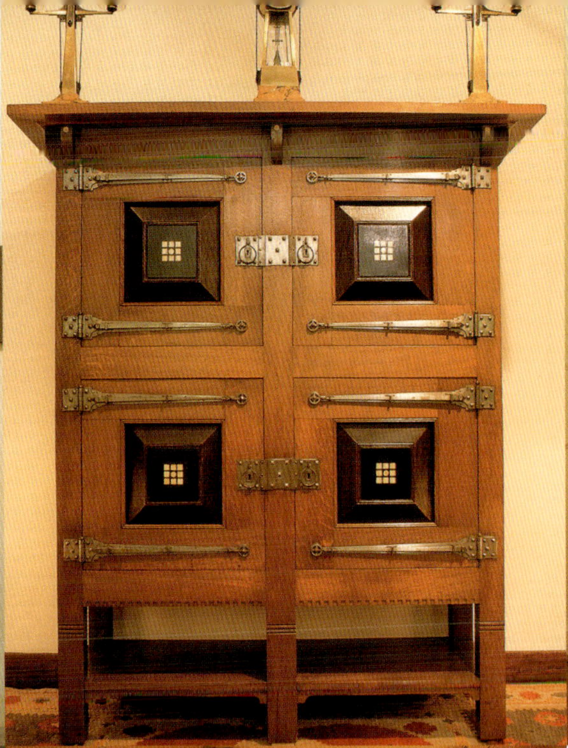
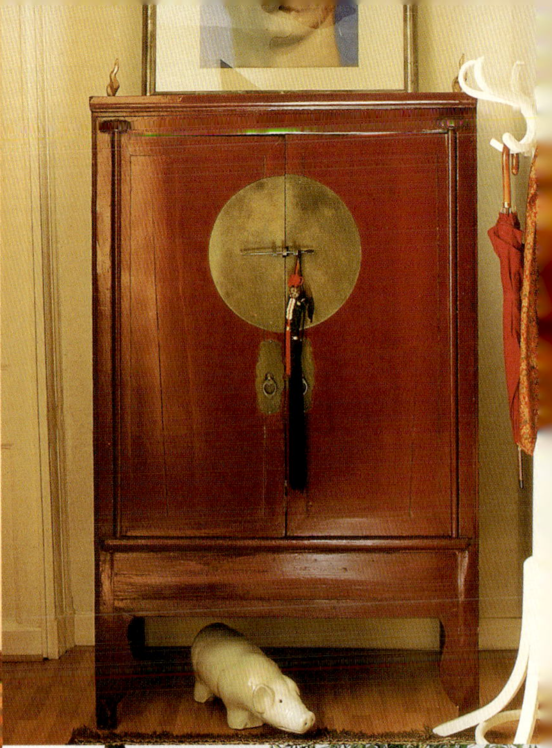
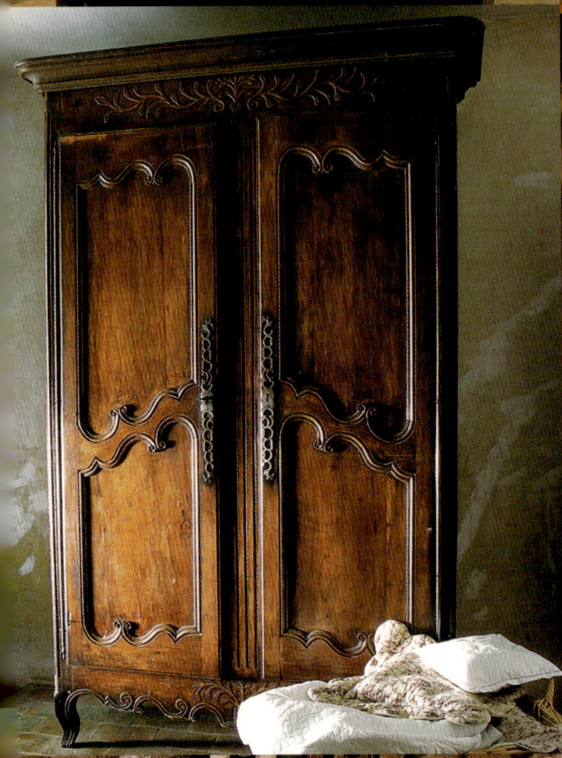
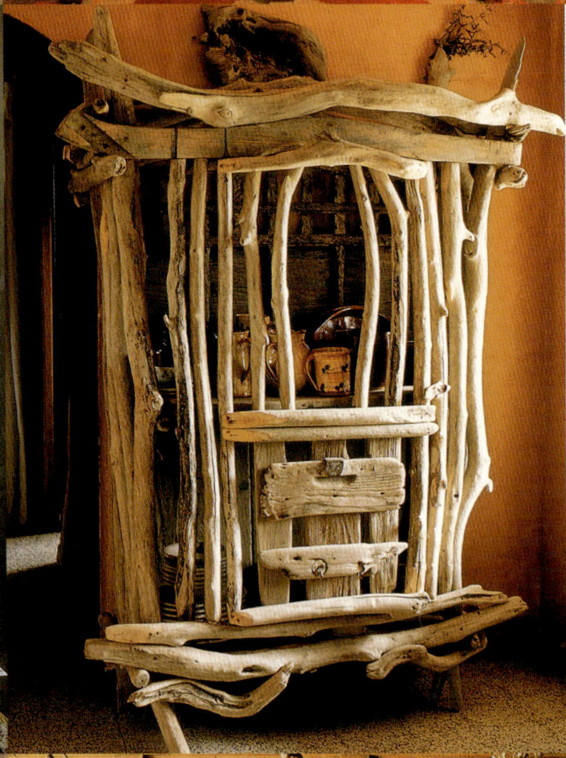
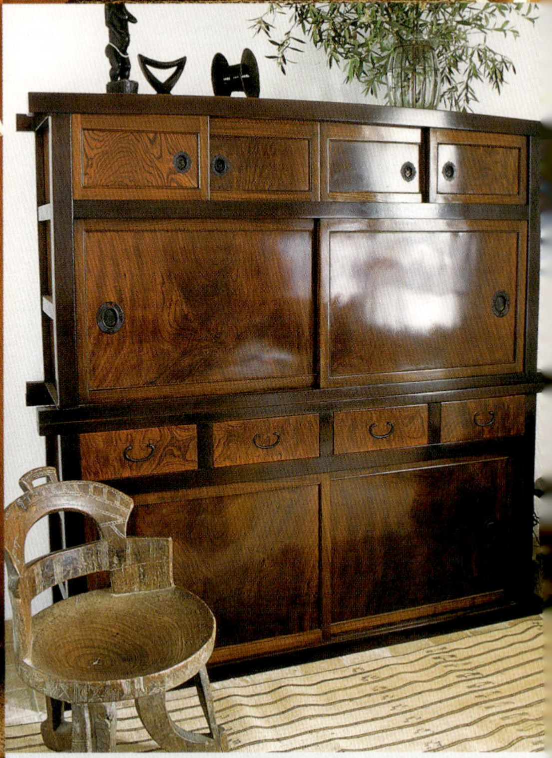
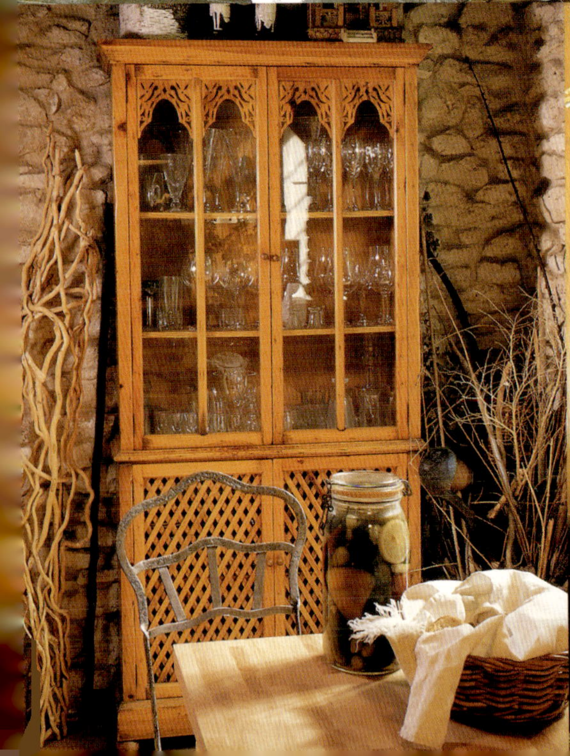
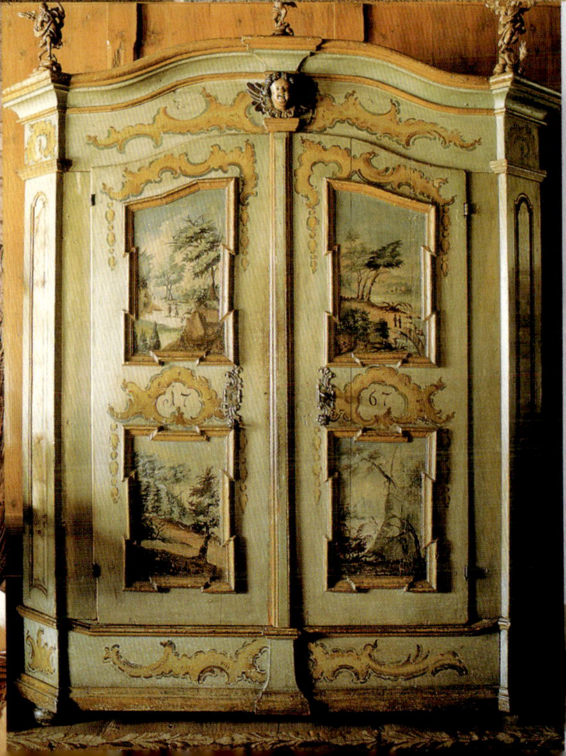
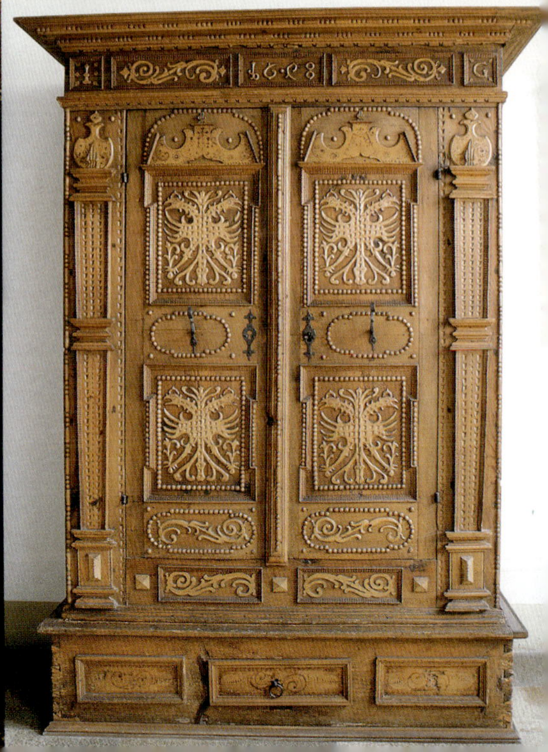

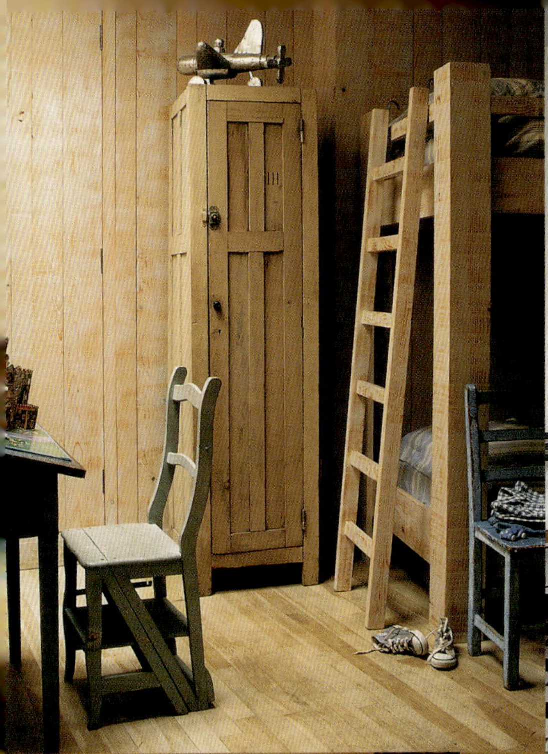
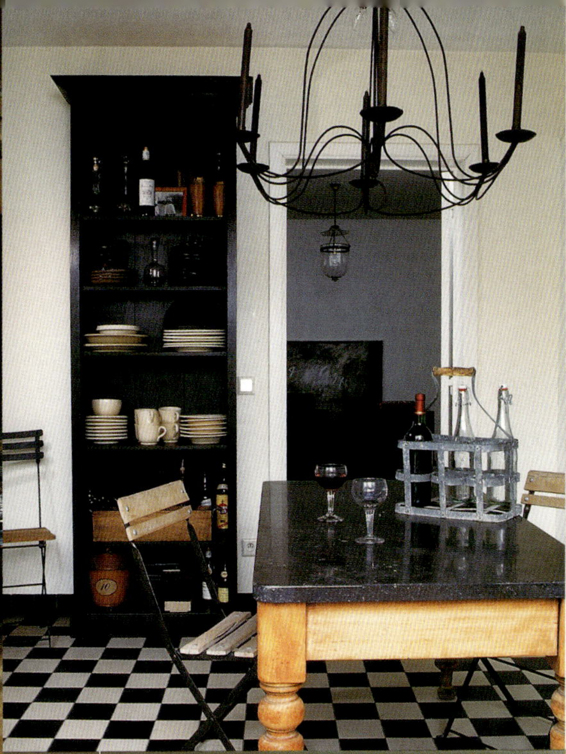
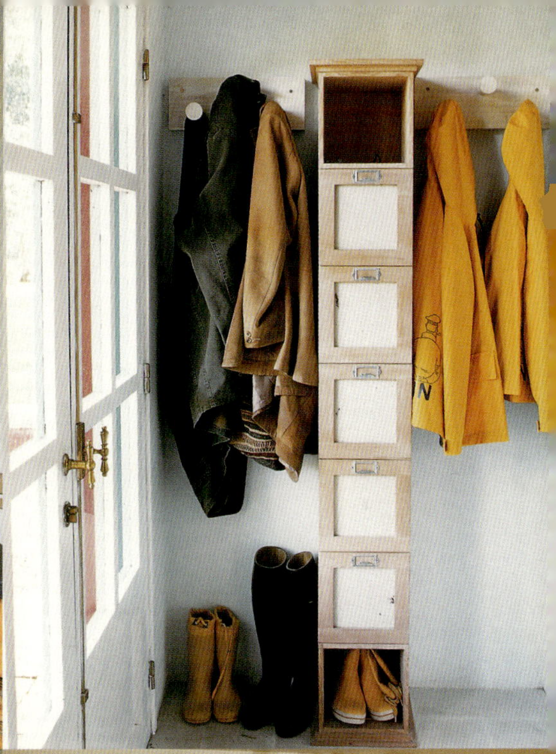
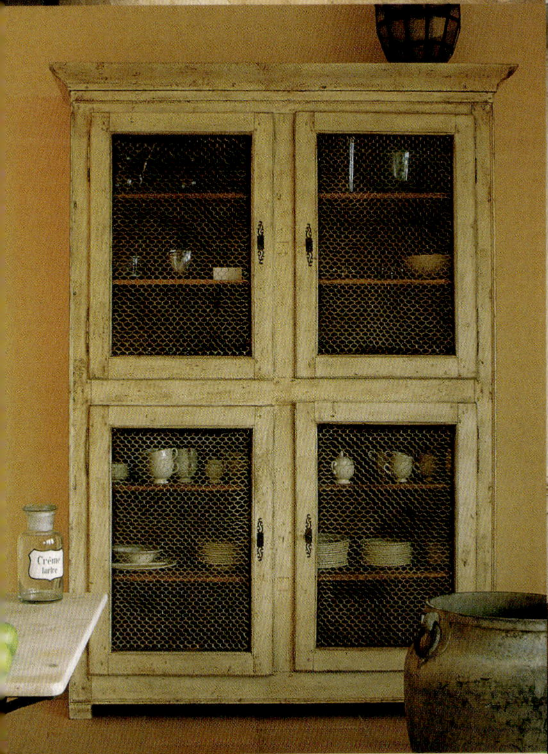
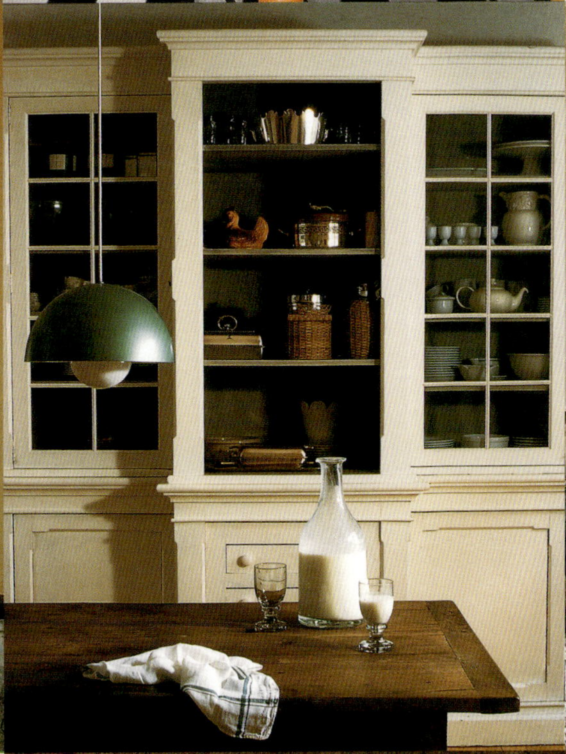
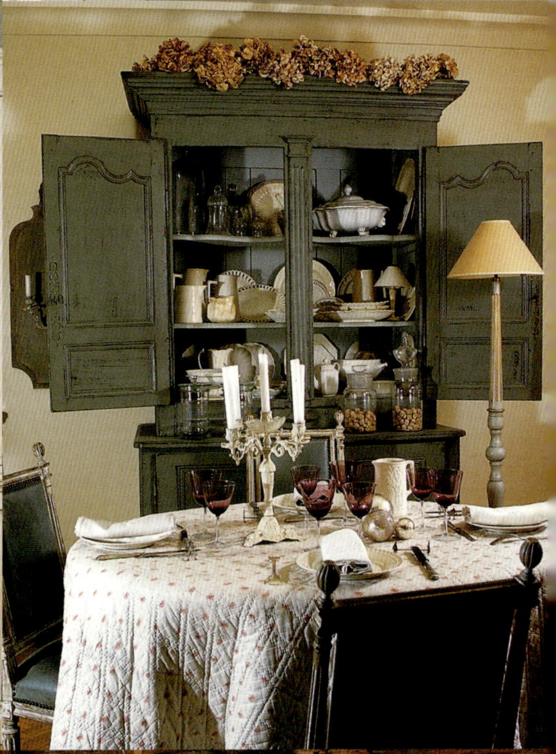
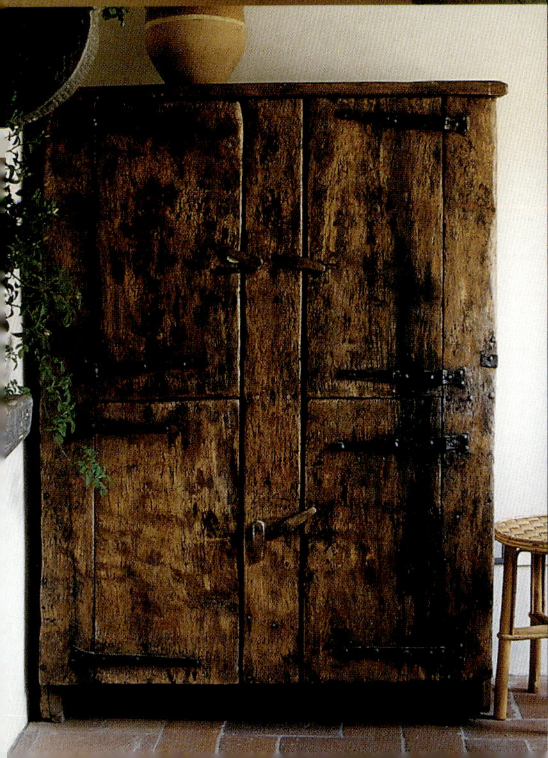
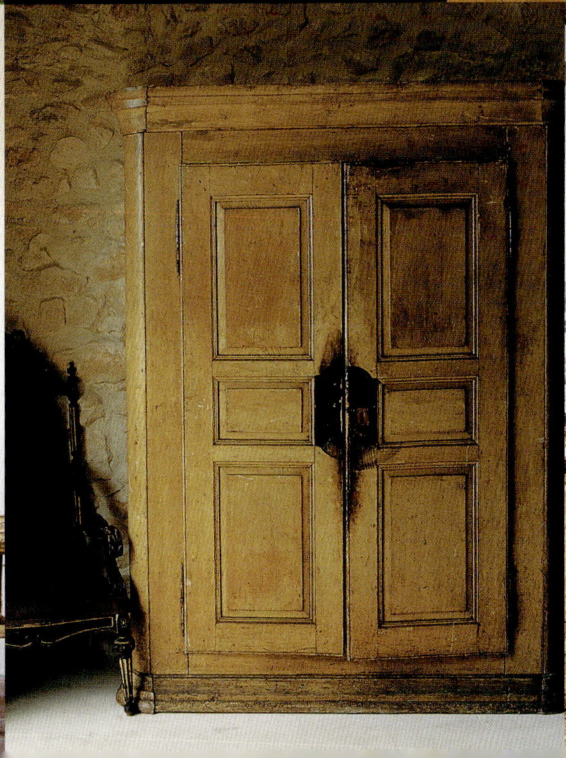
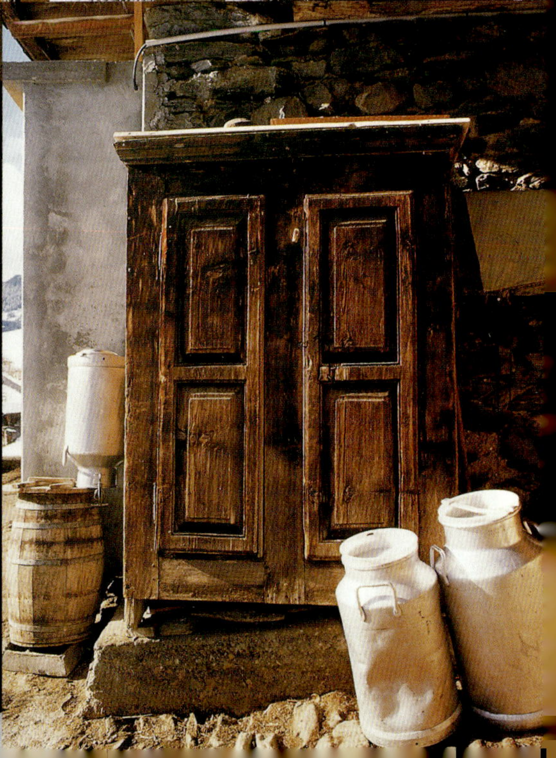

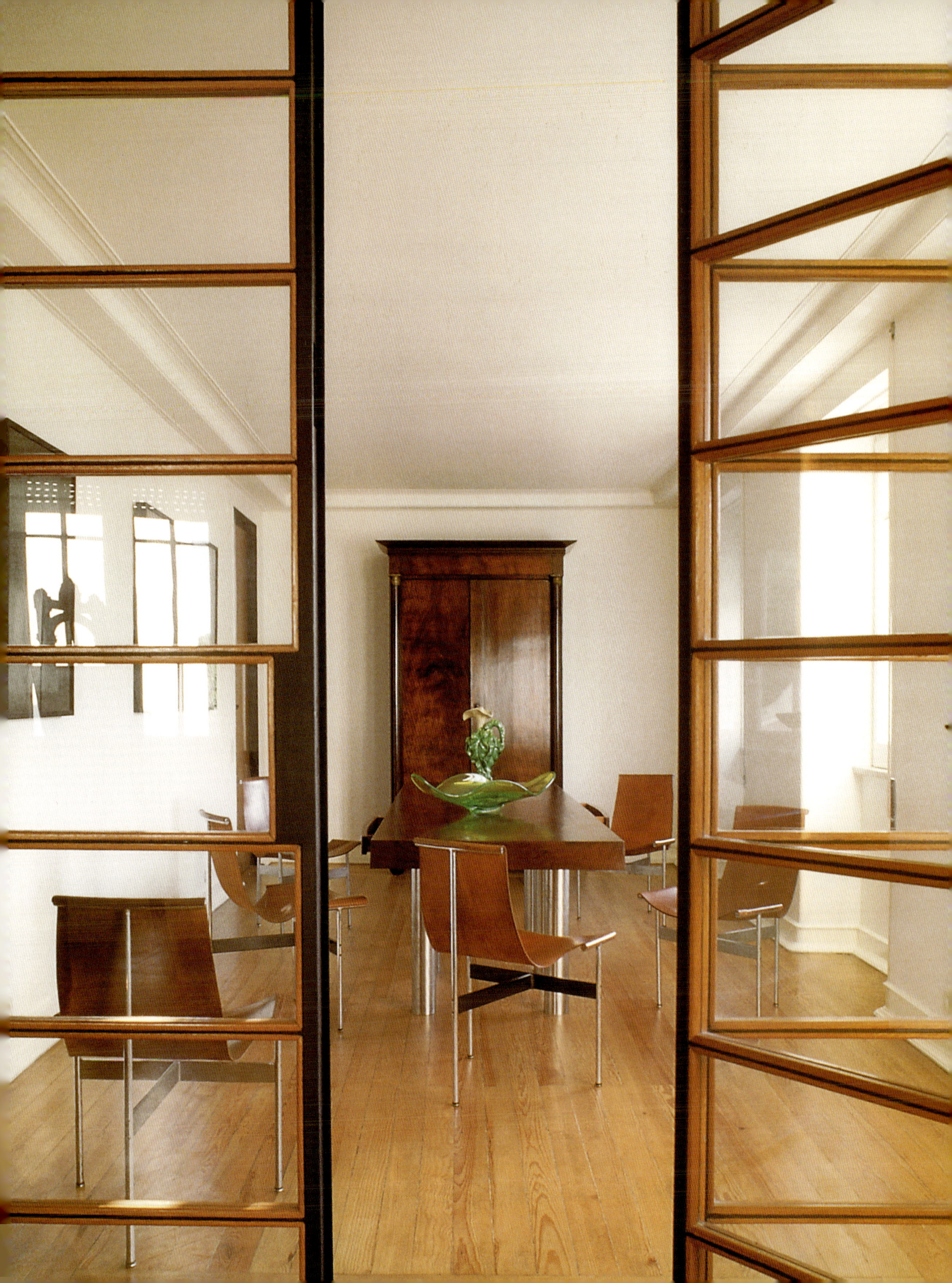

戸棚・食器棚

戸棚・食器棚

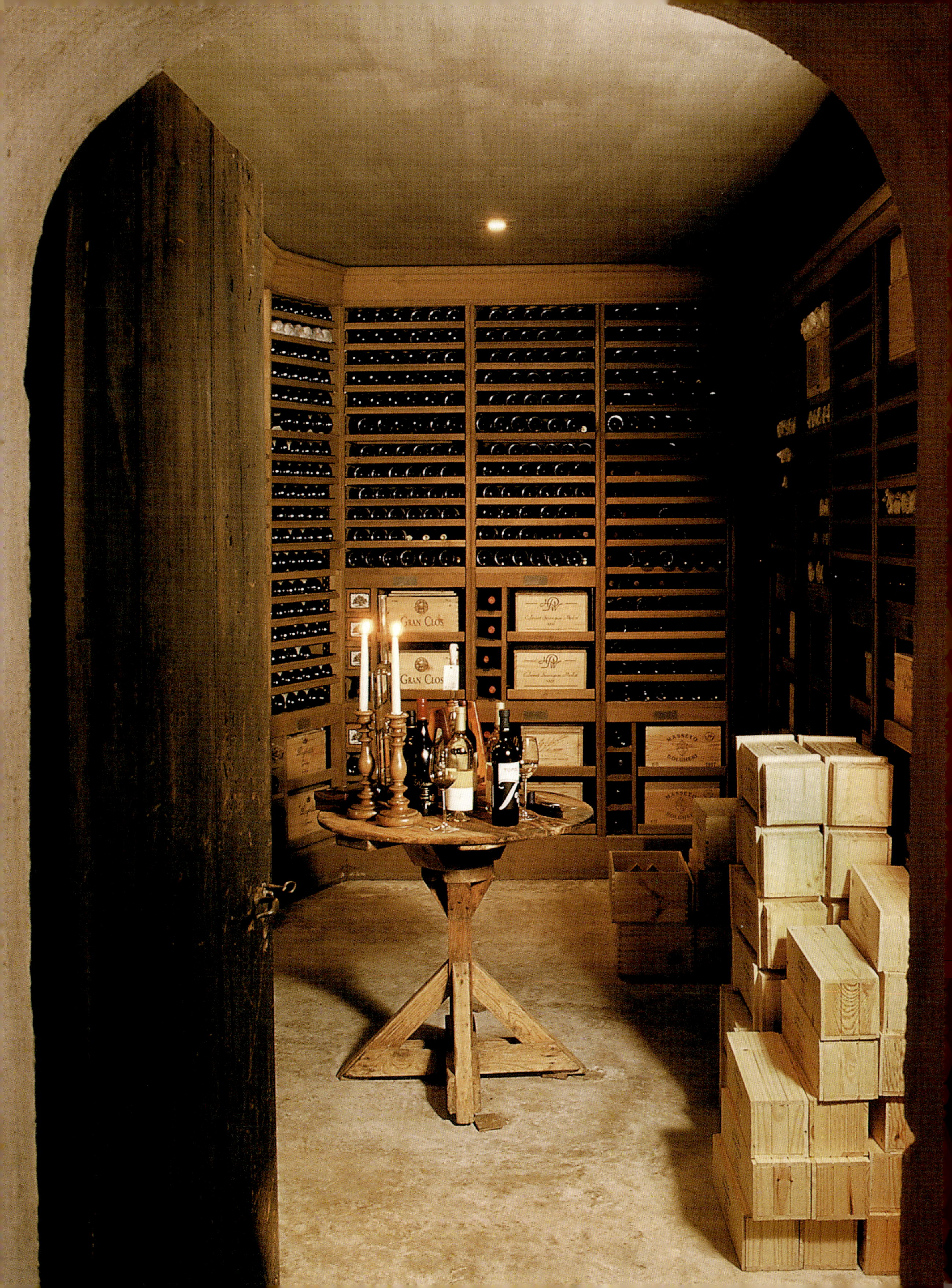
GRAN CLOS
GRAN CLOS
MASSETO
BOLGHERI

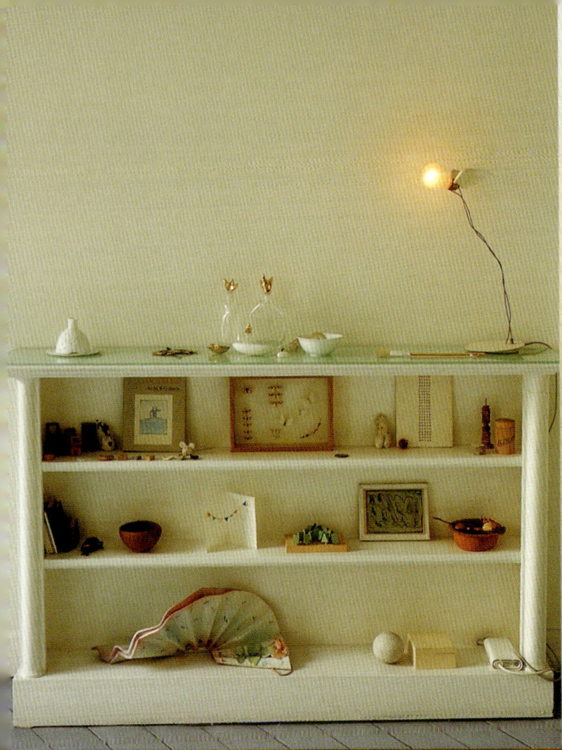
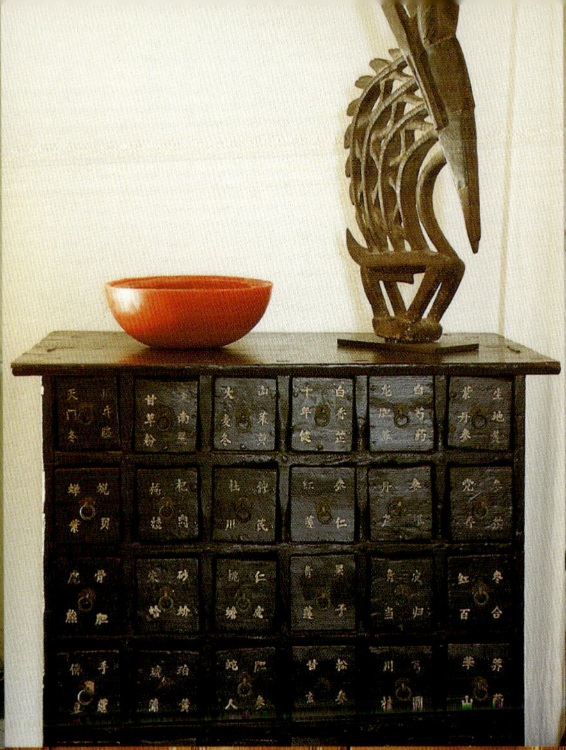
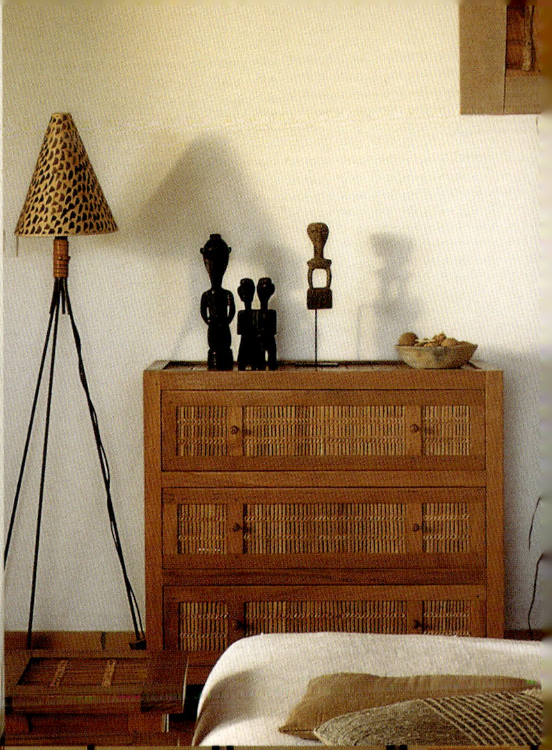
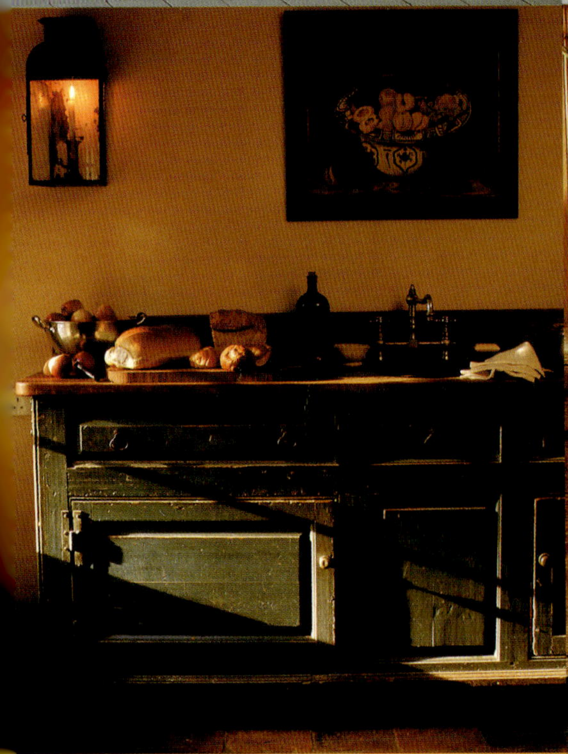
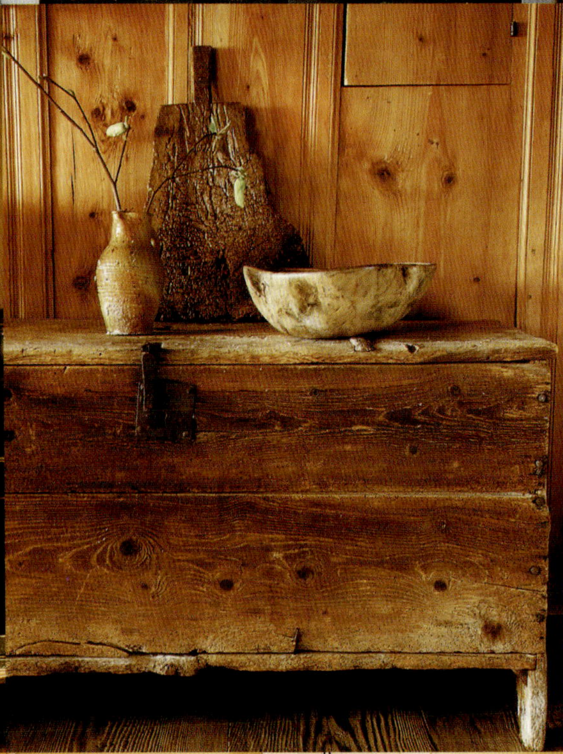
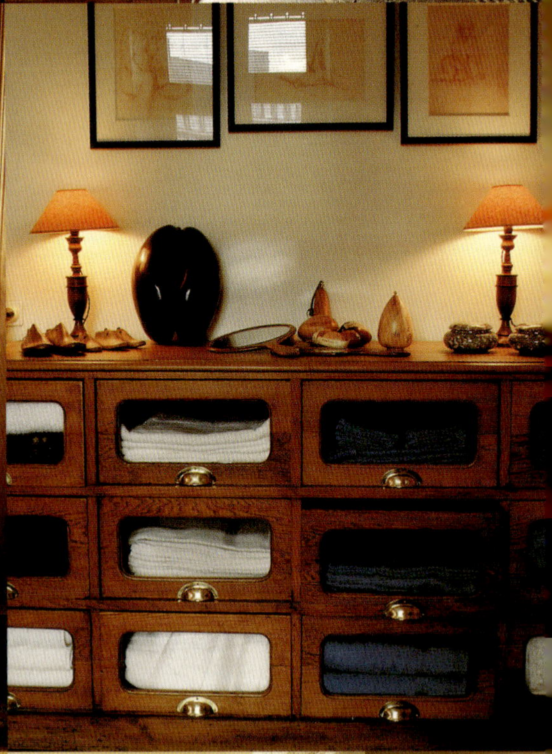
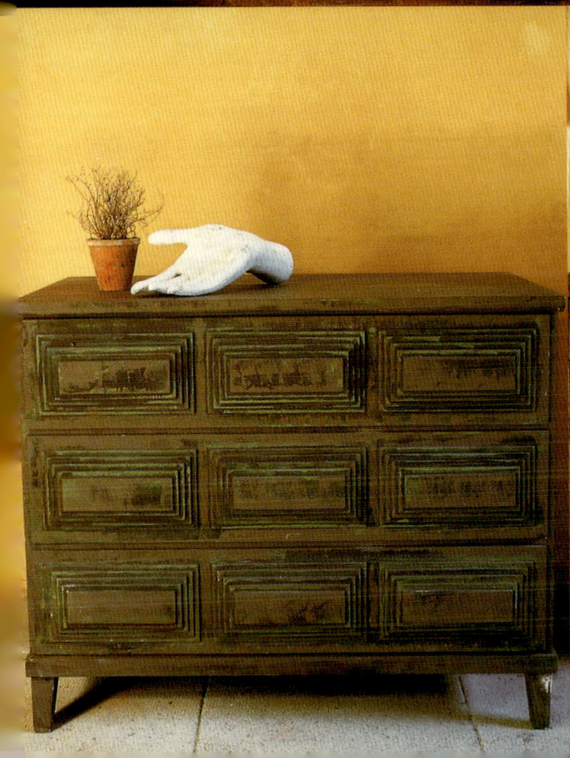
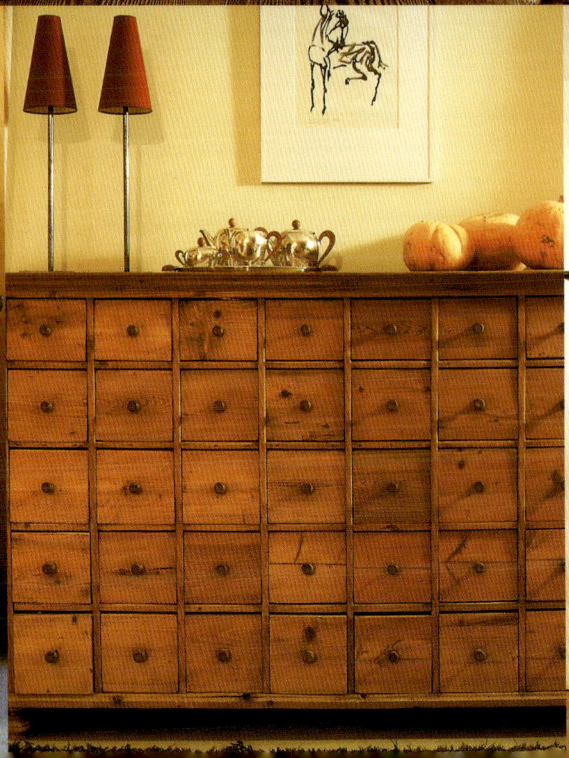
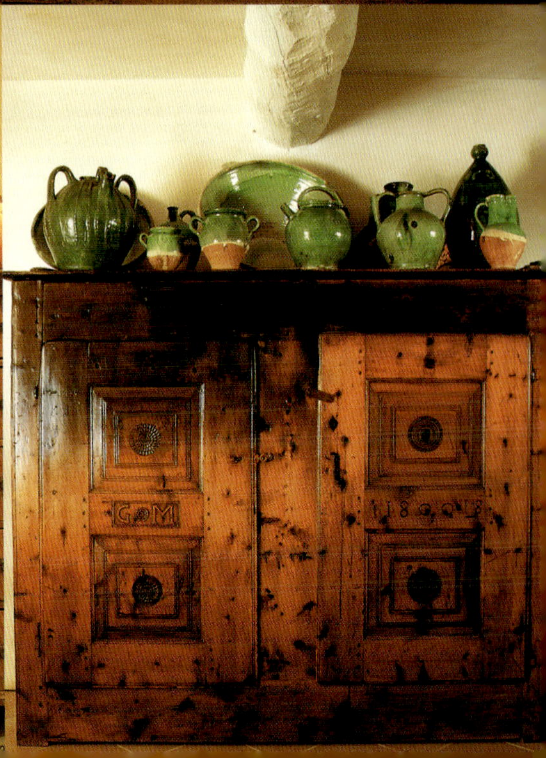

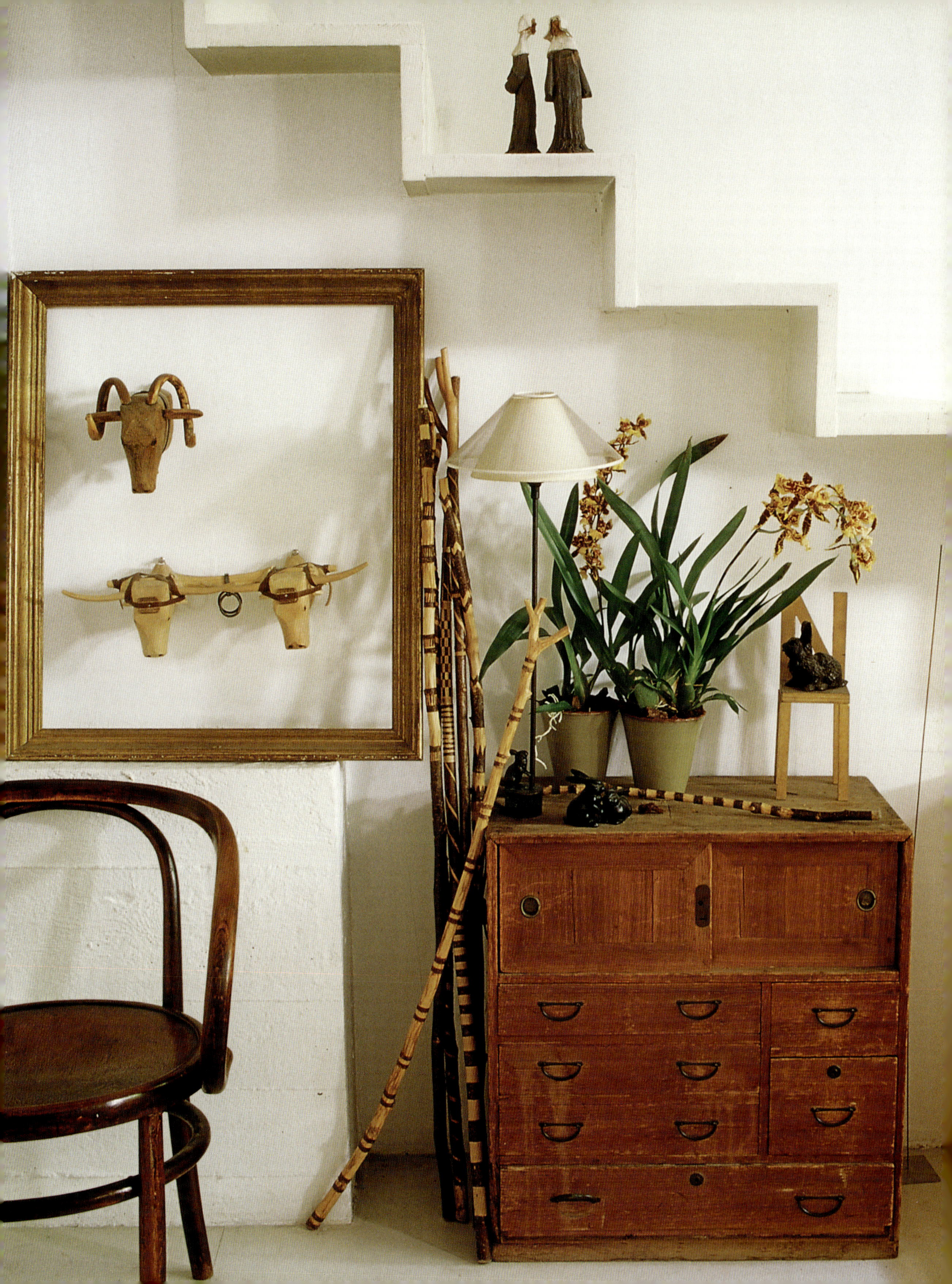

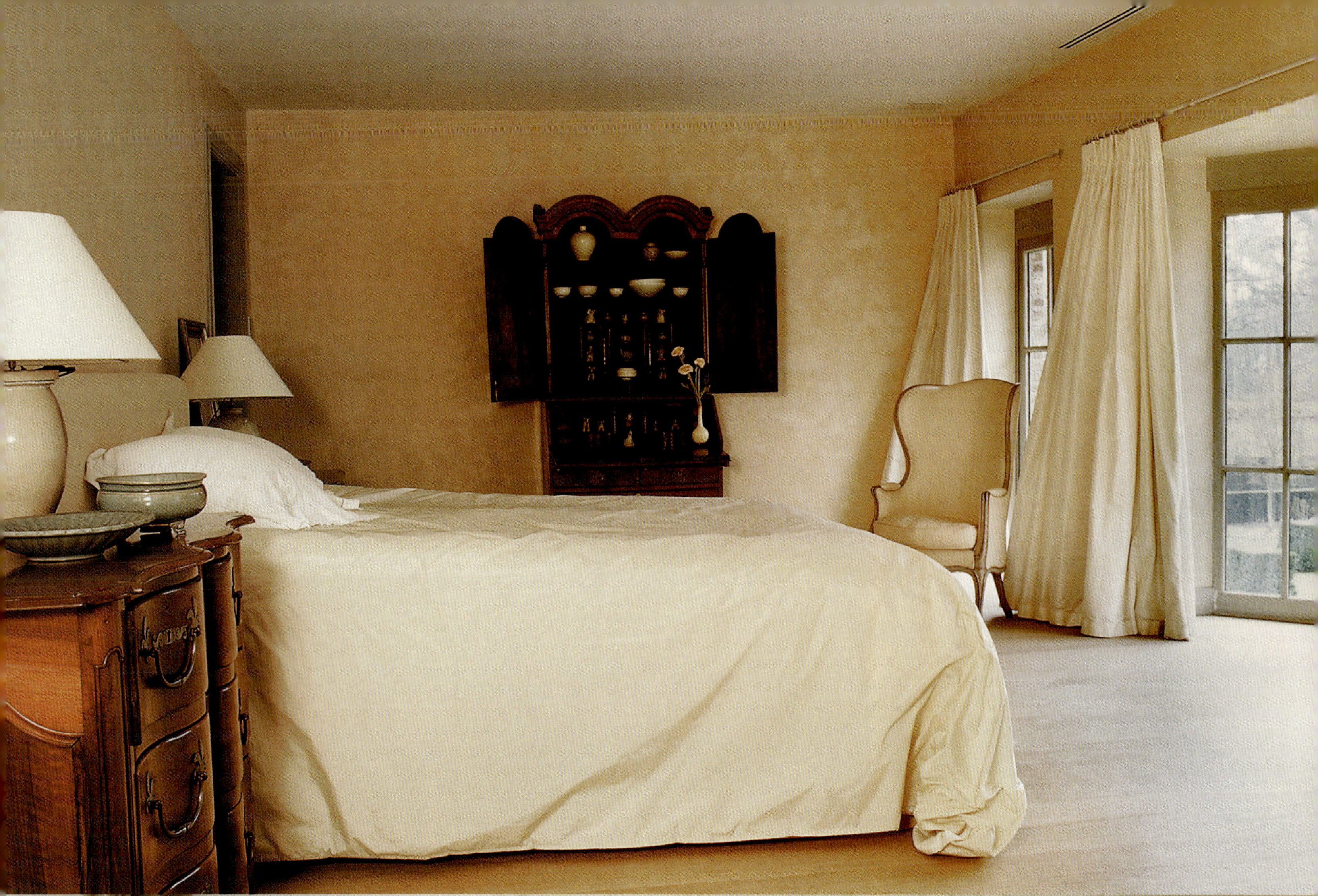

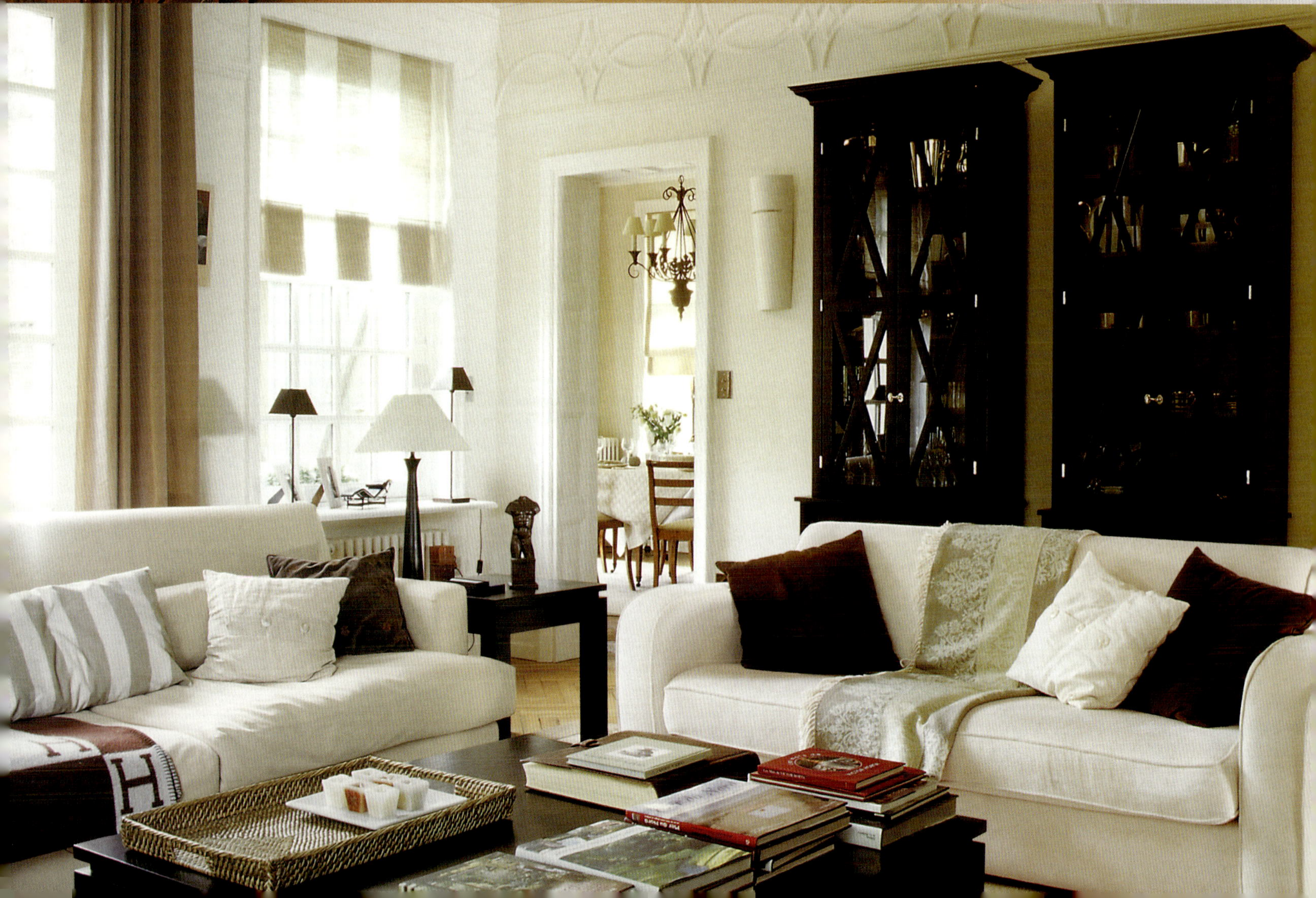

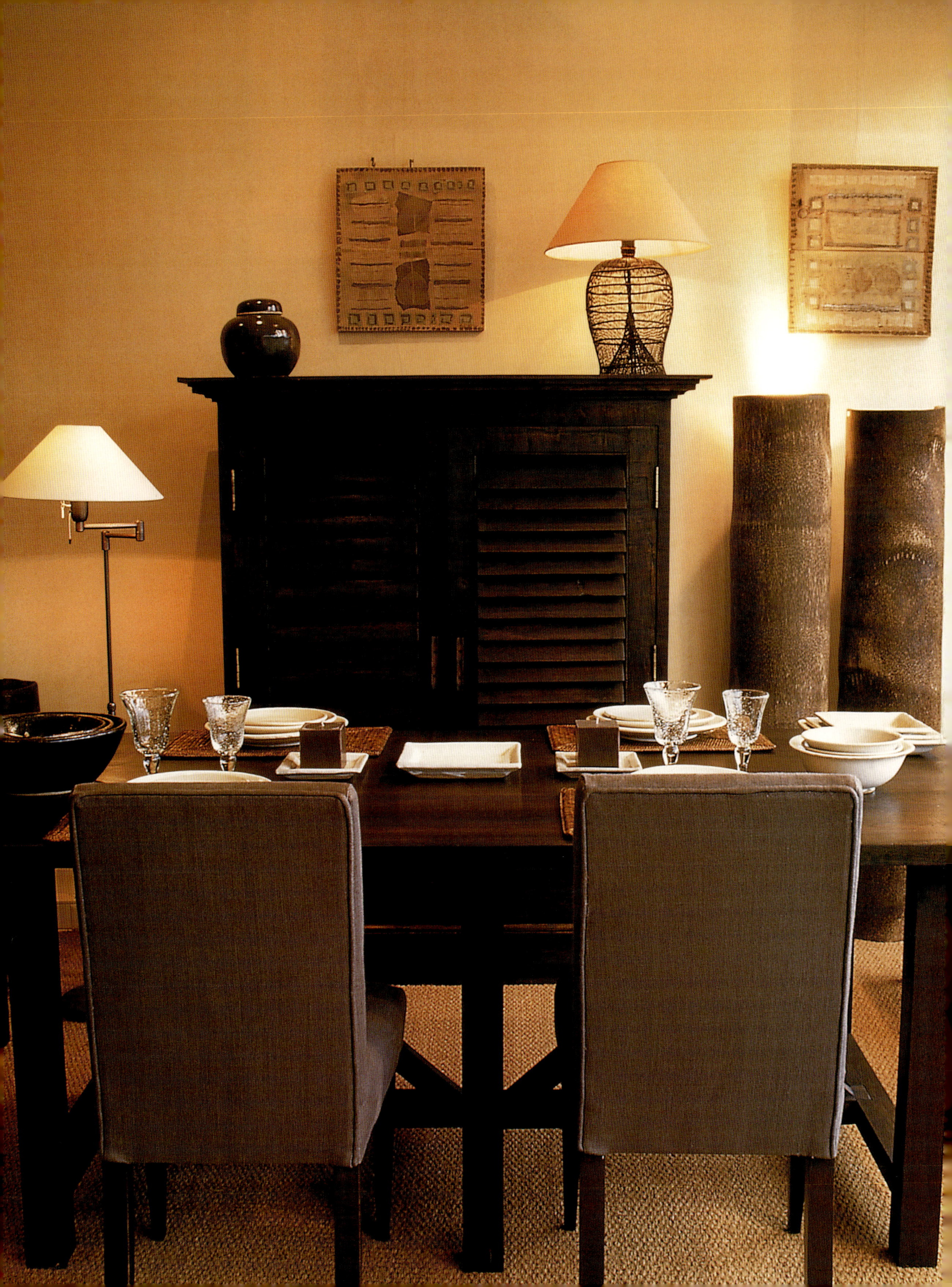

戸棚・食器棚

戸棚・食器棚

プライベートコーナー

Quiet Corners

住まいが広くても、狭くても、ひとり暮らしでも、大家族でも、どこかの部屋に小さなコーナーを用意しましょう。デスクと、座り心地の良い椅子と、使い勝手の良いライトを、できれば窓際に置くのです。これだけで、住まいに、時を忘れるような特別の空間を生み出すことができます。どの部屋にするか、という点については、朝日が射し込む場所、眺めの良い場所、心が落ち着く静かな場所など、人それぞれ好みがあるでしょう。たとえ一日中外で働いていたとしても、自宅に、手紙や本、ノートパソコン、趣味の道具などを置きっぱなしにできる場所があるというのは、とてもいいものです。別に、書類や電話類、そしてきつい仕事を連想させる物たちで山盛りになるような巨大なデスクは必要ありません。今では様々な大きさのテーブルが手に入ります。壁付けのテーブル、ライティング・デスク、蛇腹式の蓋が付いたデスクもあります。これに収納用の小さな棚や引き出し、そして生花が加われば、さらに良いでしょう。このスペースは、娯楽や家事に用途を絞るべきですが、もちろん、家で仕事をしているなら話は違ってきます。その場合は、仕事に没頭できる部屋が必要かもしれません。家族やペット、テレビや料理に、気を取られないようにするためです。家の中のスペースをすべて使い切ってしまったり、仕事場を作ったために、家の中でくつろげなくなってきたりしたら、作家のディラン・トマスやチャールズ・ディケンズという先達のスタイルを真似ることができます。つまり、心の平穏と静けさの得られる場所を、庭の隅にある納屋で見つけるのです。

Whether your house is large or small, whether you live alone or with a big family, setting aside a small corner of one room – preferably near a window – for a desk, a comfortable chair and an efficient lamp, can create one of the most beguiling and special places in your home. Everyone will have a preference over its position – a spot where you get the morning sun, a nice view or simply a bit of peace and quiet. Even if you work all day in an office, a place at home where you can leave your letters, your books, your laptop or your hobbies out on a table, will be very appealing. I don't mean an enormous desk covered with papers, telephones and all the inherent pressure that spells hard work. There are all sorts of interesting tables you could use, large or small, as well as consoles, writing bureaus and roll-tops. And if there are a few shelves, a cupboard, storage drawers and fresh flowers – even better. Keep it domestic, unless, of course, you work from home. If that's the case, you may need a devoted room – keep it away from the temptations of family and pets, TV or cooking. Should you run out of space or your work starts to take over your home-life, you can always follow the lead of such writers as Dylan Thomas and Charles Dickens who found peace and quiet in a shed at the end of the garden.

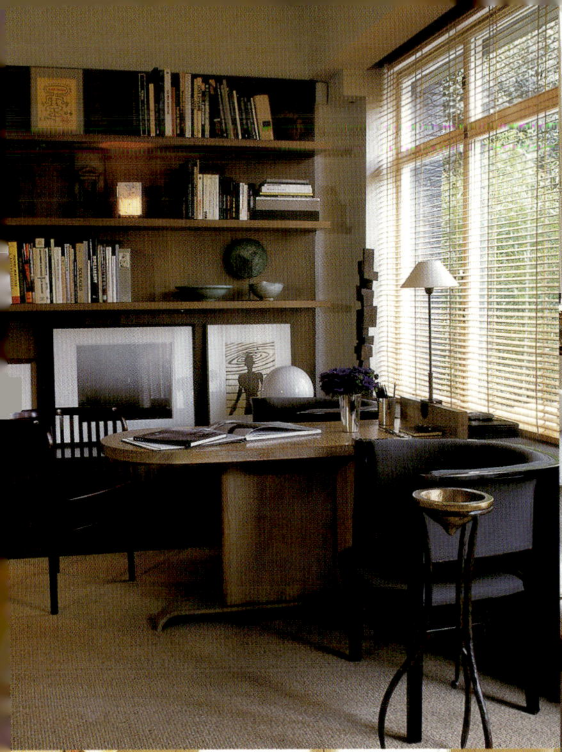
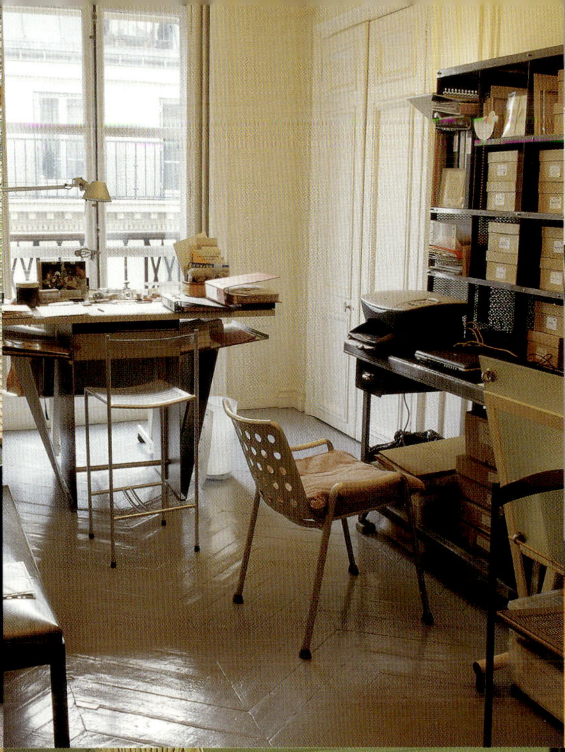
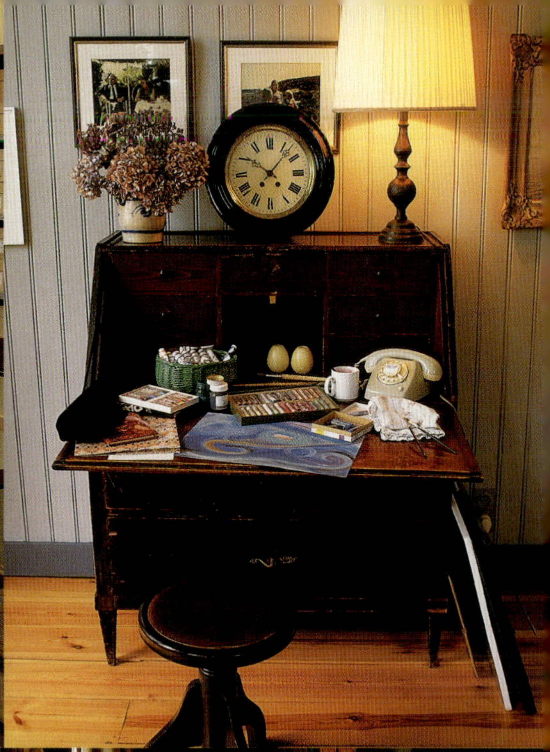
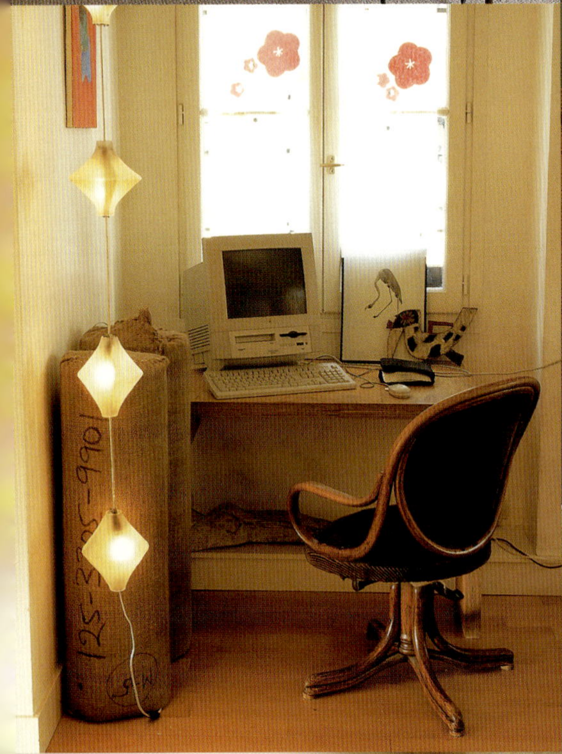
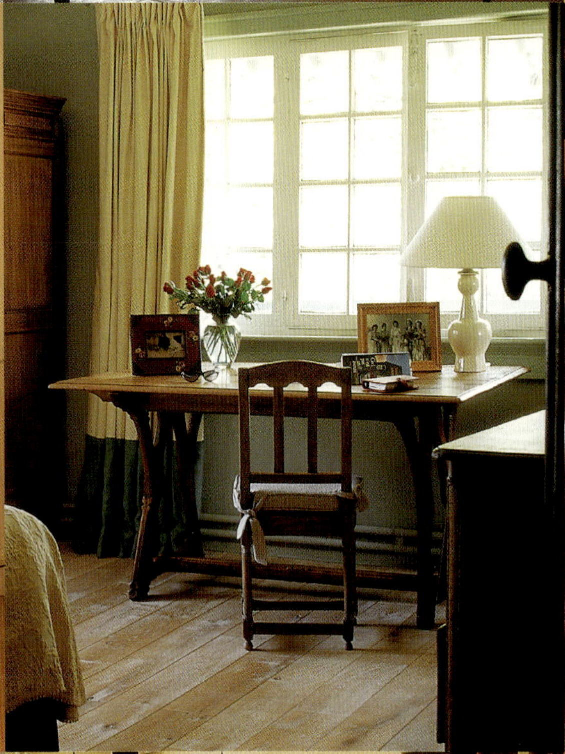
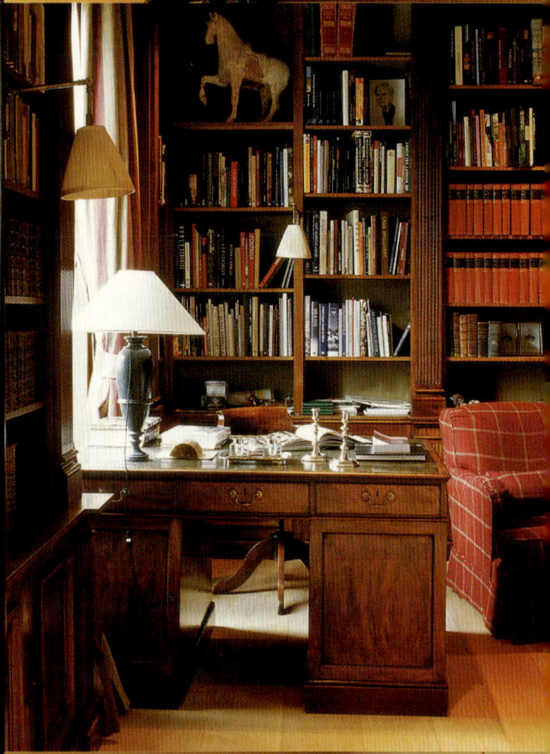
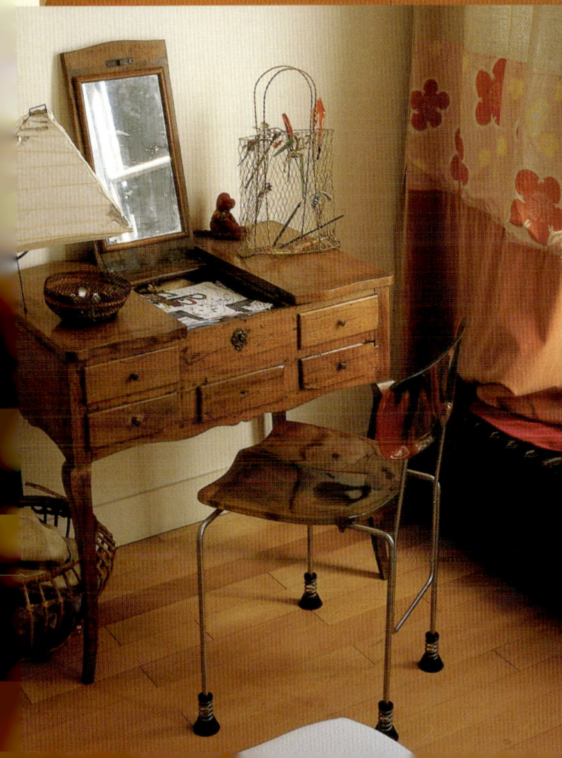
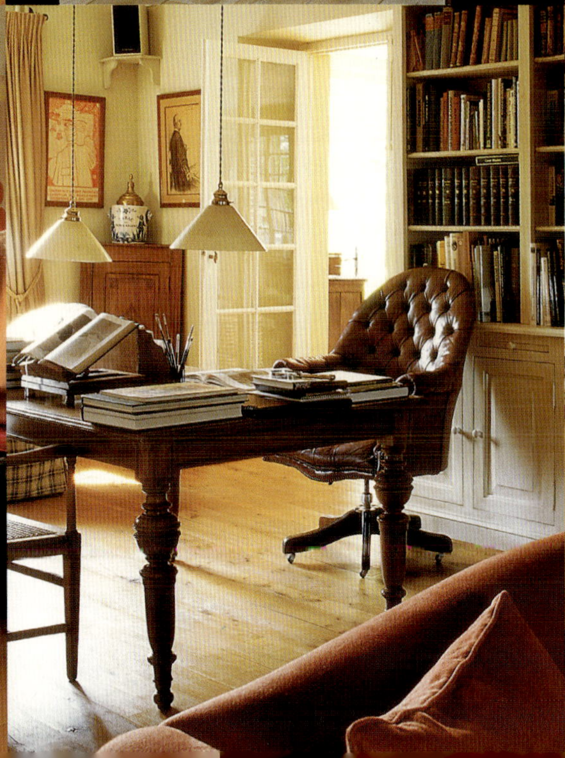
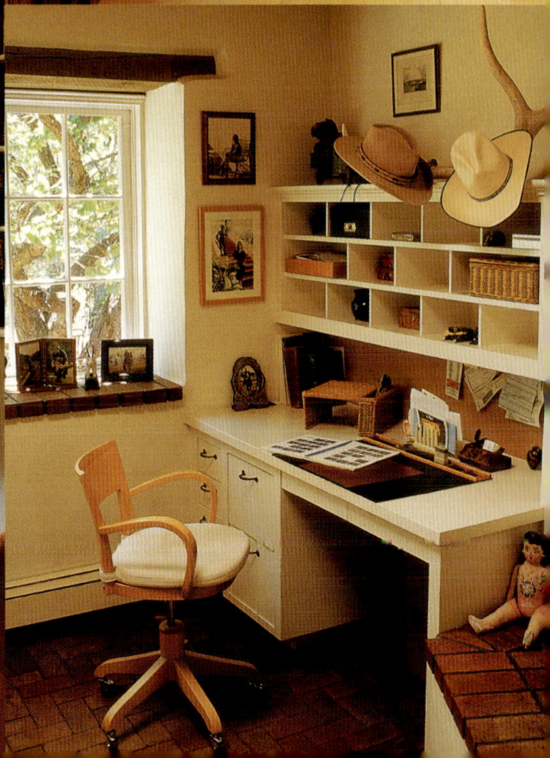

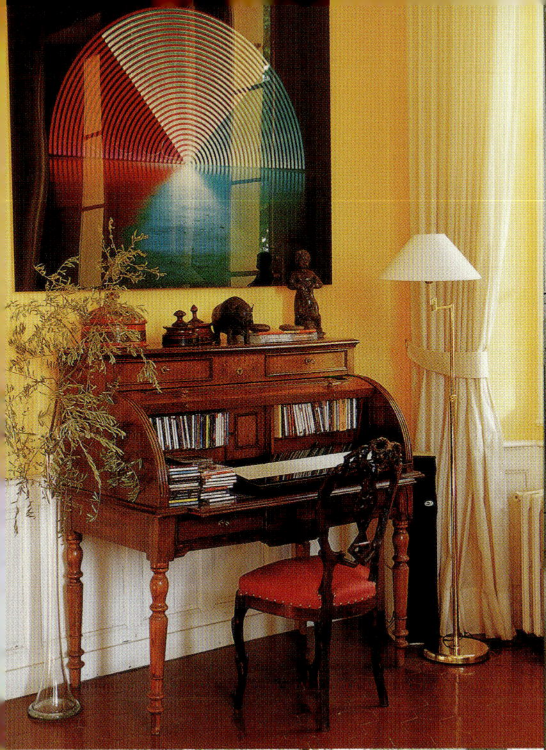
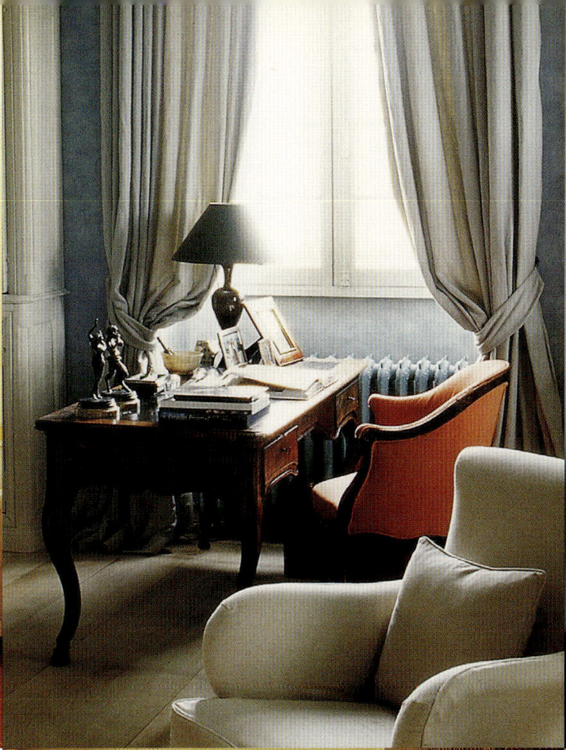
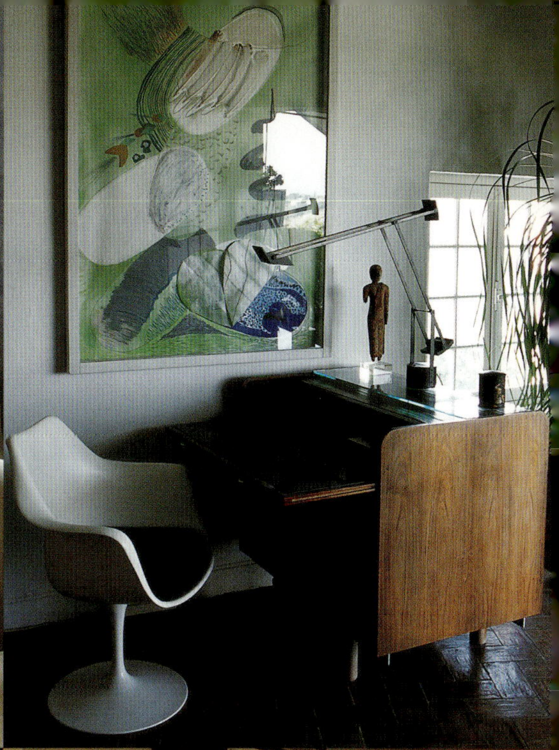
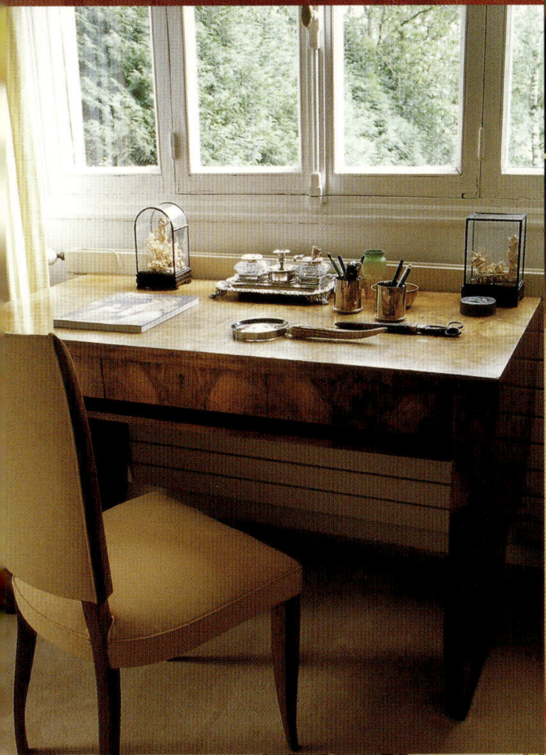
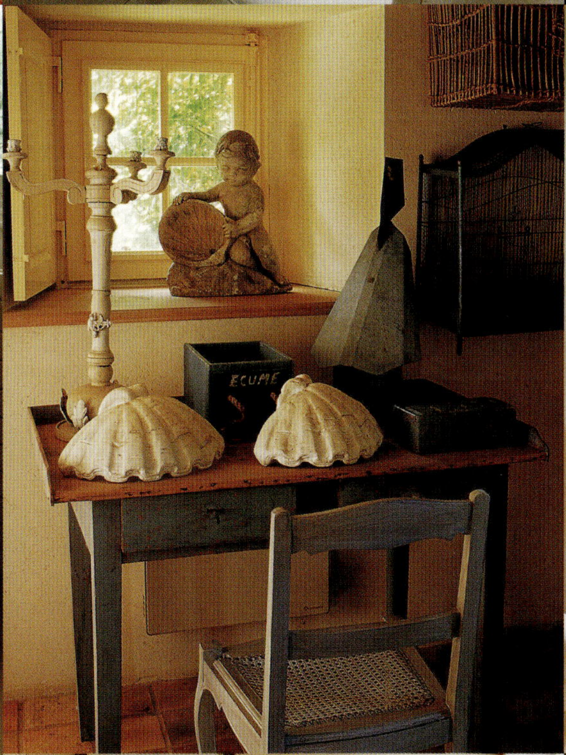
ECUME
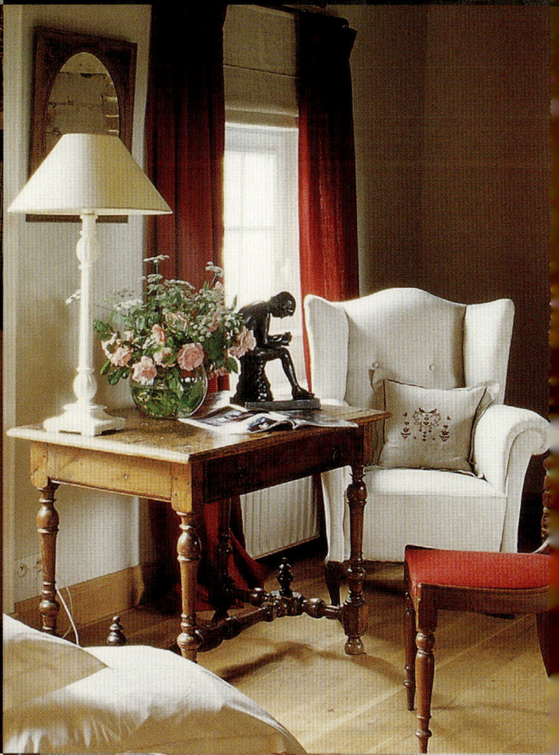
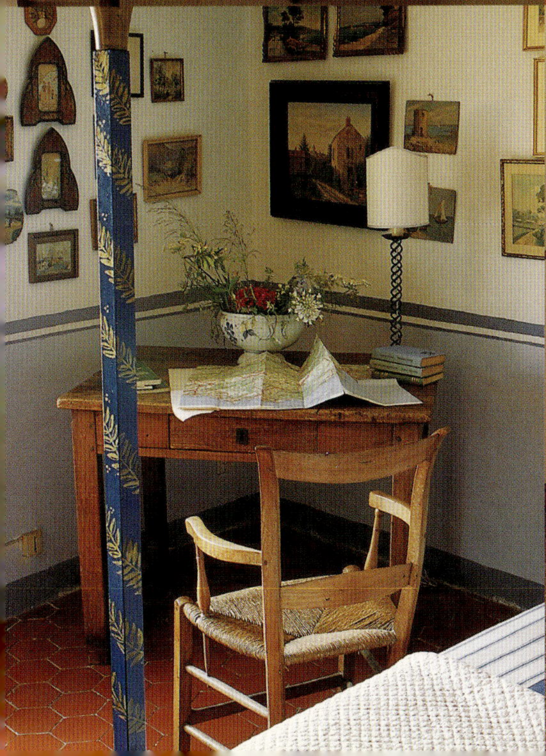
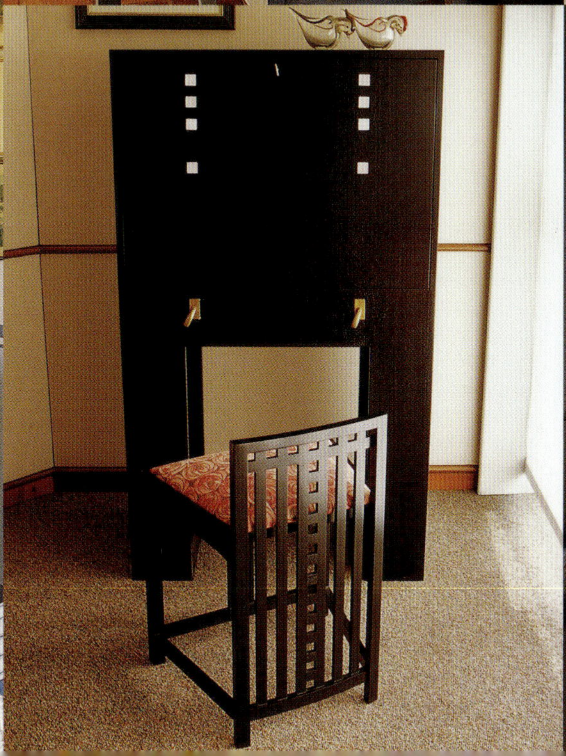
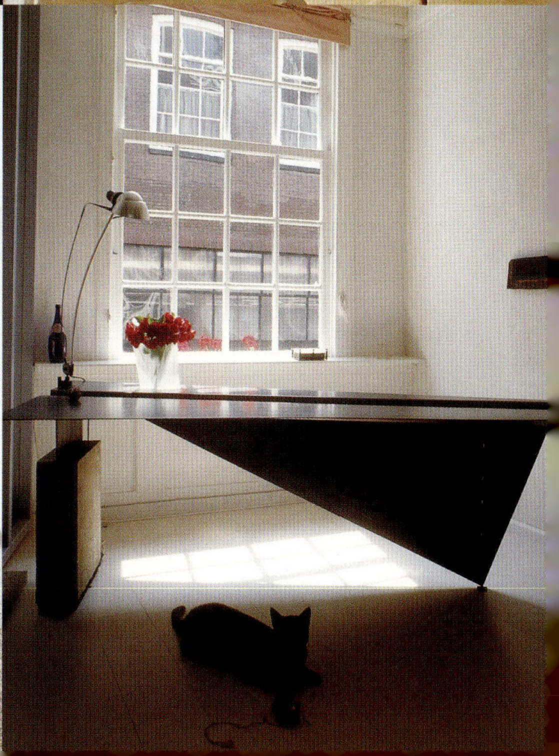

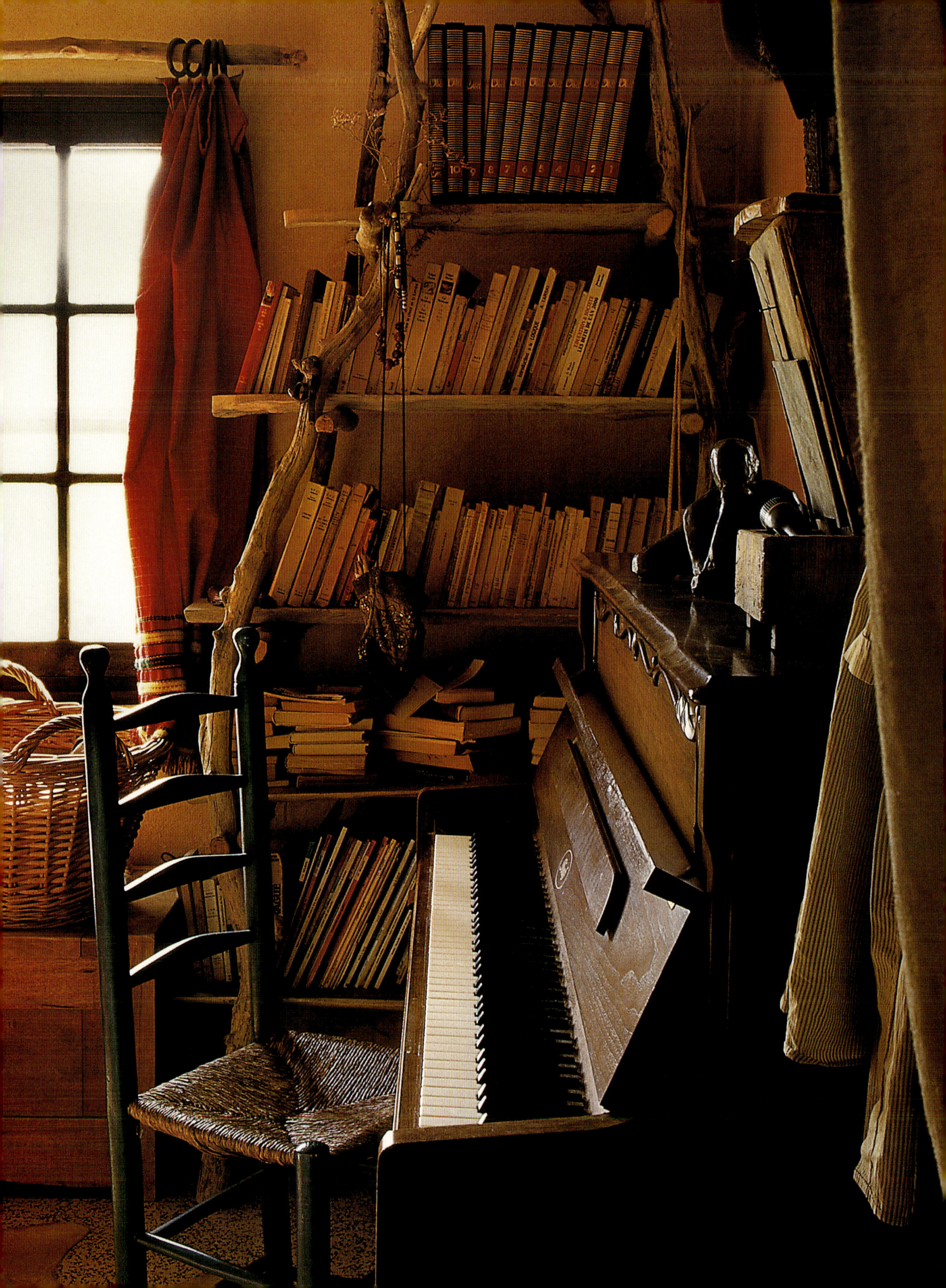

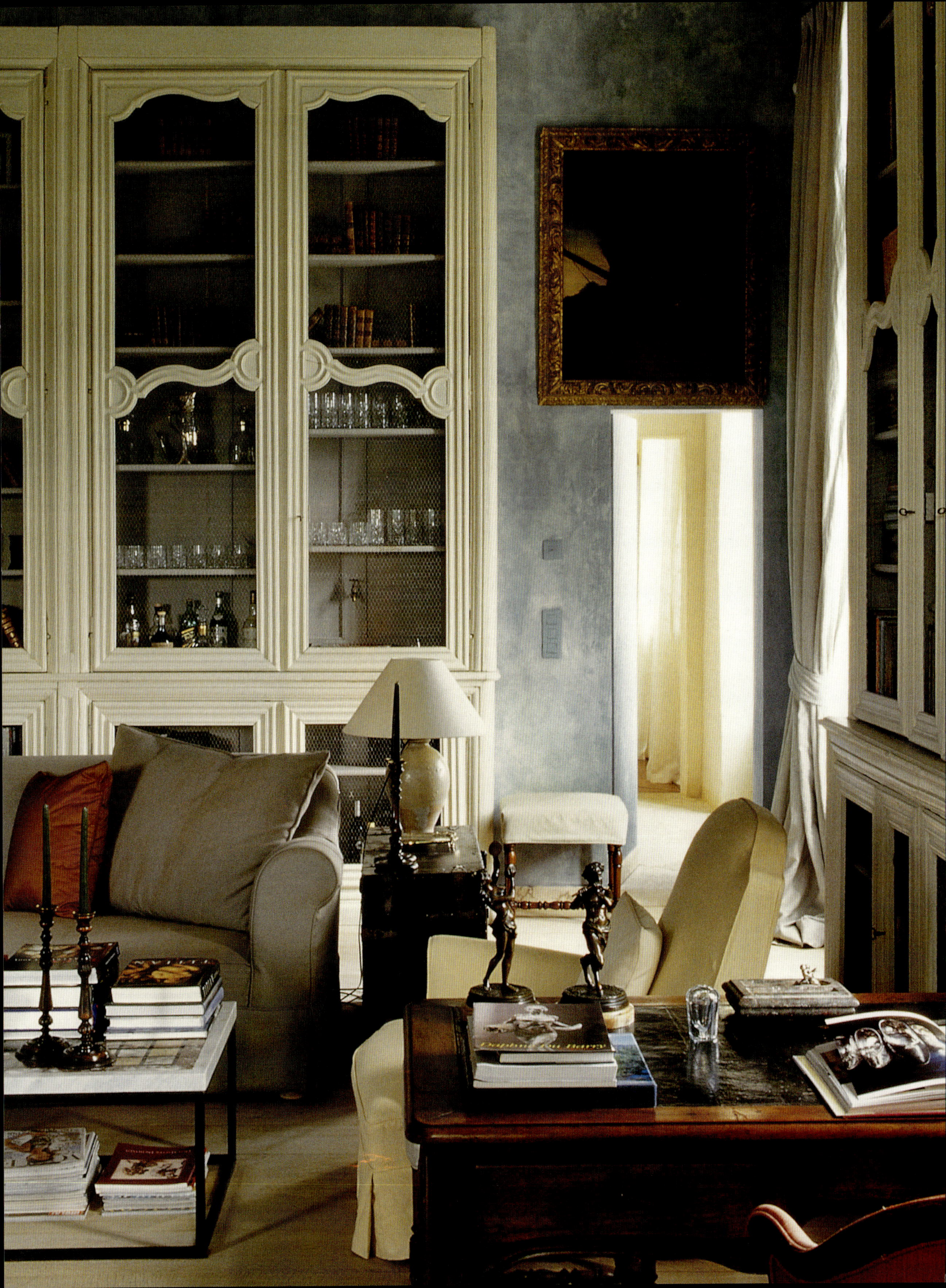

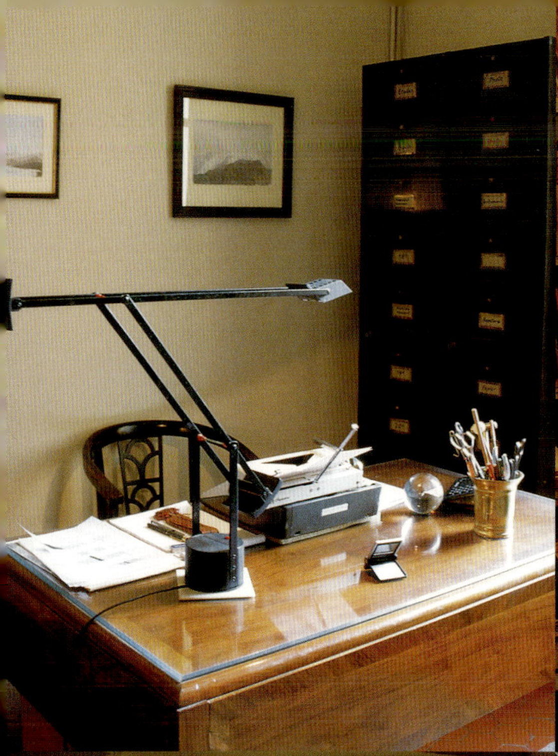
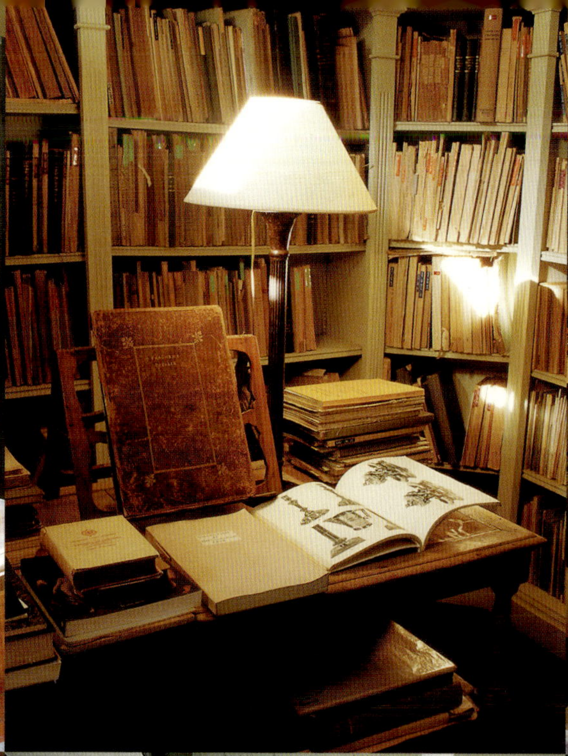
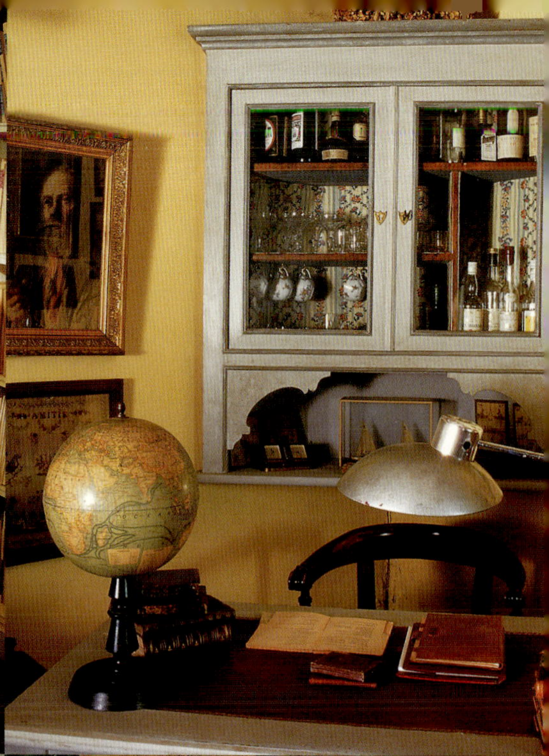
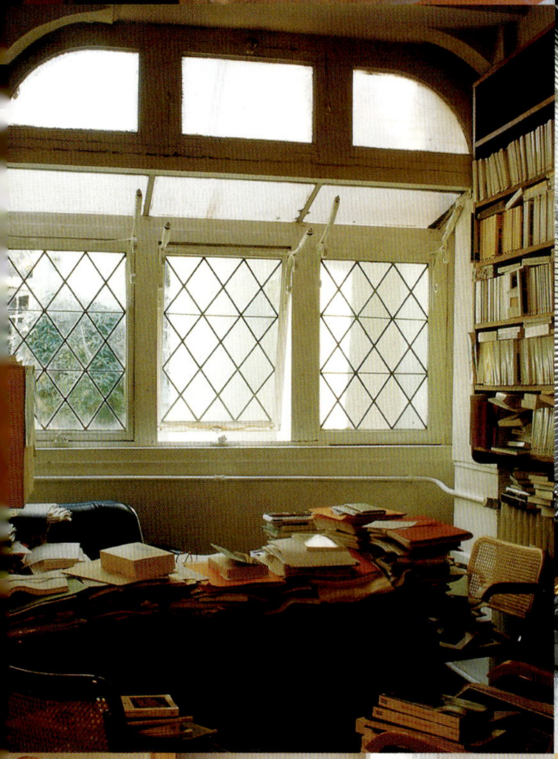
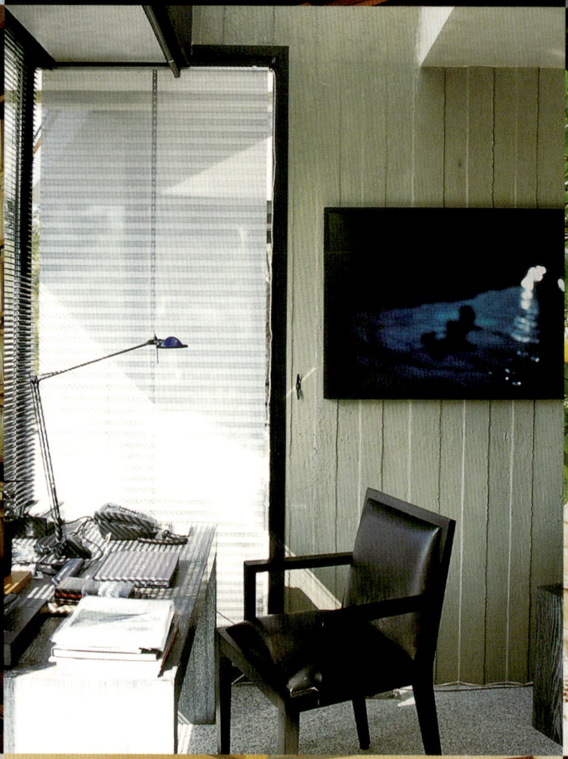
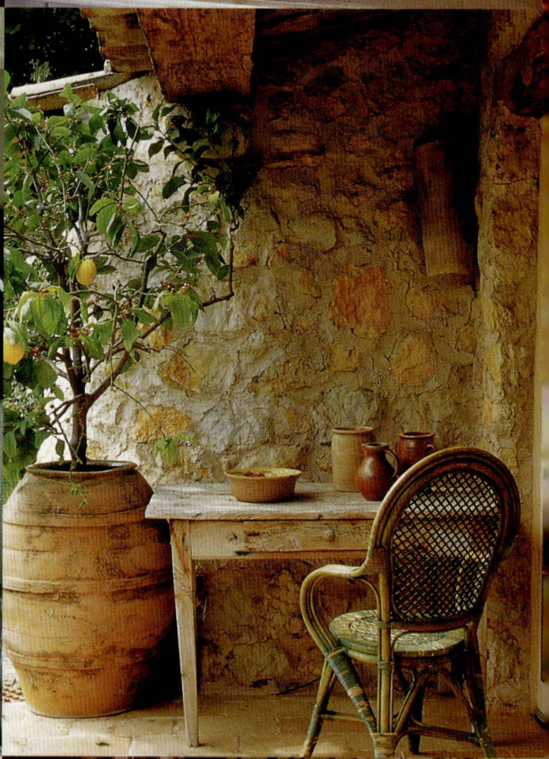
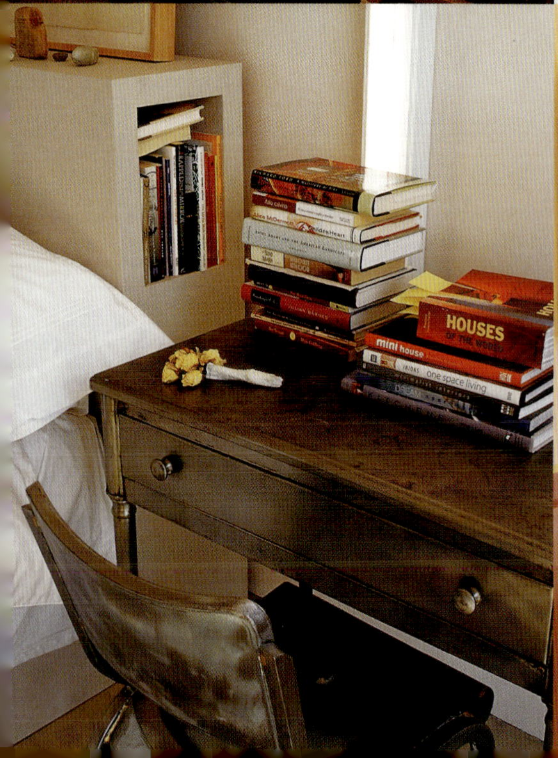
HOUSES
mini house
one space living
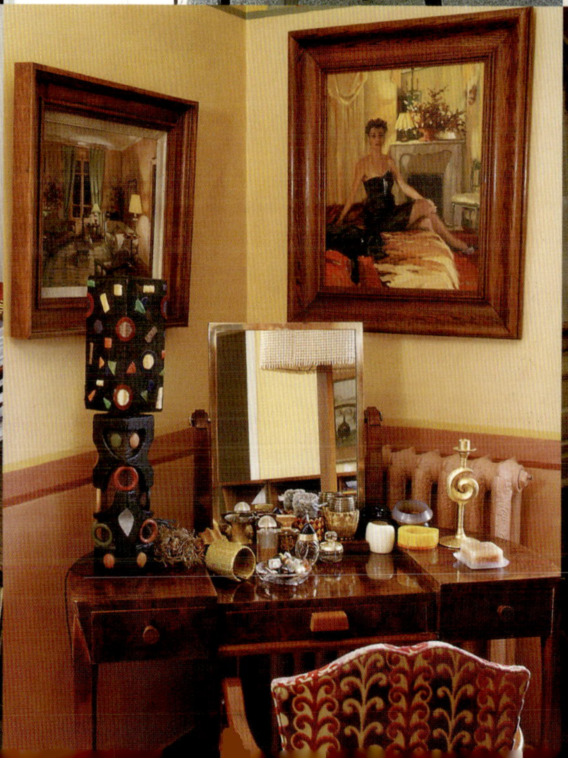
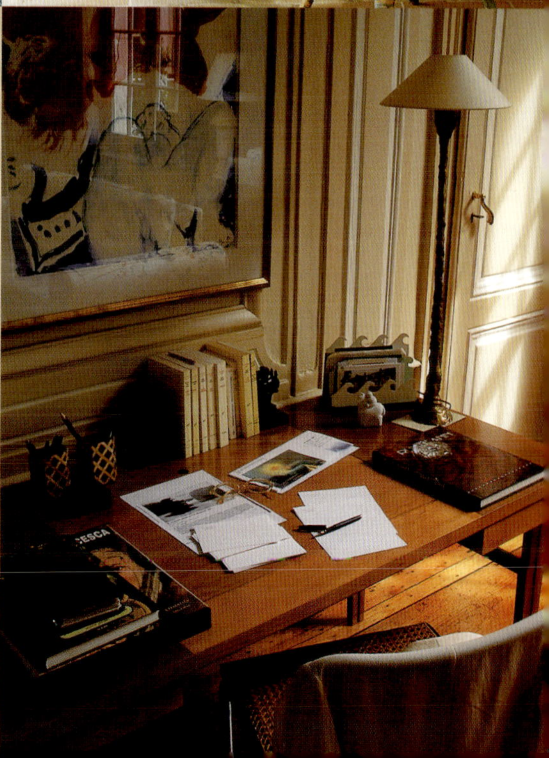

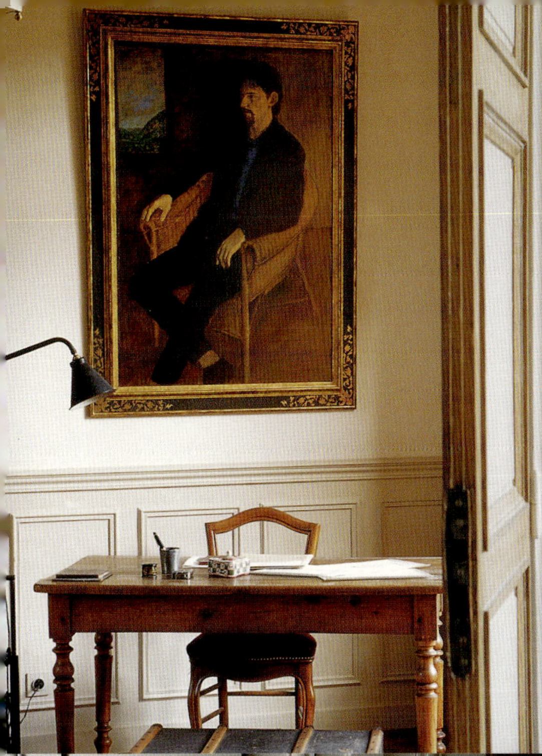
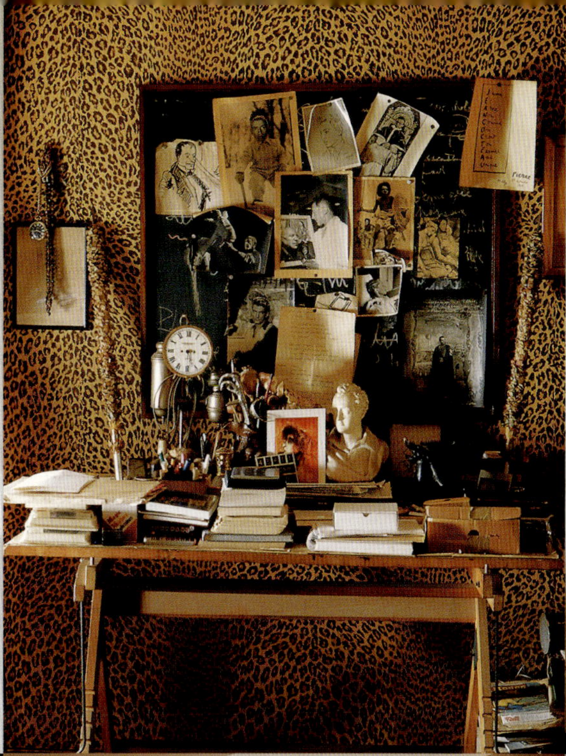
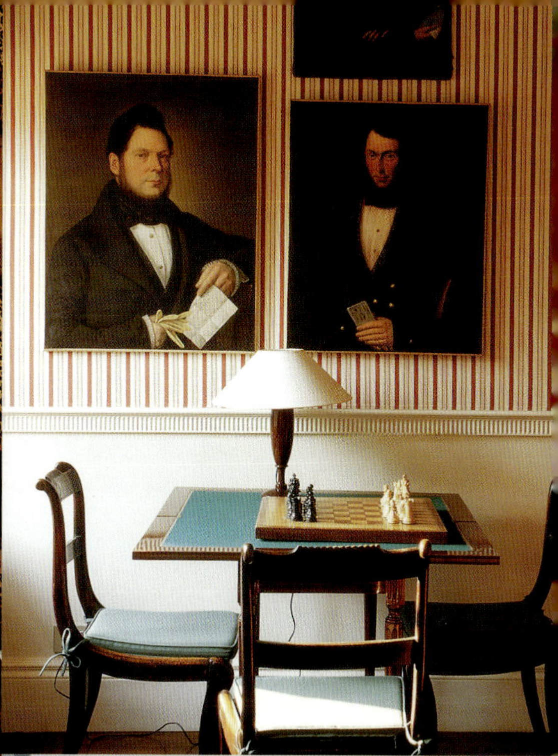
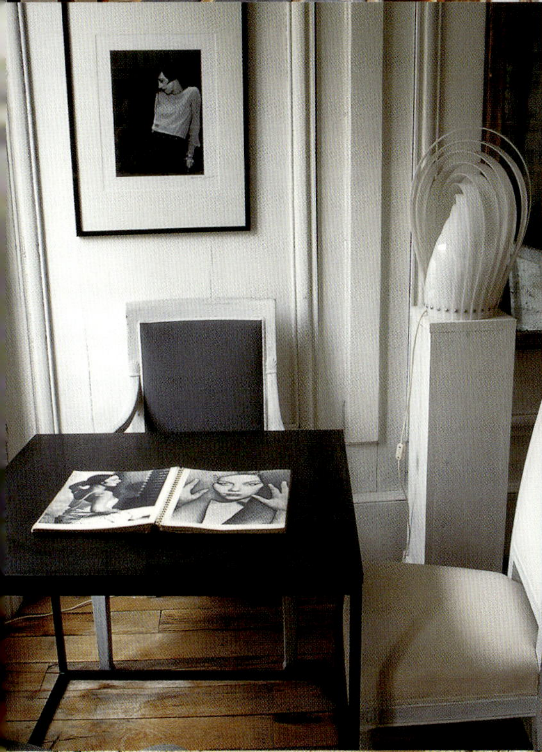
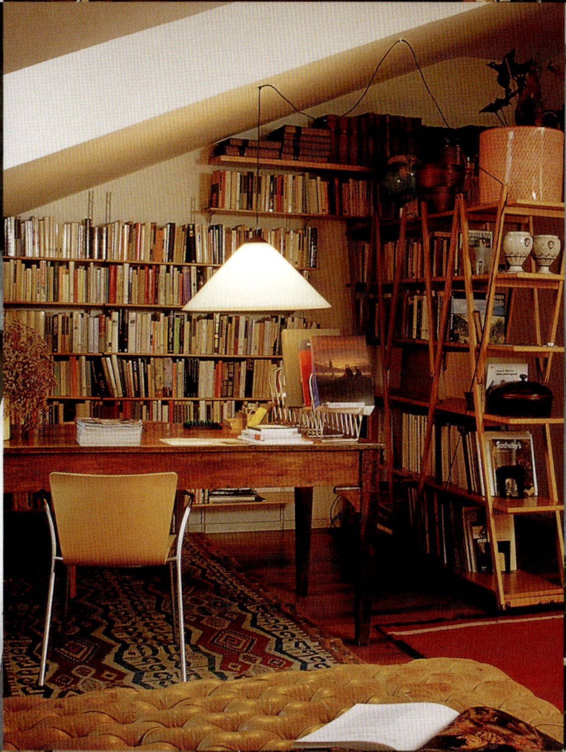
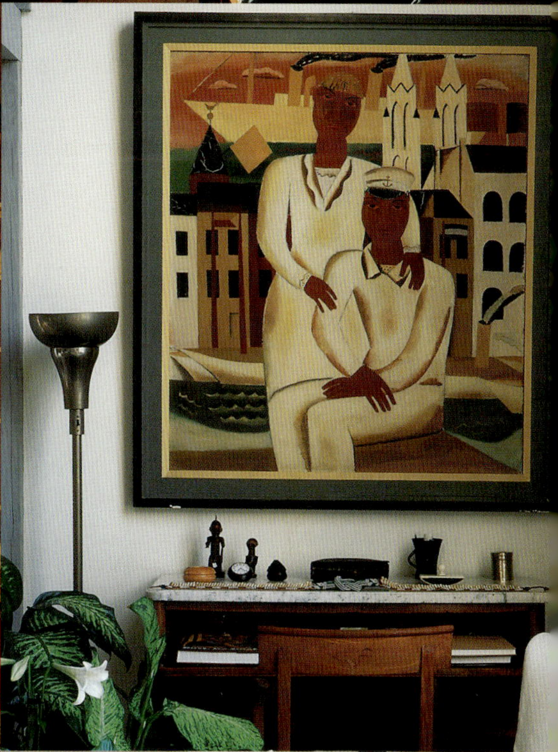
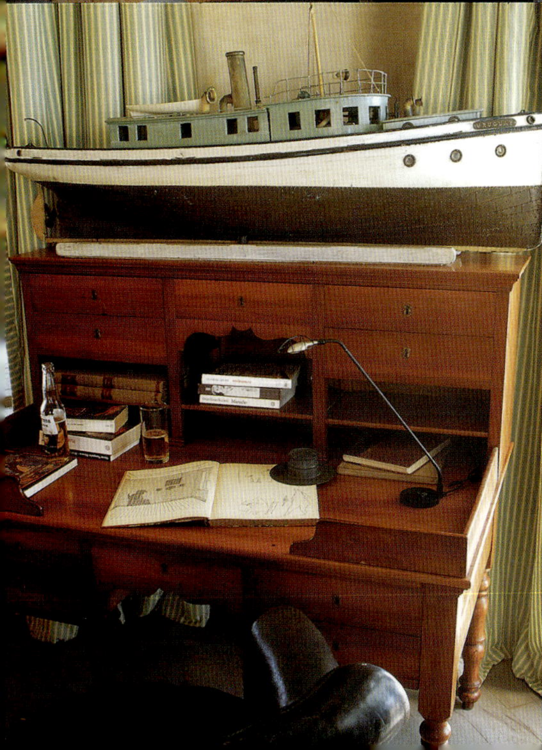
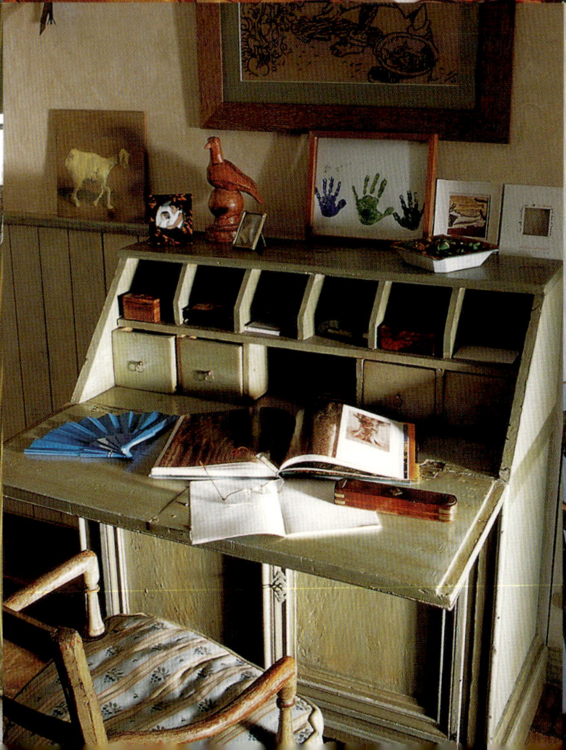
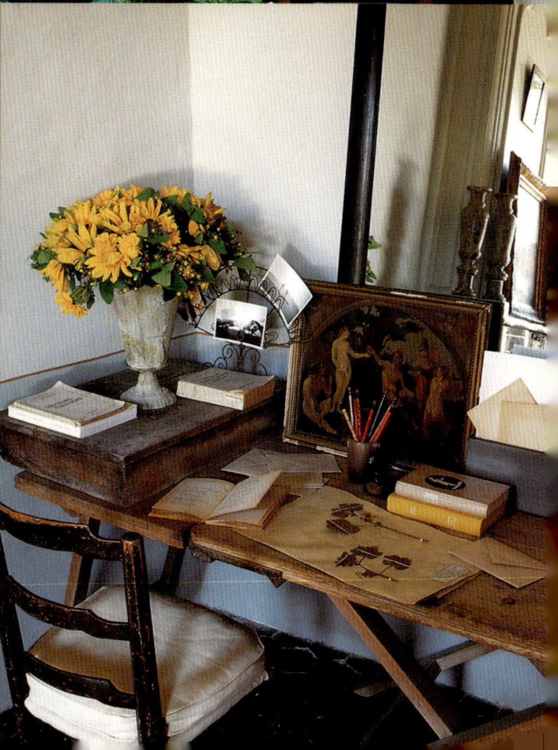

プライベートコーナー

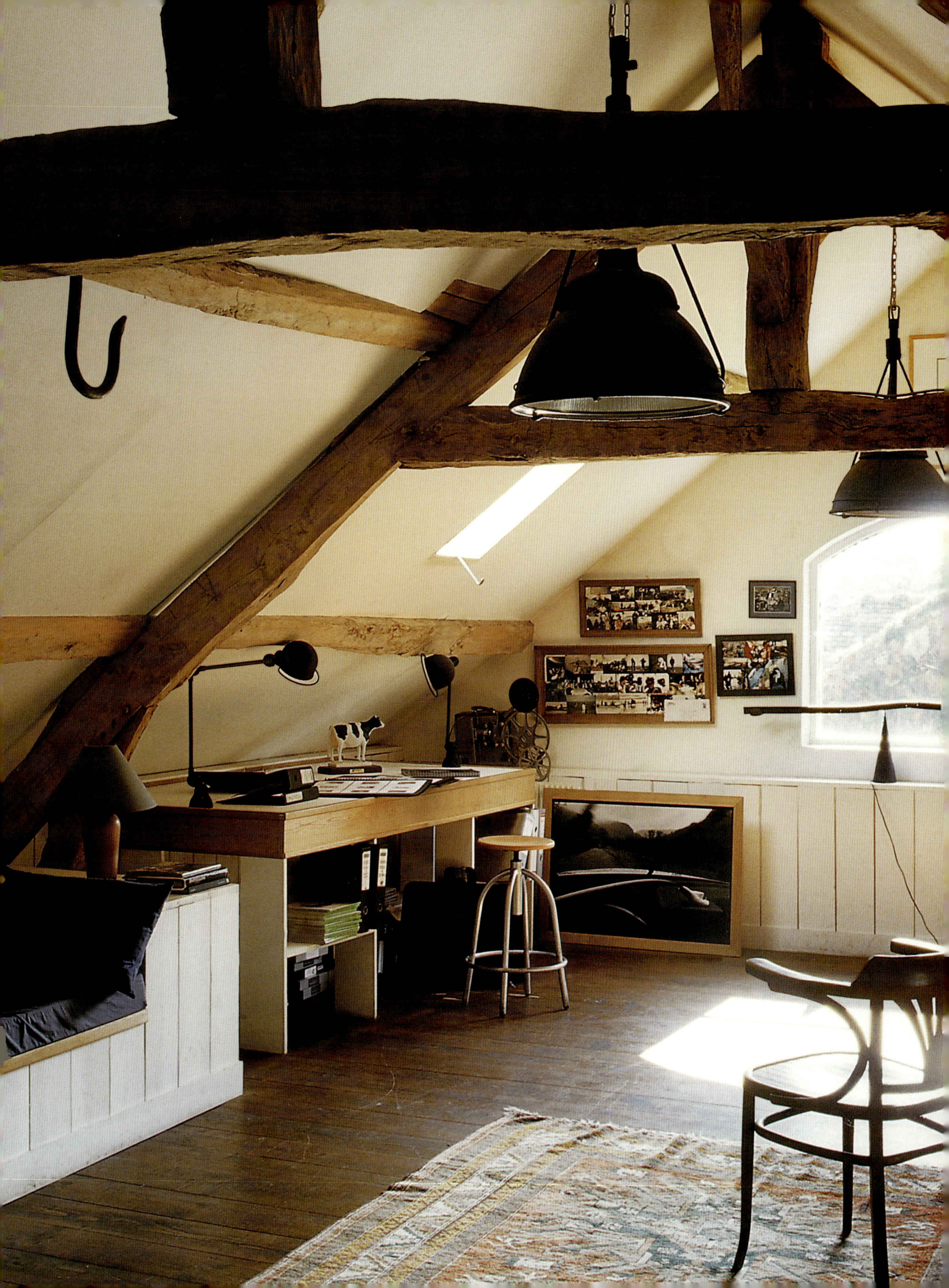

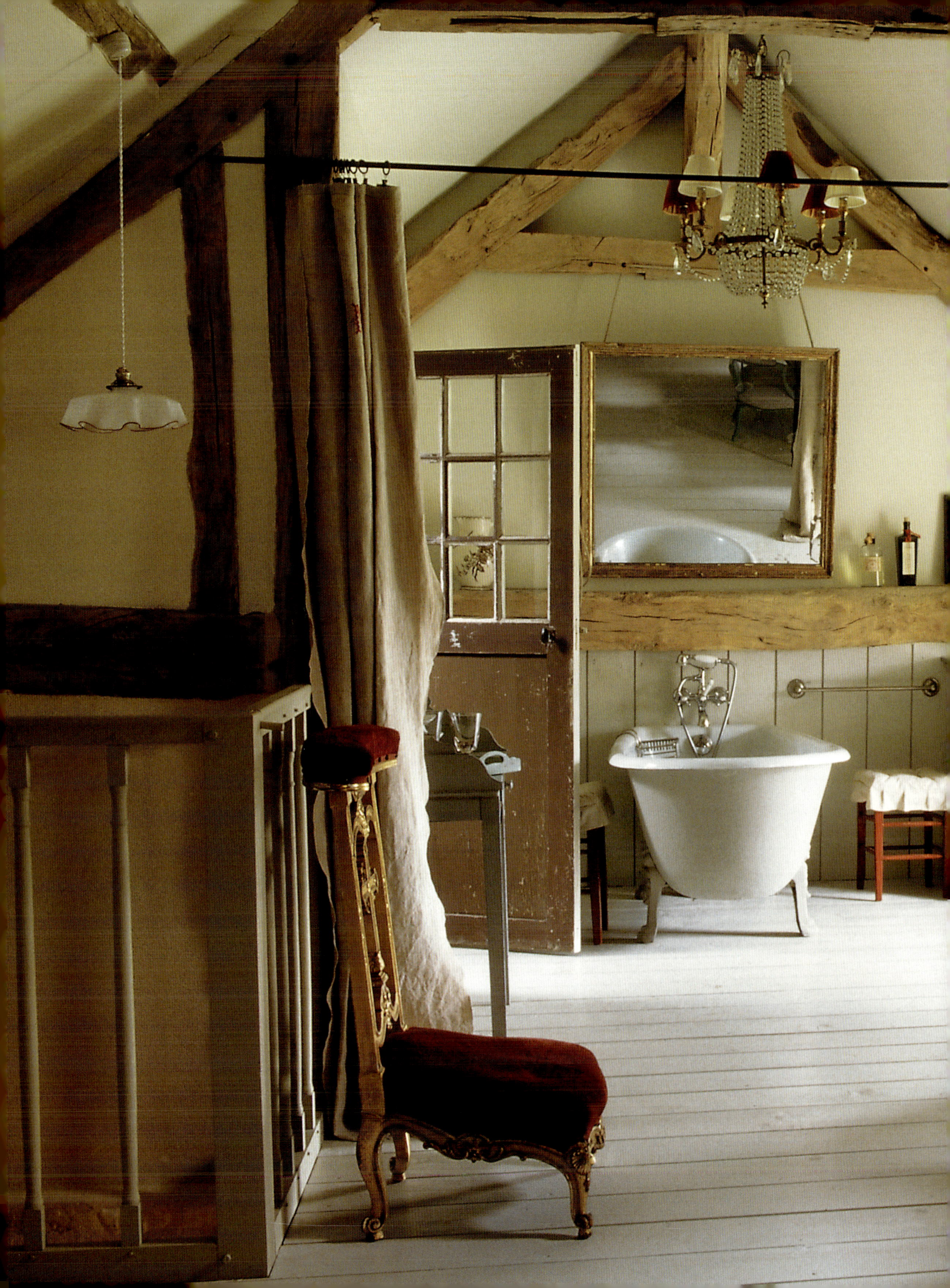

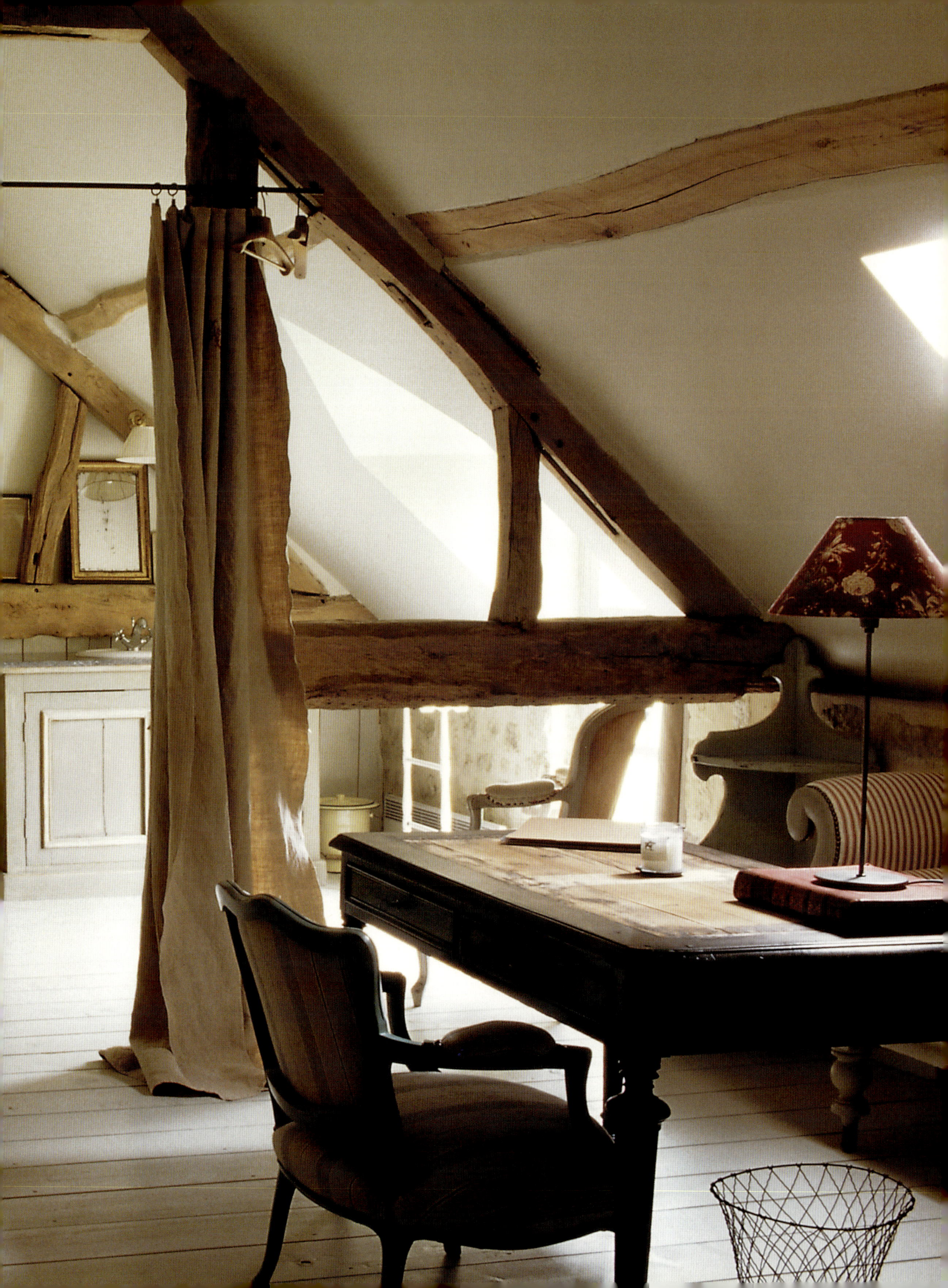

プライベートコーナー

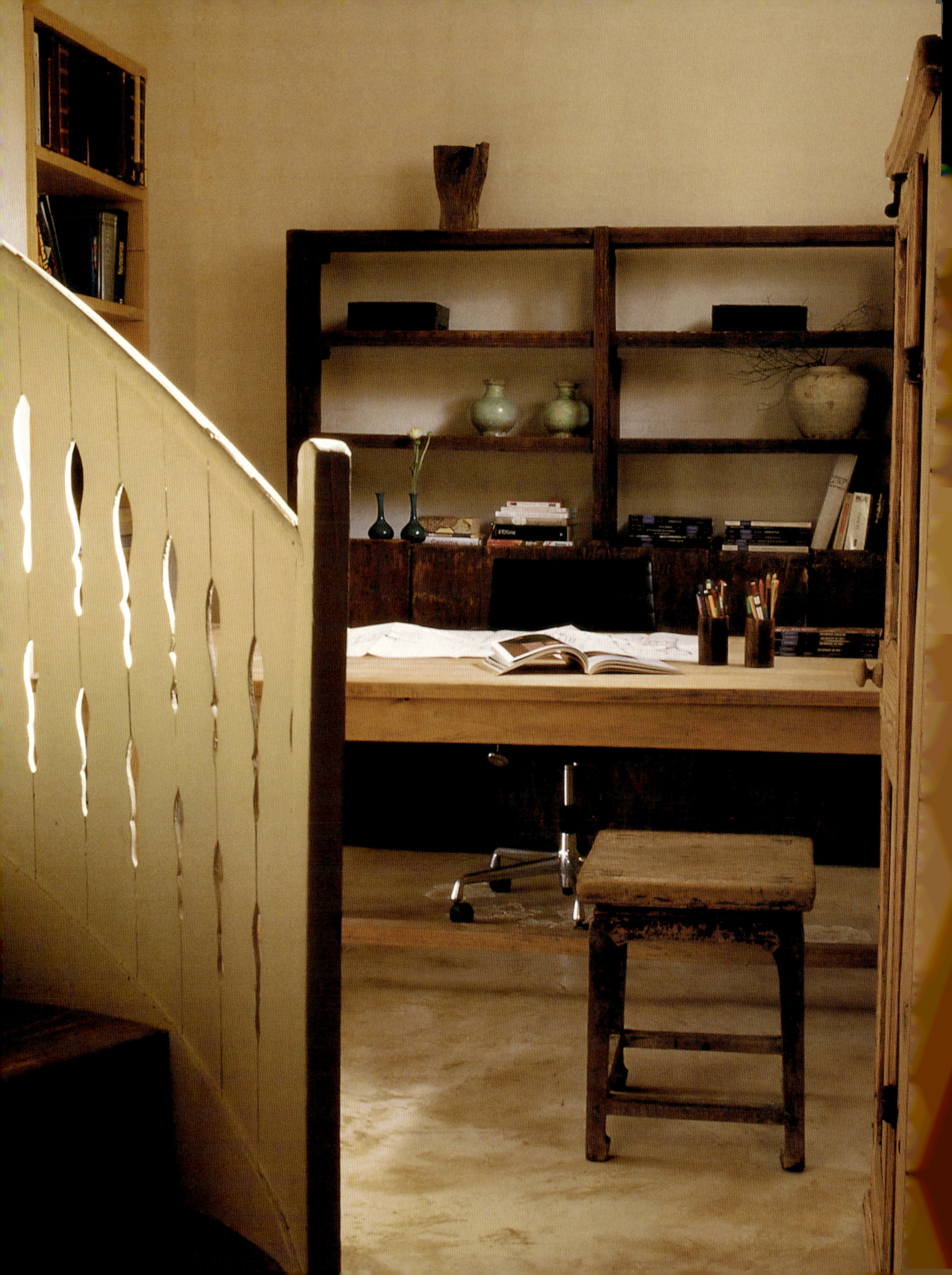

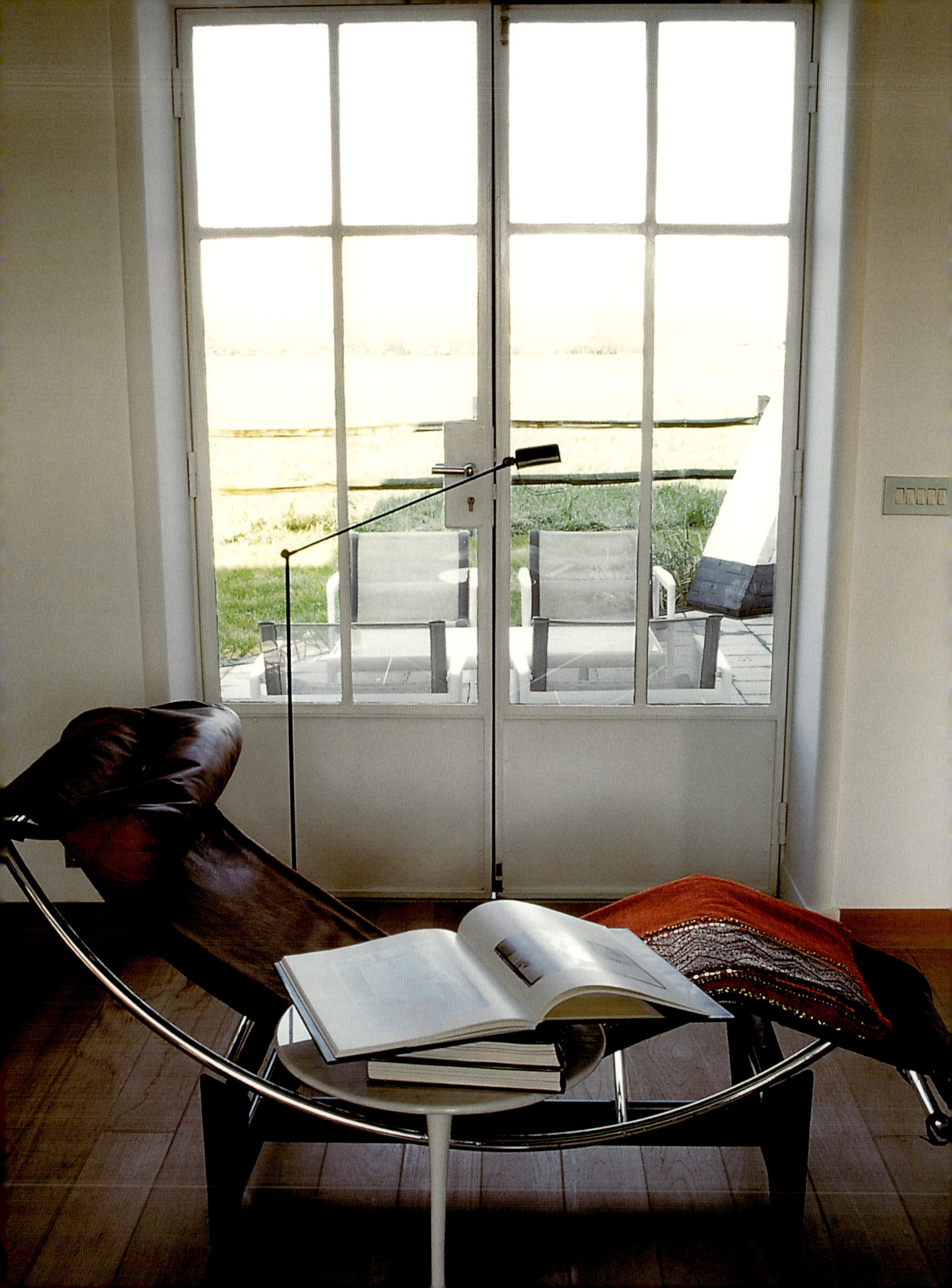

プライベートコーナー

壁の装飾

Walls Of Wonder

部屋は、多くを語ります――画家や、作家や、収集家や、有名な探険家の、自宅を開放した博物館を訪ねたことがあれば、この言葉が理解できるでしょう。こういった住宅は、日々の生活臭こそ消えていますが、思い出に満ちあふれています。その家が、とても個性的だとしたら、住んでいた人の持ち物がそう感じさせるのです。何を収集し、どのように棚やキャビネットに飾っているか、そこに住む人の個性が表れます。特にその人らしさが出るのが、壁の飾り方です。デザイナーやアーティストは、写真、絵画、版画など、額に入れた思い出に囲まれて暮らすことを好みます。探検家は、地図や、ポスターや、バスの切符など、旅を思い起こさせる品々を持ち帰ります。子どもがいる人は、その子が学校で描いた絵を飾るでしょう。しかし中には、個人的な物や、一風変わった物などを壁に飾るためには、自信が必要だという人もいます。「一番見映えの良い場所は？ ぴったりの額は？」と、決断するのに勇気がいると言うのです。まず、廊下とか、寝室といった小さいスペースだけ飾ってみることをおすすめします。飾ろうとする壁を、ギャラリーの壁というよりも、スクラップブックのページのようにとらえるのです。高価な絵画や、希少な芸術品を飾らなければ、などと思わないでください。風変わりで、個人的な物を飾るほど壁は面白くなり、多くの誉め言葉の元になり、長期間、自分自身の目をも楽しませることになるでしょう。

Rooms tell many stories – as you'll know if you've ever visited the museum homes of painters, writers, collectors or famous explorers. Though no longer stuffed with the clutter of everyday life, these houses are filled with memories. If it's a house full of character, that identity will come from the person's possessions, what they collected and how it is displayed on shelves, in cabinets, on tables – or most importantly on the walls. Designers and artists love to surround themselves with pictures, paintings, prints and framed mementoes of all kinds. Explorers bring back maps, posters, bus tickets and things that remind them of their journeys. People with children will put up school drawings. But for some, having the confidence to hang things, personal things, quirky things on the walls, takes a certain bravery that they may not have. Where's the best position? What's the most suitable frame? Perhaps the solution is to concentrate first on one small space – maybe in the hall or a bedroom. Approach the wall as a page in a scrapbook rather than a gallery wall, and don't think that you have to use expensive images or one-off artworks. Displaying the most unusual and personal things often proves to be the most interesting, generating the most compliments and engaging your eye for the longest time.

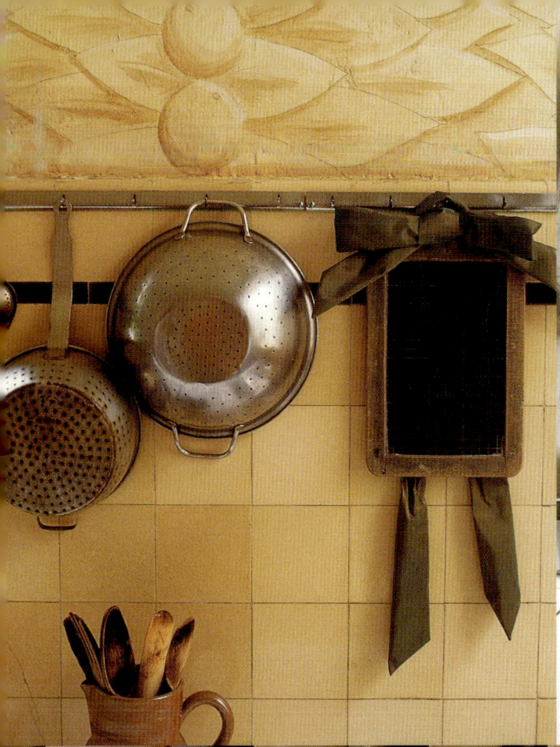
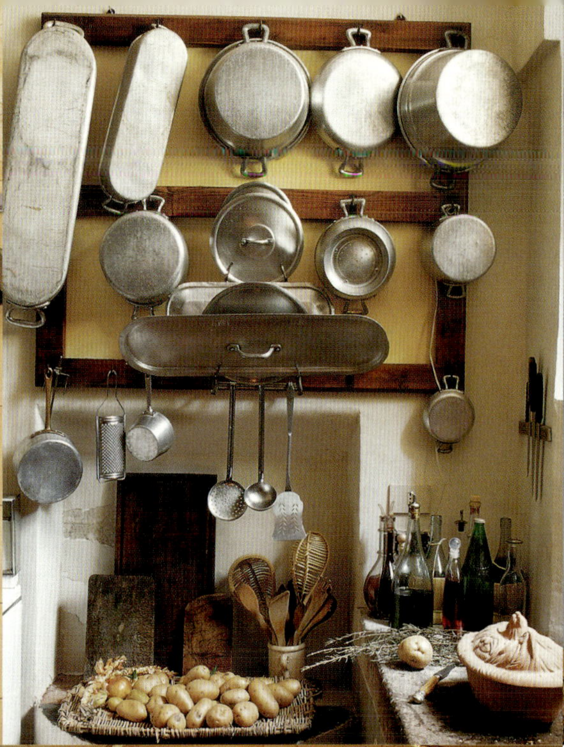
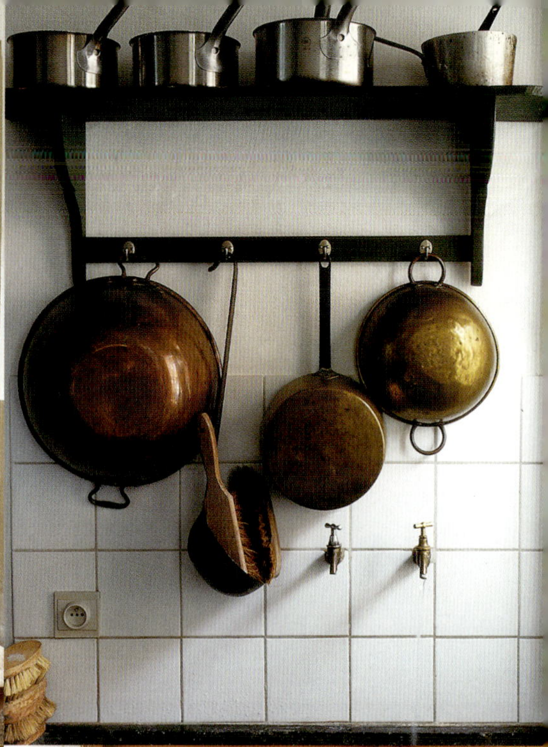
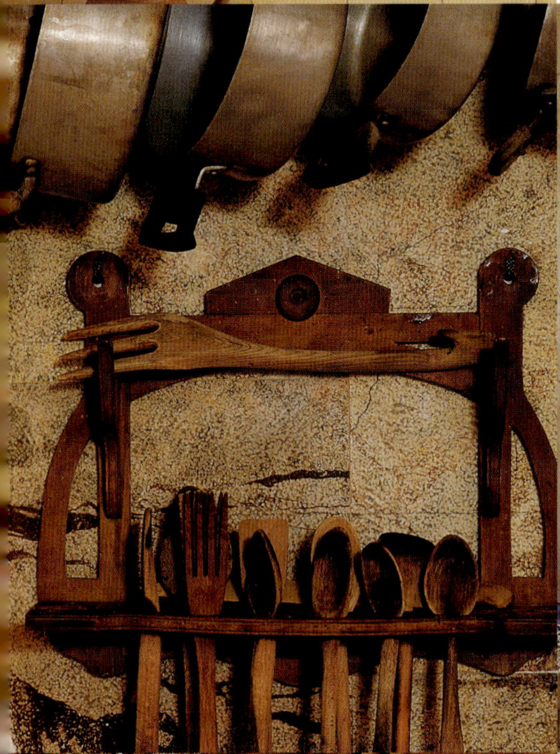
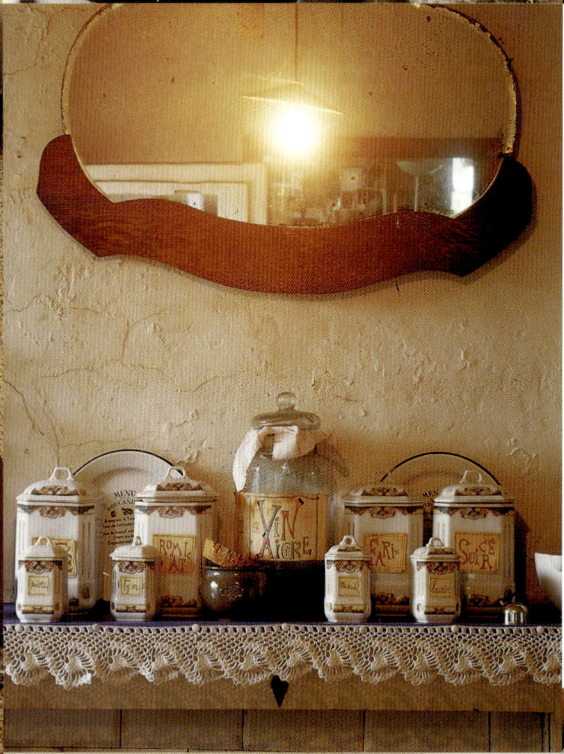
VIN AIGRE
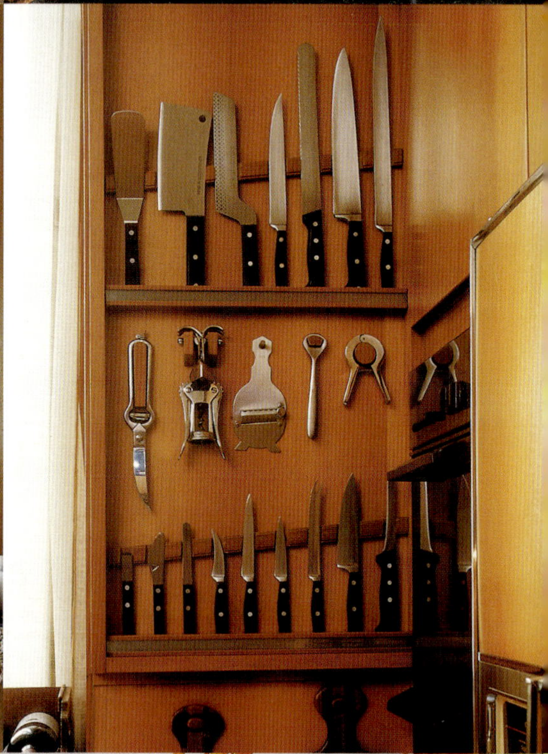
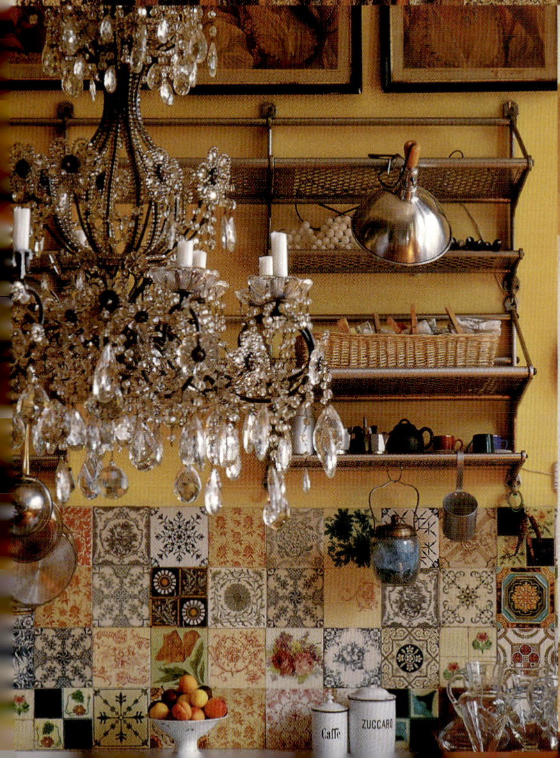
ZUCCARO
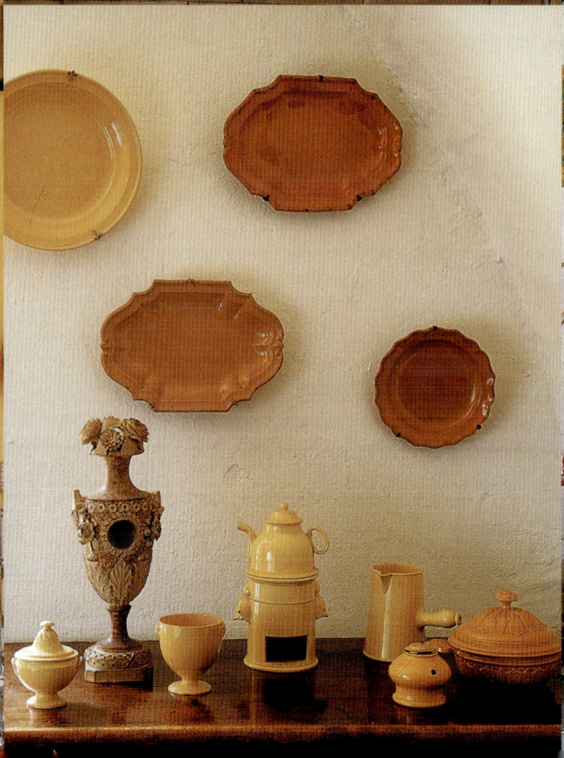
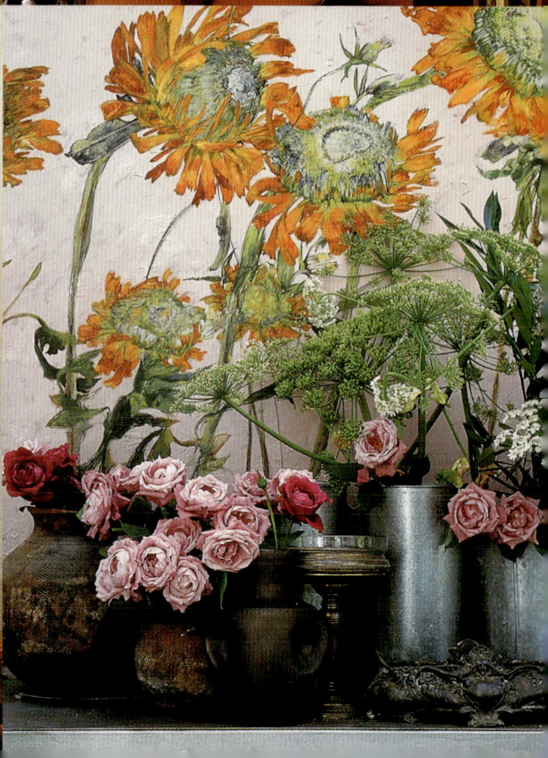

vendredi
6
DECEMBRE

DESSUS

壁の装飾

壁の装飾

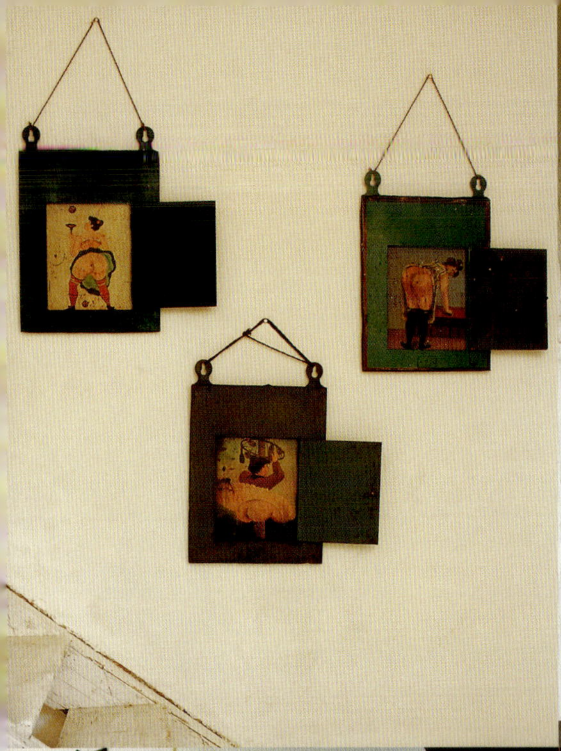
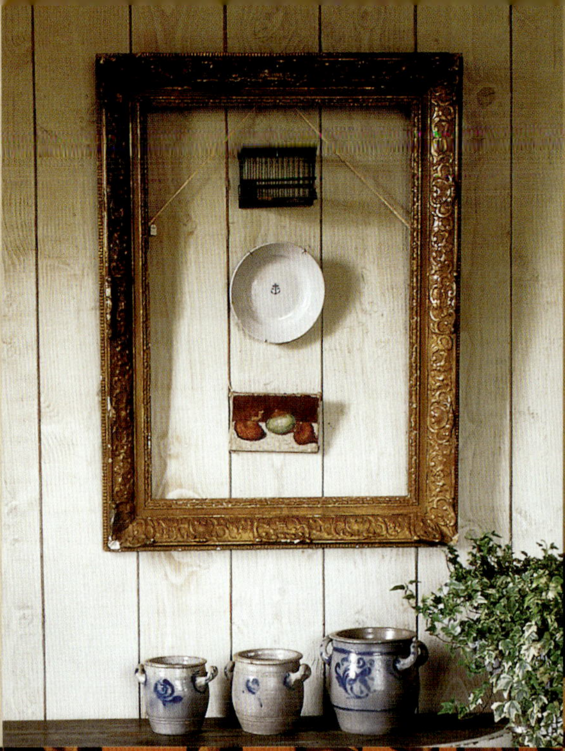
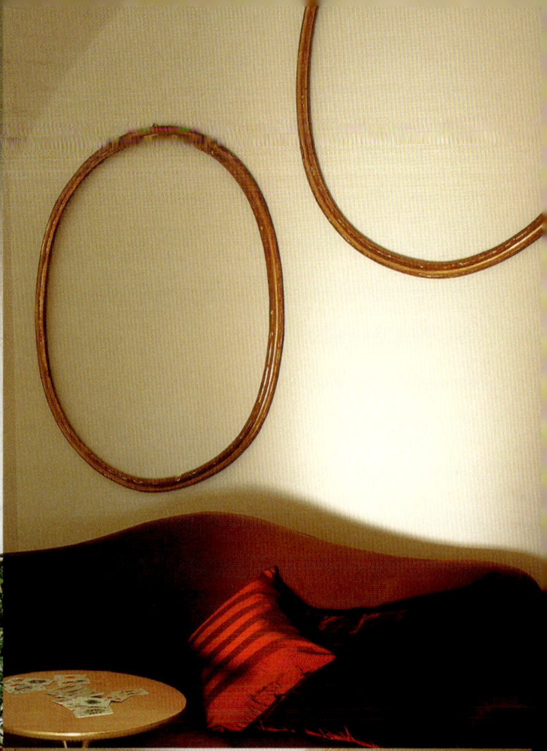
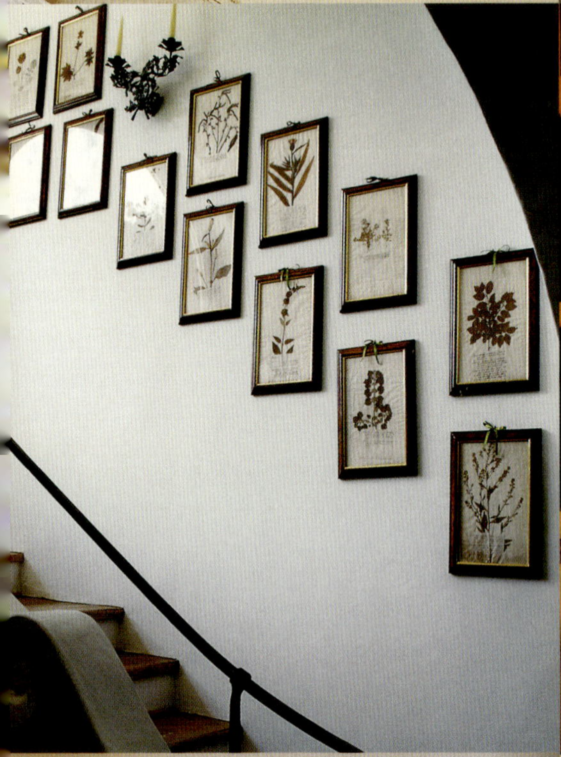
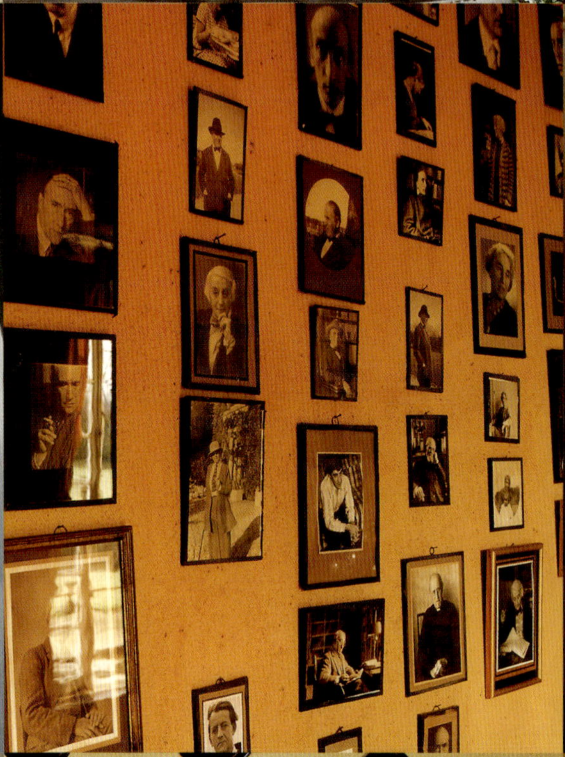
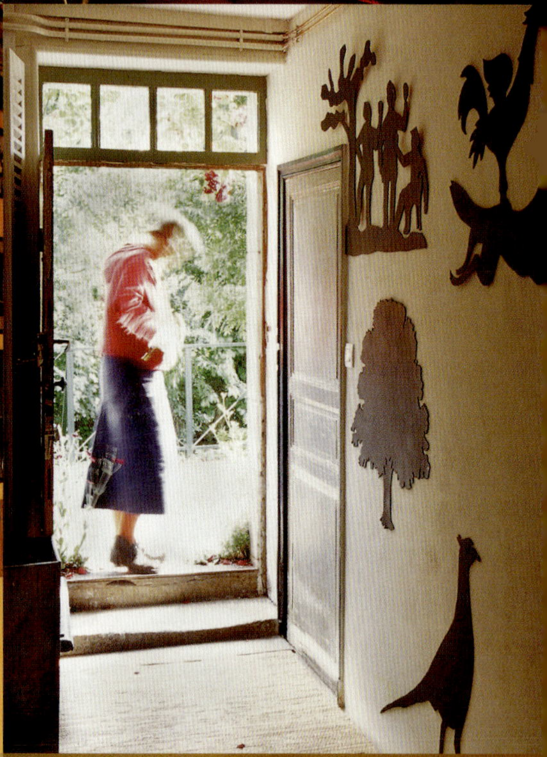
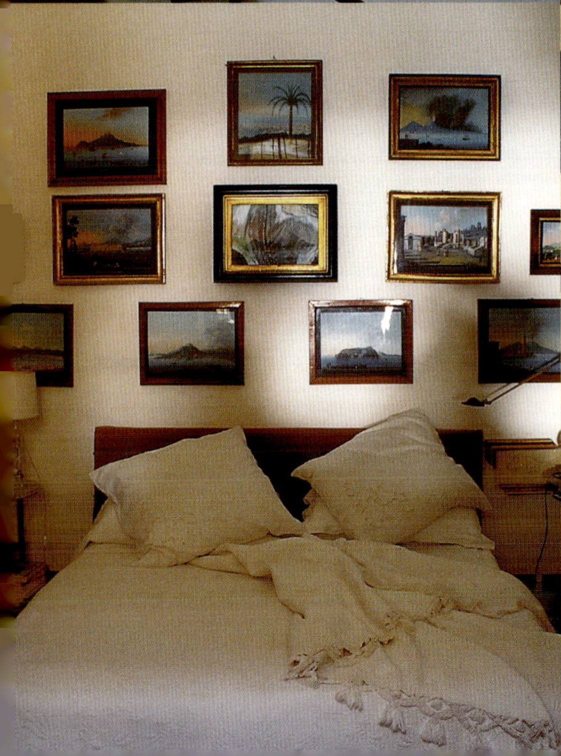
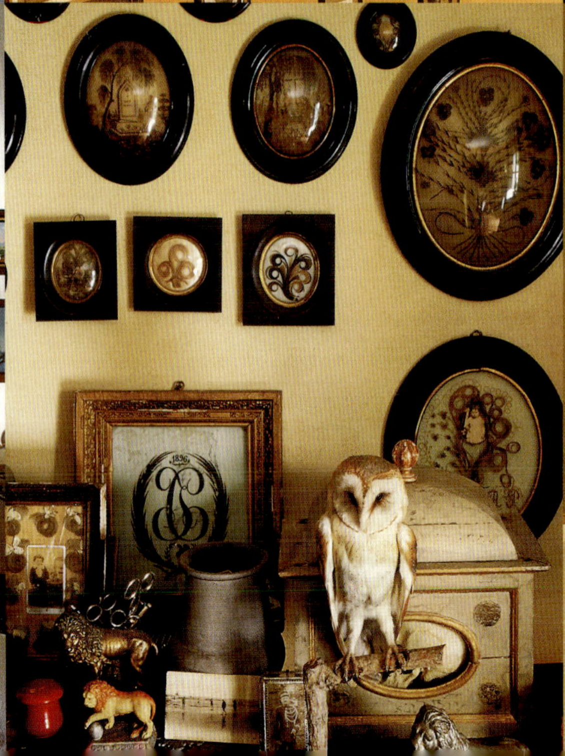
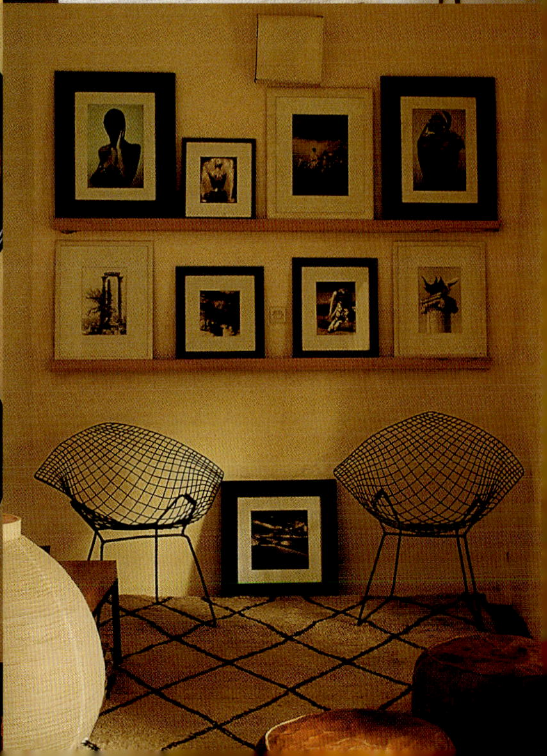

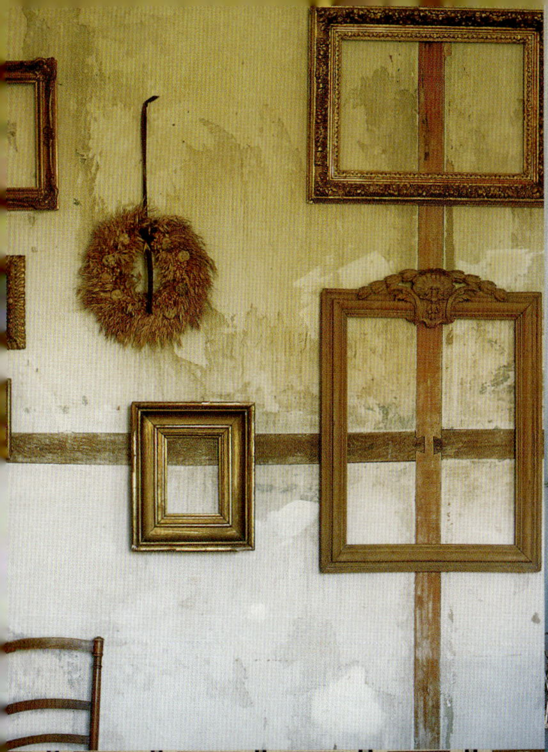
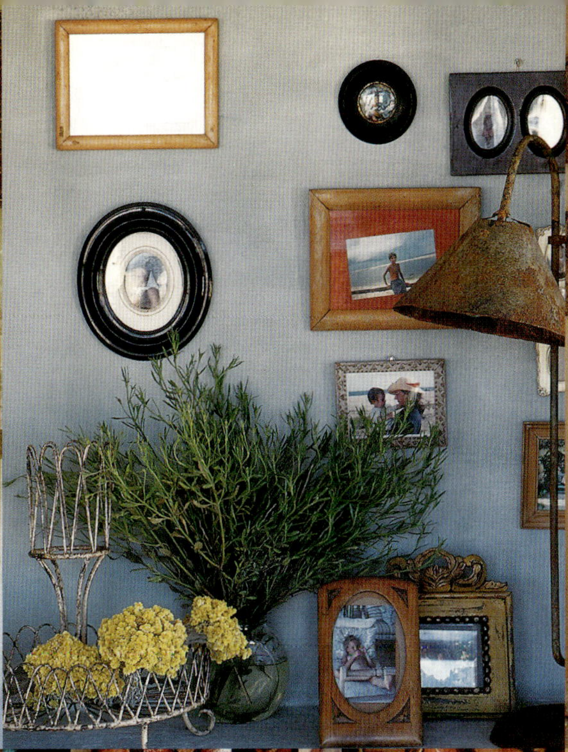
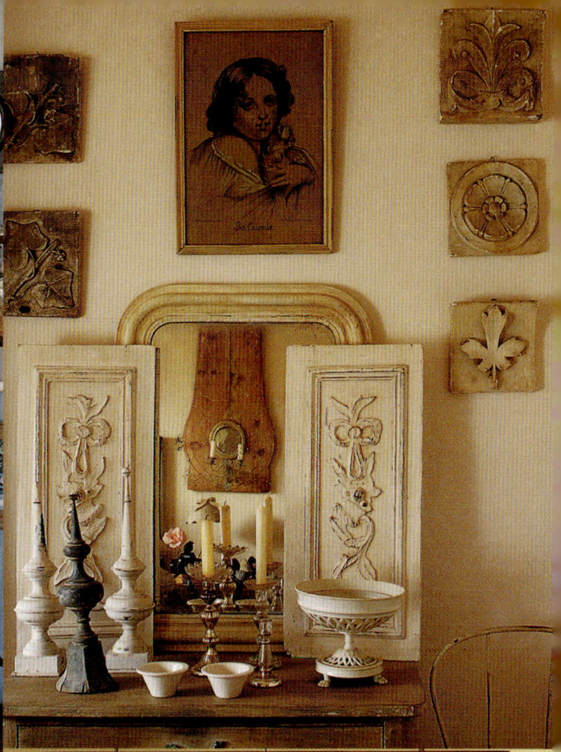
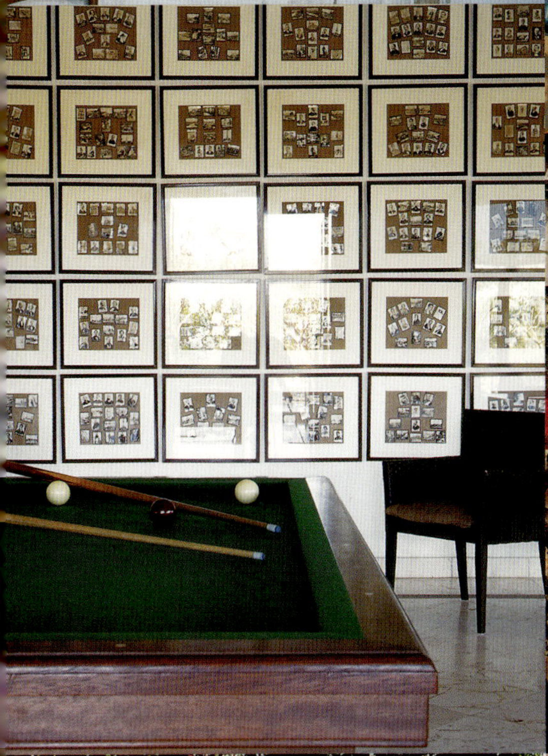
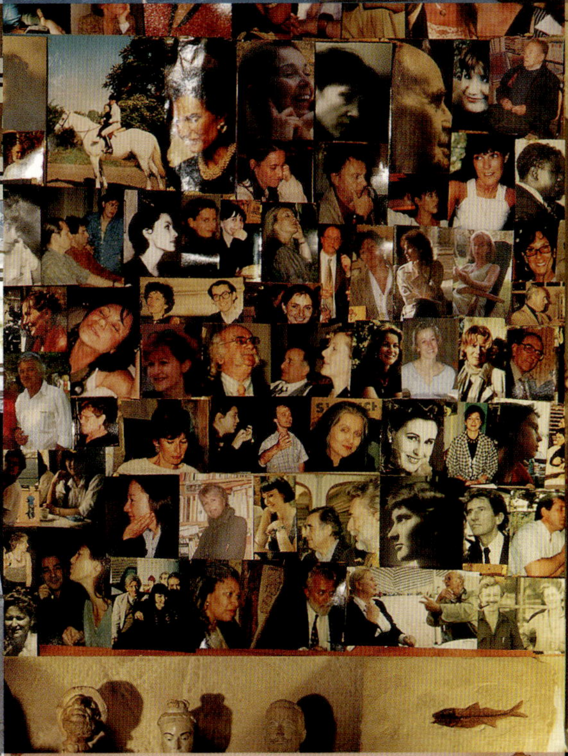
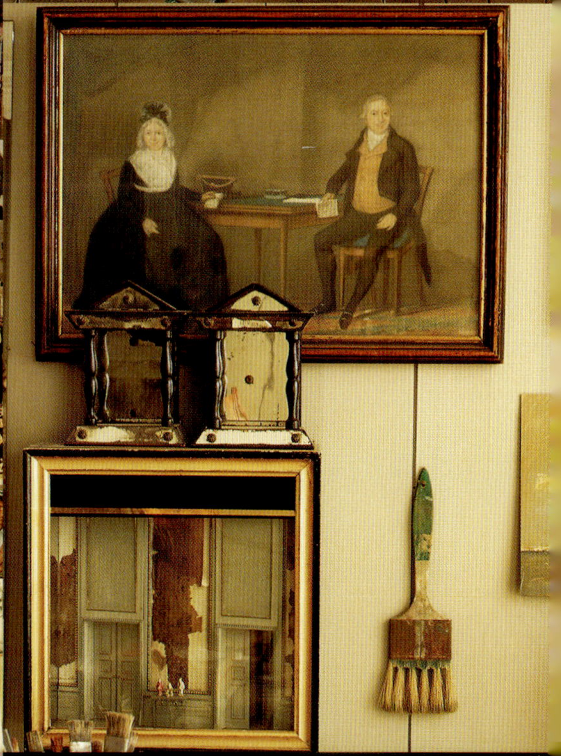
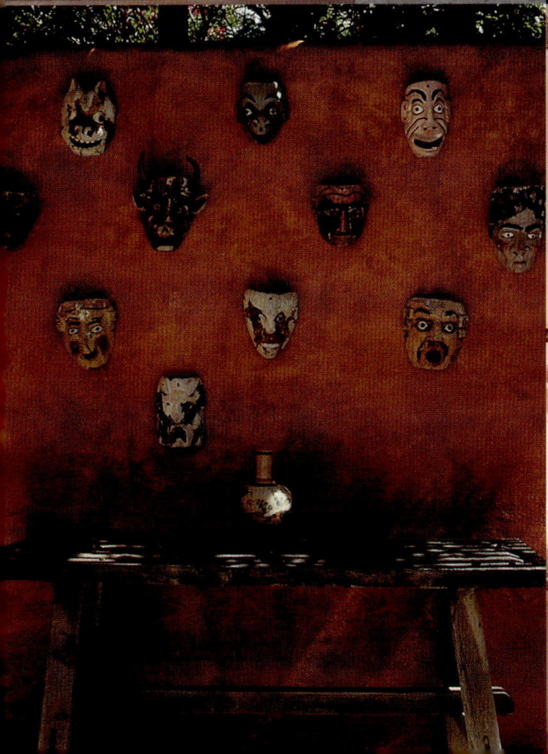
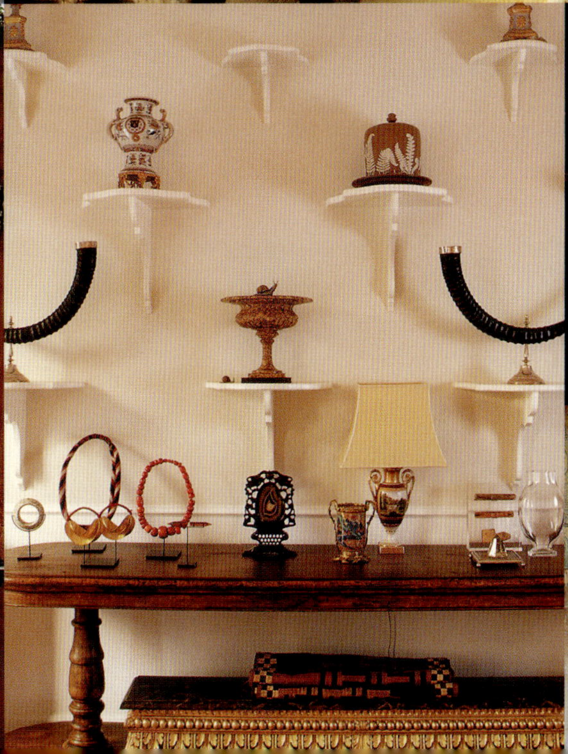
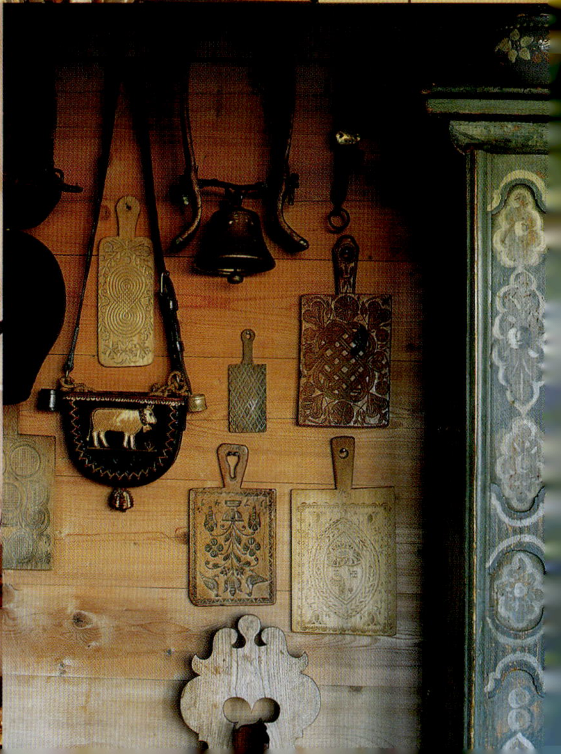

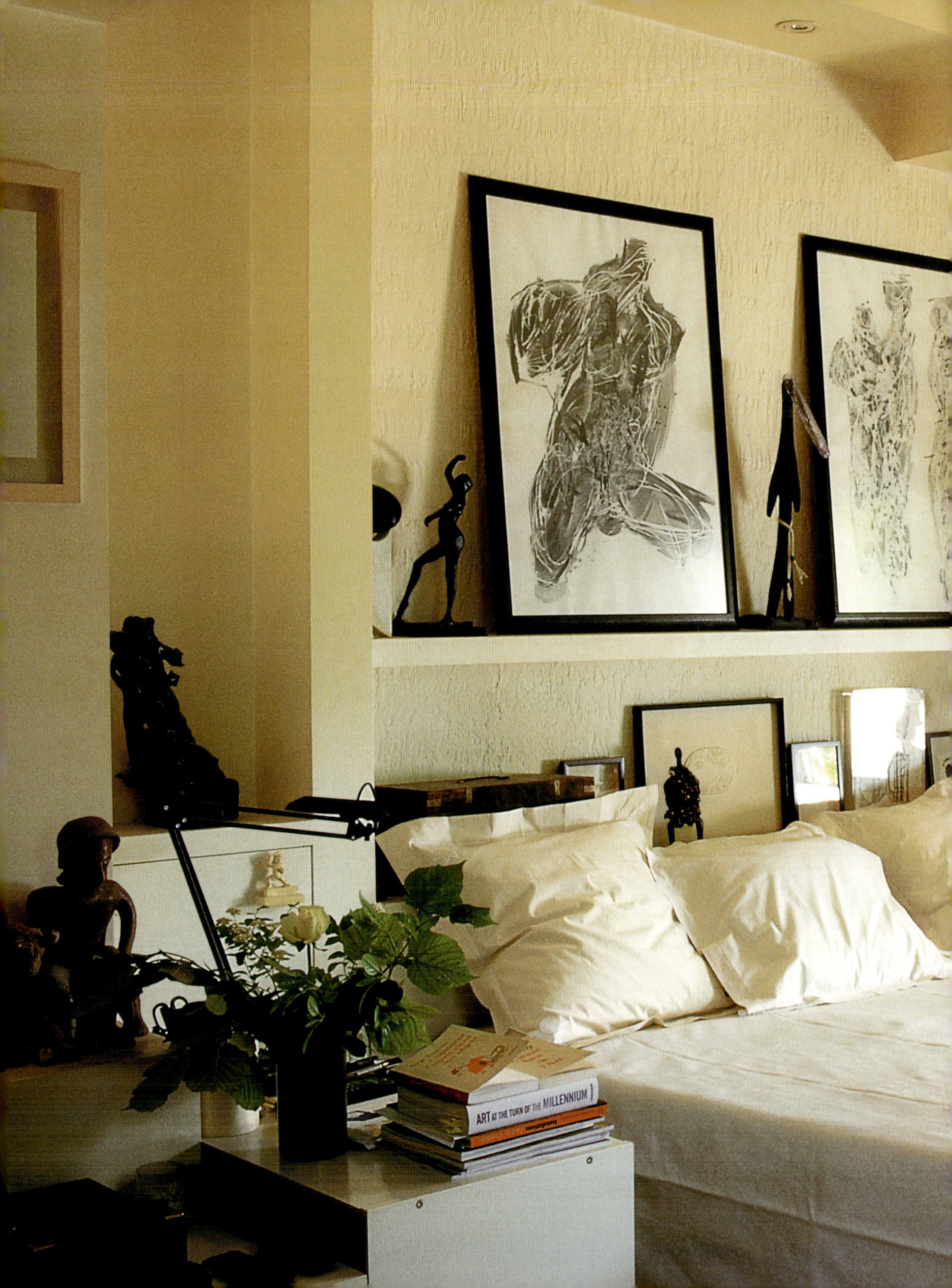
ART AT THE TURN OF THE MILLENNIUM

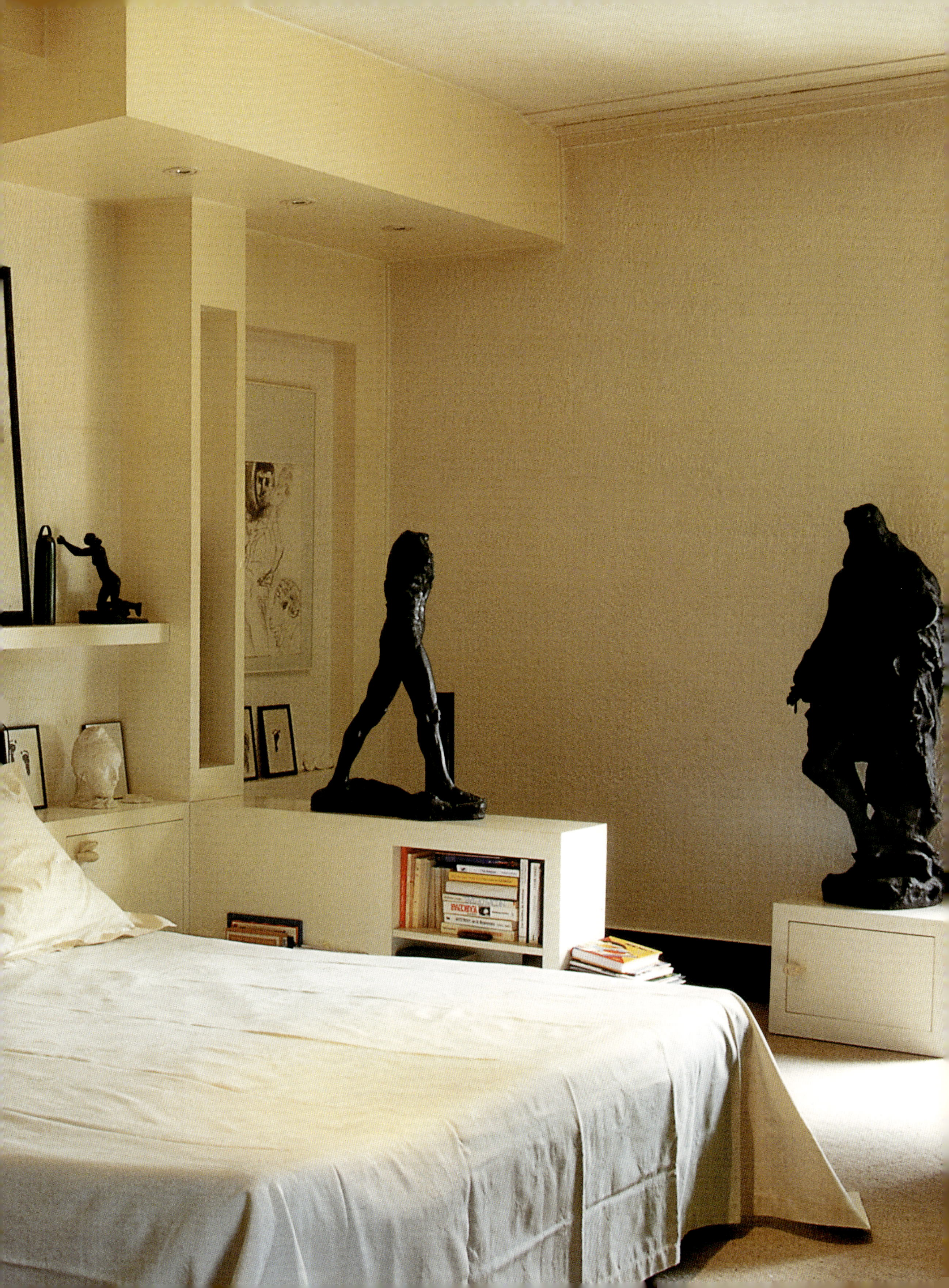

暖炉

Light My Fire

どんな部屋に、どんなスタイルの暖炉がマッチするでしょうか？　暖炉を、家の建築スタイルや、インテリアに合わせて選ぶべきでしょうか？　マントルピースの大きさが、どの程度の暖炉が欲しいですか？　そもそもマントルピースはどうしても必要でしょうか？　正方形や円形の、シンプルな飾り枠では代用できないでしょうか？　マントルピースの要・不要に関しては、暖炉に「本物」の火を使うかどうかで違うのでは、と思われるかもしれません。しかし今日では、様々な意匠を凝らした暖炉があるため、ルールはほぼないも同然です。決断する決め手は、「熱」かもしれません。もし暖炉の火で部屋を暖めたいなら、その希望に合う製品があります。しかし、煙道、煙突、開口部のサイズ、安全性といった条件もまた、考慮せねばなりません。しかし、ゆらめく炎を眺めたい、トロフィーを飾る棚が欲しいといった装飾の目的で暖炉を設置したいとお考えなら、選択肢は無限にあります。選択肢が多ければ、選びやすいかもしれませんし、かえって選びにくくなるかもしれません。メーカーのショールームに足を運び、どのような製品があるか見てみましょう。きっと驚くことになるでしょうから、覚悟しておいてください。並んだ白い小石や陶器の松ぼっくり、はたまた、ごちゃごちゃとしたアルファベットの文字から、炎が立ちのぼっているのを目にすることになります。「炎を使った芸術品」とか、スイスのスキーロッジのイメージに近い暖炉などが揃っています。お望みなら、コーヒーテーブルの中央に設置したガラスの筒の中で、煙の出ない炎を楽しむということだってできるのです。

What style of fireplace goes with what style of room? Should you match it to the architecture or your home furnishings? Do you want a fireplace with a big mantelpiece or a small one? Do you need a mantelpiece at all? Perhaps a simple cut-out surround would suffice – maybe a square or framed circle. You might think that it depends on whether you want to have 'real' flames, but now – with many types of 'designer' fires available, there are almost no rules. The deciding factor might be heat. If you want your fire to heat the room, there are specific products to suit your needs. But there are also requirements to consider concerning flues, chimneys, size of opening, safety and so forth. On the other hand, if it's just the decorative elements that you're after, a flickering flame to look at and a shelf on which to display your trophies – then there are no limits. This might make it easier to decide, or harder. Visit suppliers' showrooms and see what's on offer – and be prepared for a surprise: flames flickering from a row of white pebbles, ceramic pinecones or a jumble of letters of the alphabet; fireplaces that look more like framed artworks or something from a Swiss ski lodge. You can even have a smokeless fire in a glass cylinder in the centre of a coffee table.

暖炉

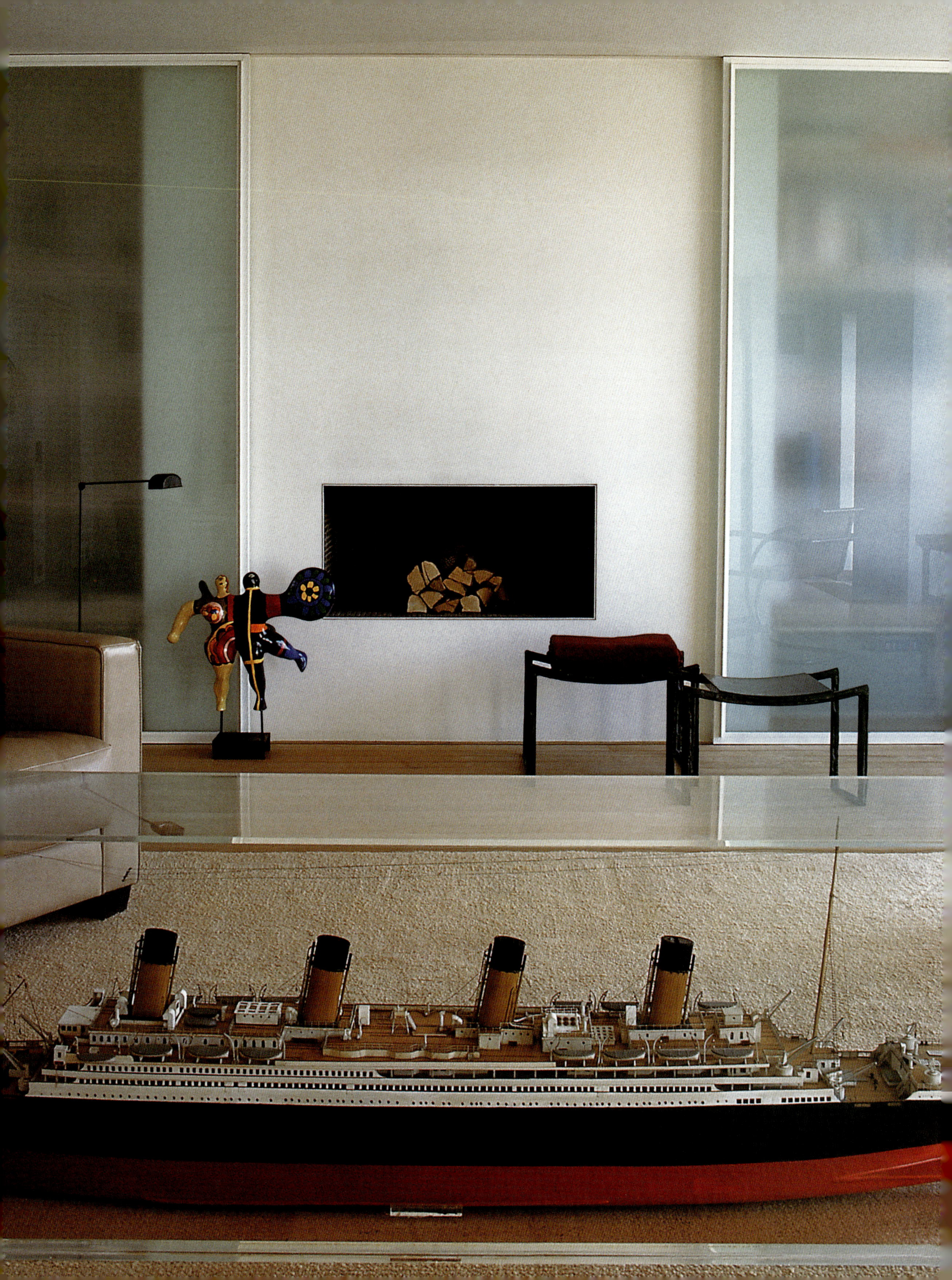

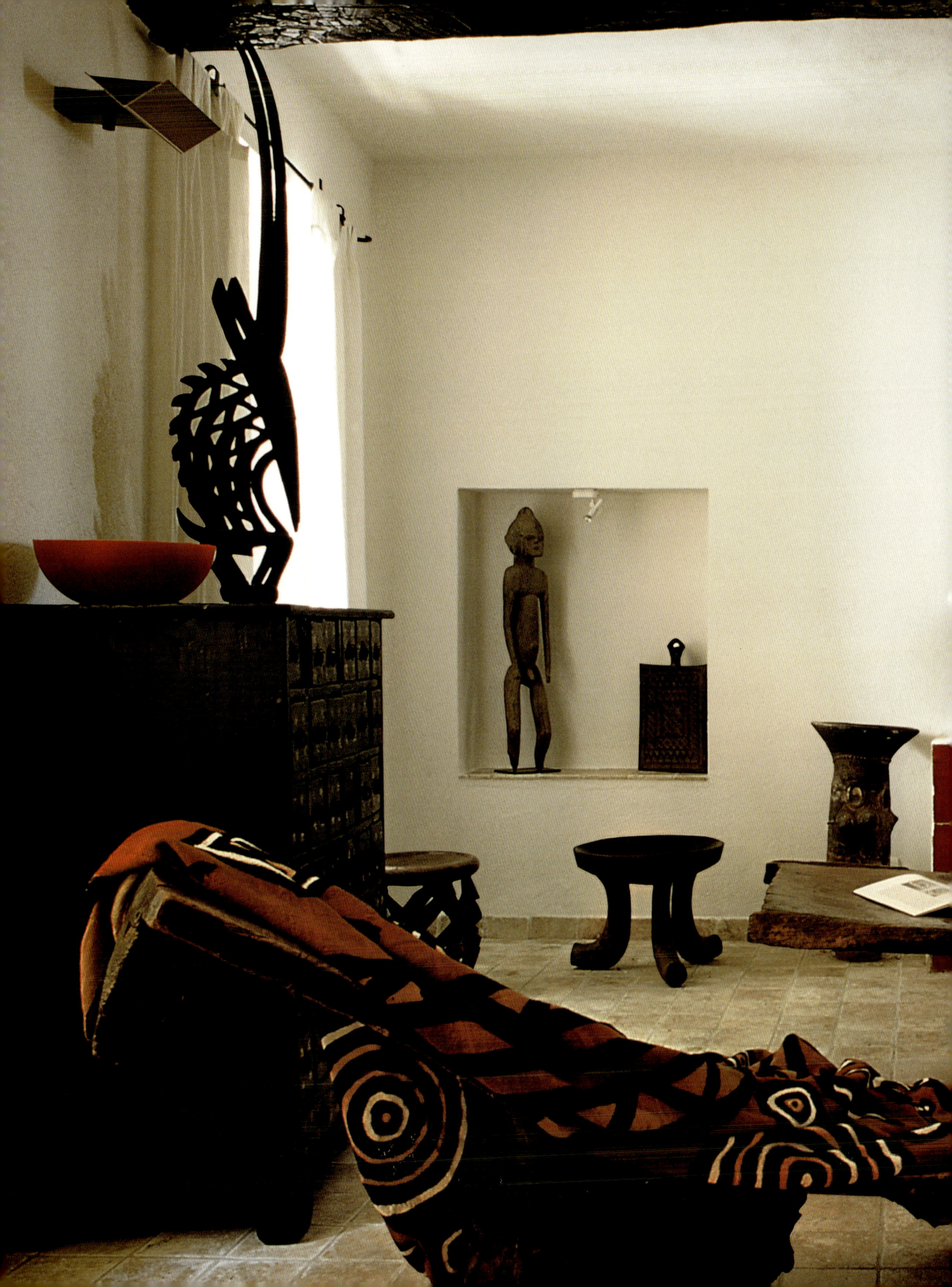

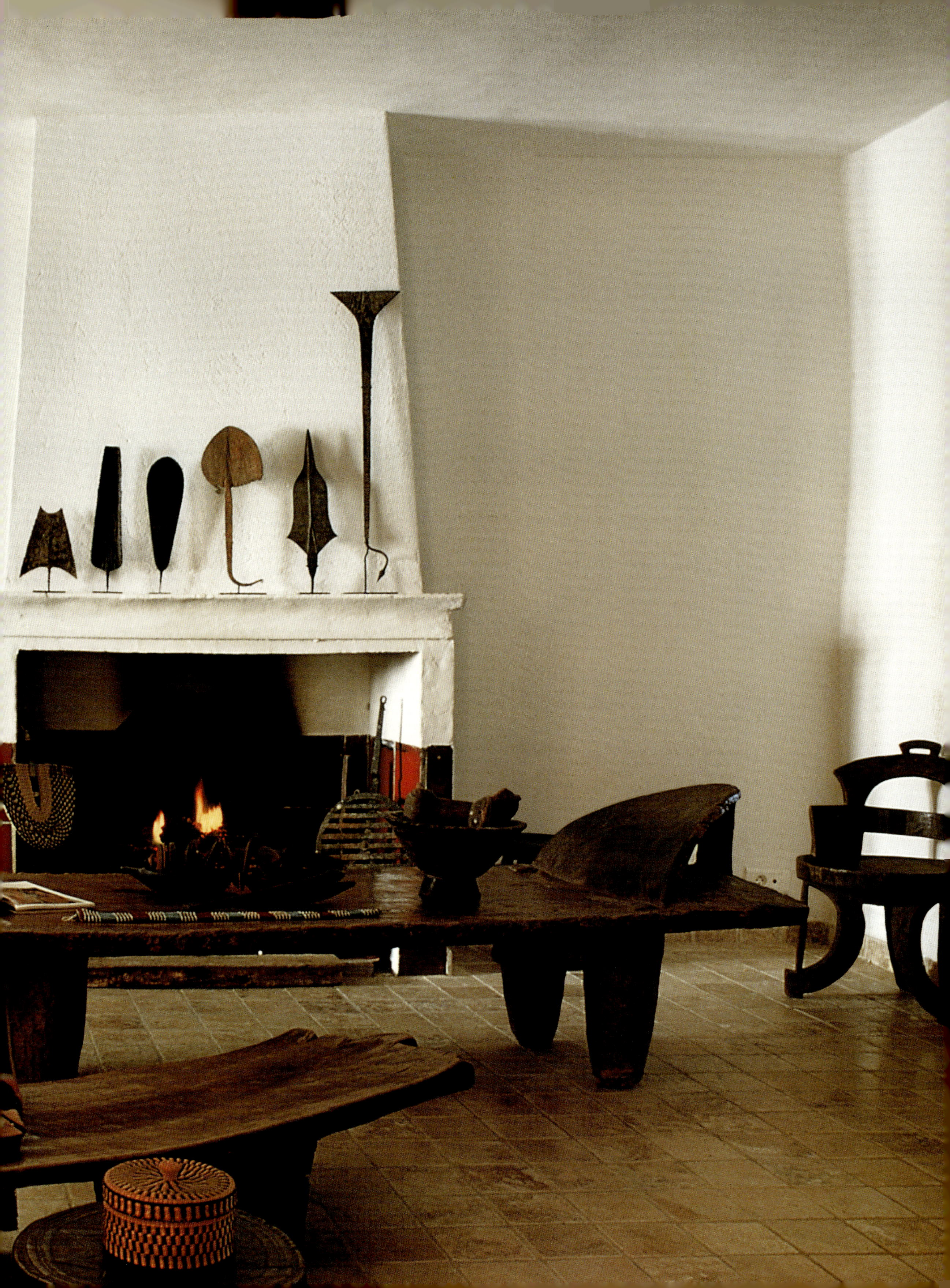

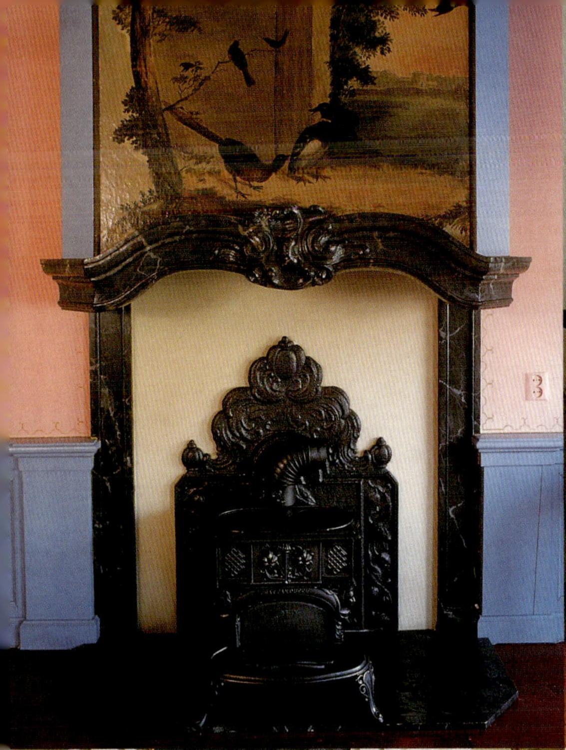
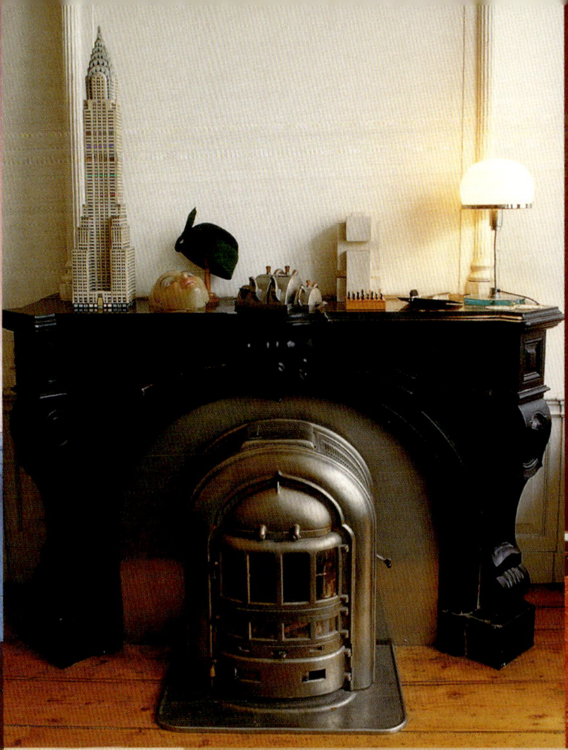
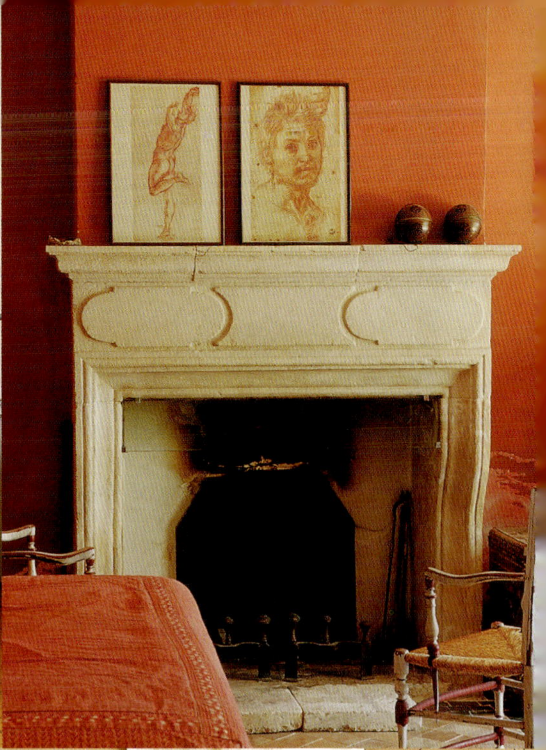
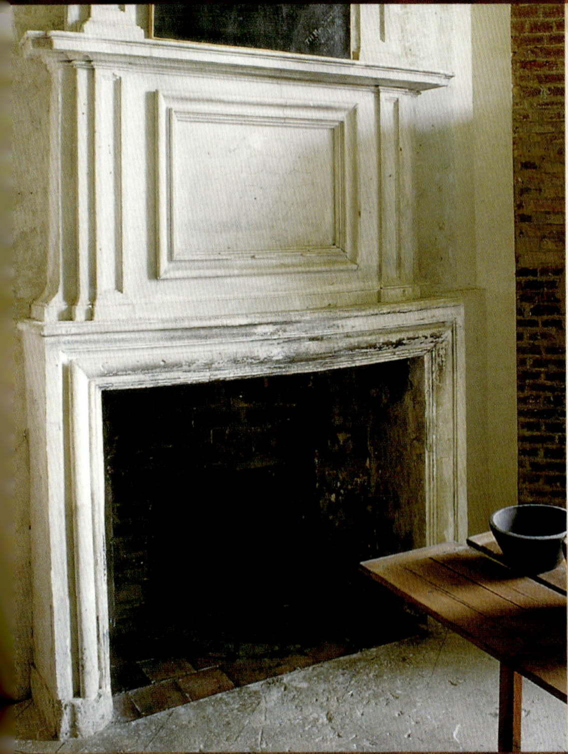
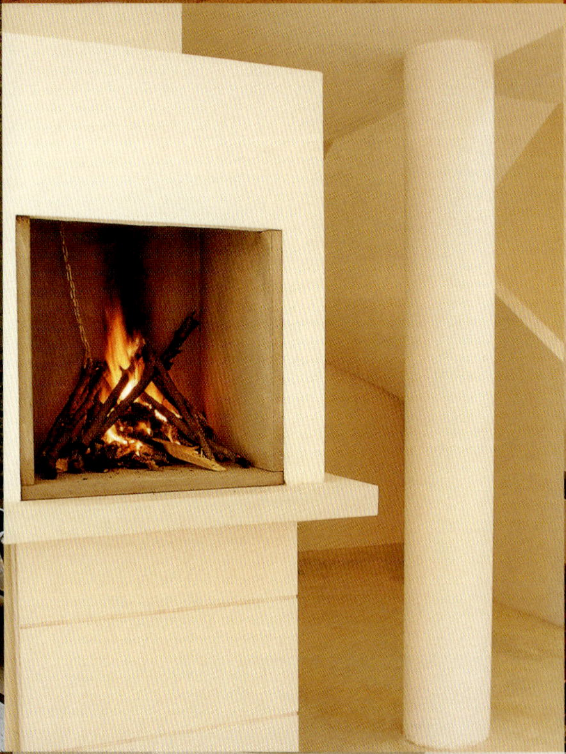
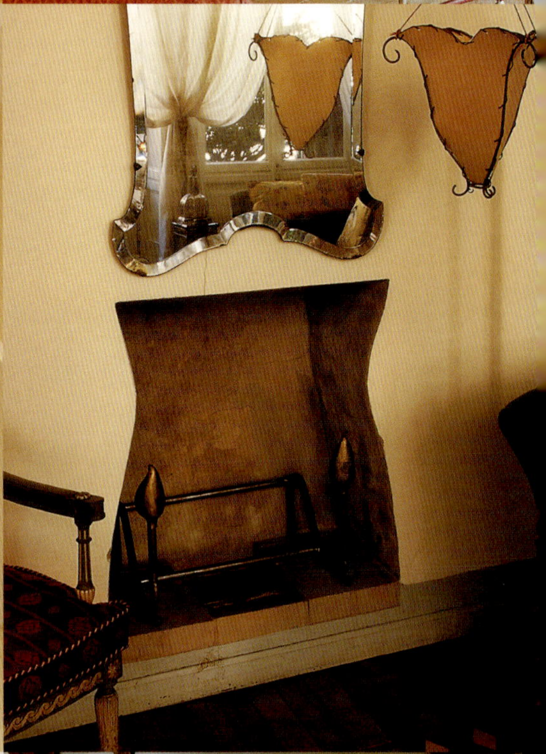
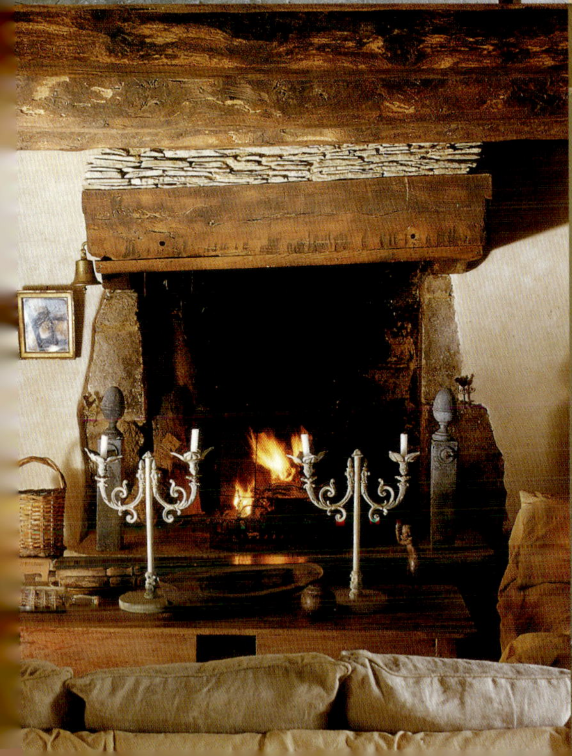
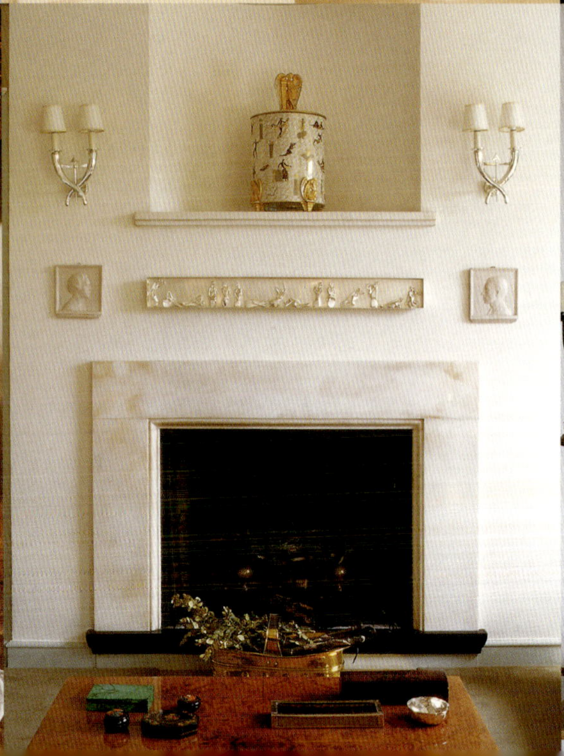
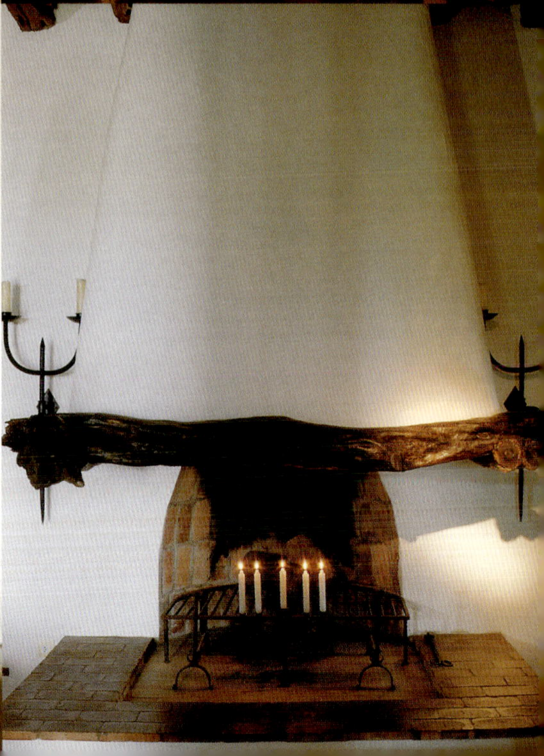

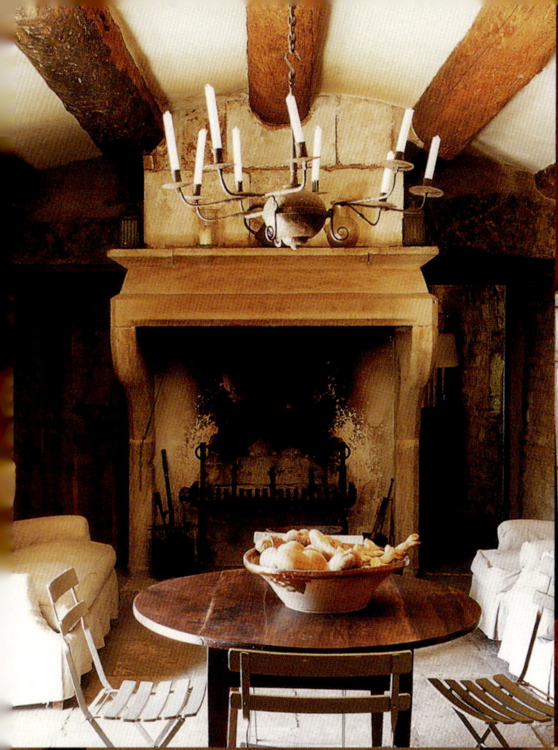
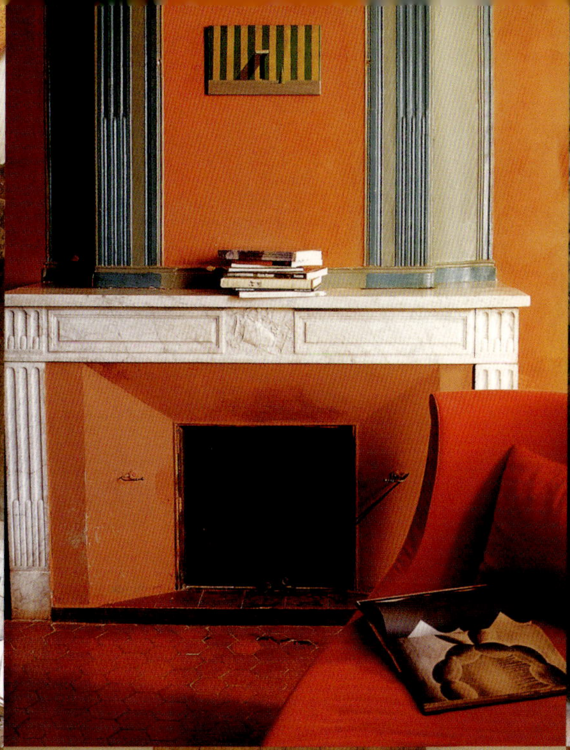
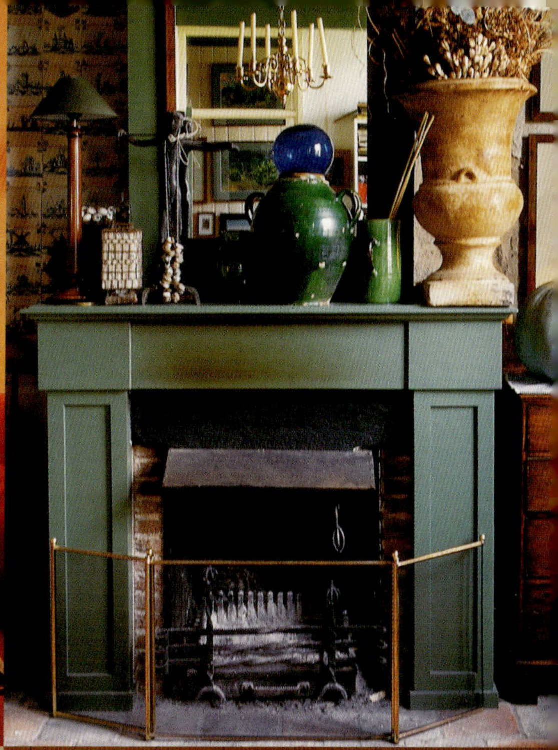
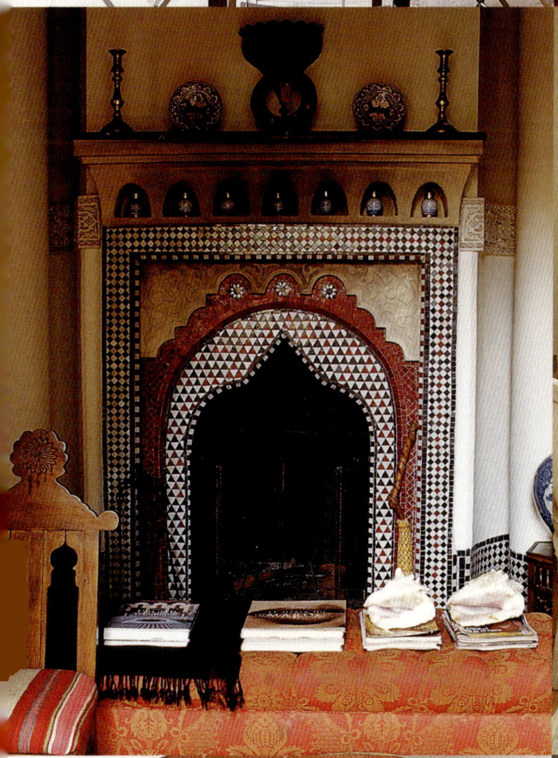
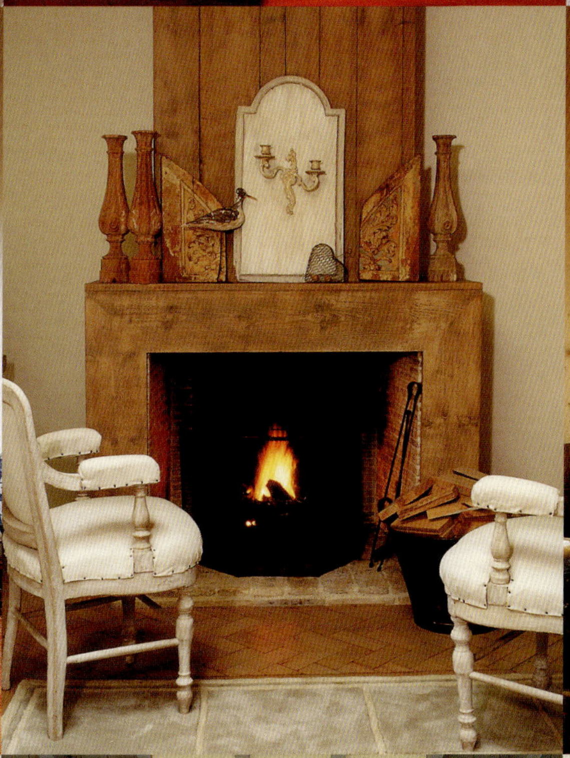
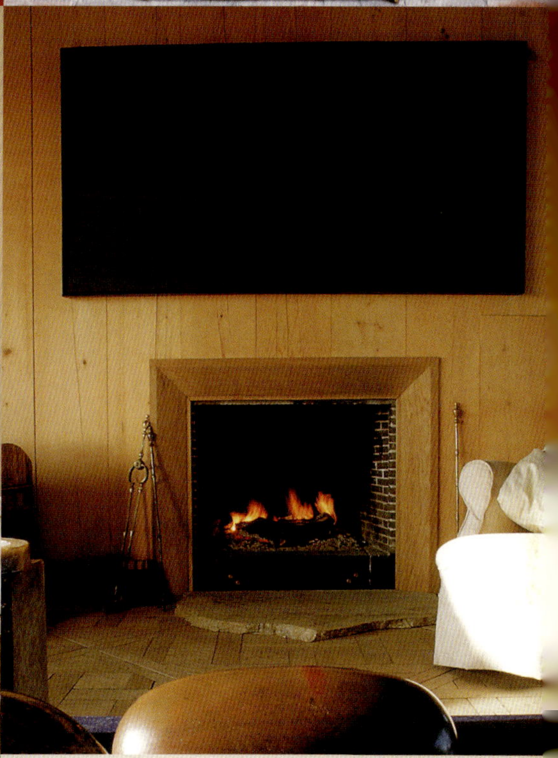
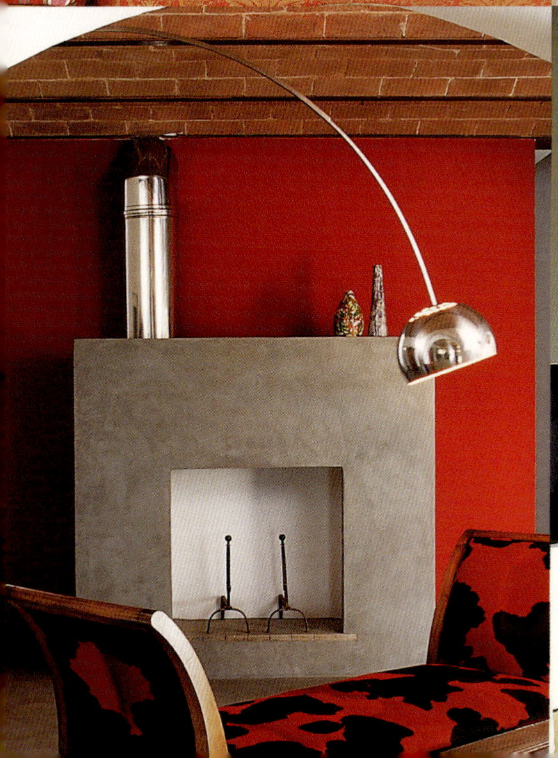
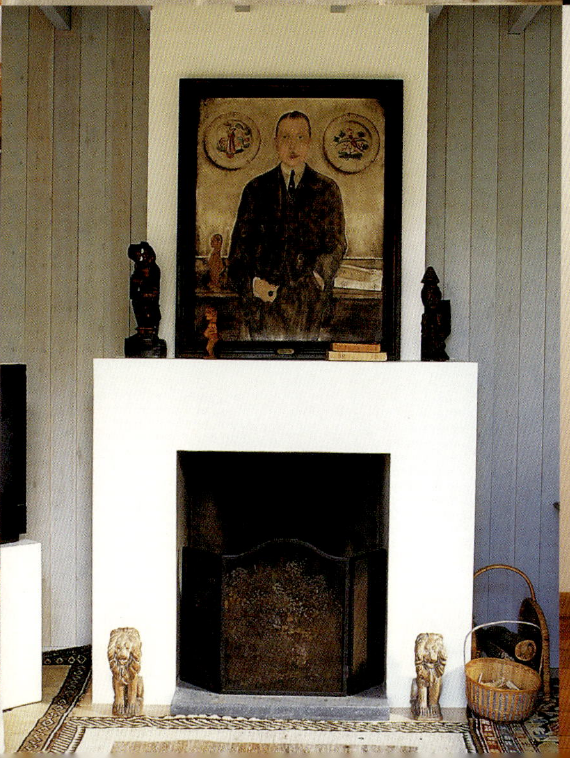
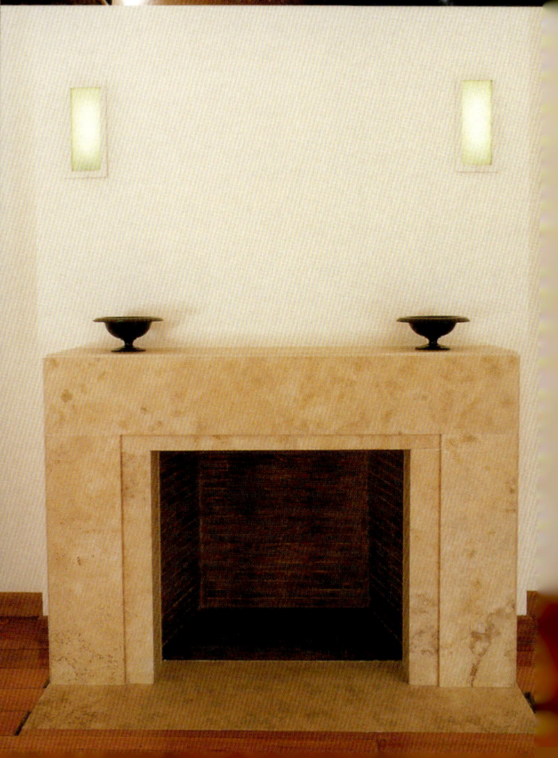

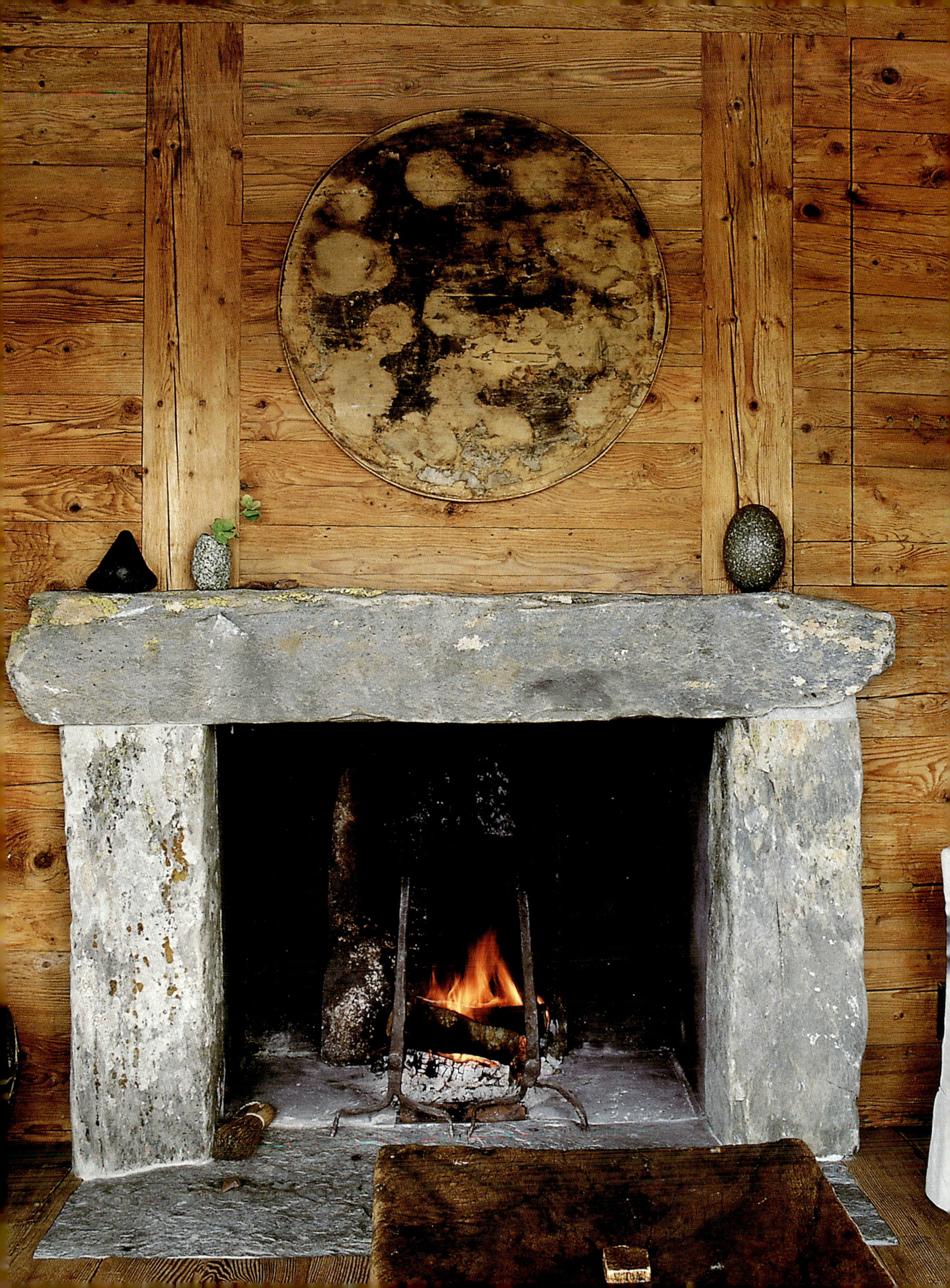

暖炉

暖炉

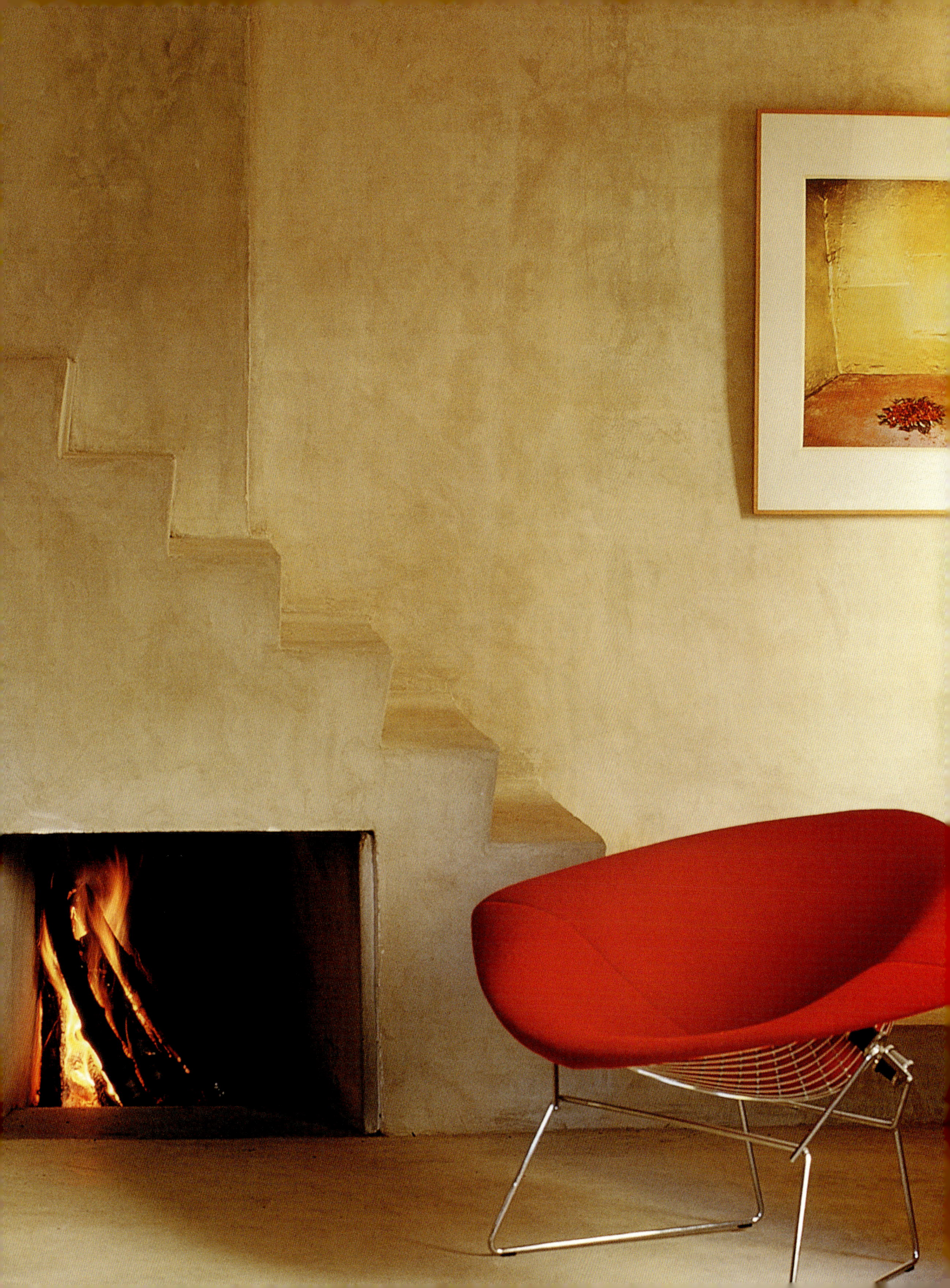

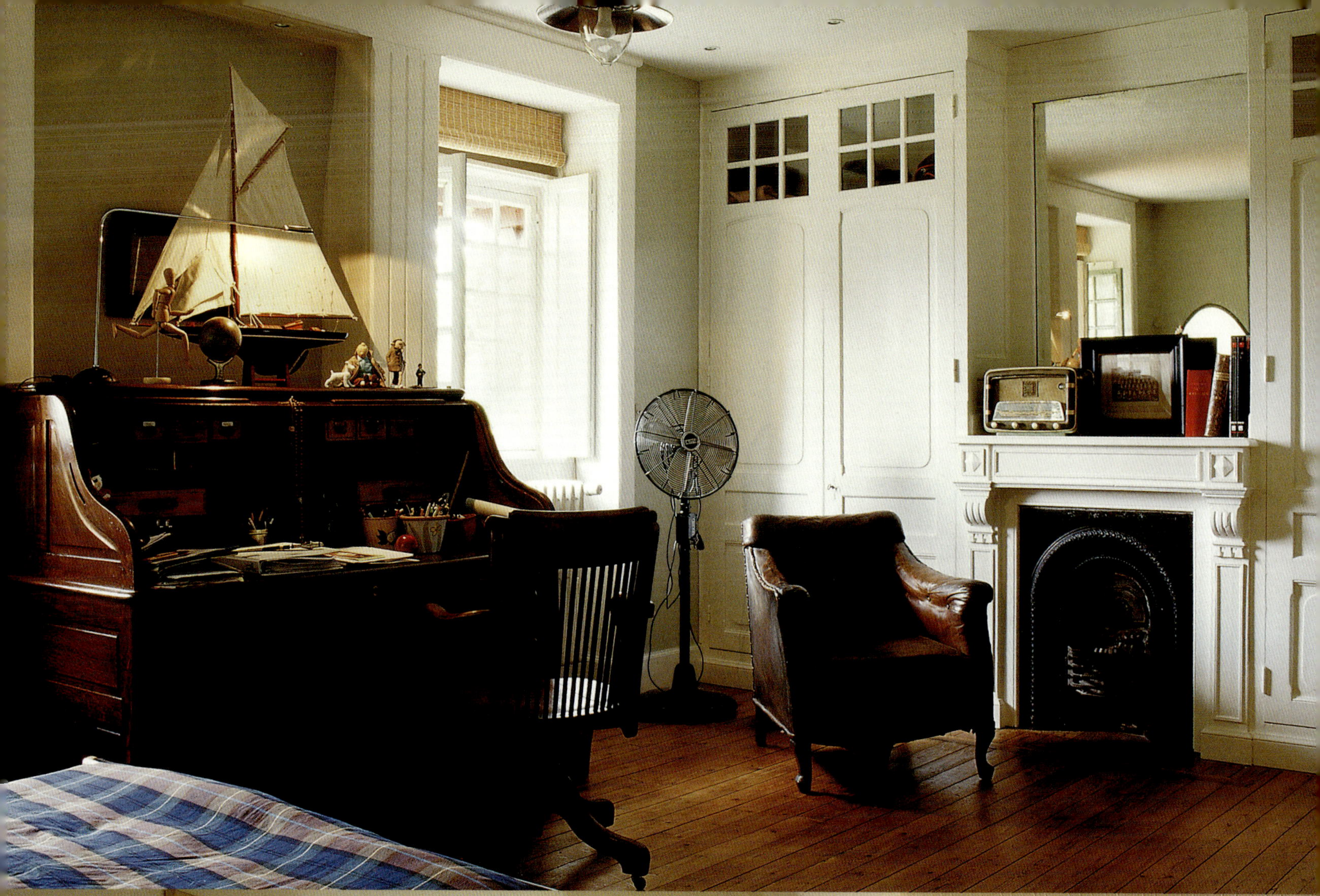
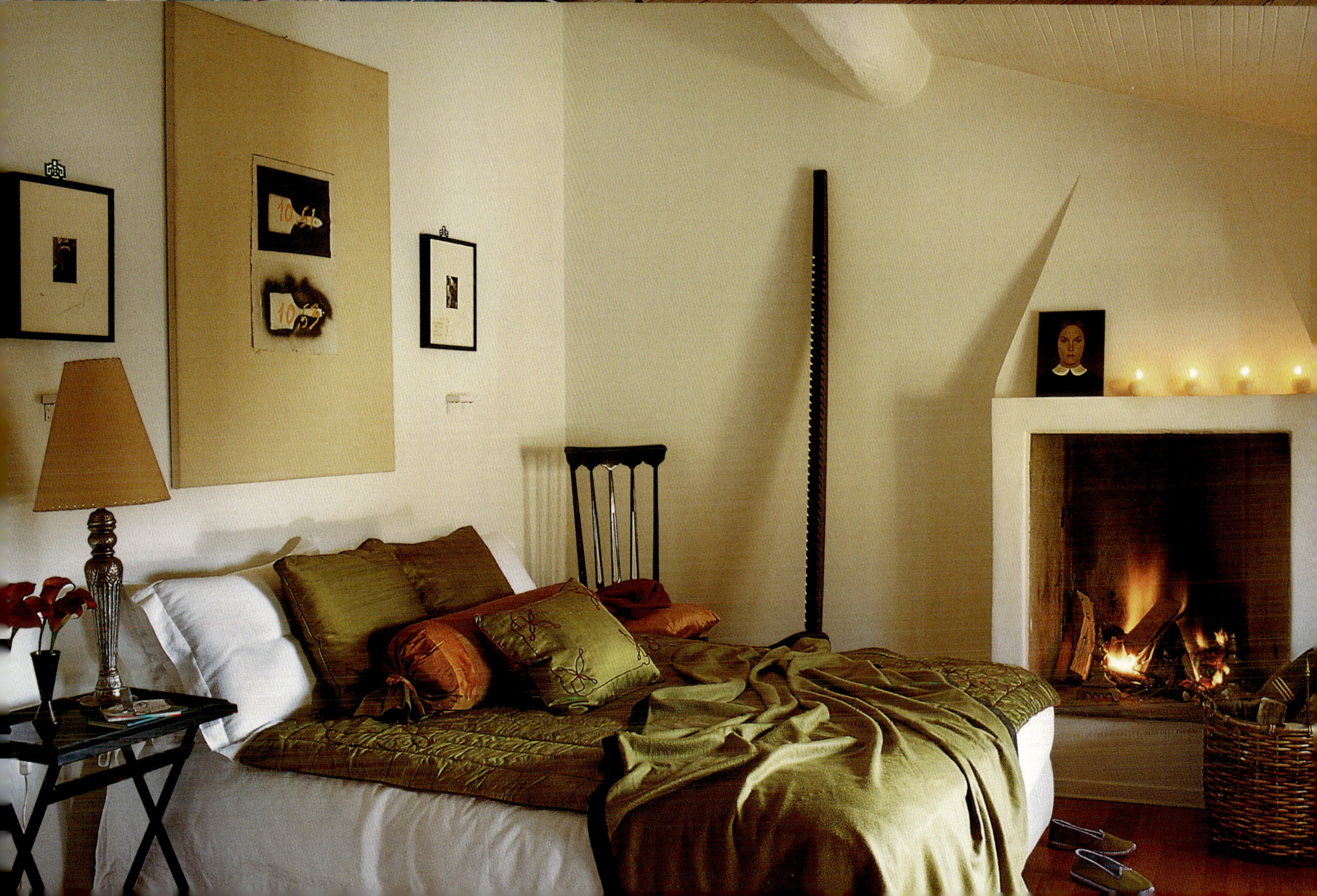

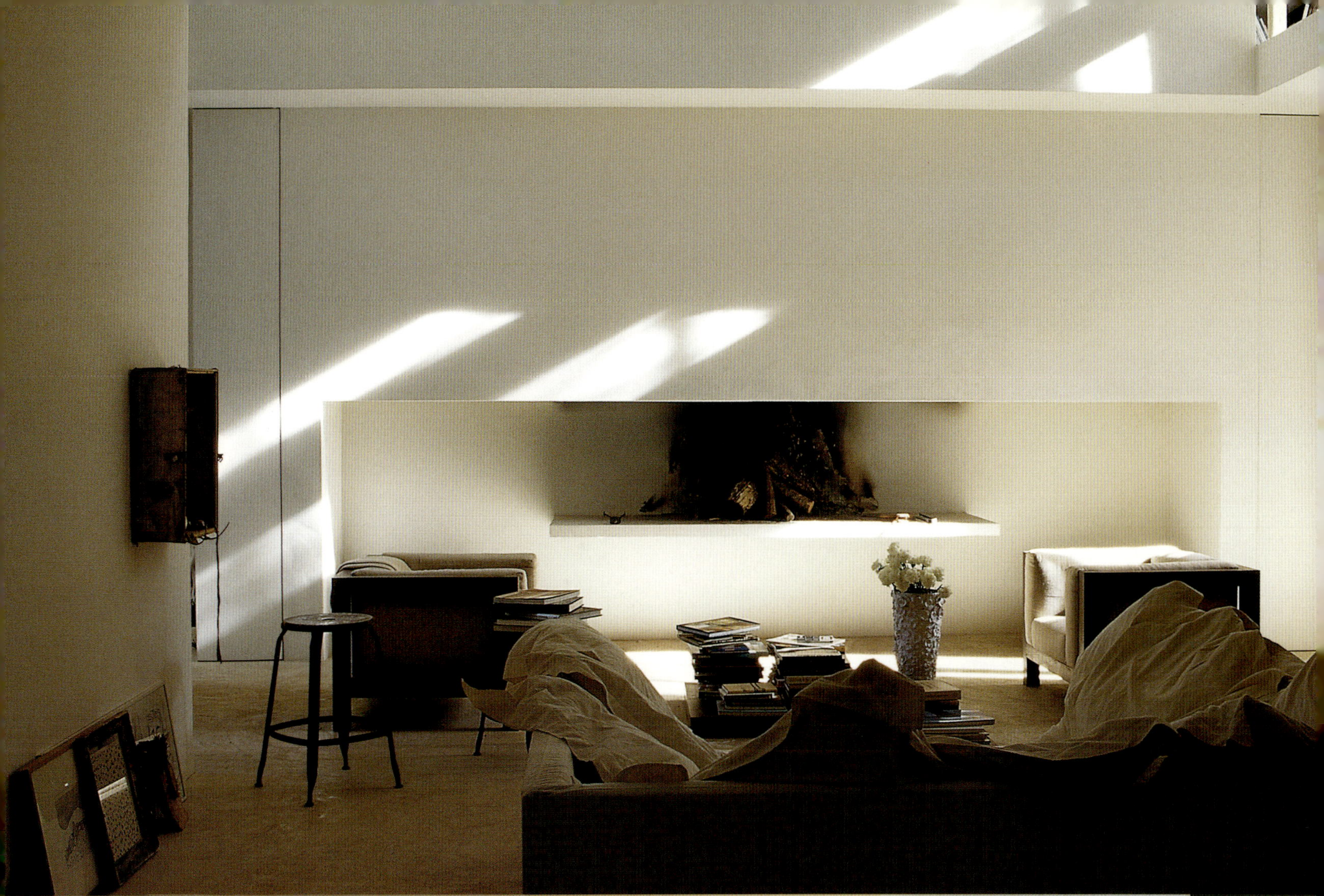
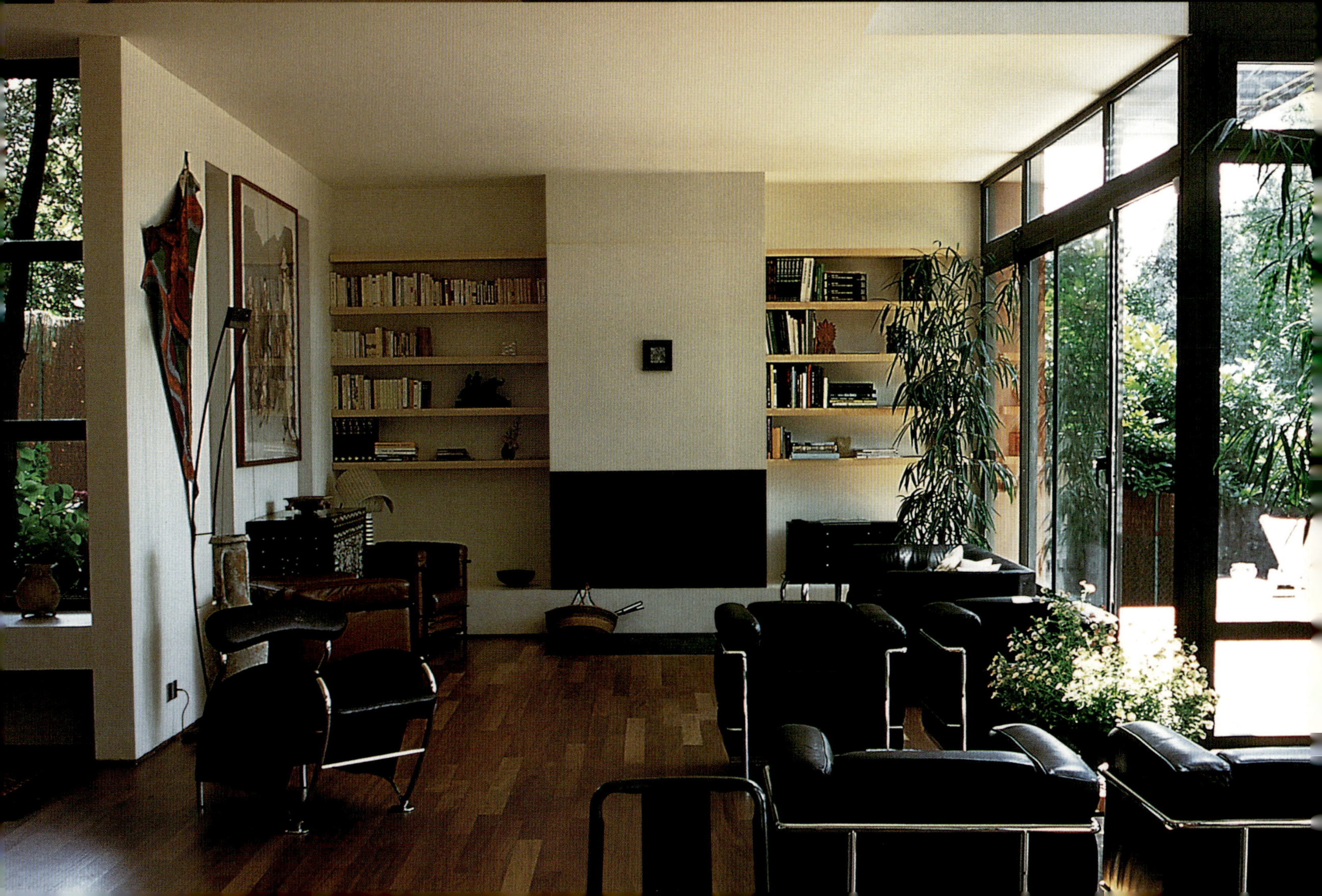

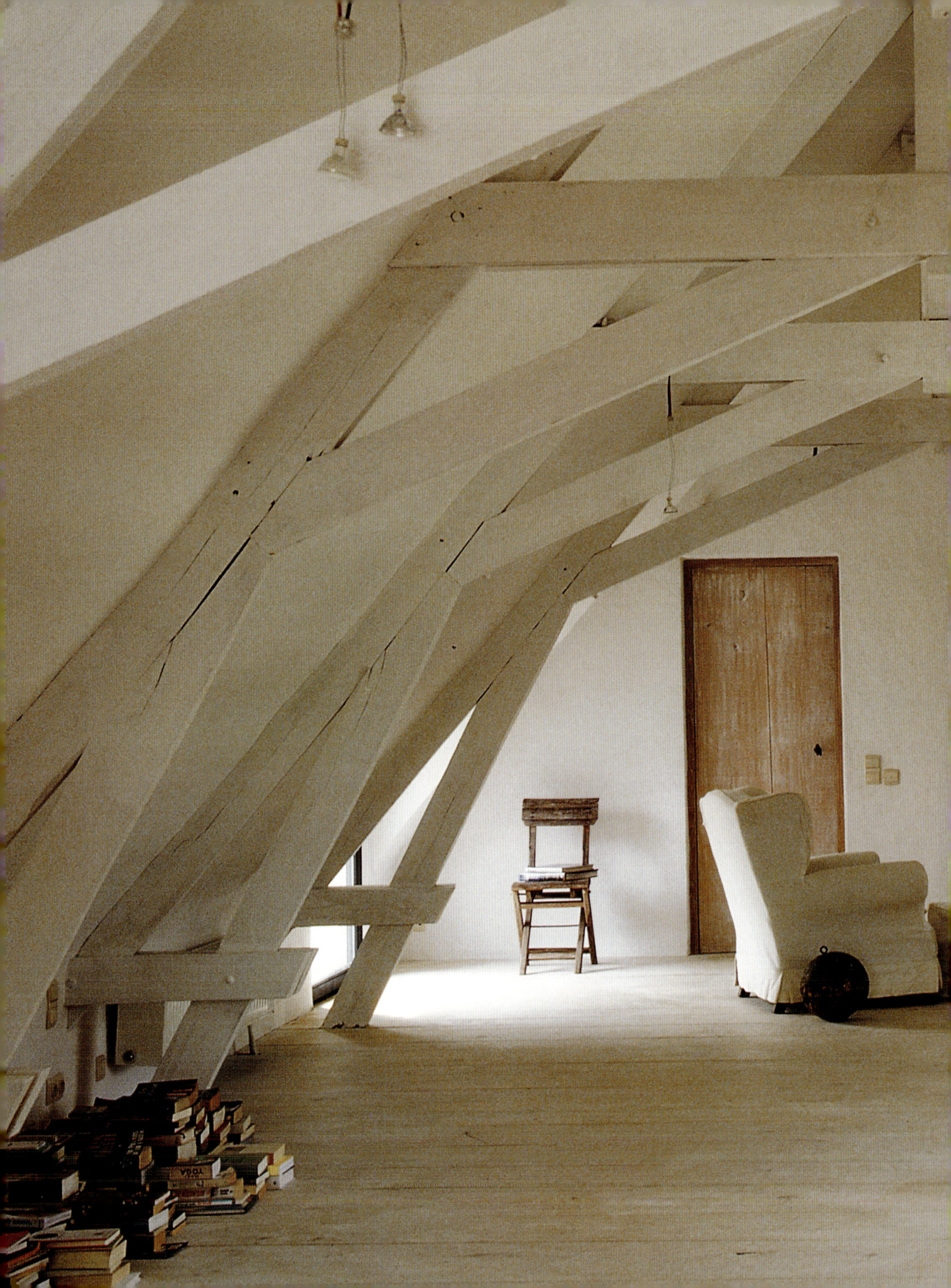
YOGA

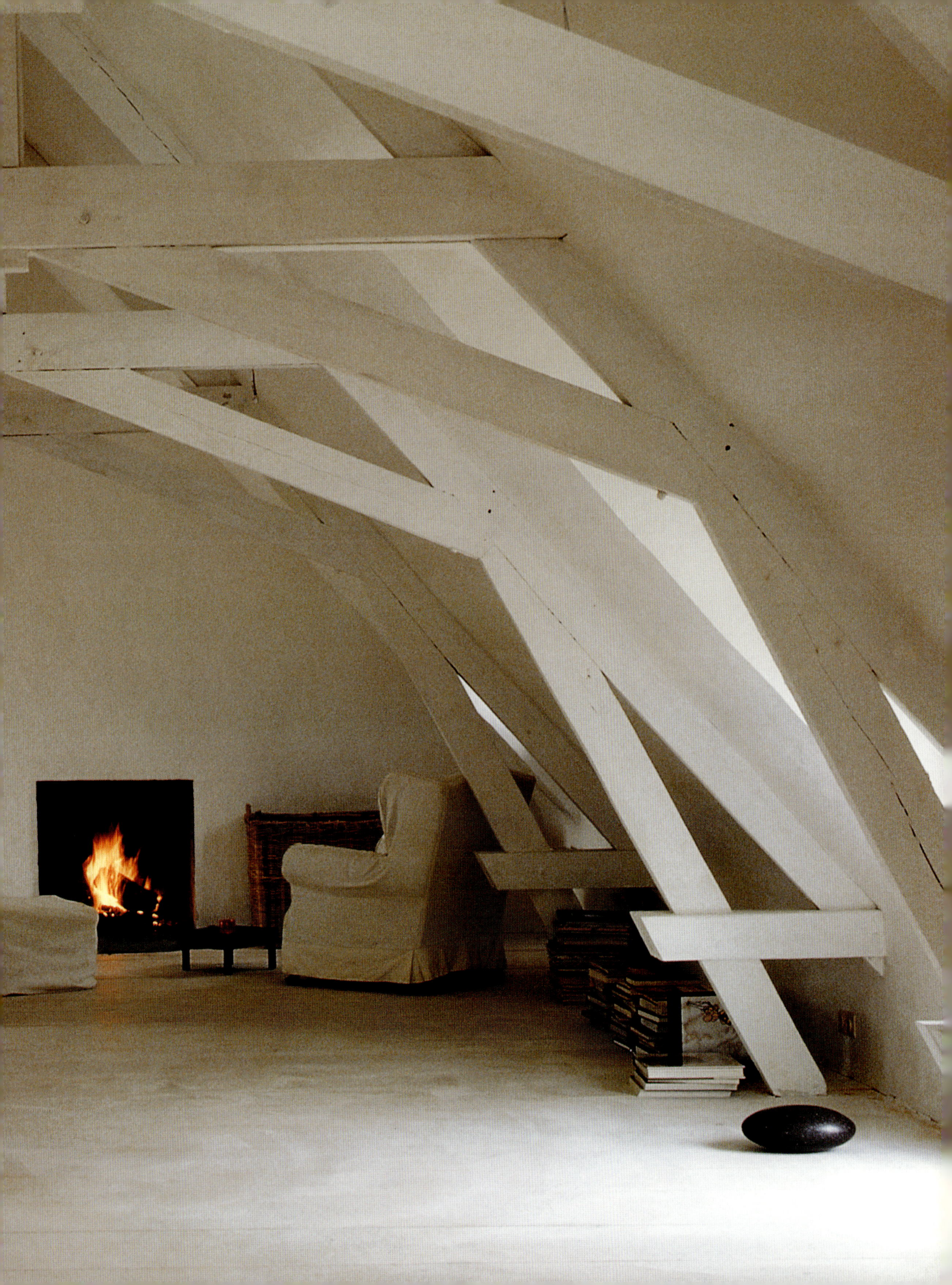

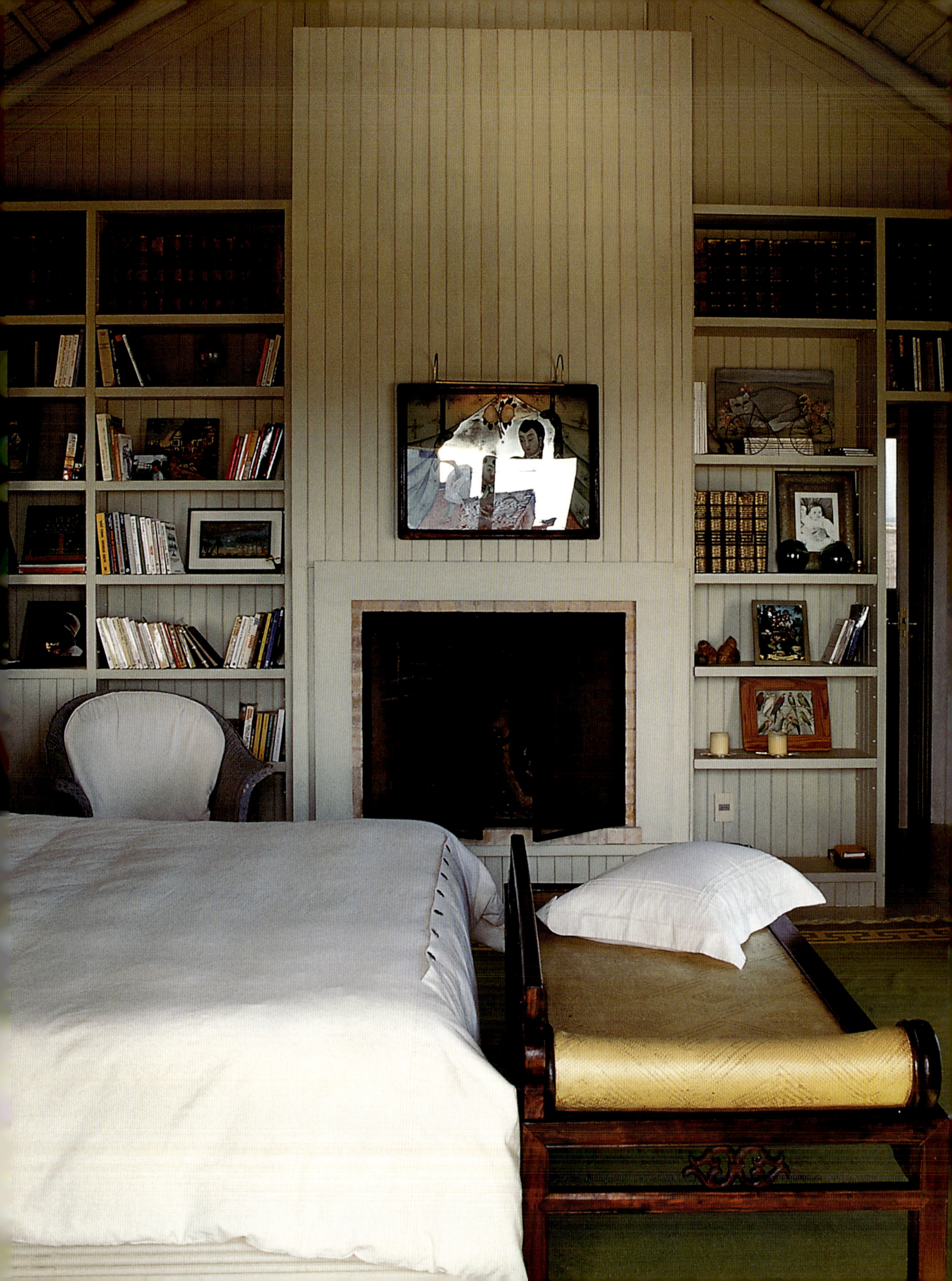

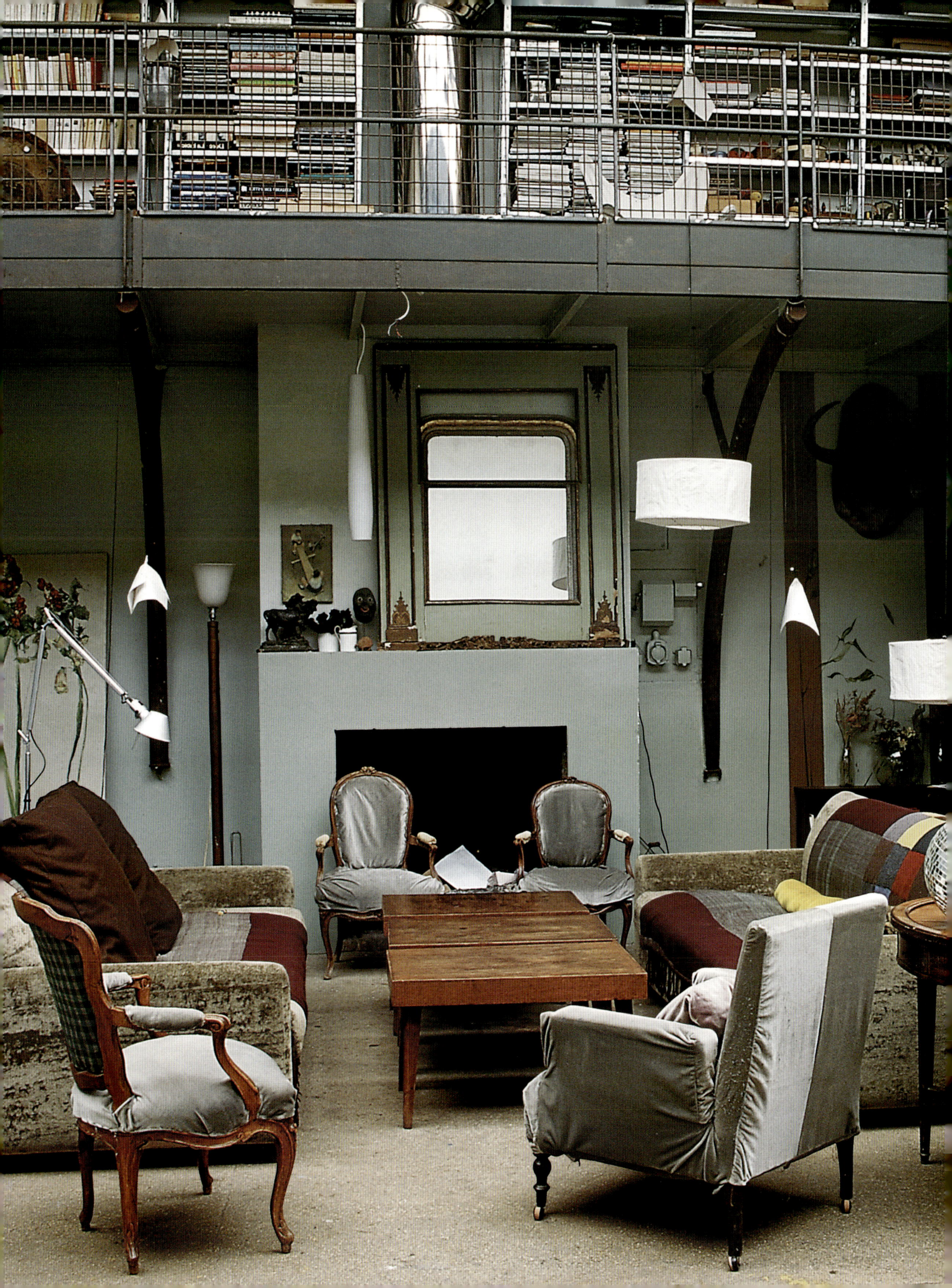

色と素材感

Colour & Texture

「落ち着いて。そう感情的にならないで」誰かにこう言われた経験がきっとあるでしょう。しかしそれは、リビングルームに関する話でしょうか？　自分自身で部屋を装飾する様々な手法の中で、色を加えるというのは、もっとも個人的で、もっとも感情的な方法と考えられています。色は、私たちの幸せの基本です。色彩心理学という分野で、色が人の気分にどのような影響を与えるかという、多くの研究がなされてきました。道路標識、交通信号、注意書きに使われている色を、思い浮かべてみてください。幼い頃から、私たちは特定の色に反応します——危険は赤、お悔やみは黒（文化によっては、白）といった具合に。住まいに白を使うと、光を反射し部屋を明るく見せることで知られています。青と緑は、バスルームに向くみずみずしい色です。赤は心地よく、温もりを感じさせます。色を取り入れるのは、簡単そうですが、実は容易ではありません。色に加えて、素材感——光沢や浮き出し模様の有無——という要素があります。不動産業者が口を揃えるのは、家を売り出す際に、できるだけ多くの人の関心を集めて、早々と買い手を見つけるには、家の色をニュートラルにするべきだということです。家を売る話は別として、なぜ、私たちは部屋の色を変えるのでしょう？　色は取り入れるのが簡単だからです。——朝食と、昼食の間の時間で、部屋を塗り替えることだってできます。ドア、窓枠、壁1枚といった、小さなスペースから始めてみましょう。自分自身のひらめき——つまり気分を信じてください。色とは、マーラーの演奏会を締めくくる、壮麗なシンバルの音です。これを聴かずして、どうして家に帰れるでしょう？

'Calm down and don't get so emotional.' I bet somebody has said that to you before – but have they said it about your living room? Of all the things that you can do to a room, adding colour is considered the most personal, the most emotional. Colour is fundamental to our wellbeing. Many studies have been done into the psychology of colour and its effects on our mood – think of those used in street signs, on traffic lights and safety notices. From an early age, we respond to certain colours – red for danger; black for mourning (or in some cultures, white). In the home, we know that a white room reflects the light; that blue and green are a good fresh palette for bathrooms; that red is cosy and welcoming. It sounds simple, but it's not. Add to this, the element of texture: gloss or matt, embossed or even perforated. Property developers all agree that if you want to appeal to the greatest number of people, and get a quick sale, then you should keep it neutral. Aside from that, why would you? Colour is so easy to apply – you can change a room between breakfast and lunch. Start with a small area – a door, maybe, or a window frame or a single wall. Trust your instincts – your emotions. Colour is the clash of cymbals at the end of a Mahler concert. How could you go home without it?

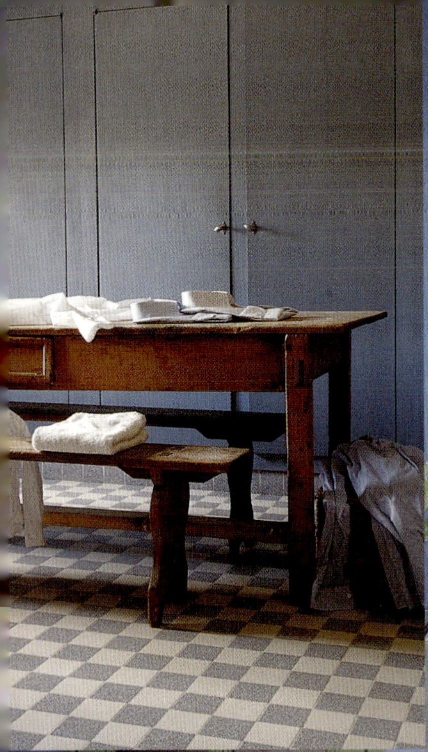
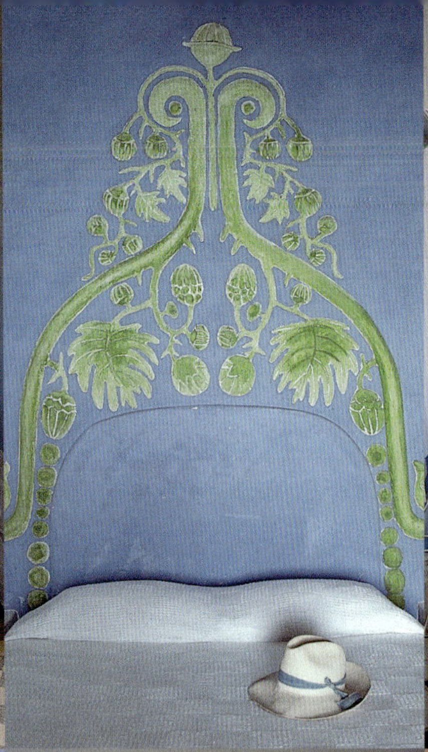
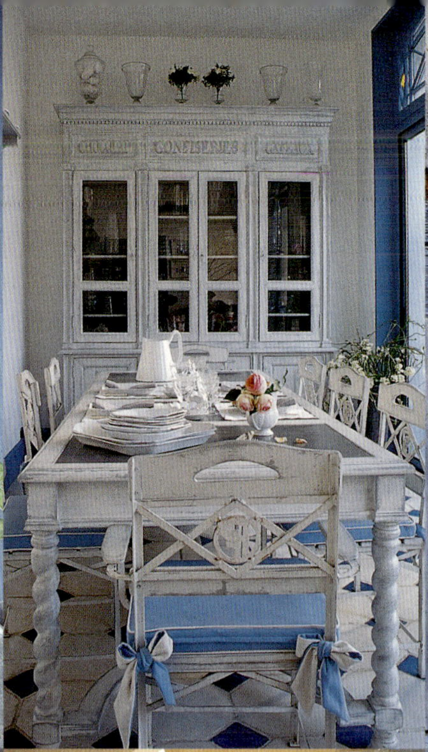
CONFISERIES
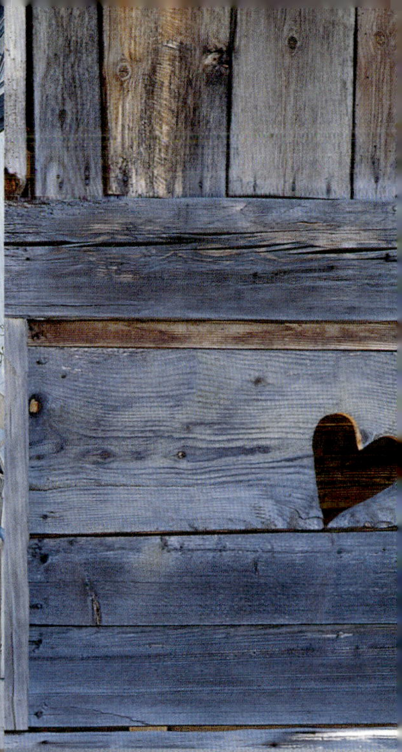
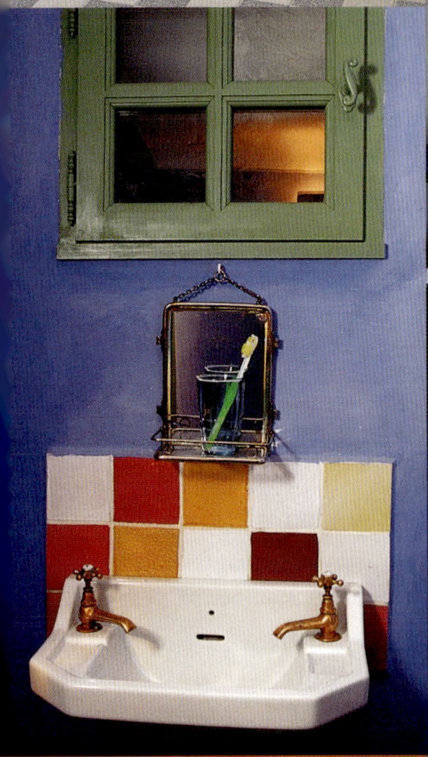
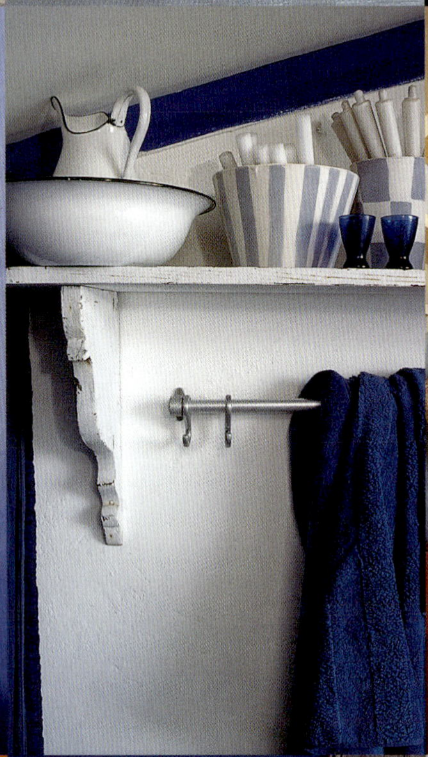
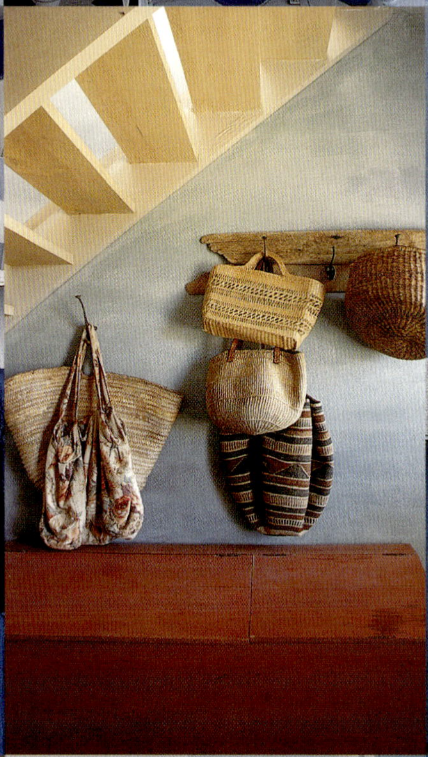
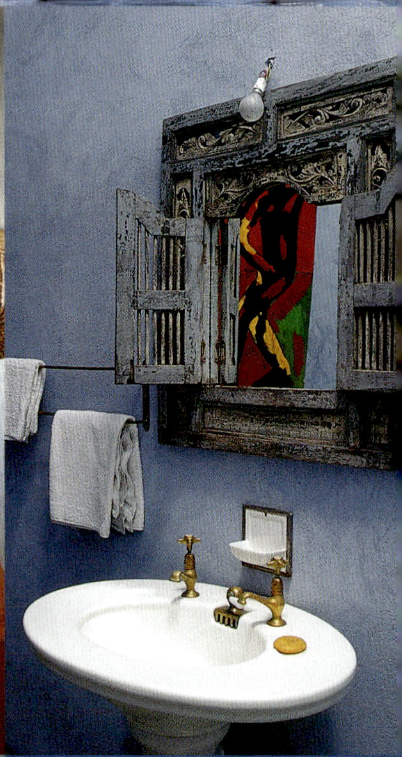
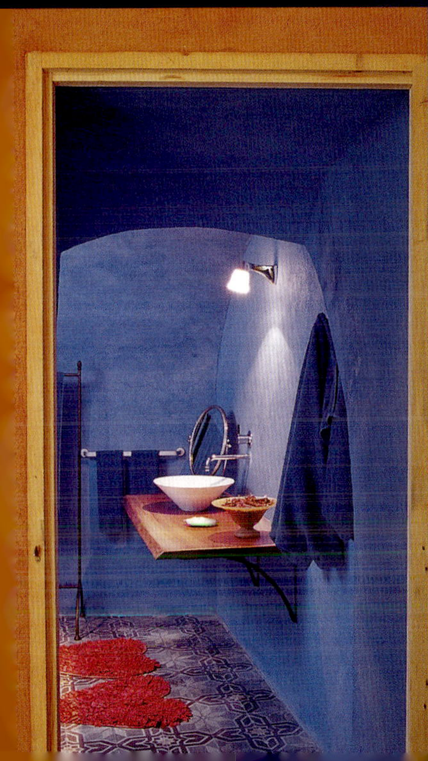
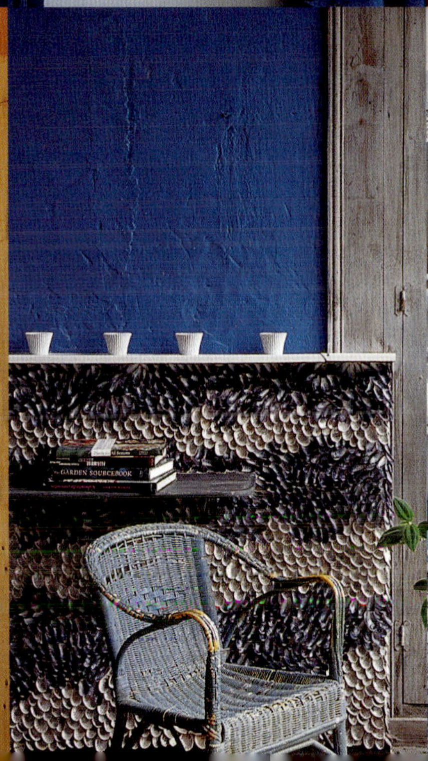
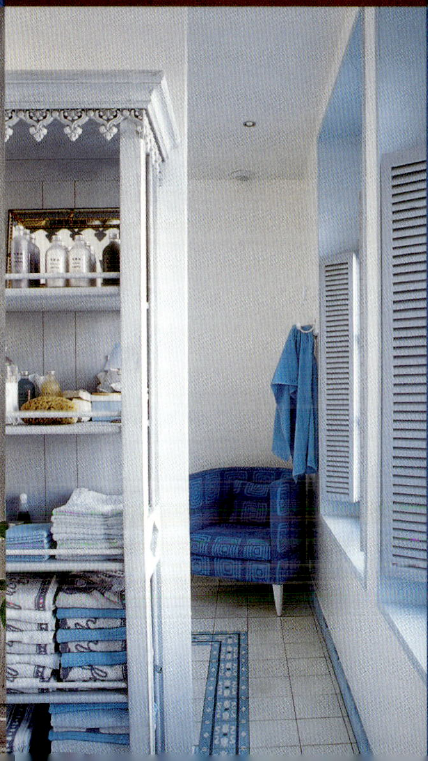
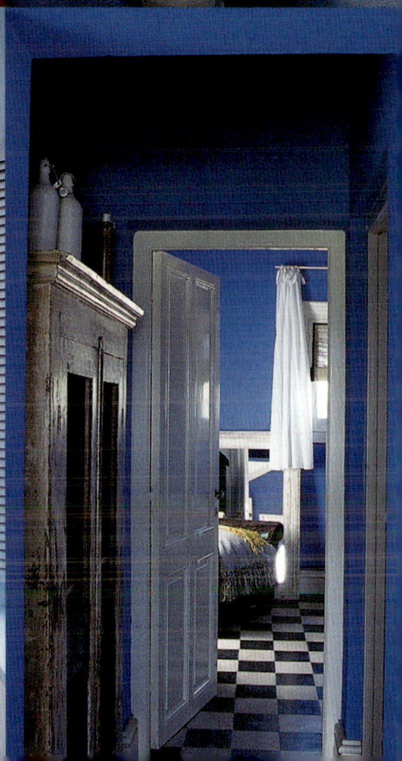

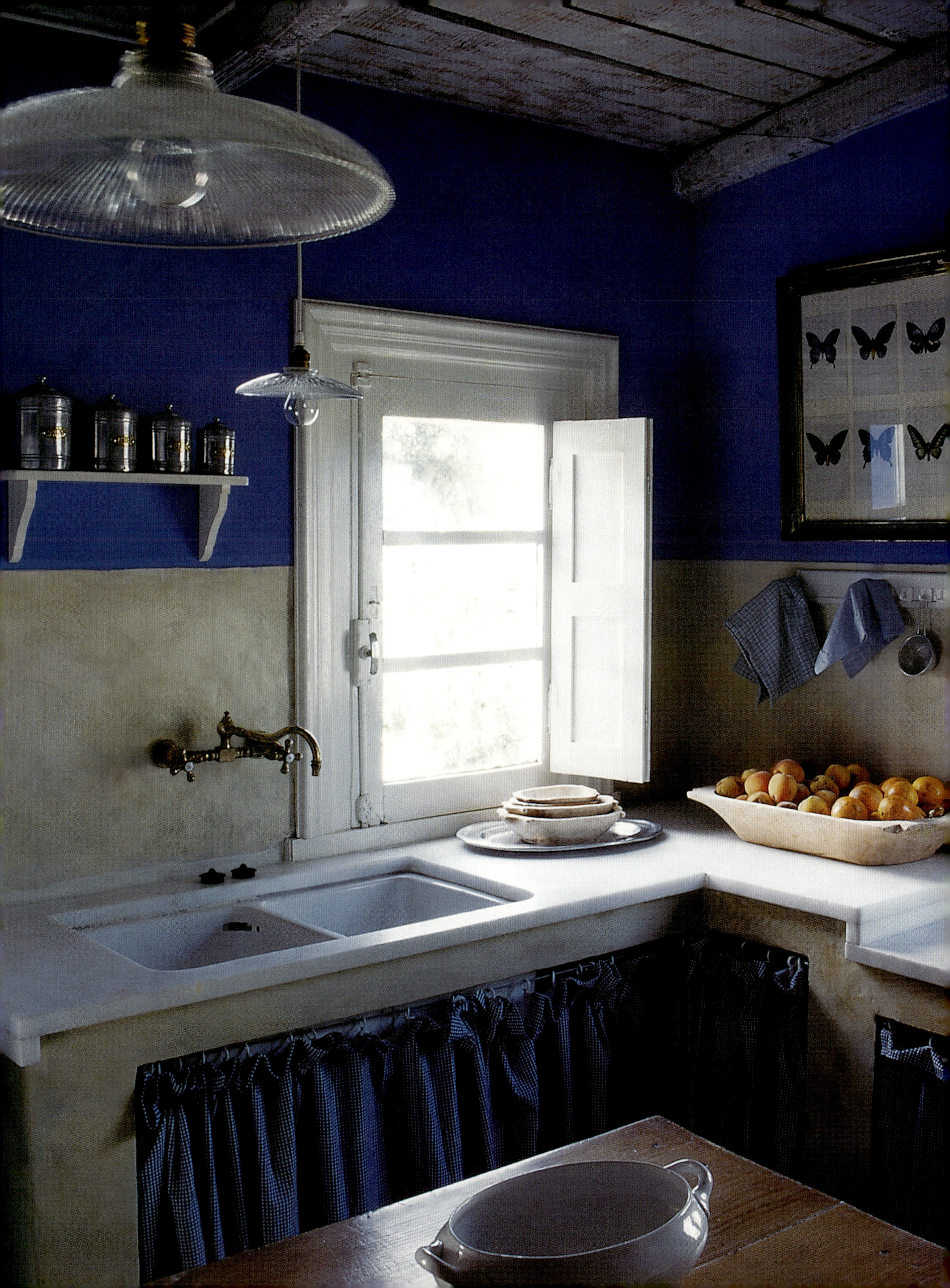

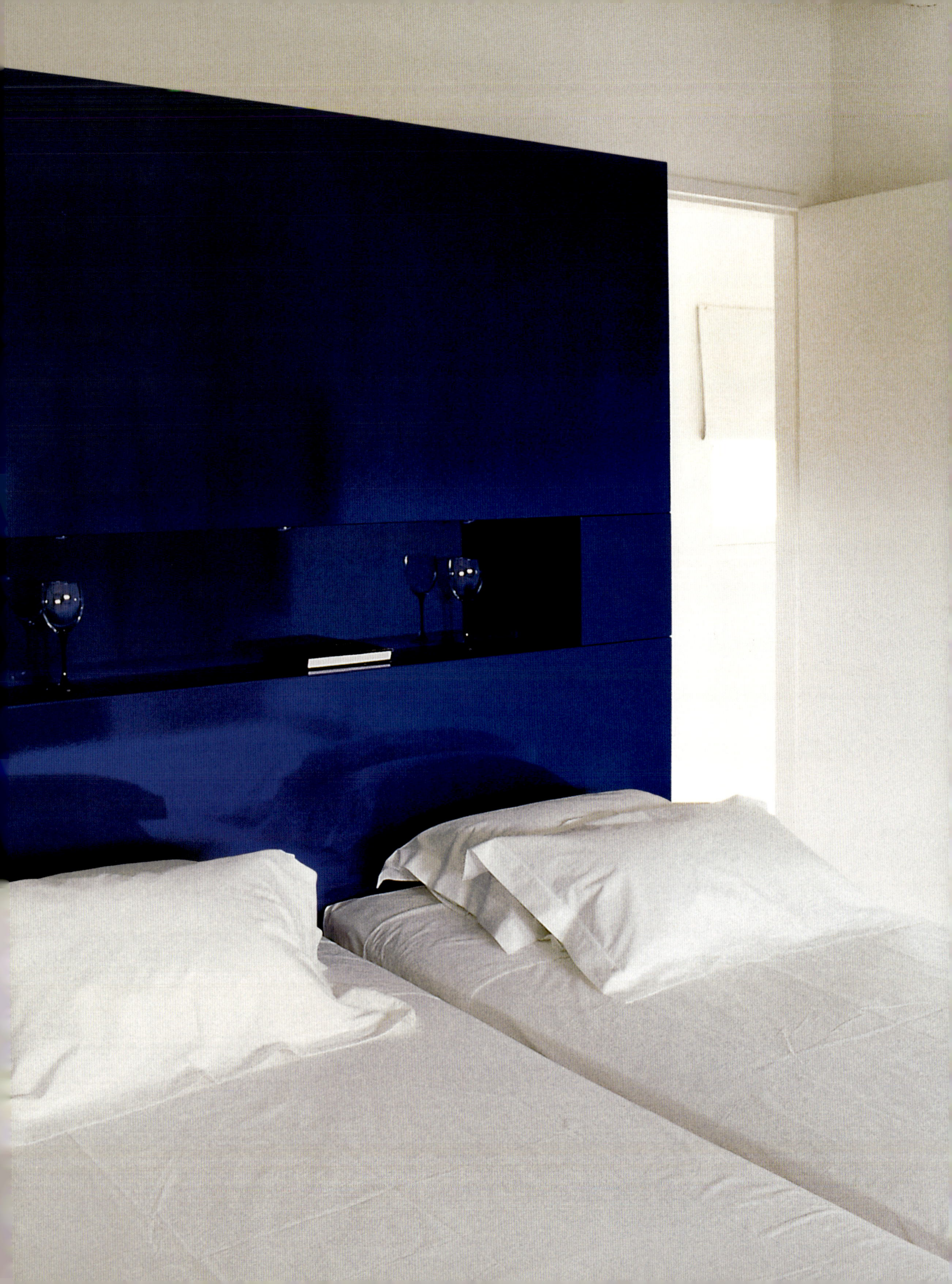

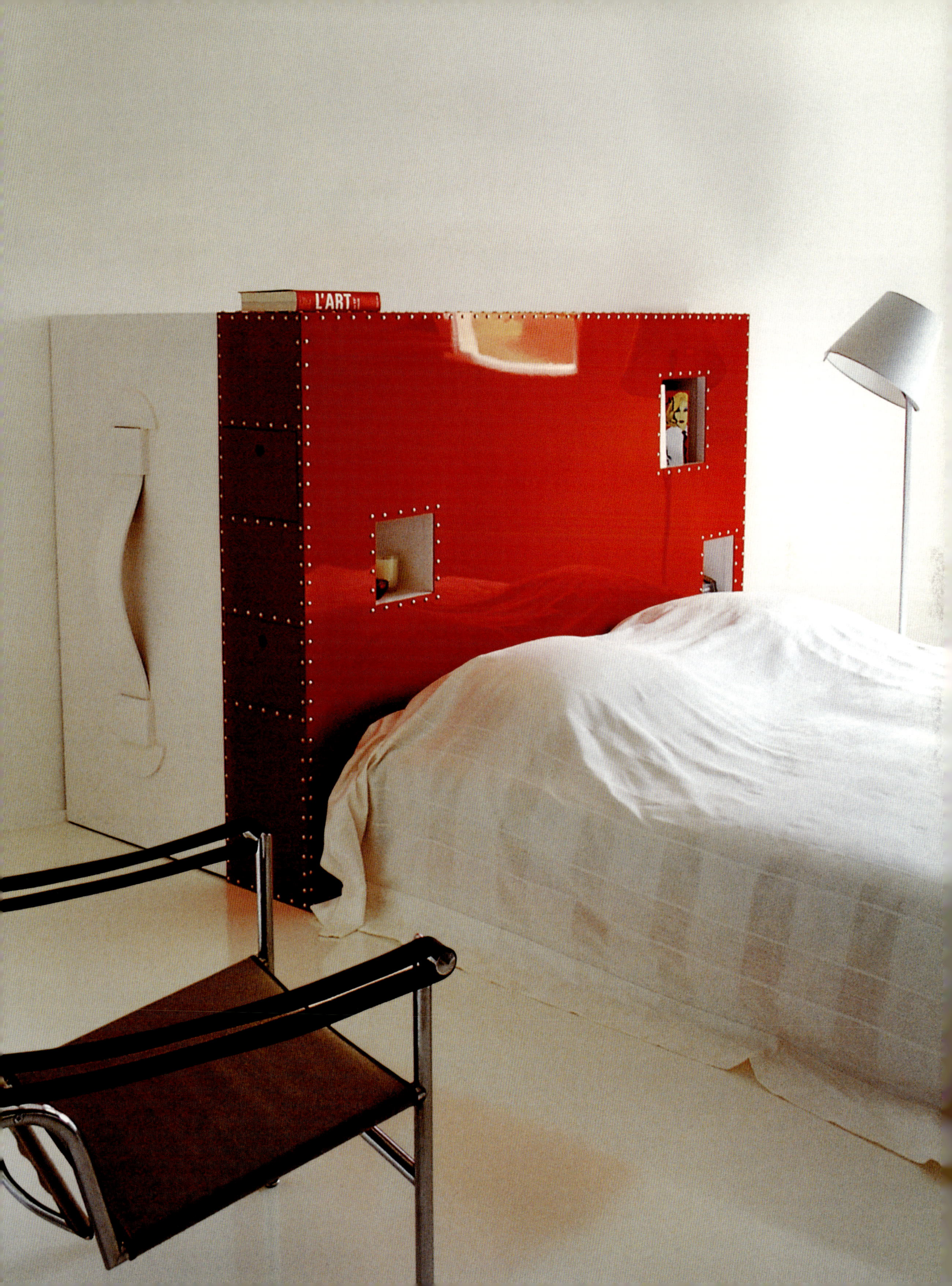
L'ART

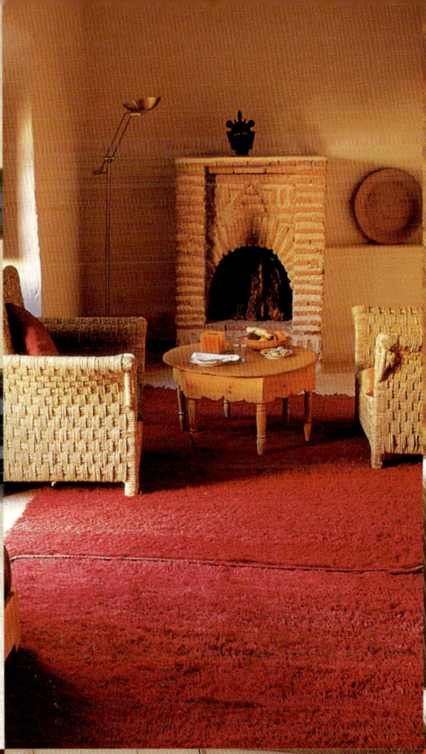
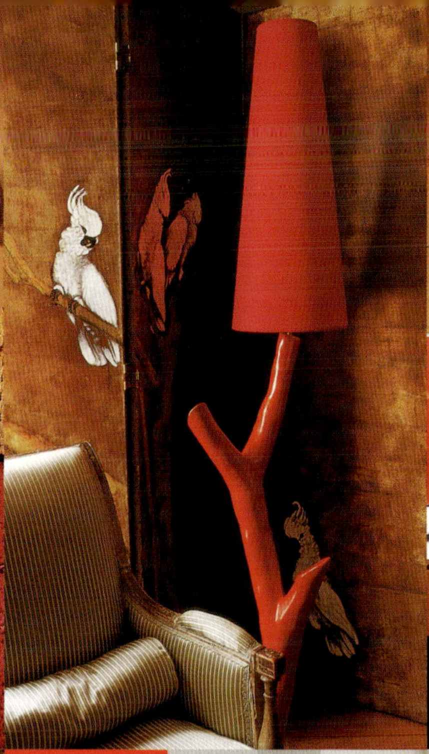
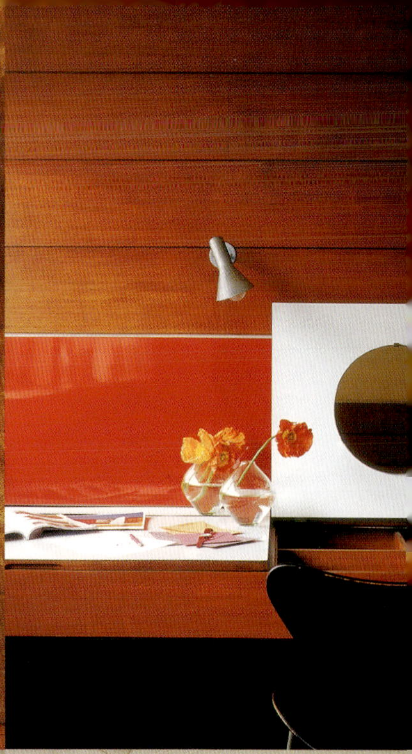
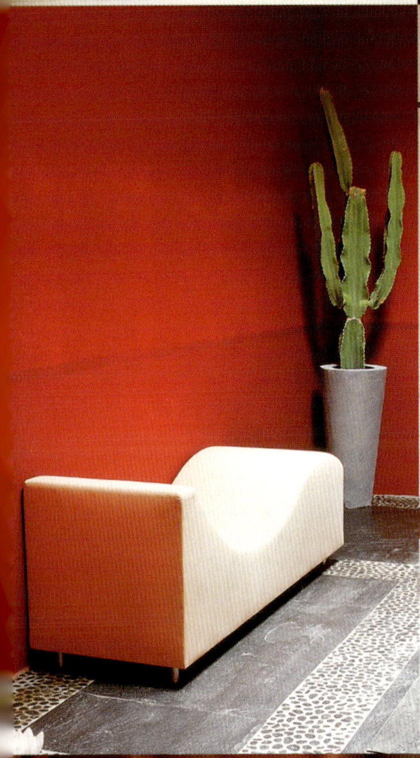
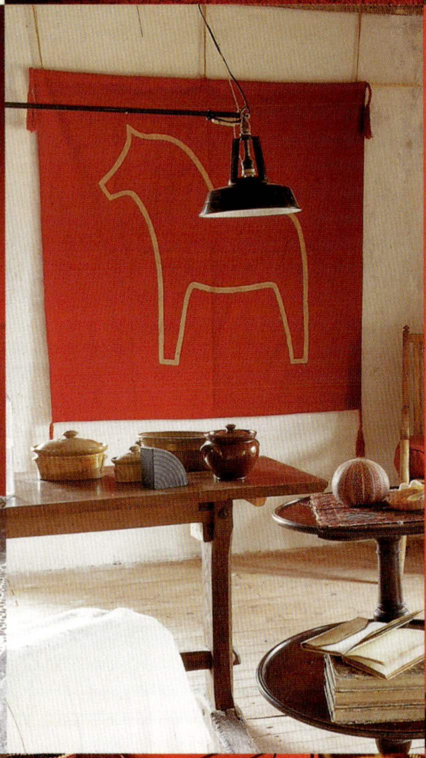
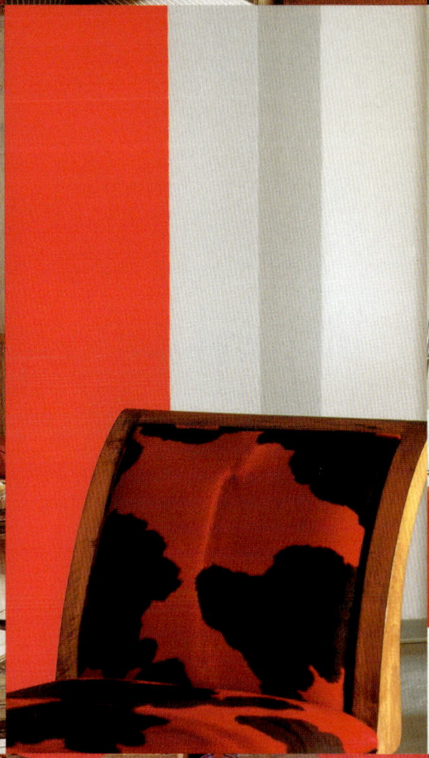
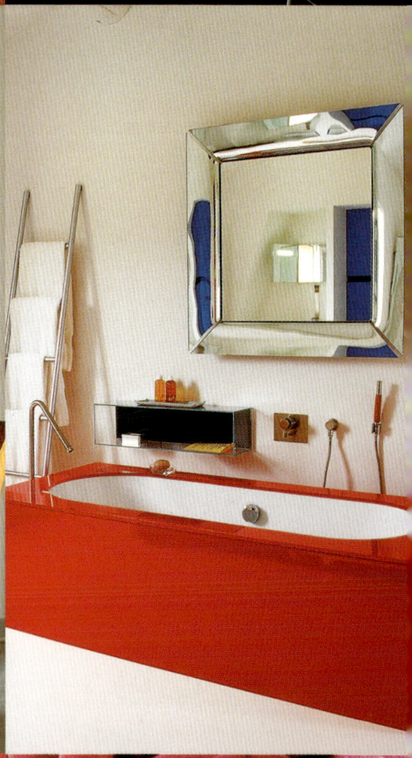
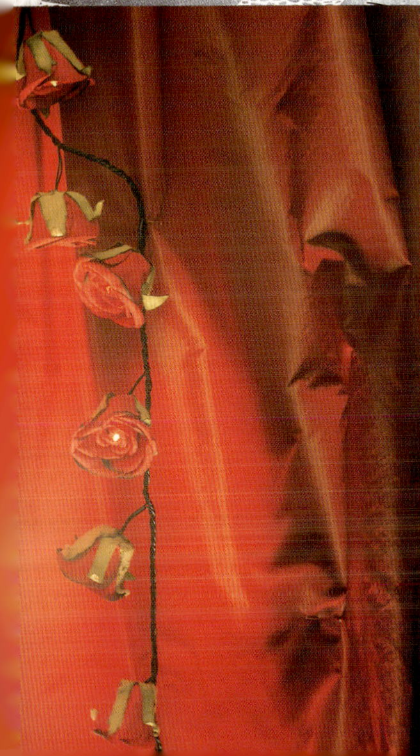
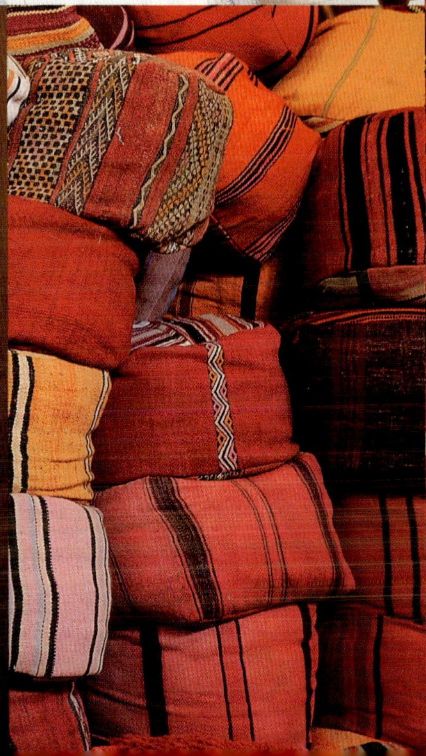
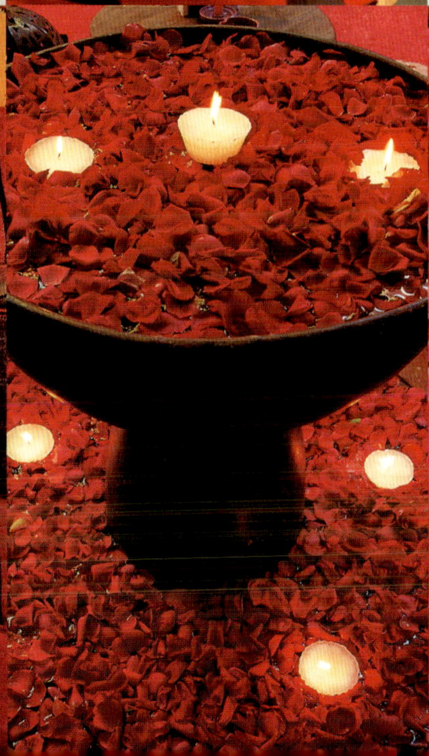
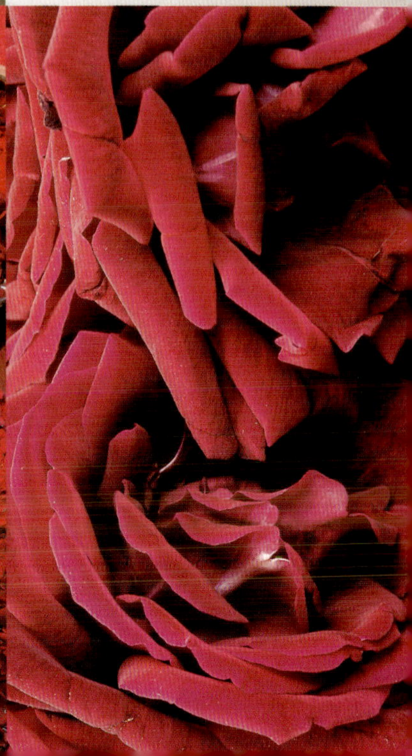

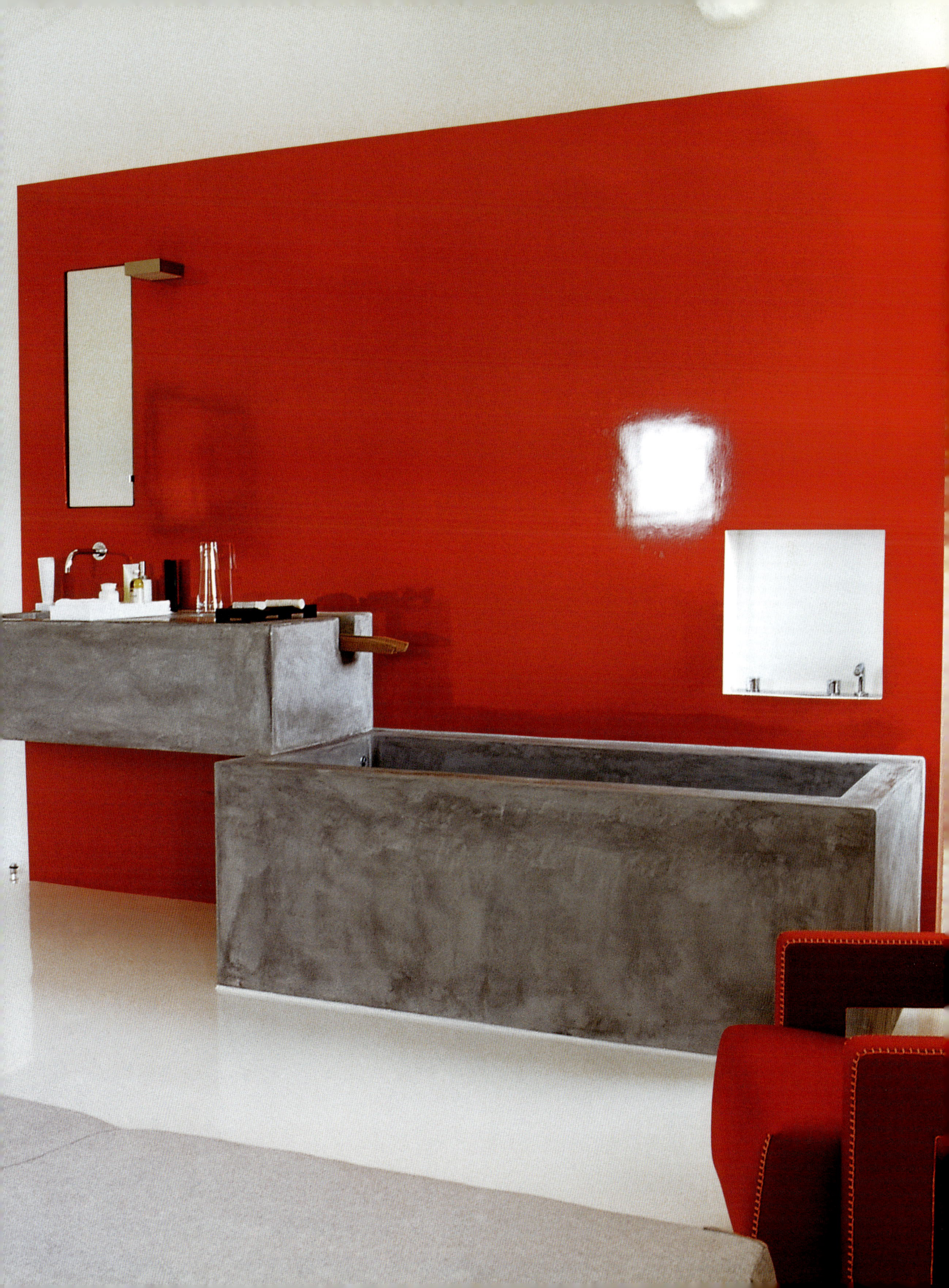

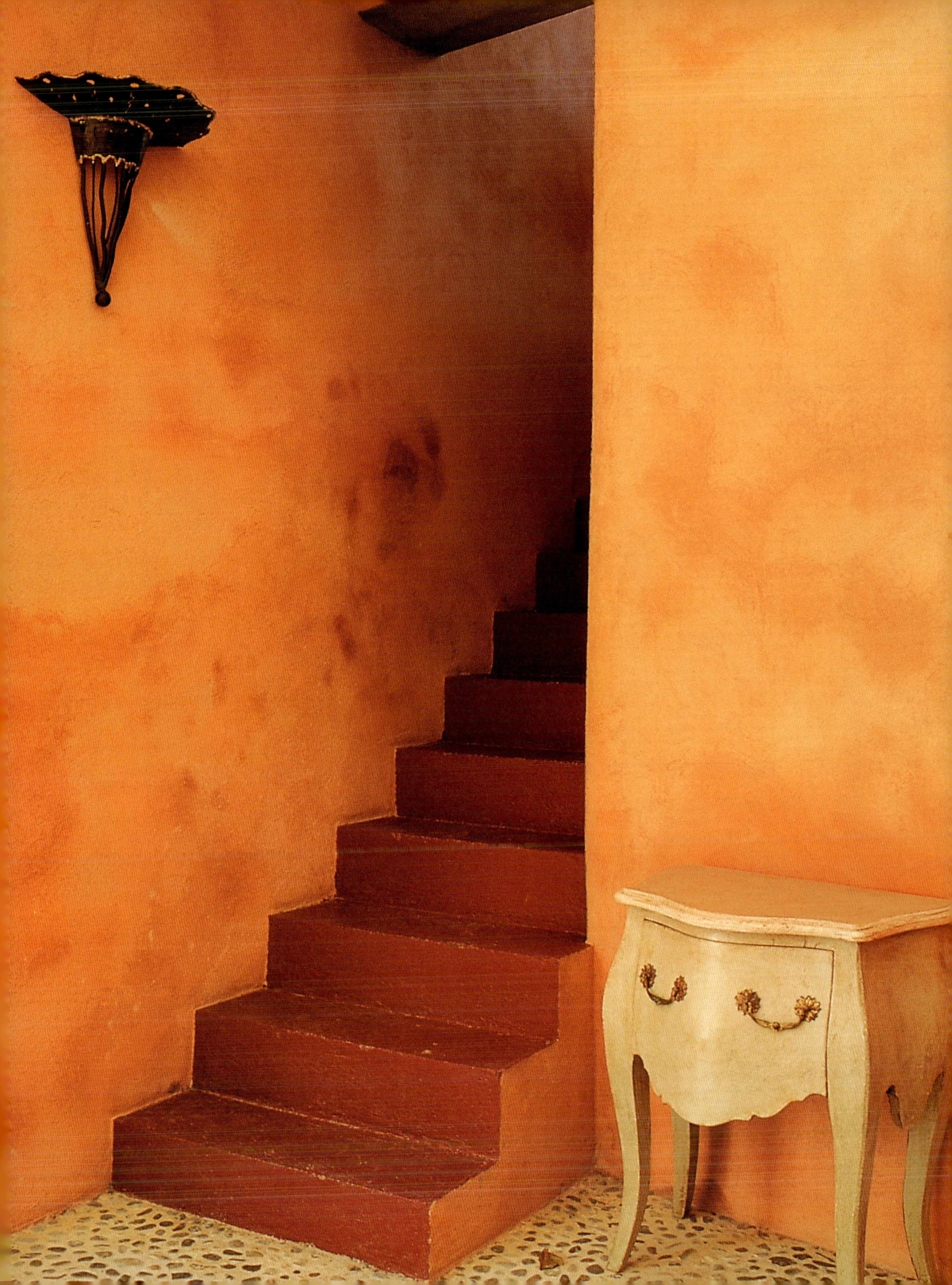

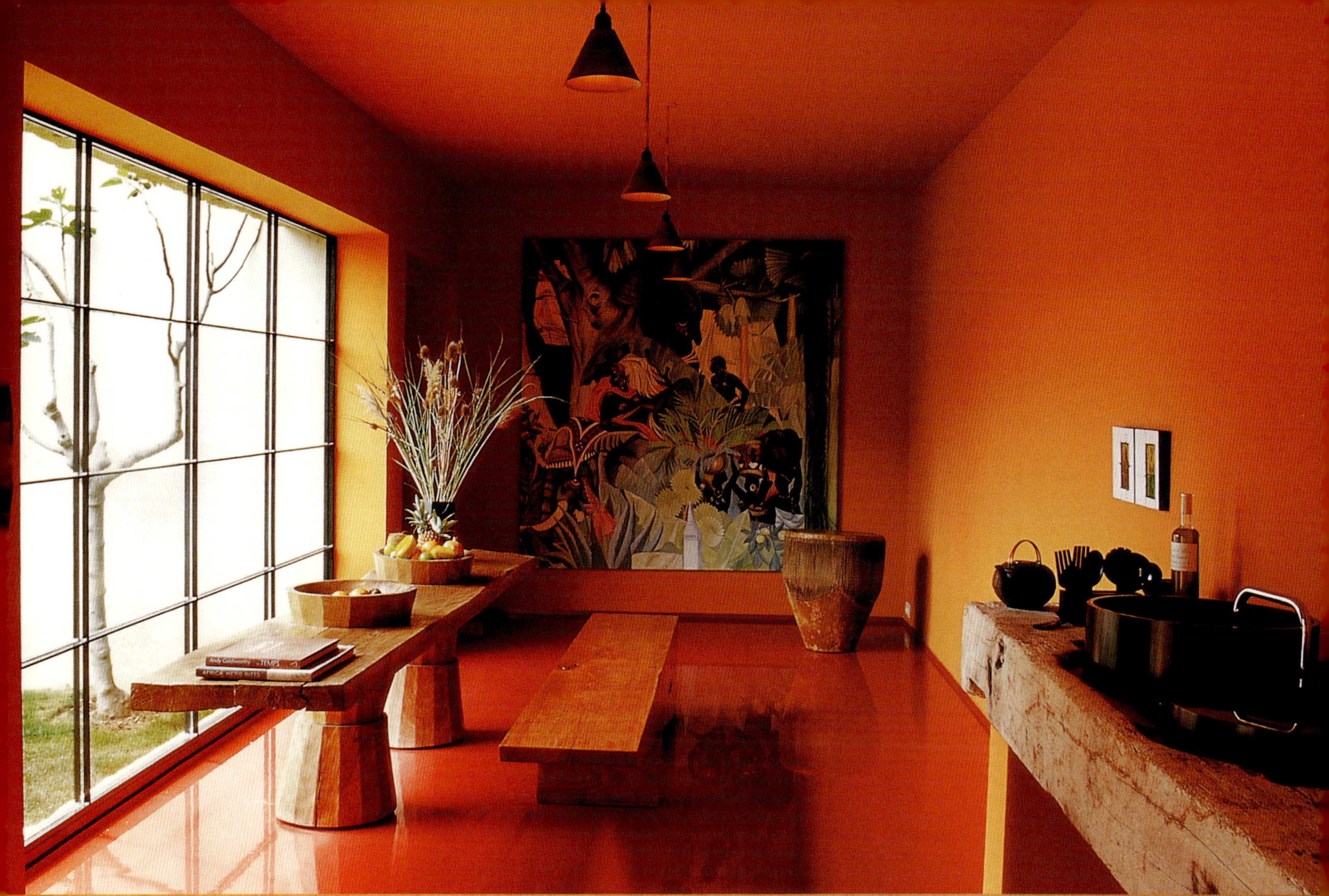

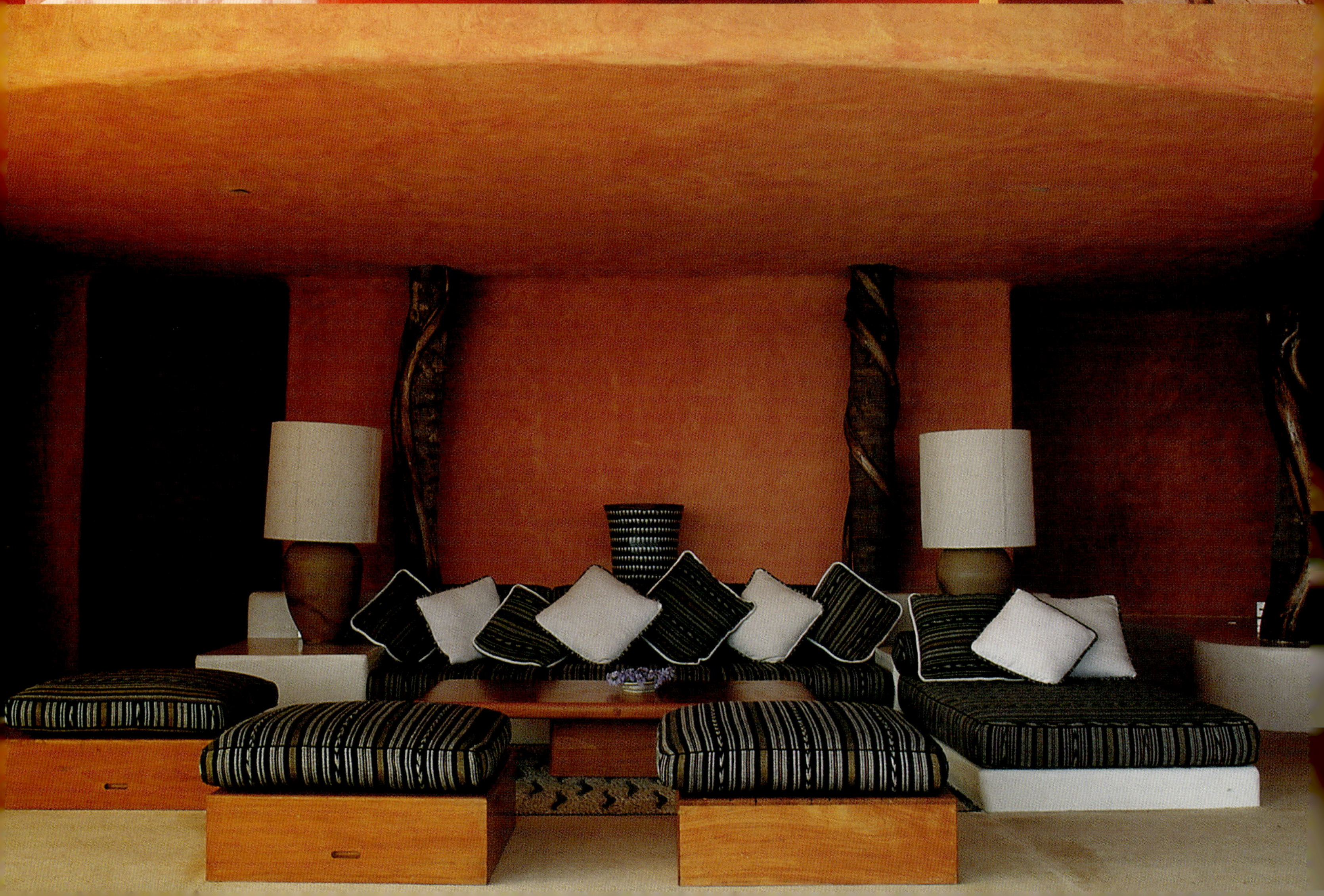

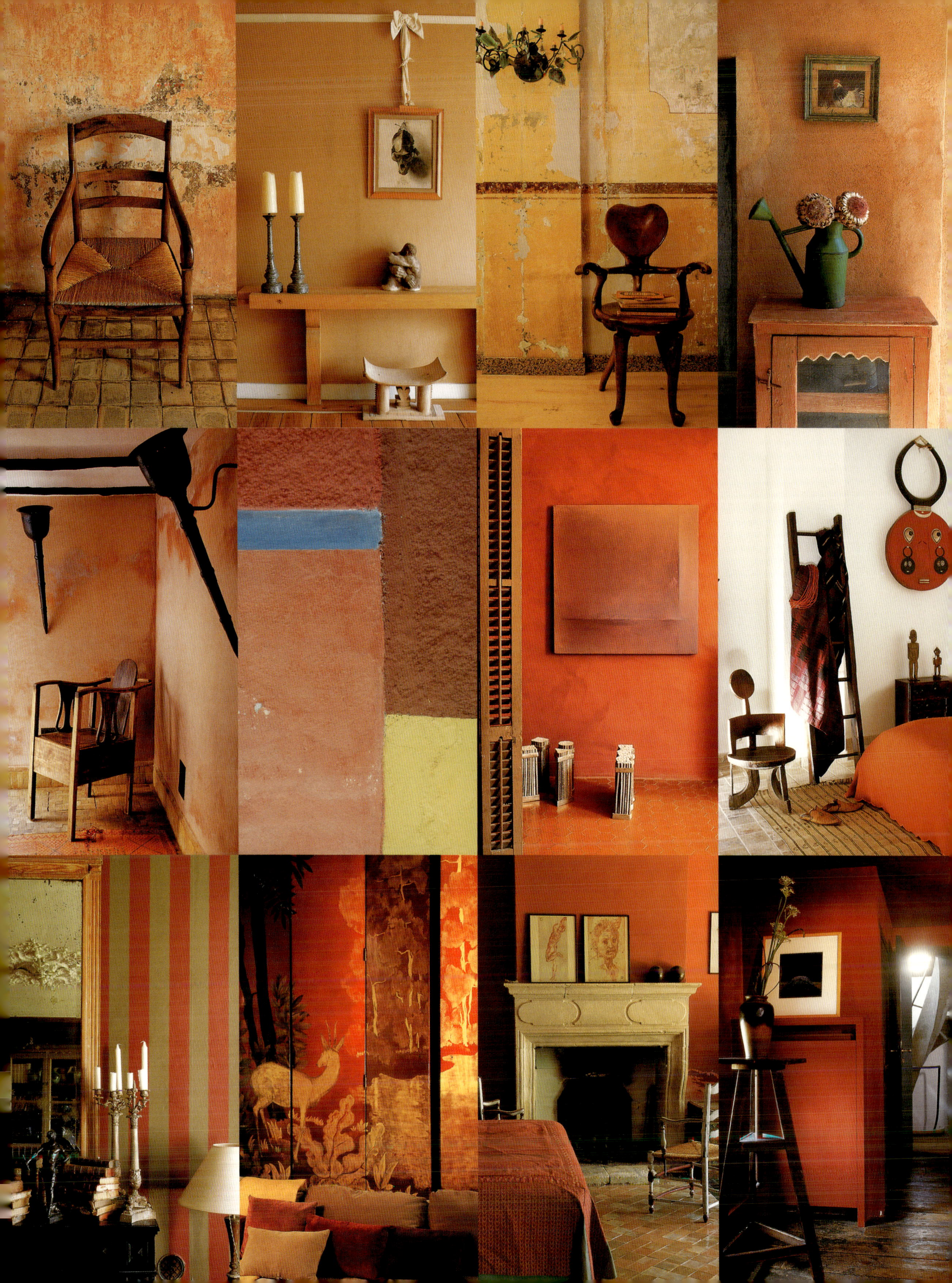

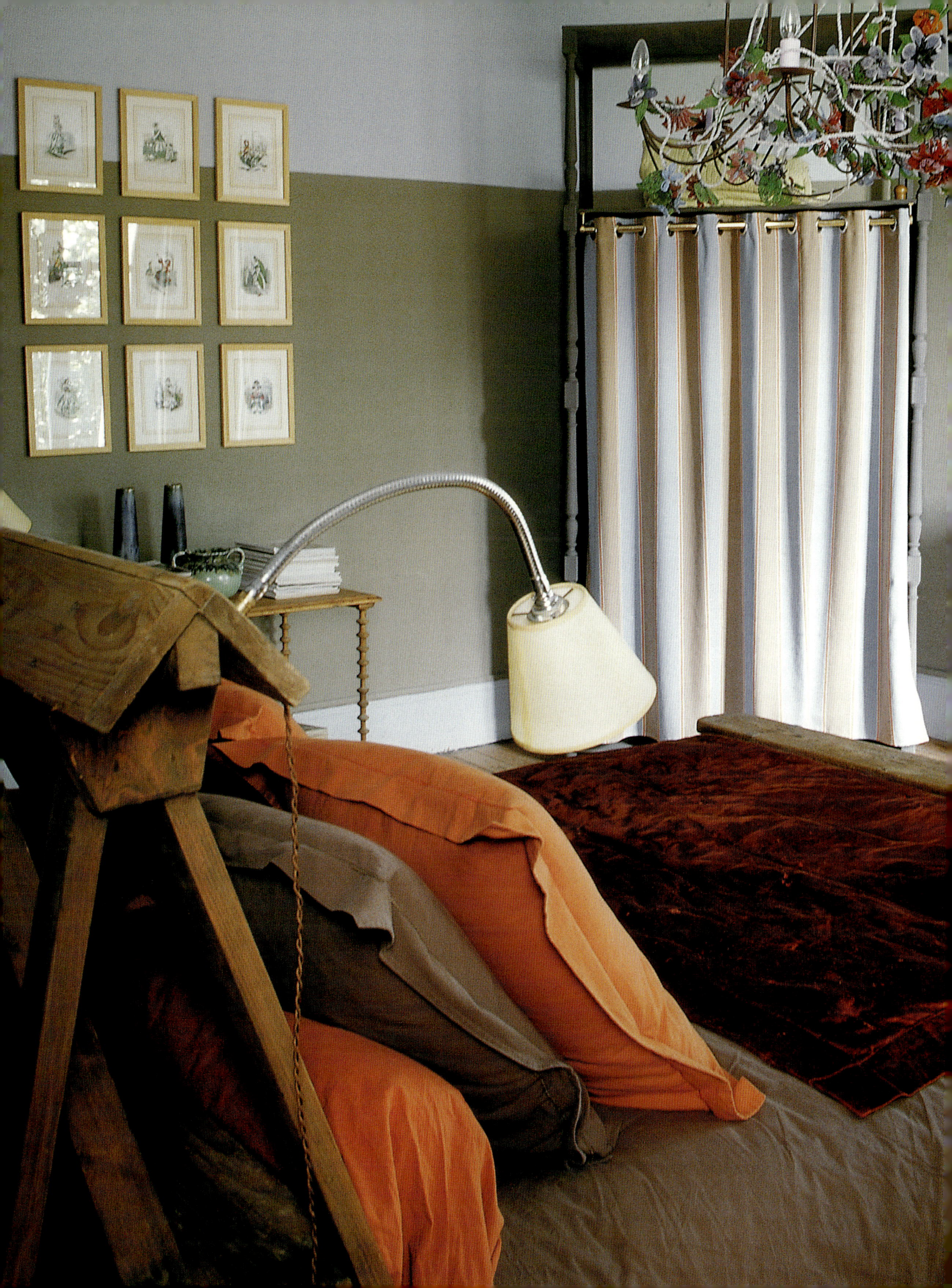

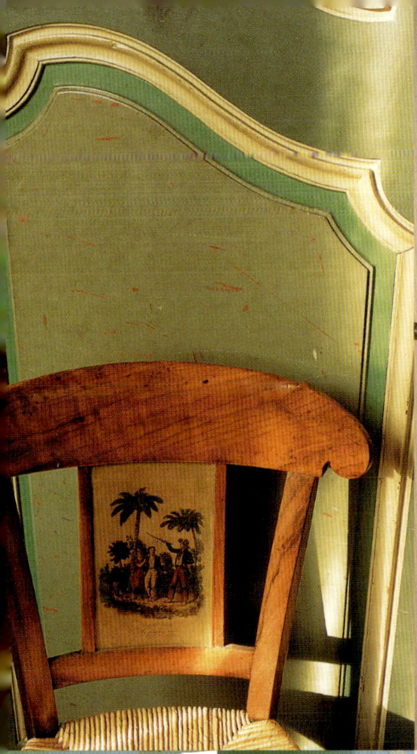
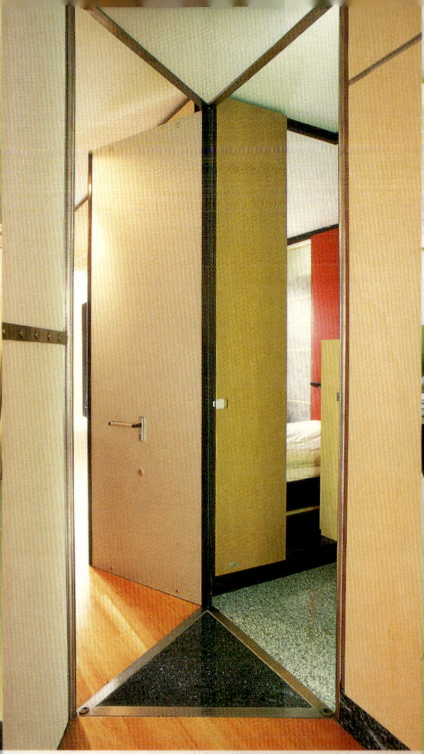
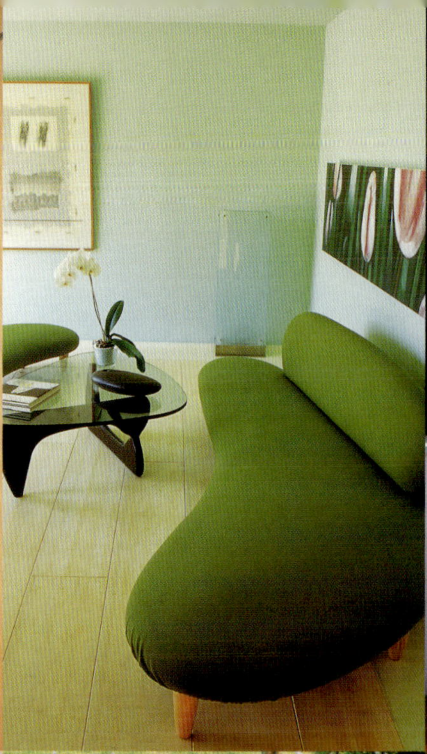
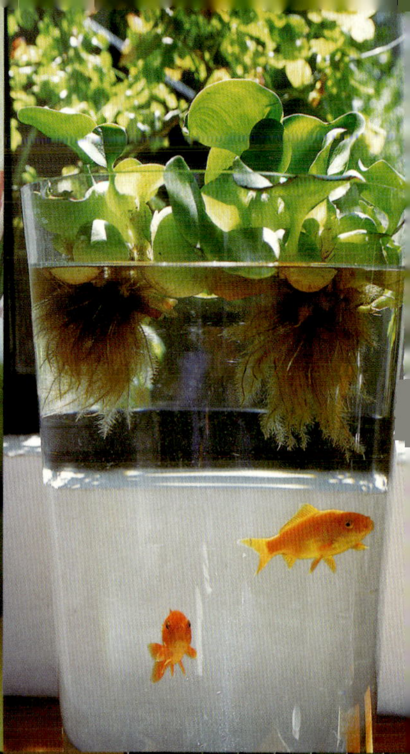
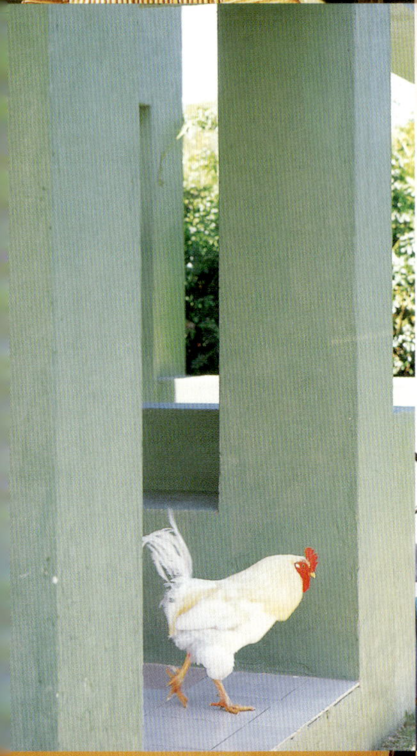
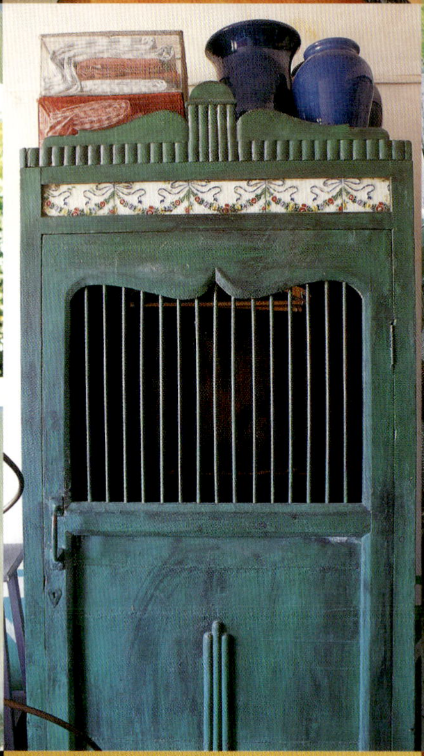
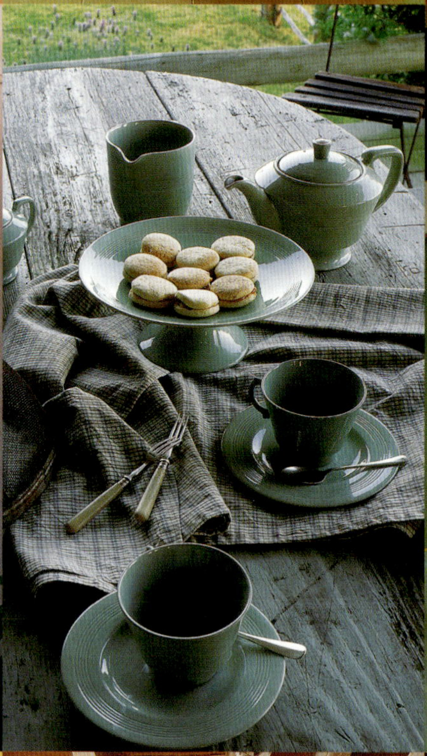
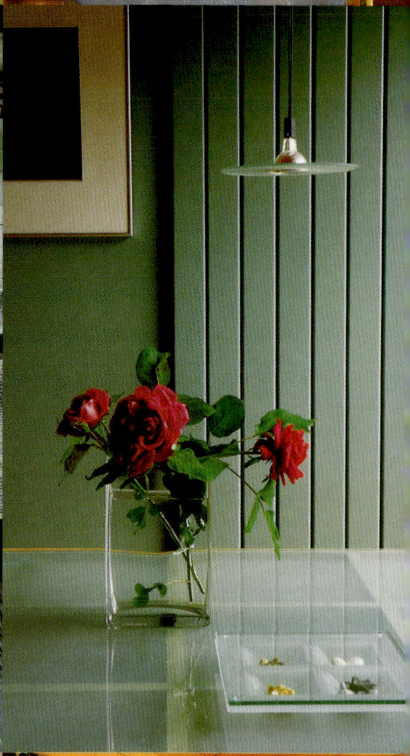
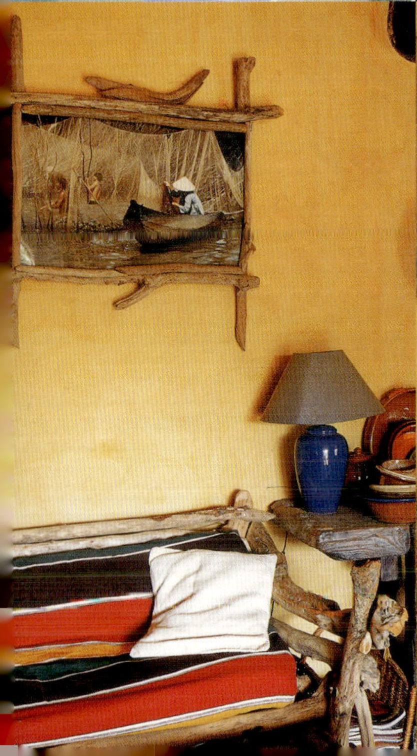
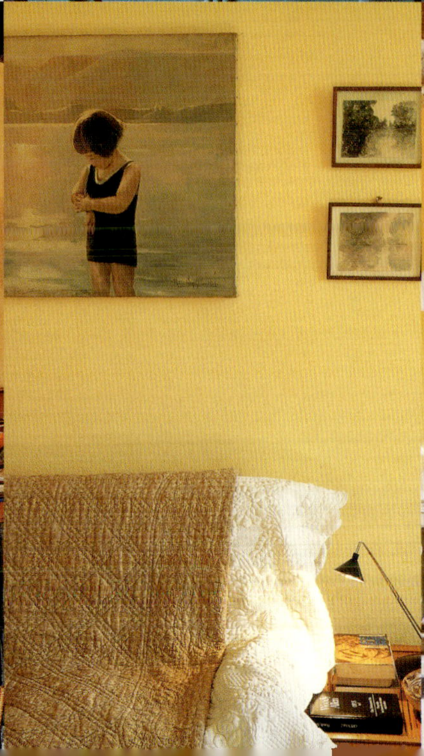
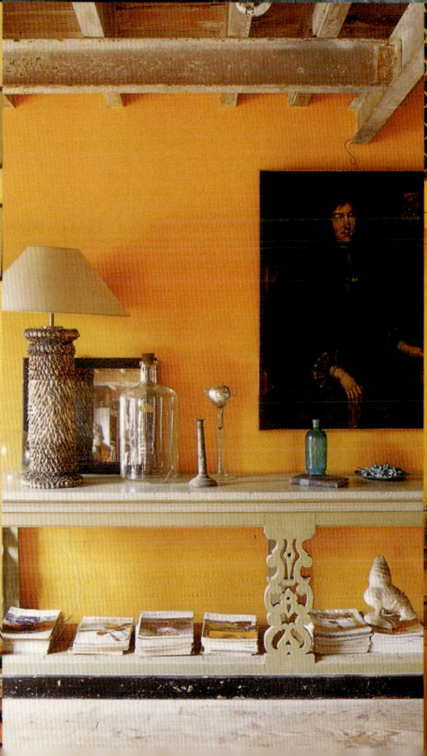
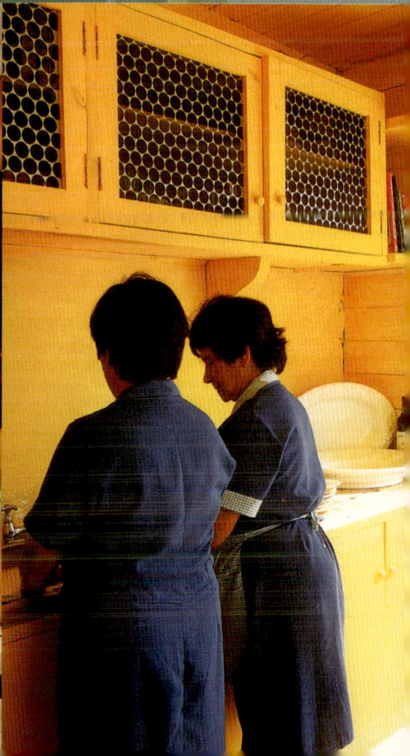

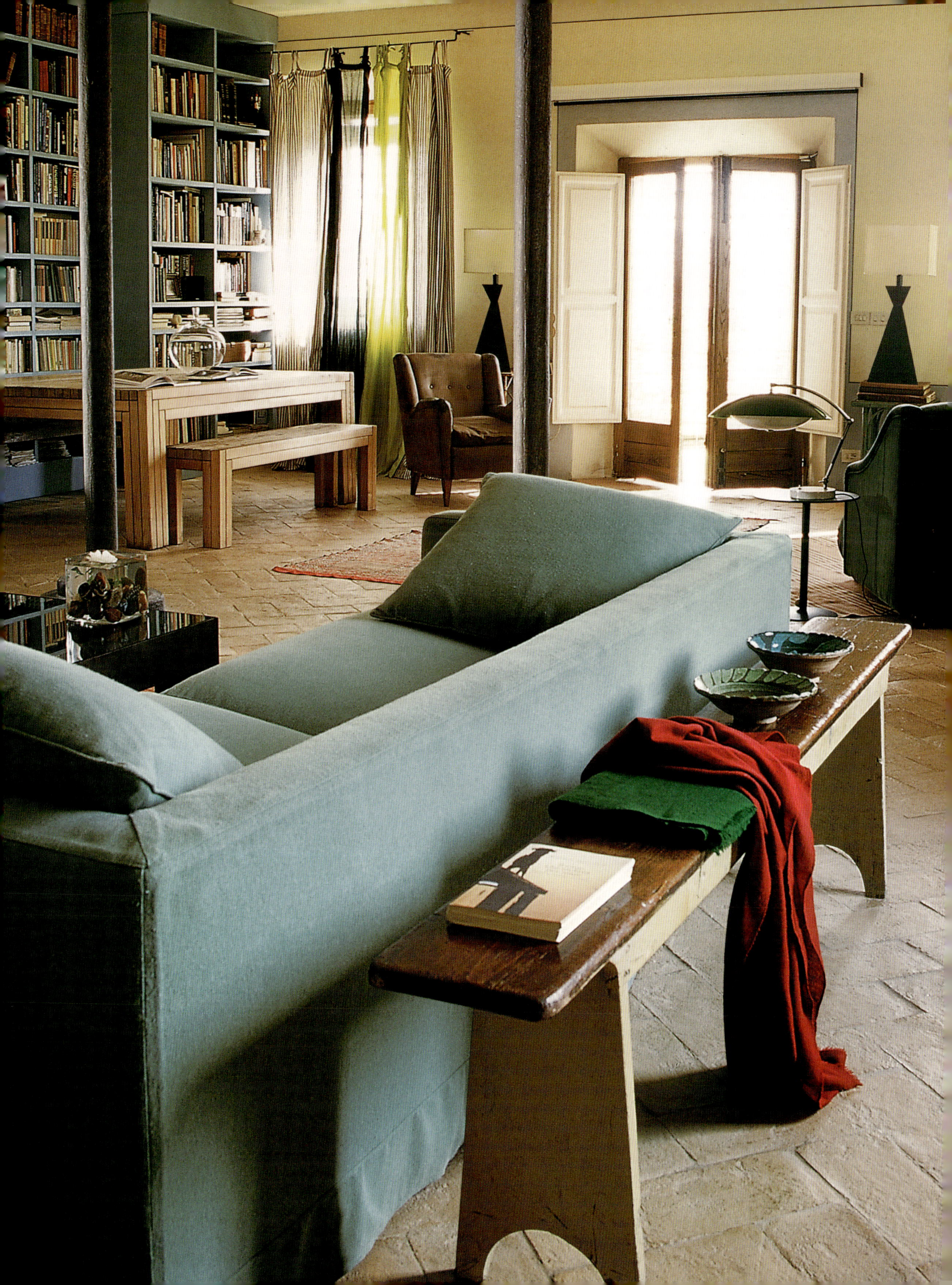

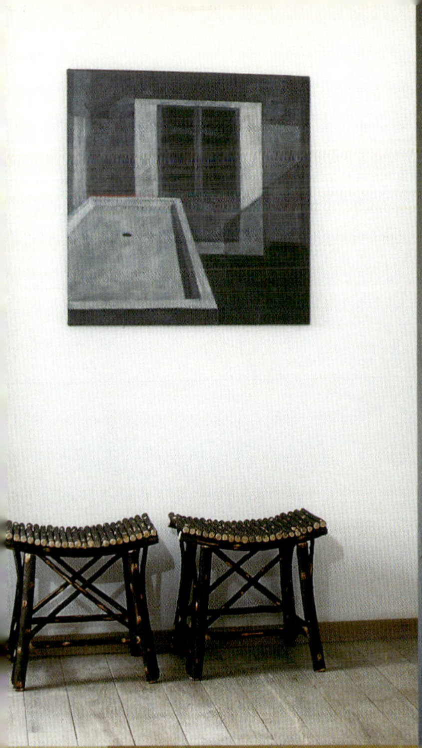
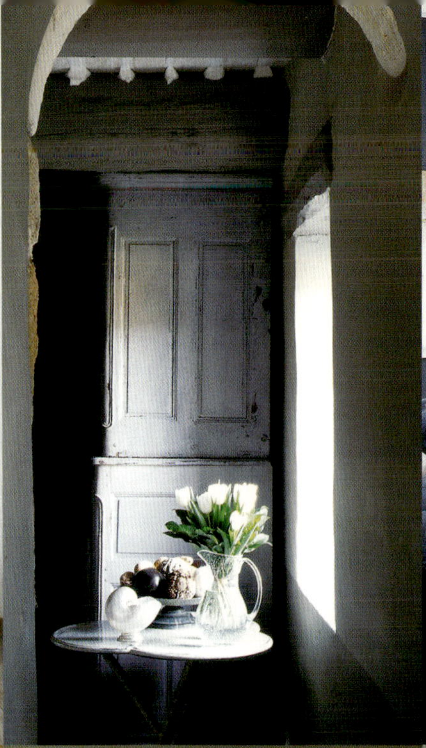
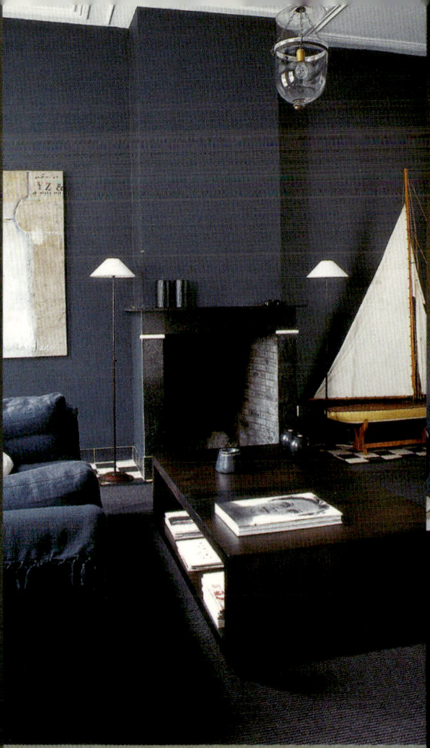
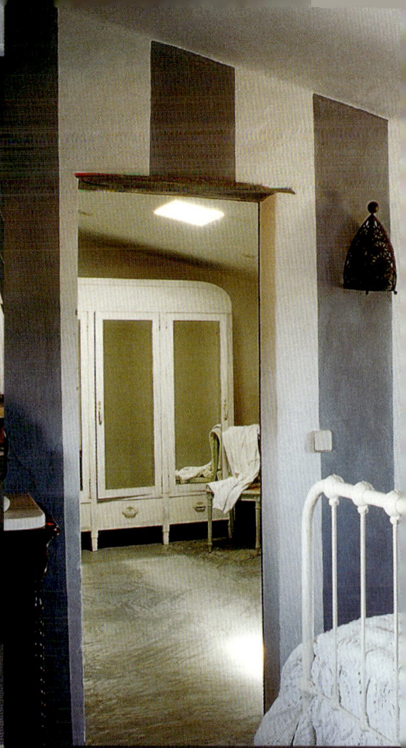
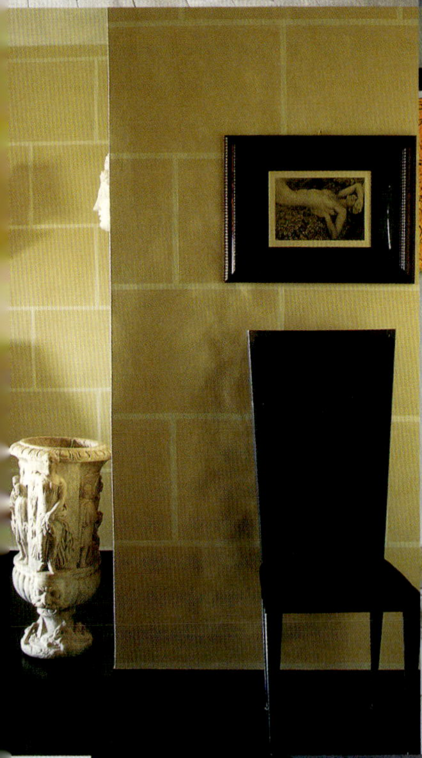
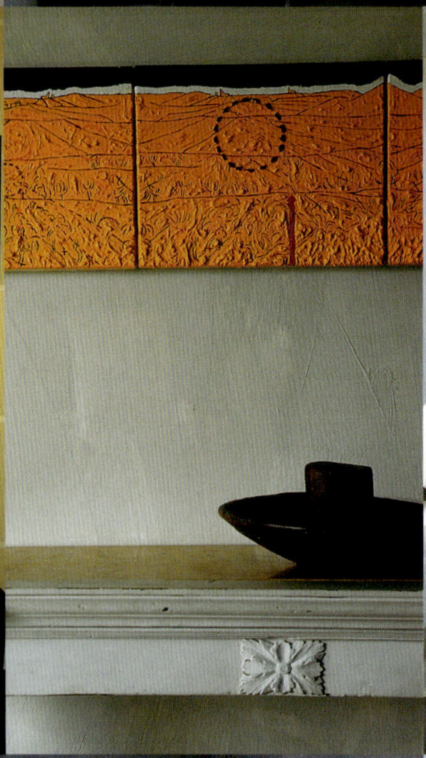
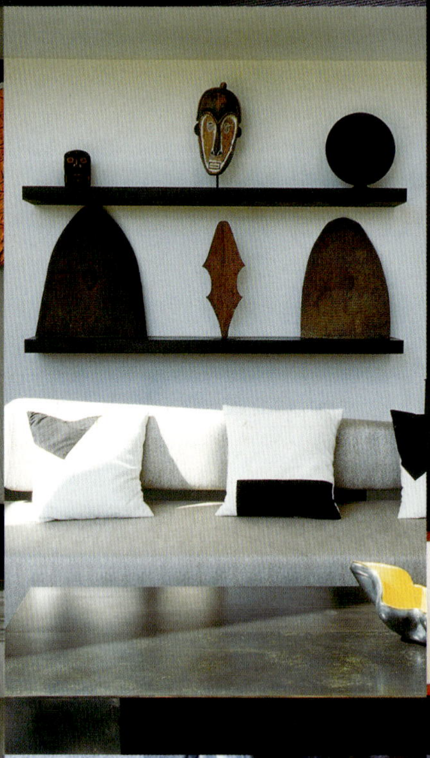
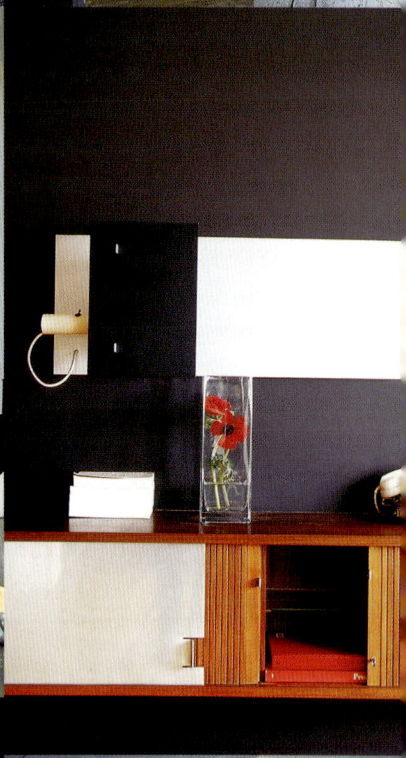
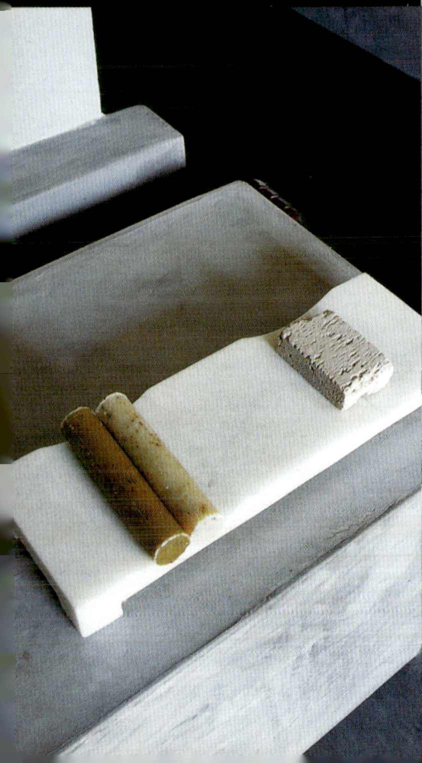
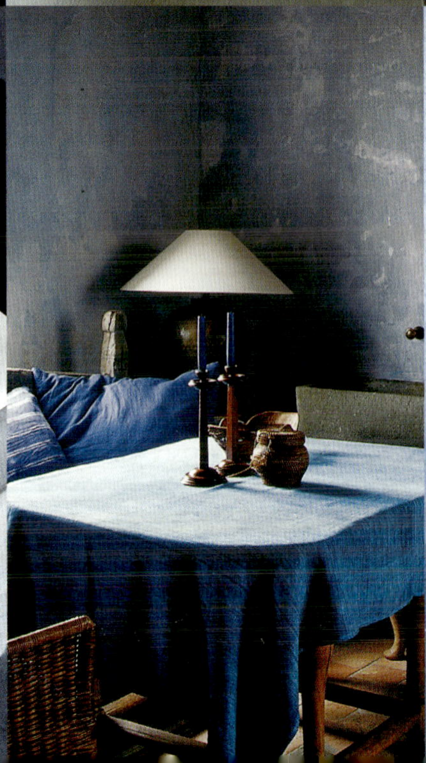
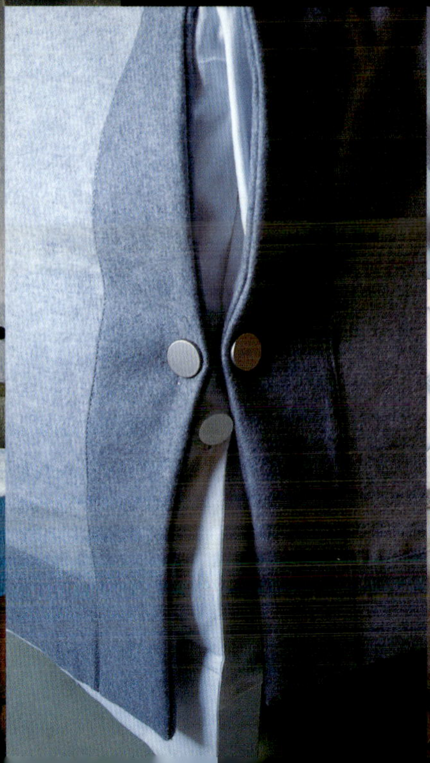
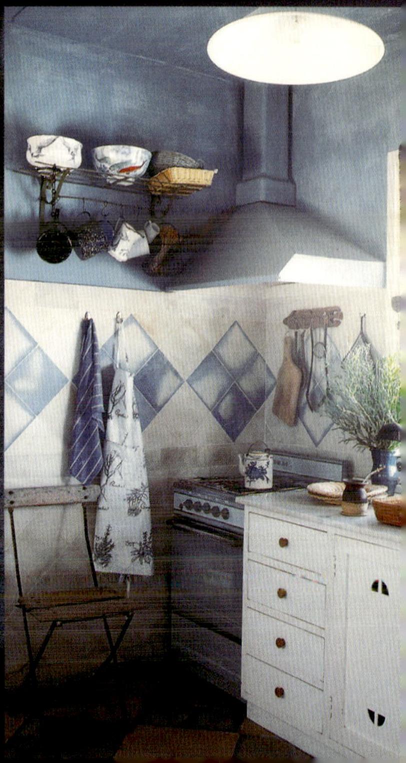

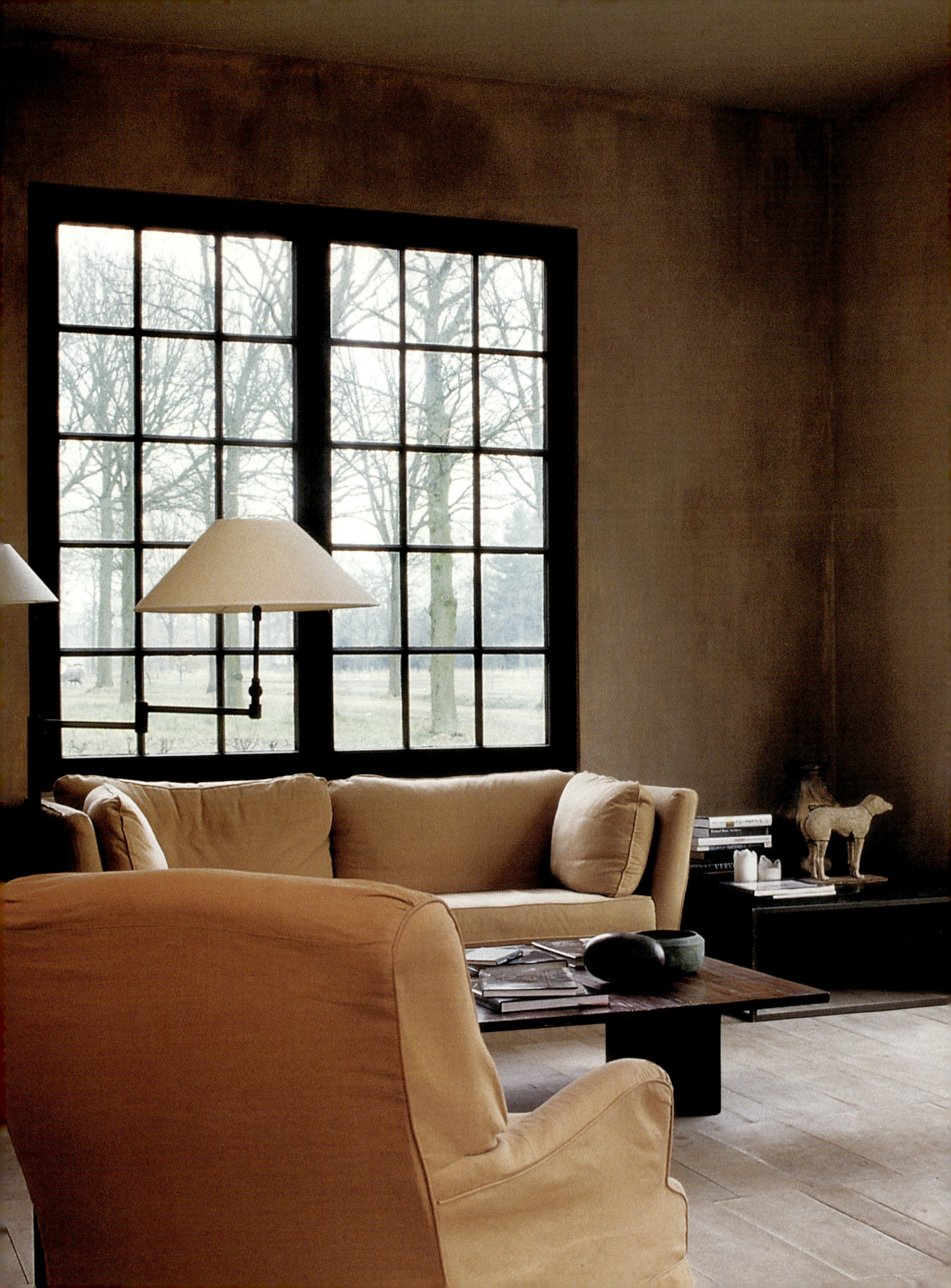

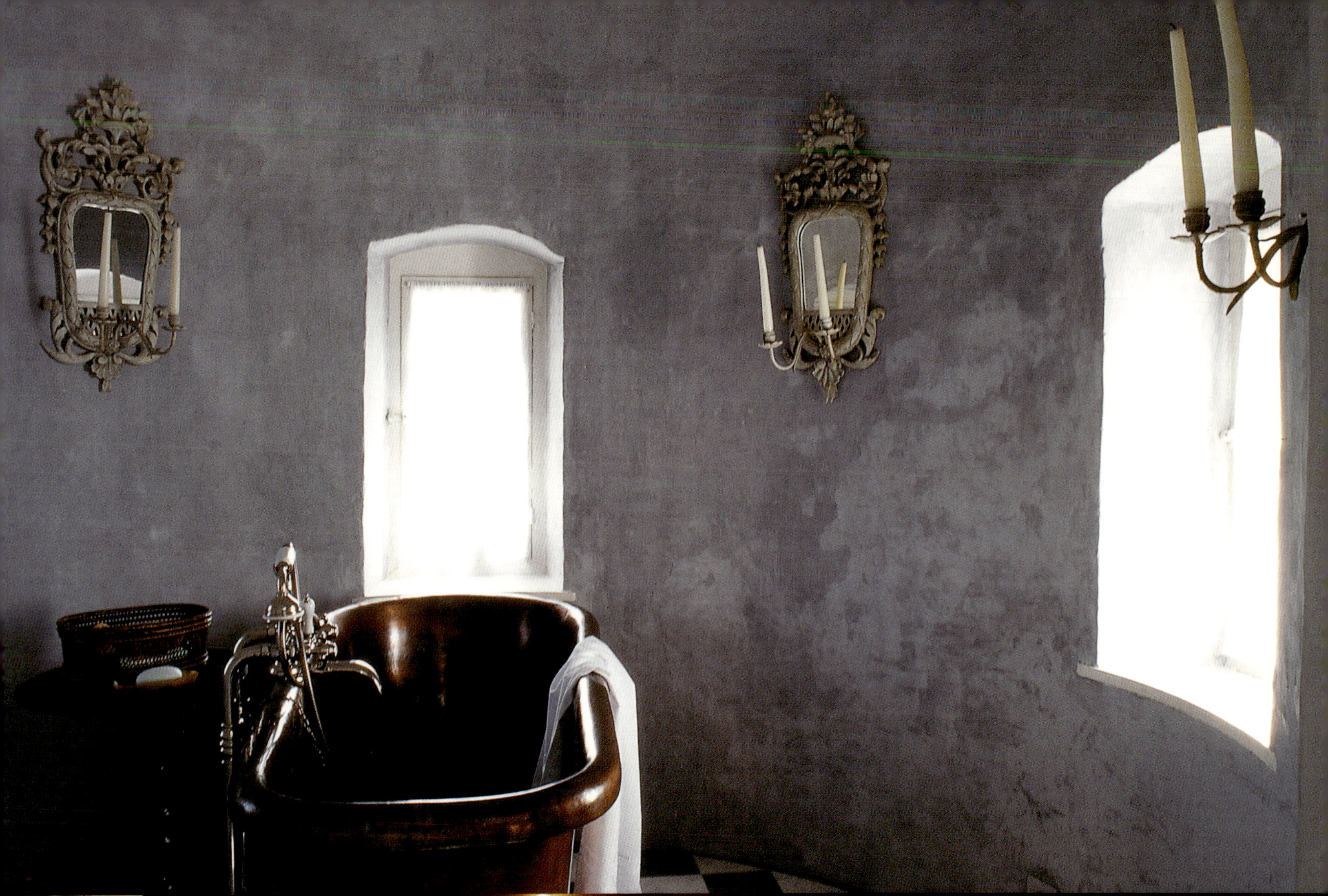

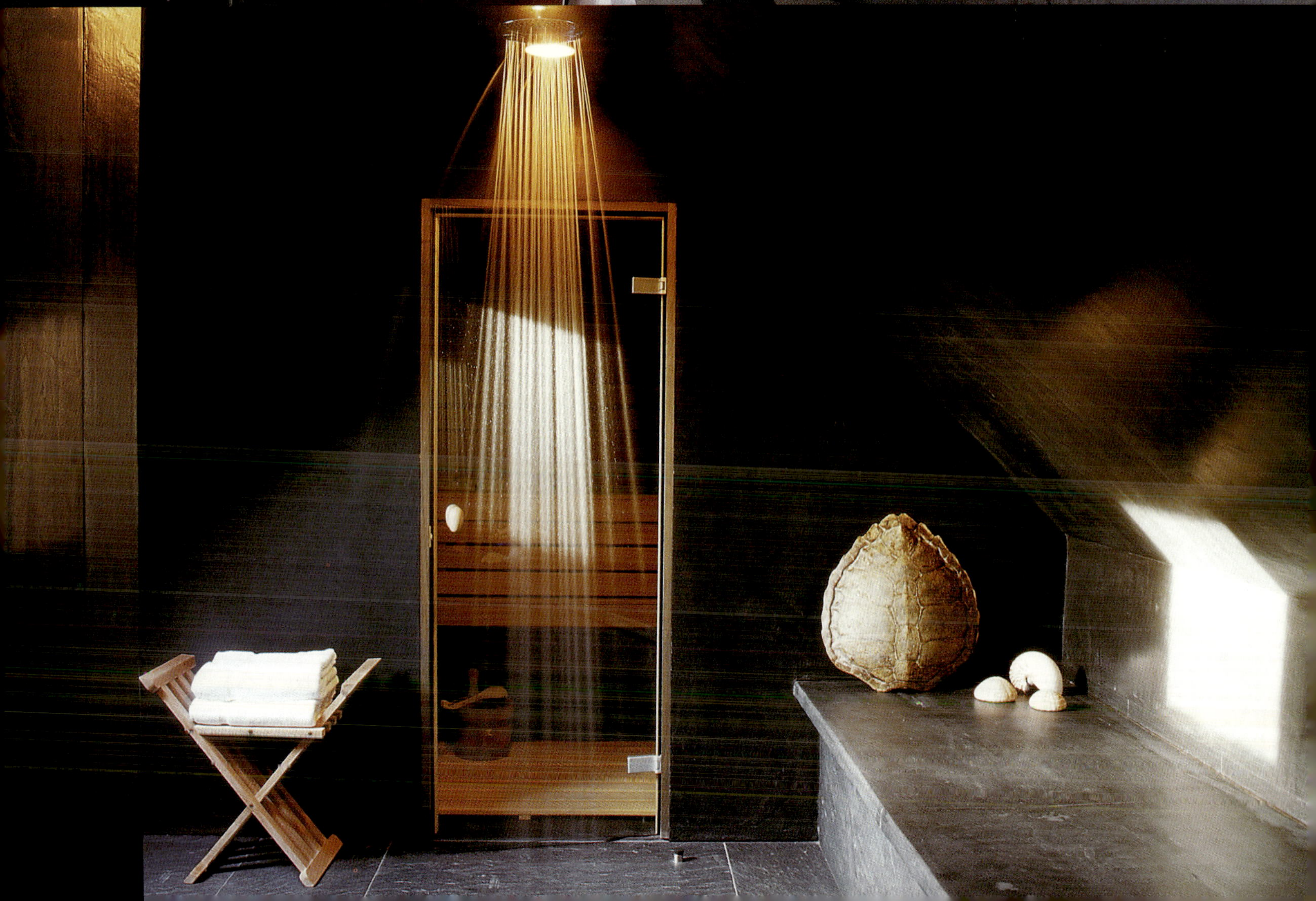

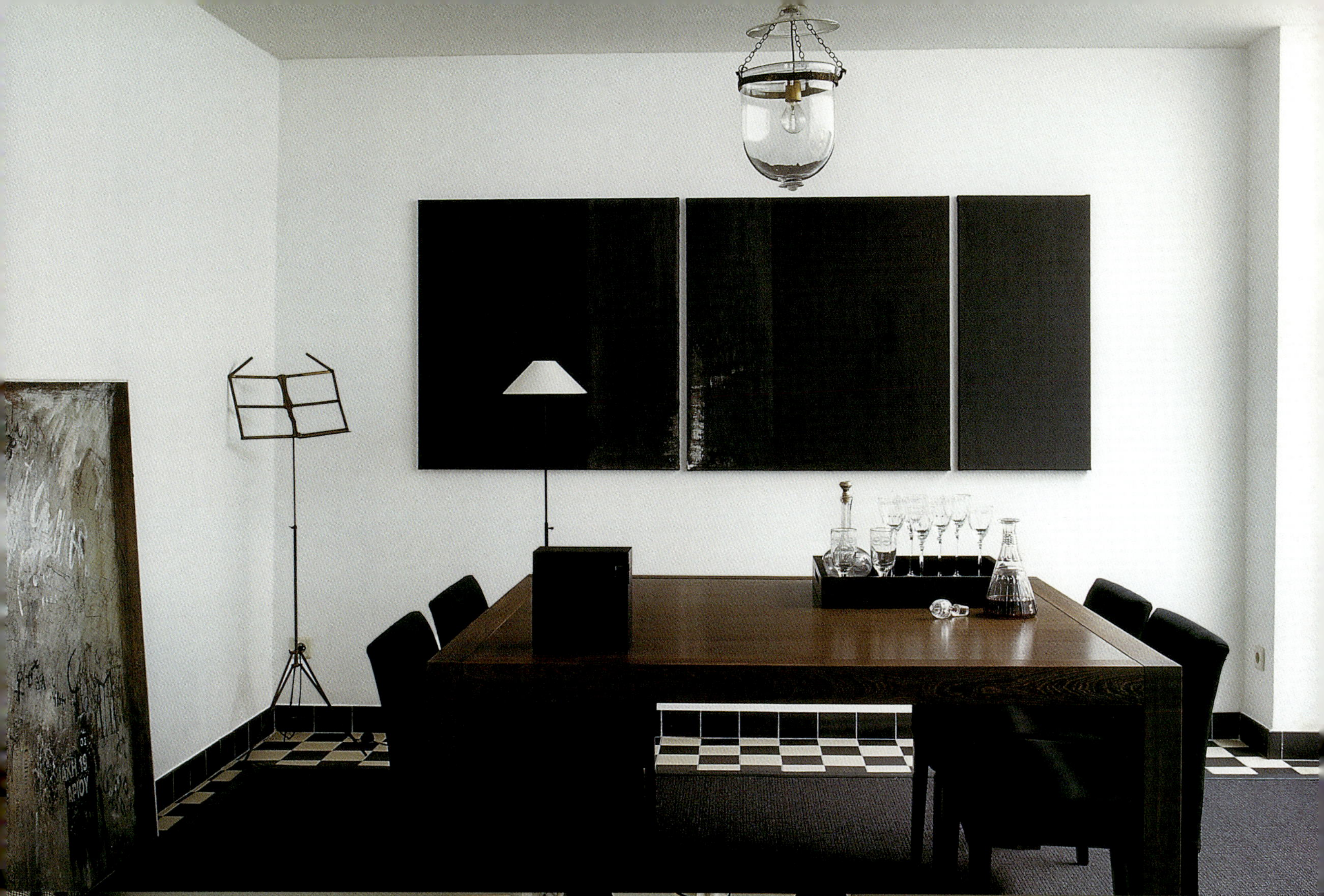

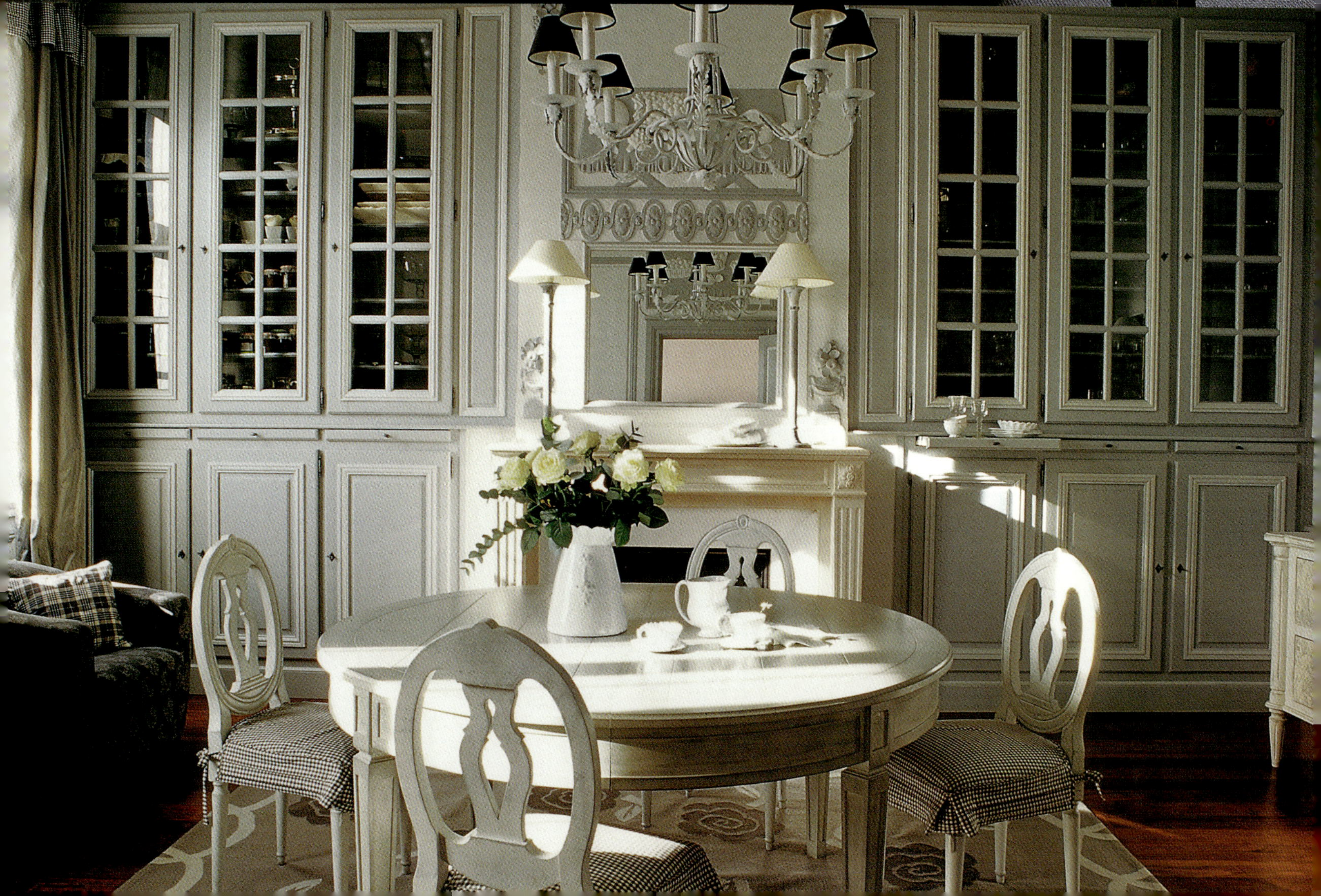

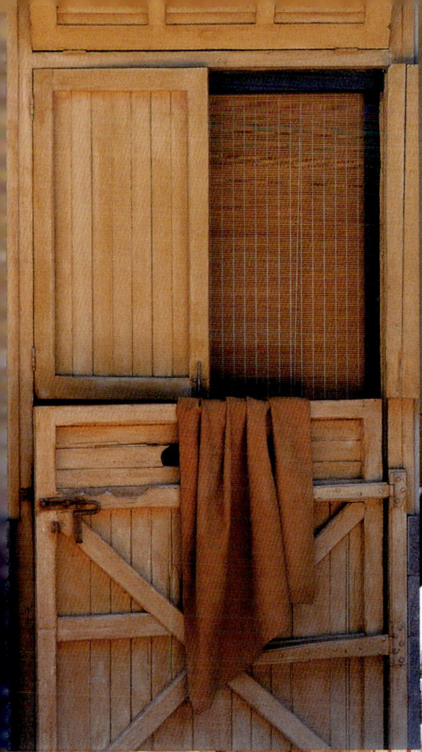
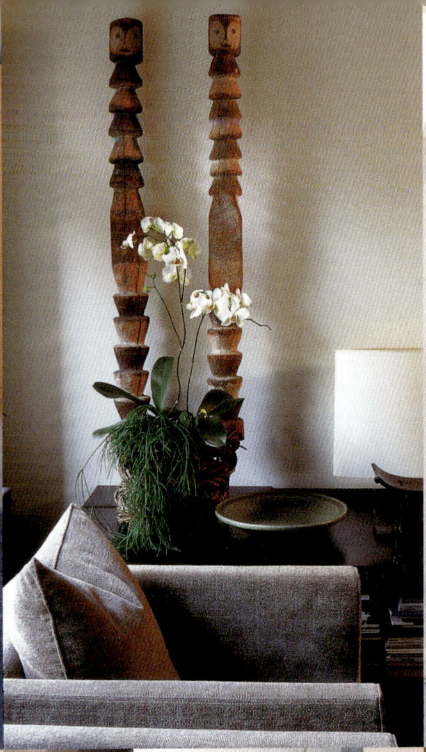
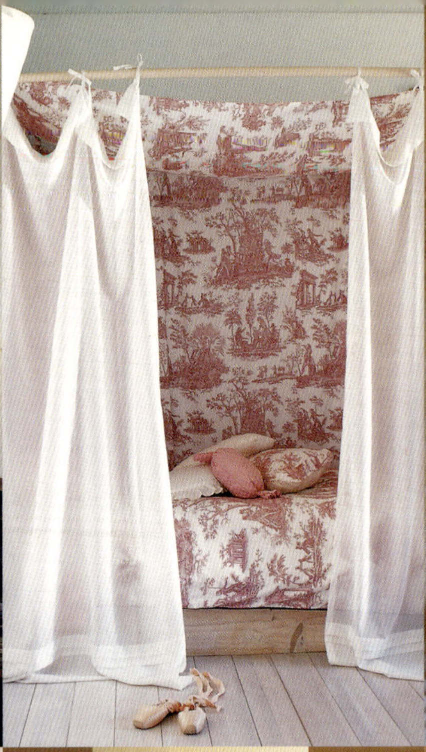
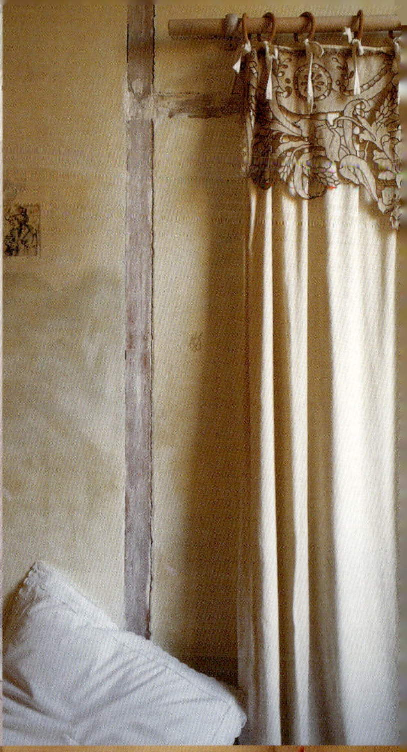
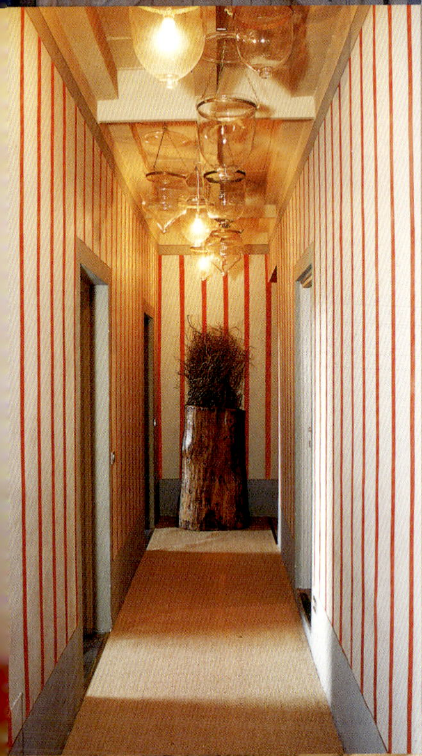
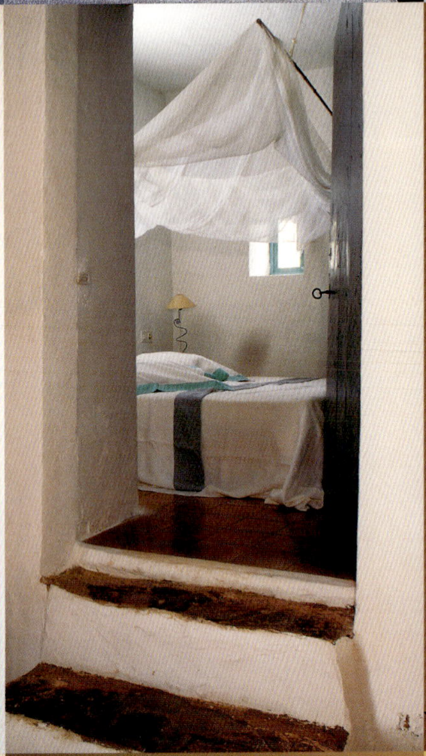
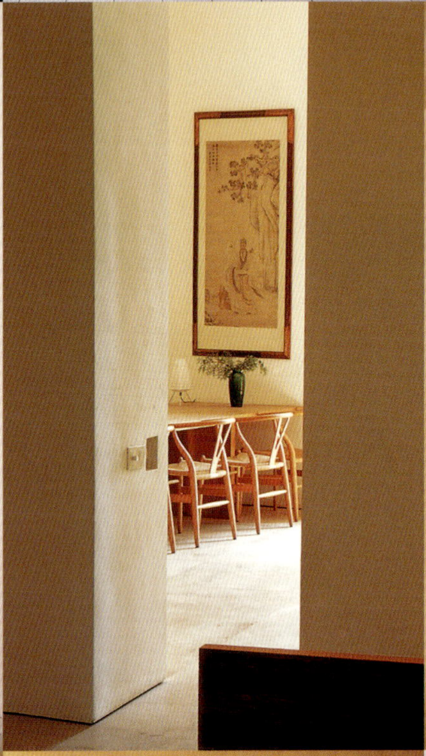

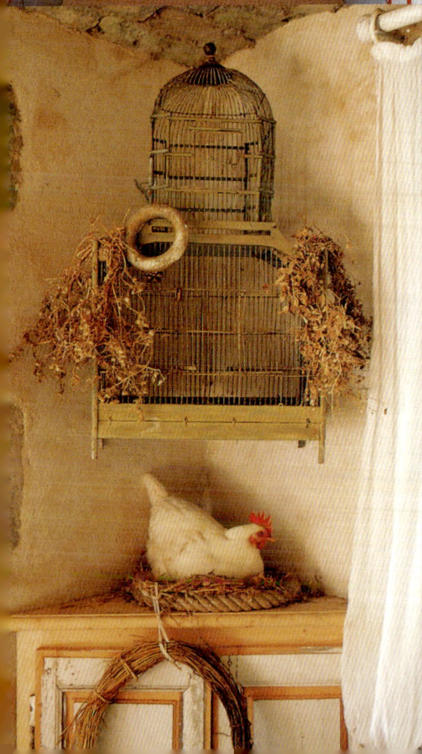
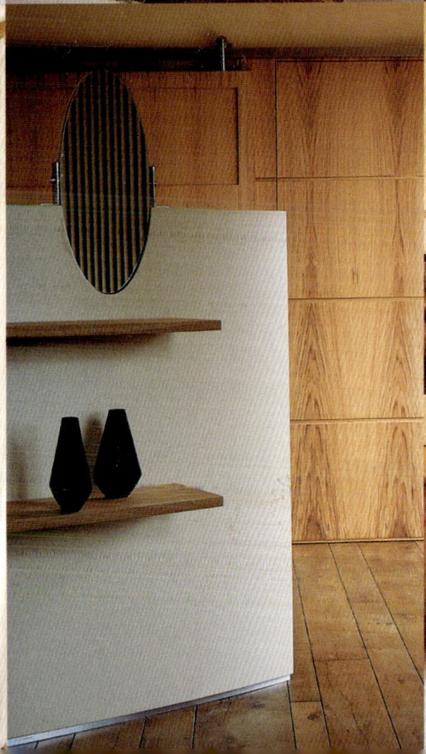
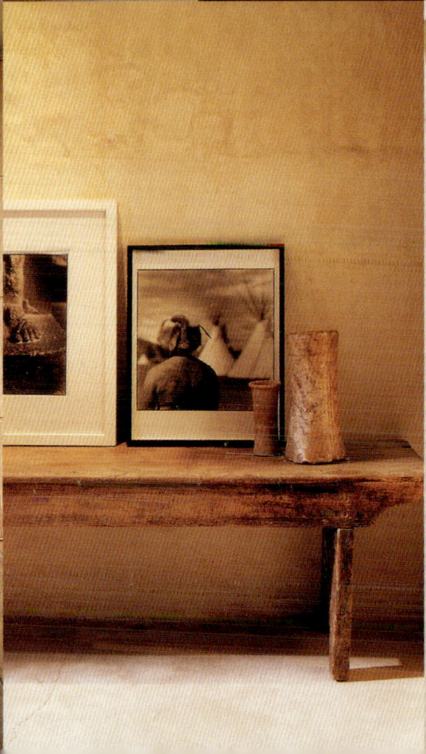
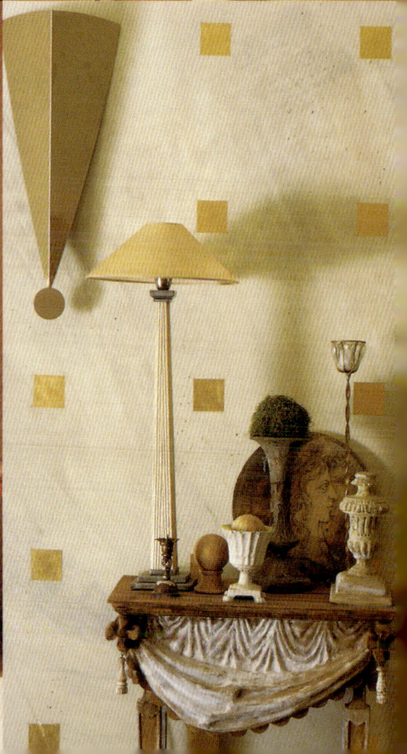

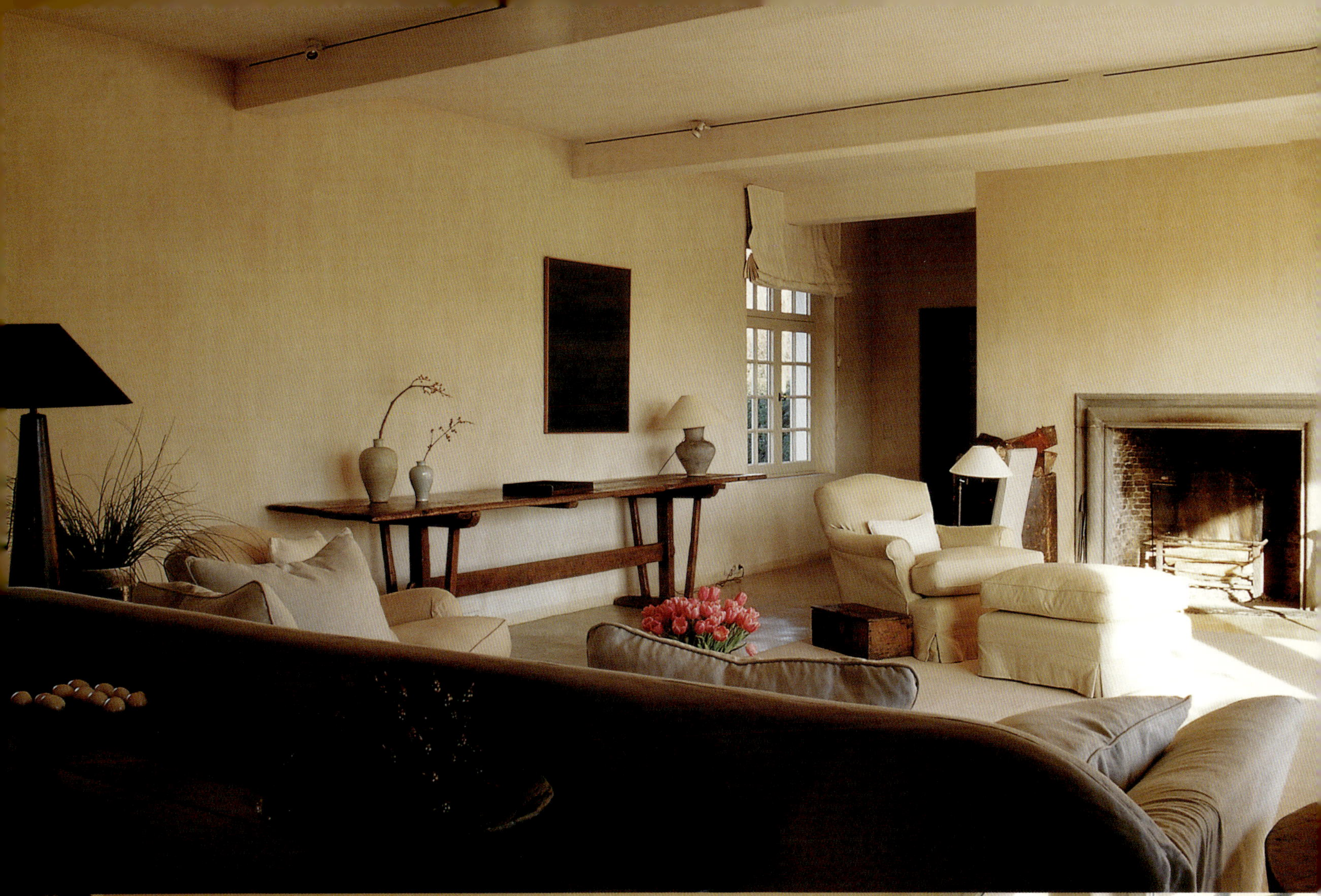

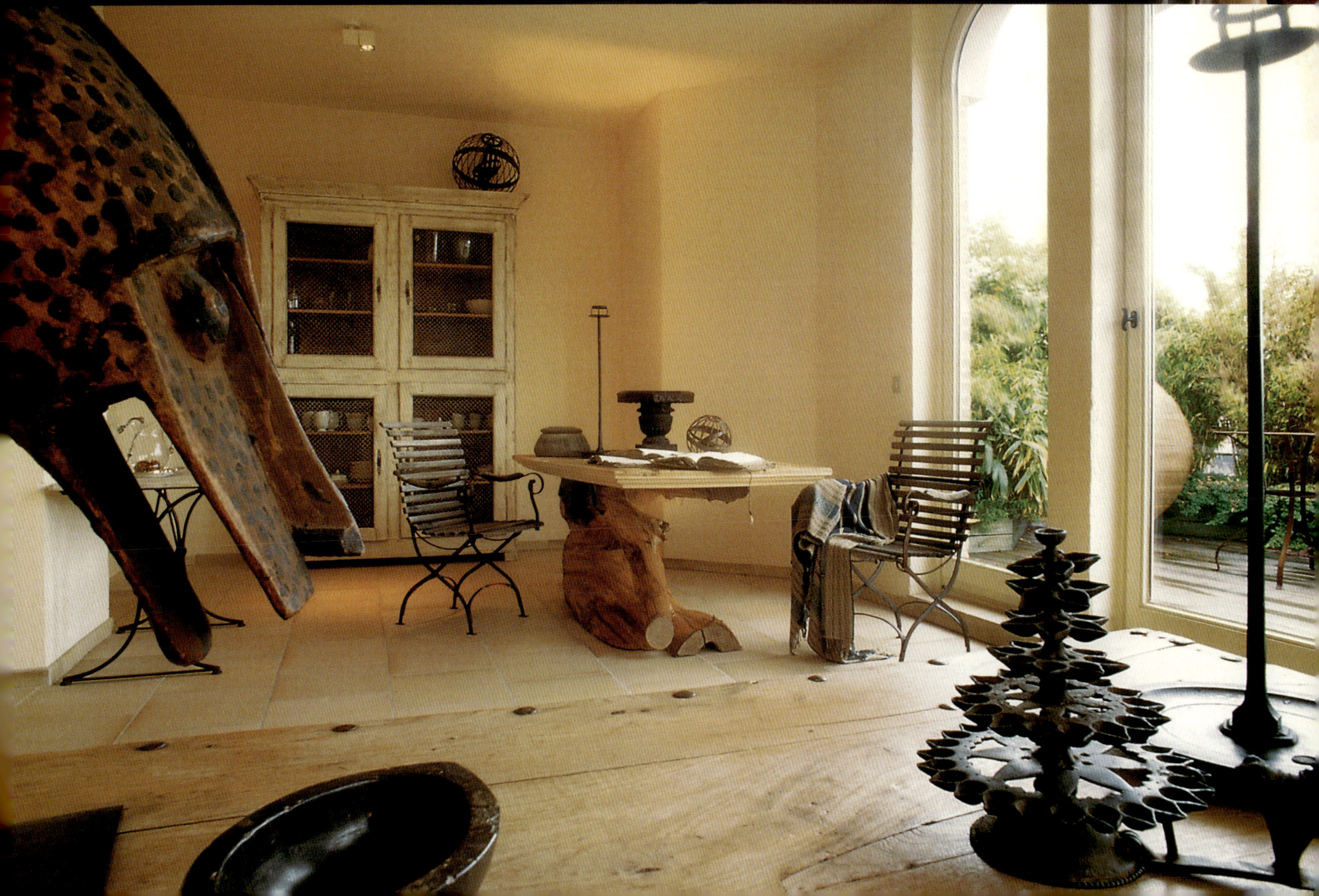

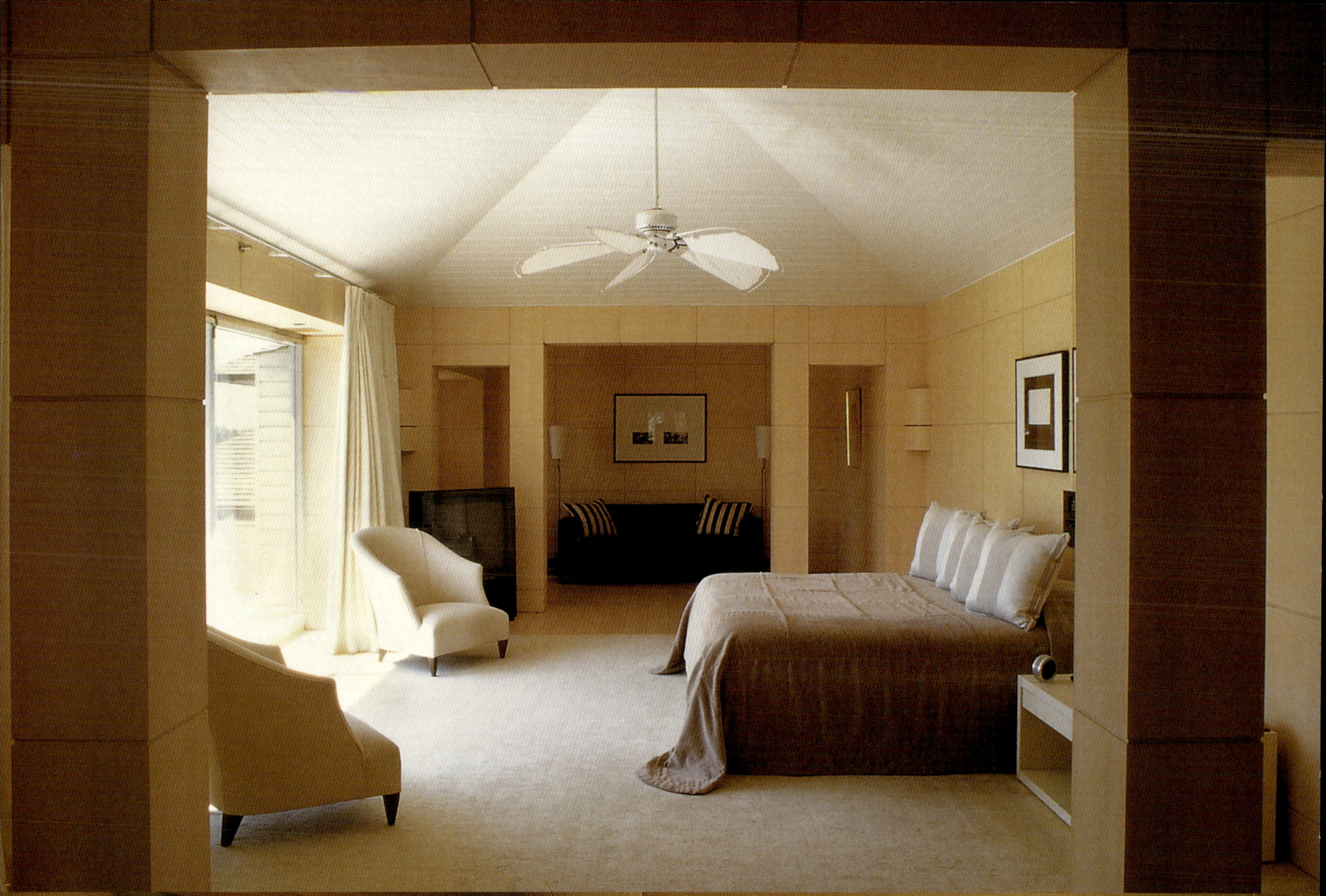

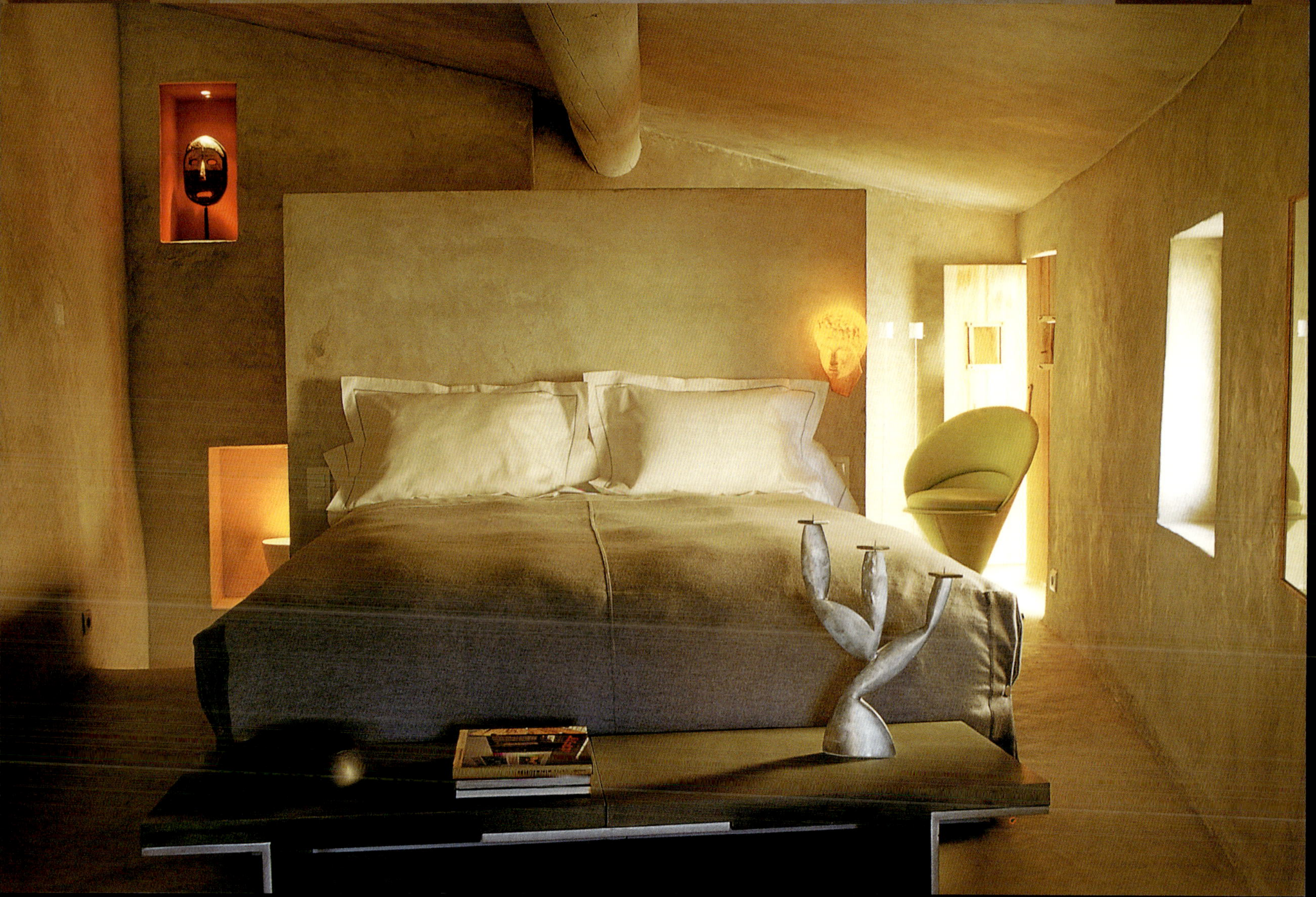

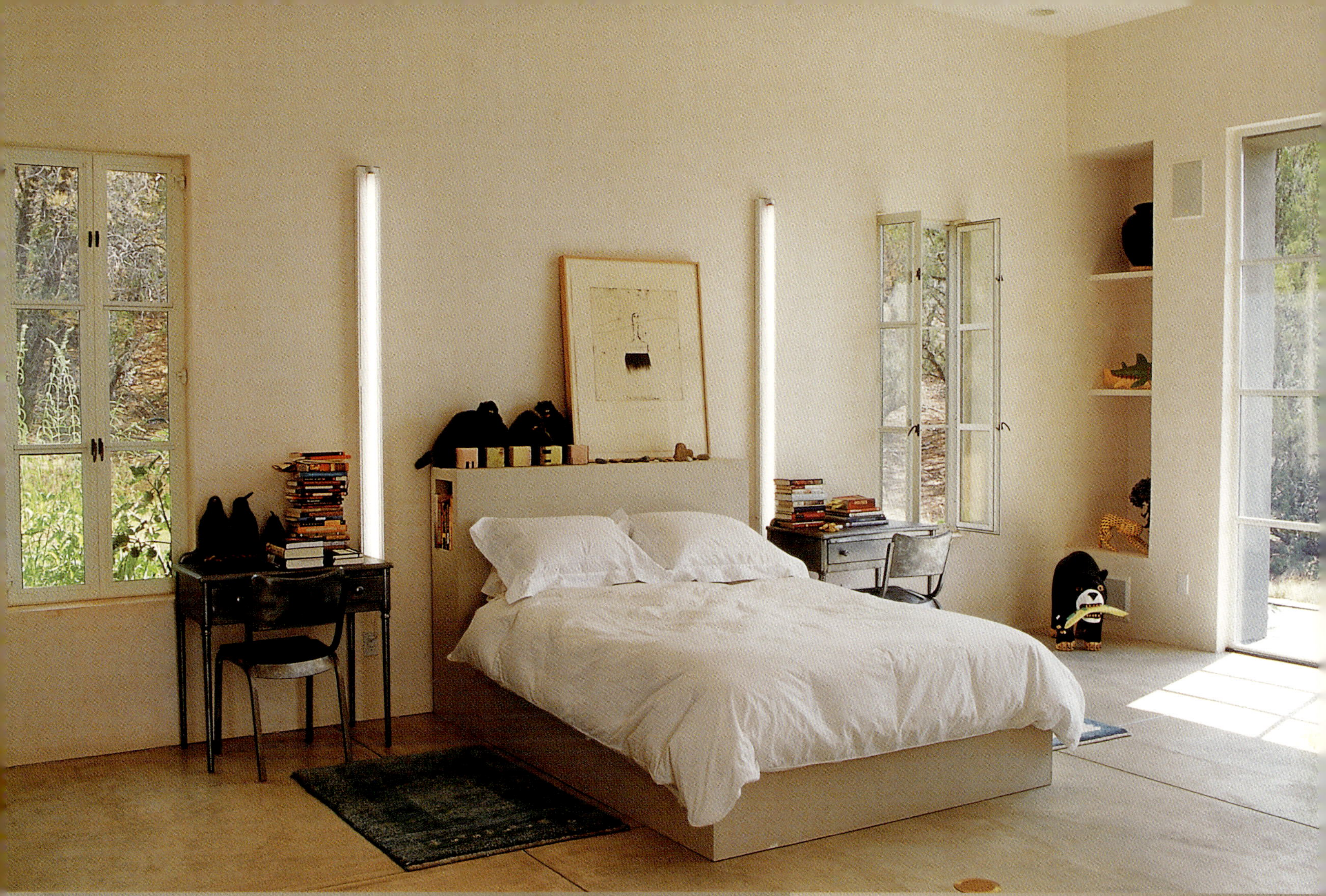
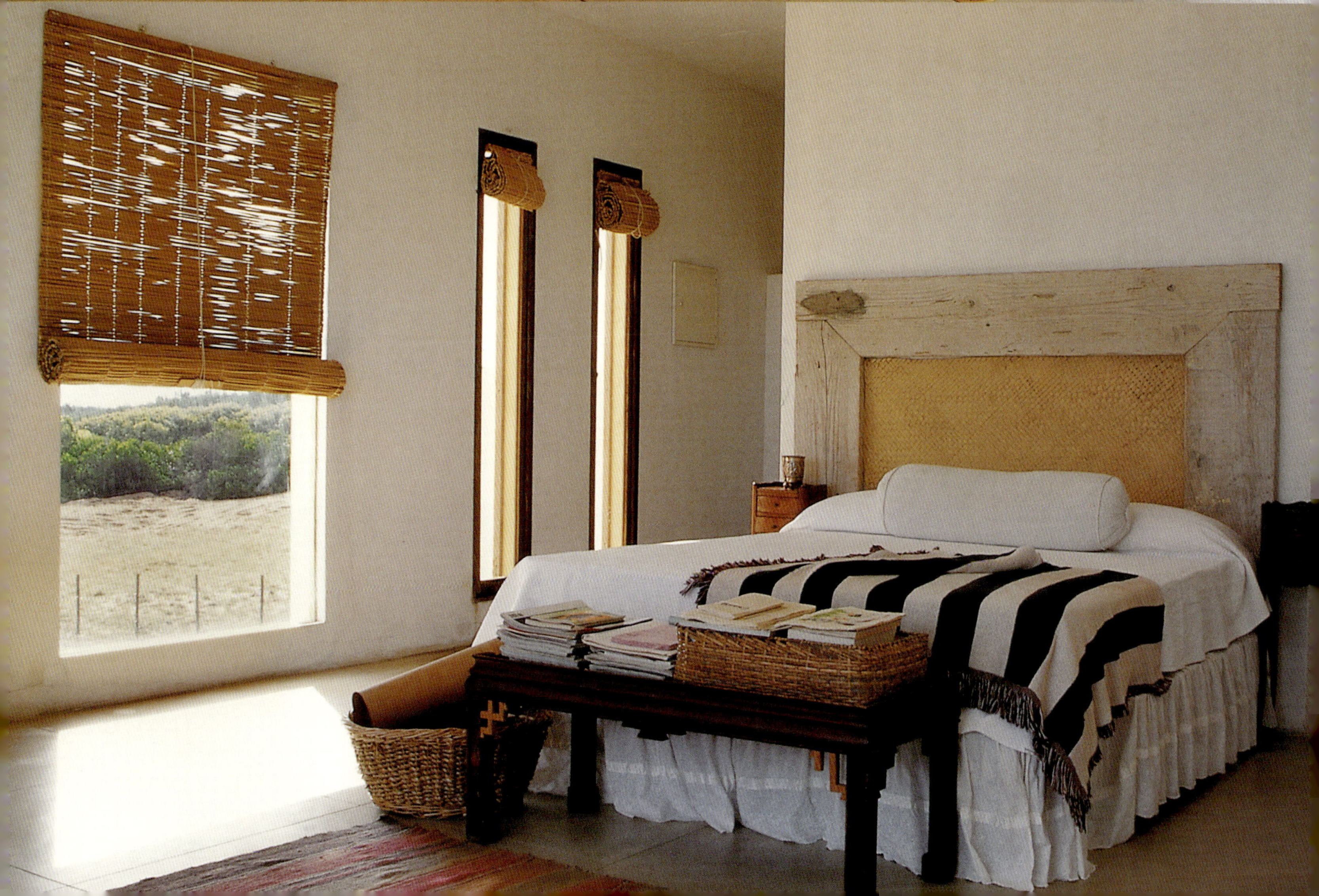

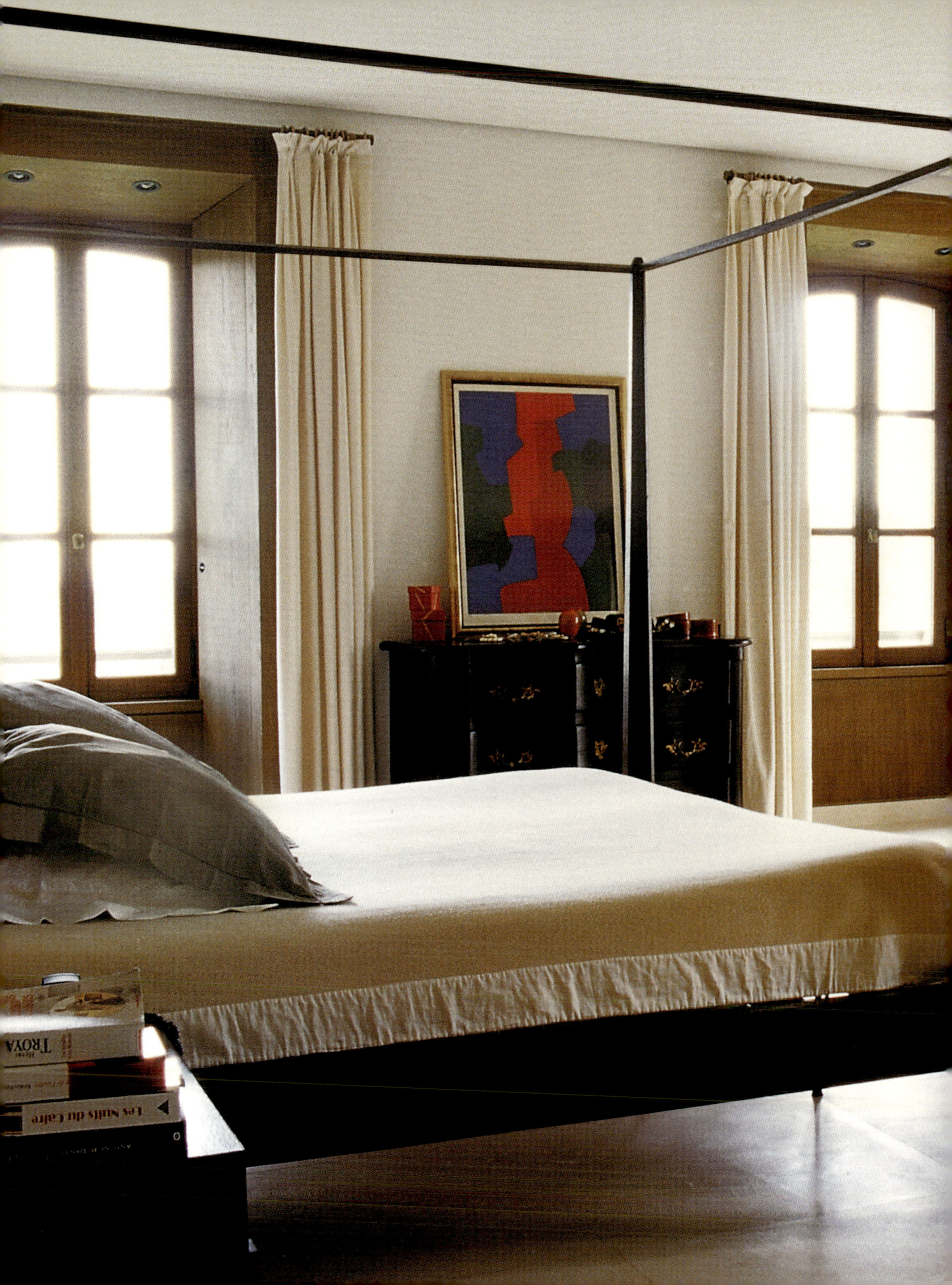
Les Nuits du Caire

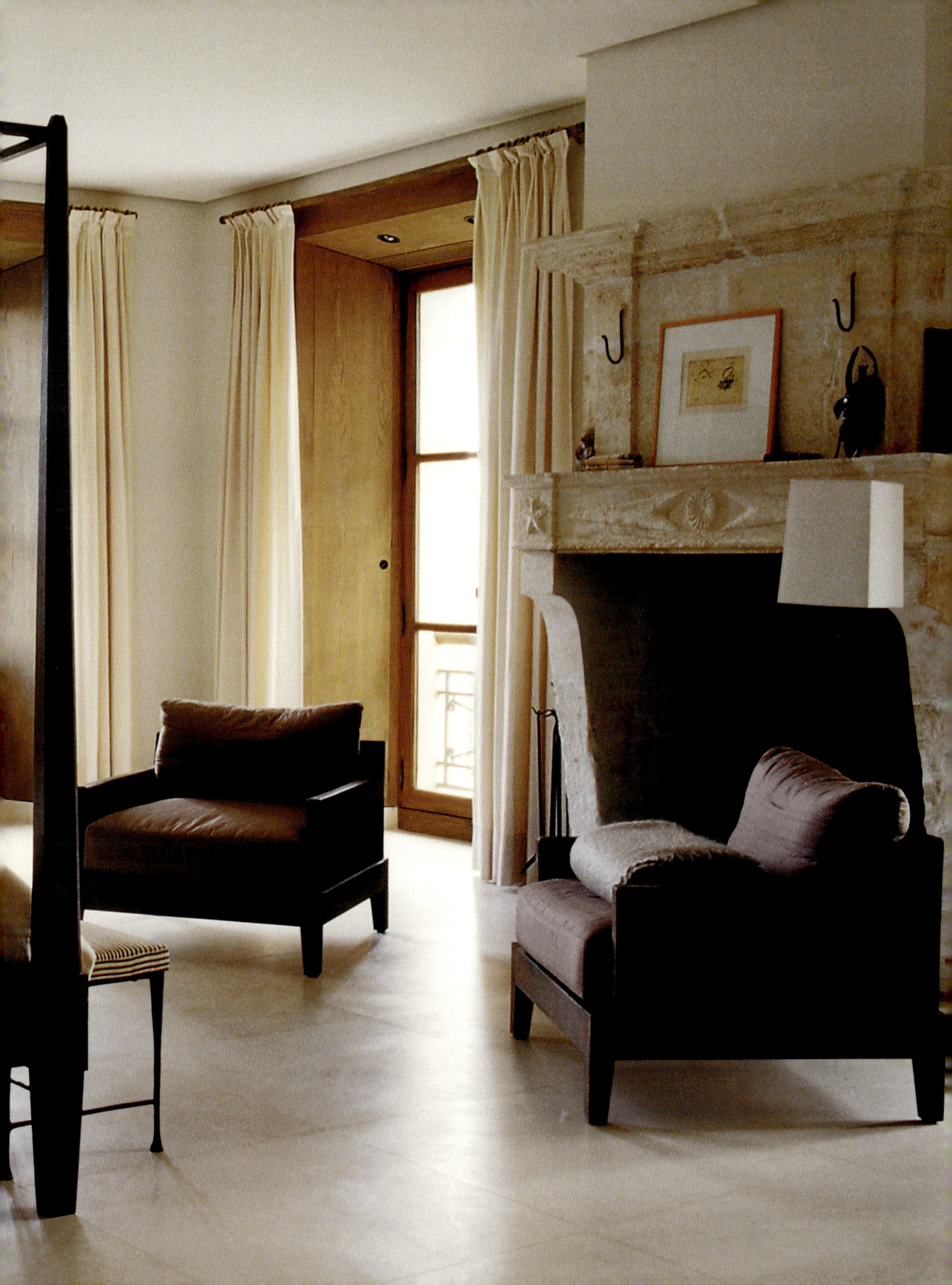

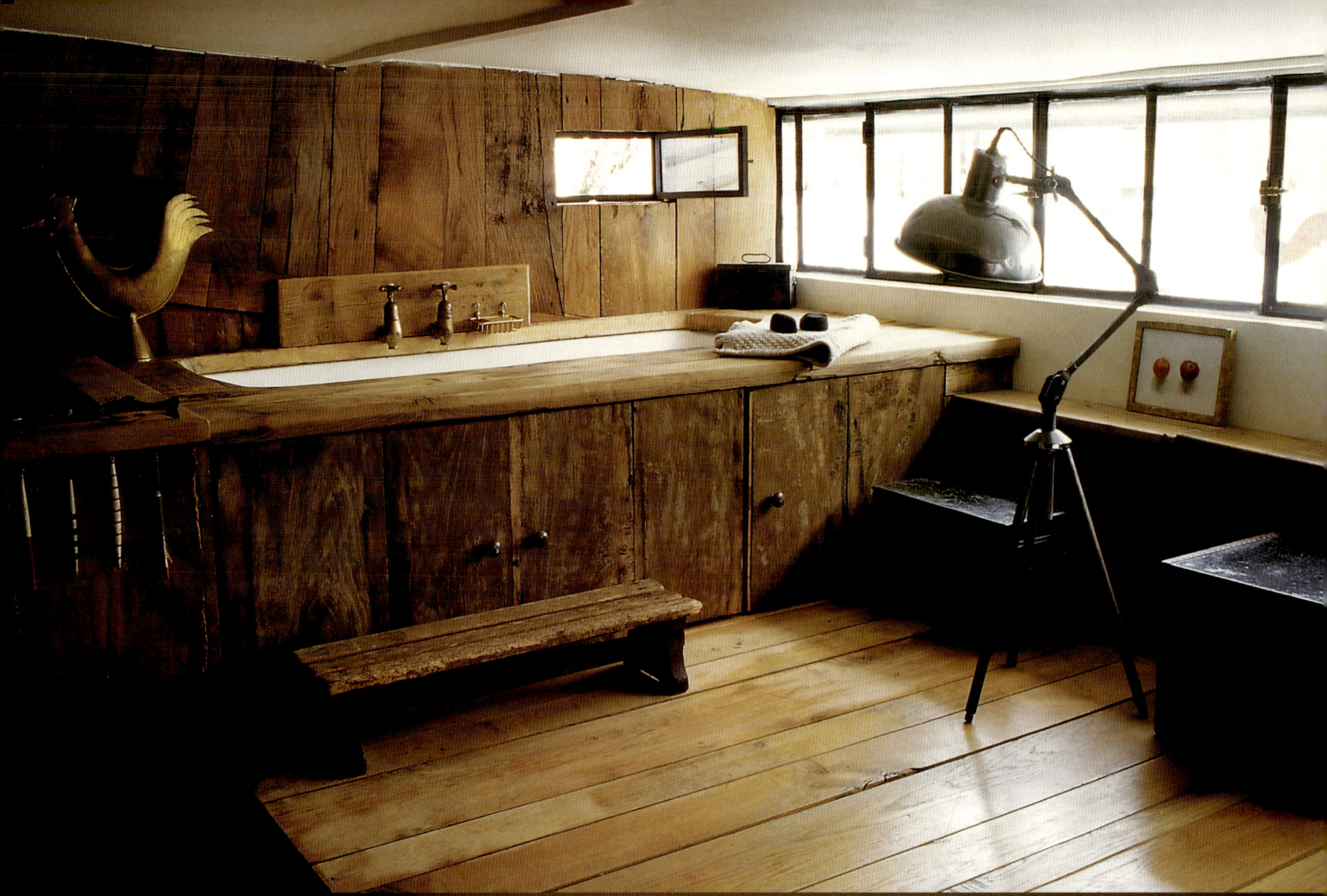
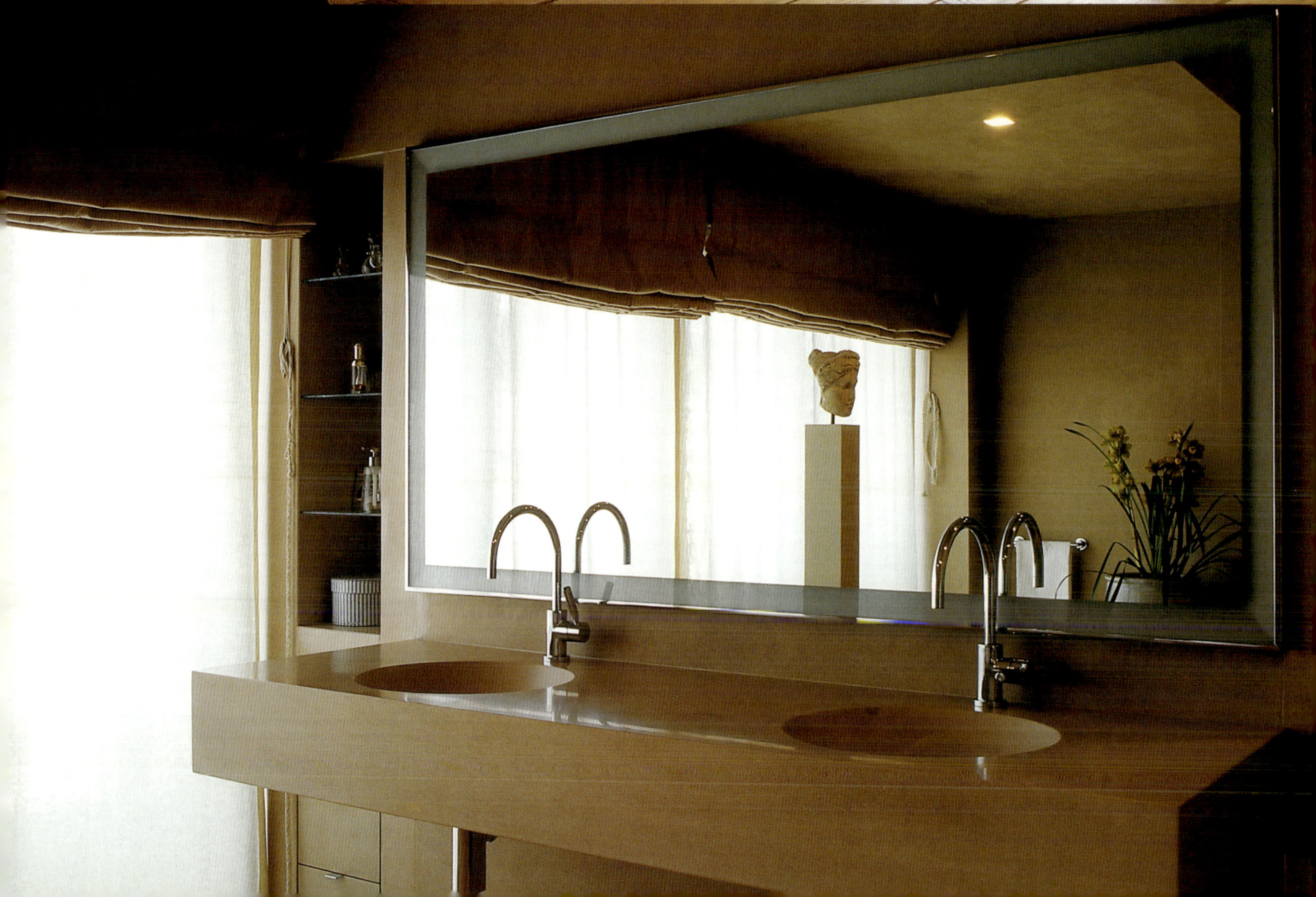

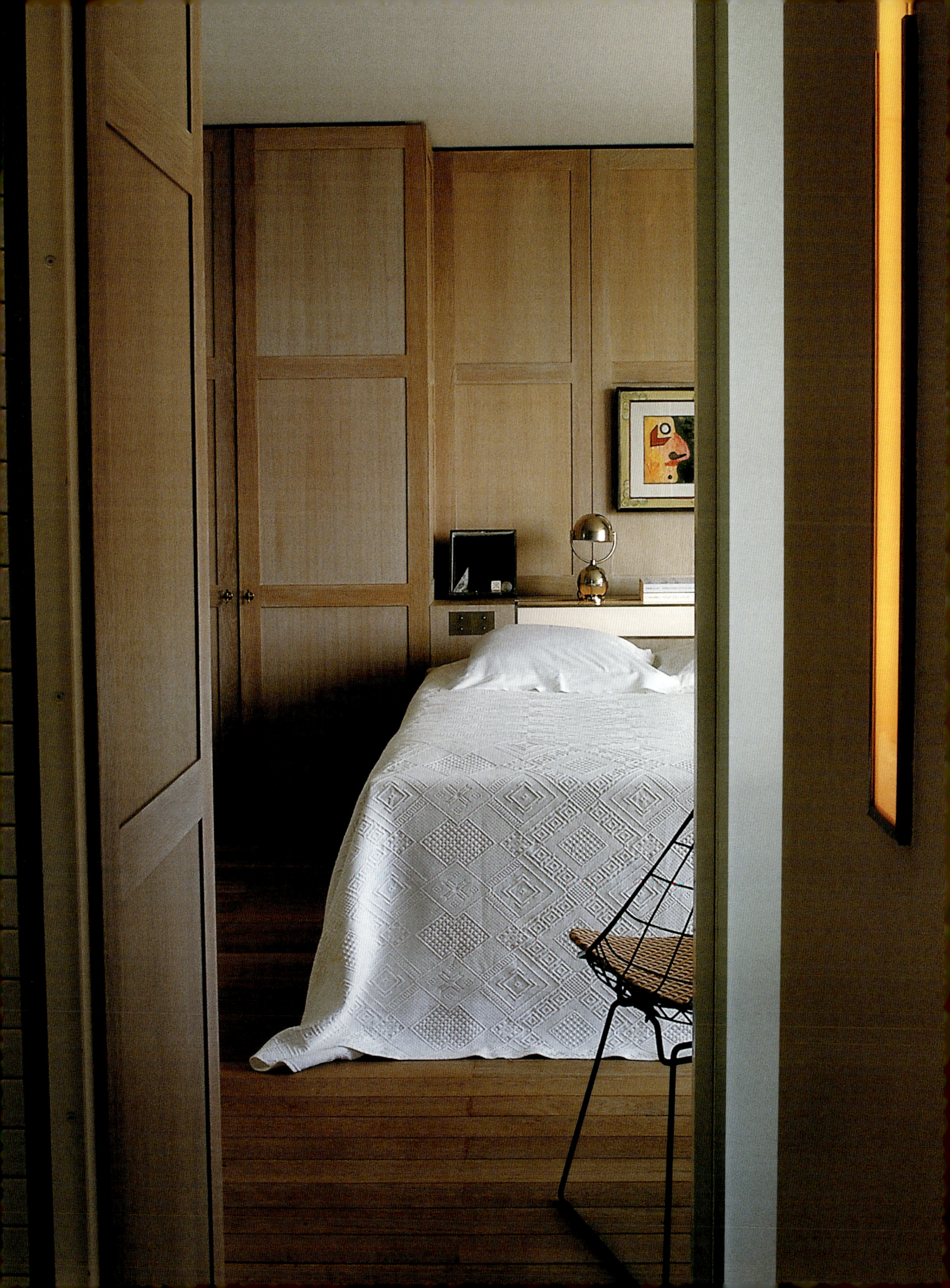

色と素材感

色と素材感

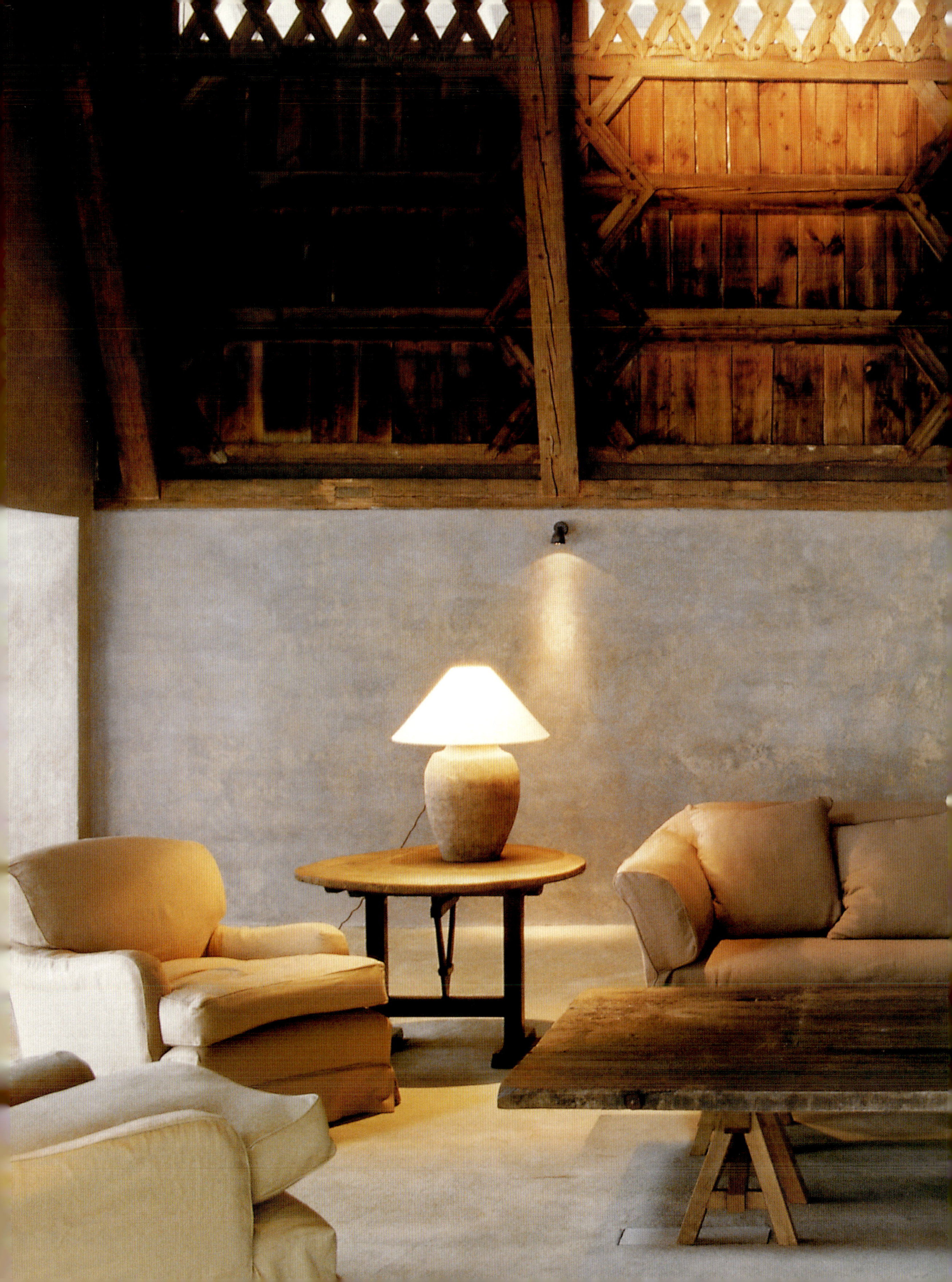

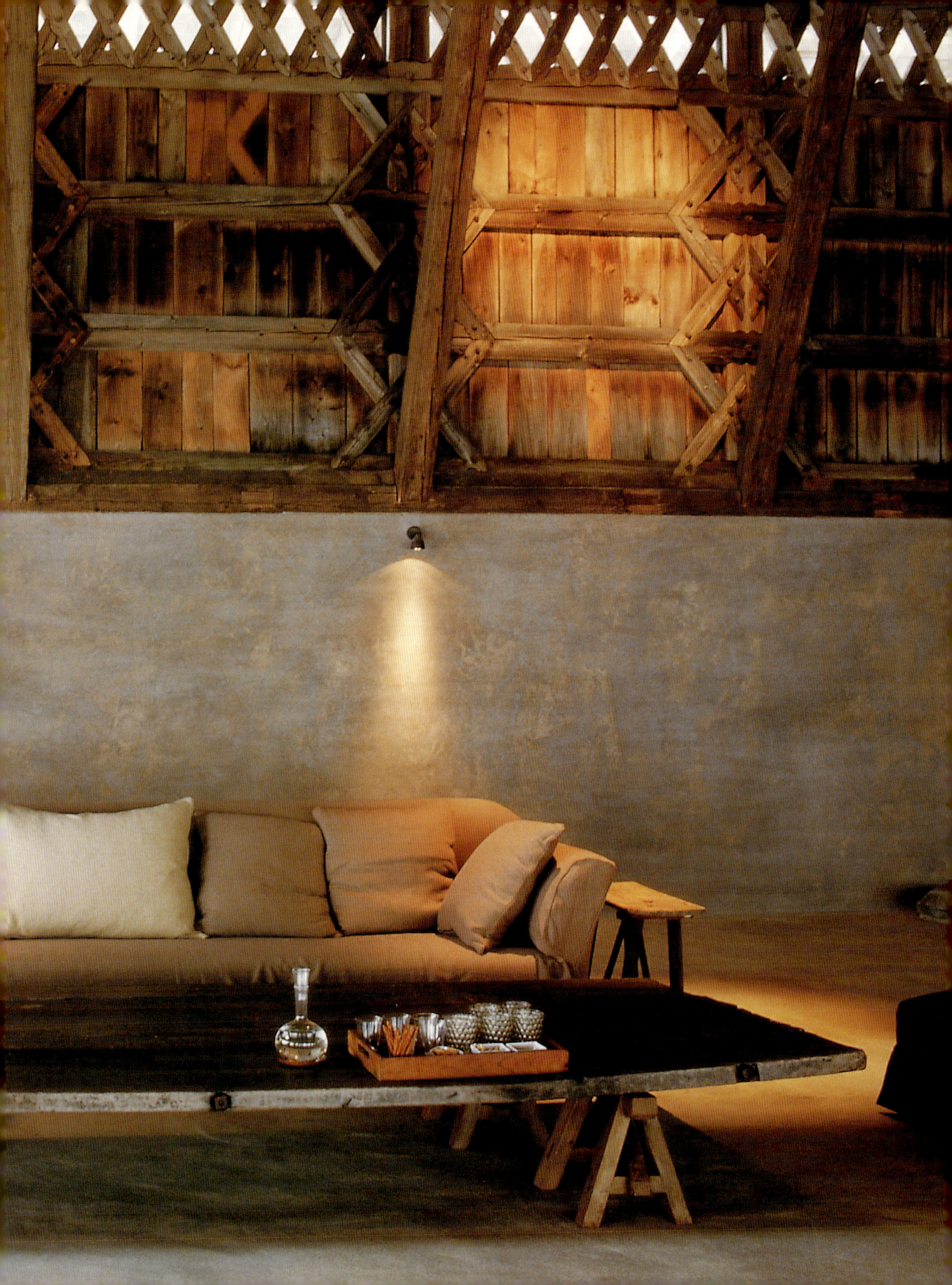

開放感

Reaching Outwards

ファッションの流行は、私たちが購入し、身に着ける物に、大きな影響を与えます。しかしインテリアに関する流行の変化はもっと緩やかです。この流行に影響を与えるものとして、デジタルテレビやLED照明のような、利用価値の高い新製品や新技術、また、家庭での生活習慣の変化や、他の国のインテリアスタイルを目にする機会が増えたという事実が挙げられます。航空運賃が下がるにつれ、異国情緒あふれる熱帯の地で、休暇を過ごす人々が増えていきました。その影響で、外気を取り入れた開放的な住空間への欲求が、長期的で、なおかつもっとも大きなインテリアの流れを生み出しています。世界には、ゾウの水飲み場を眺められるよう屋外にベッドを設けた新しいホテルがあります。生い茂る熱帯植物に囲まれたバスタブ、シャワー。水平線沿いに広がるプール。そして、自然を楽しむ方法として何より魅惑的なのは、屋外での料理や食事です。たとえ、寒さの厳しい地方でも、屋外に席を設けたカフェやレストランは珍しくありません。こうして遂に、家の裏口のドアは開け放たれるようになりました。がたつきやすかった屋外用の金属テーブルや折りたたみ椅子は、洗練された屋外デッキ用の家具に取って代わりつつあります。つまり、屋外デッキに、広々としたダイニングテーブルとチェア、またはスタイリッシュな全天候型ウィッカー・ソファ、ベンチ、コーヒーテーブルというセットを置くのです。屋外での食事をより快適にする、ソーラー照明、パティオ・ヒーティング、陶器の薪ストーブもあります。最新の天気予報がすぐに確認できるなら、天蓋付きベッドだって、室内だけの物ではないのです。

Trends in fashion have a huge influence over what we buy and wear, but trends in home furnishing change more slowly, and are affected not only by the availability of exciting new products and technology – things like digital TV and LED lighting – but by the changes in our domestic habits, and by what we see elsewhere in the world. The most radical development for many years, stimulated by cheaper air fares and our holiday trips to hotter, more exotic destinations, has been our desire for a more open-air lifestyle at home. New hotels all around the world now offer alfresco beds looking onto elephant watering holes; bathtubs, showers and infinity pools amongst tropical vegetation; and, most seductive of all, cooking and eating outdoors. Even in the coolest countries, cafés and restaurants with outdoor seating are now commonplace. At last, the back doors at home have been flung open and the wobbly metal table and folding plastic chairs can be replaced by more sophisticated cooking equipment on decking that supports a generous dining table, chairs and even stylish all-weather wicker sofas, seats and coffee tables, enhanced by solar lighting, patio heating and a ceramic chiminea. Given current predictions for climate change, canopy beds cannot be far behind.

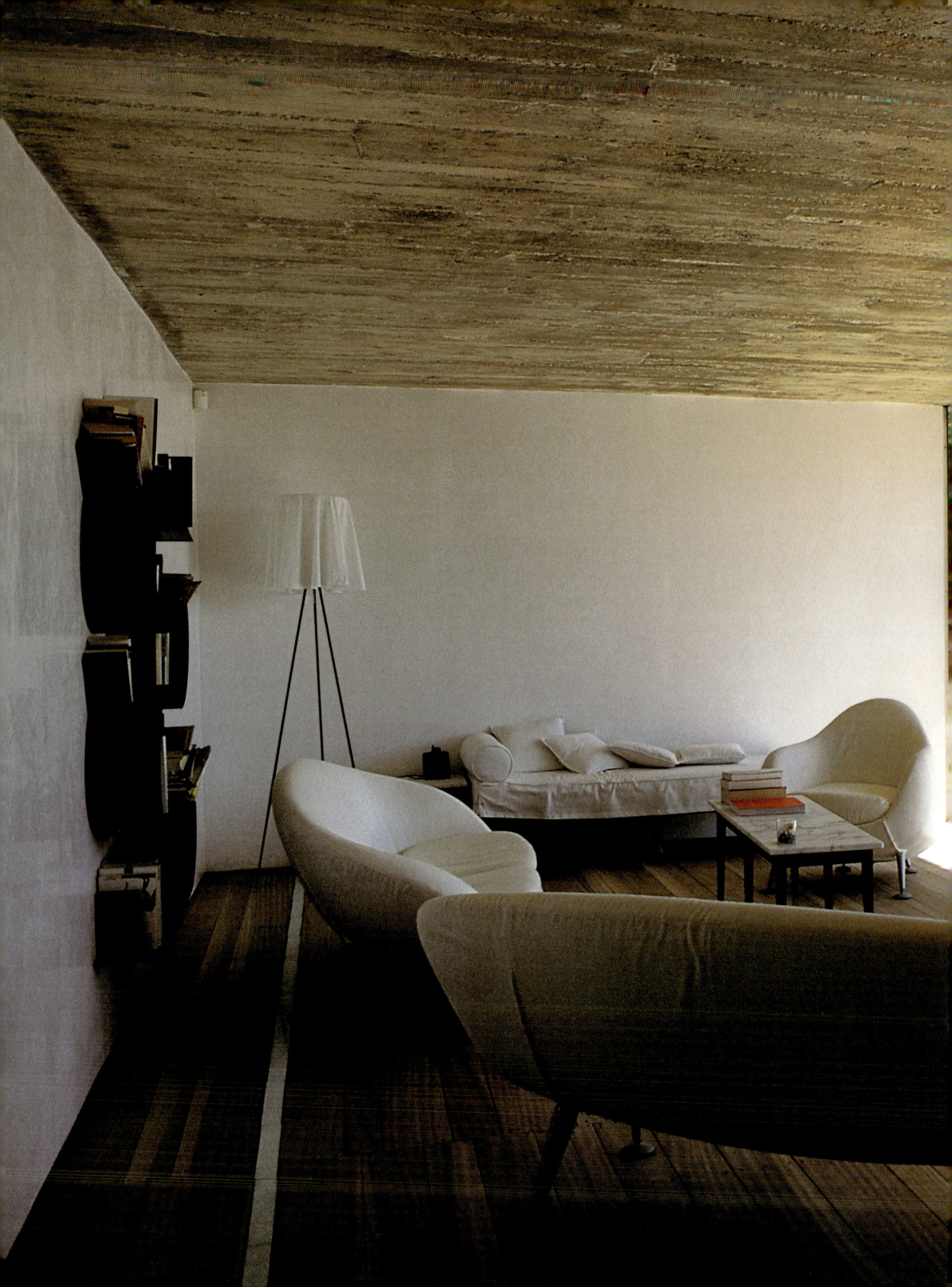

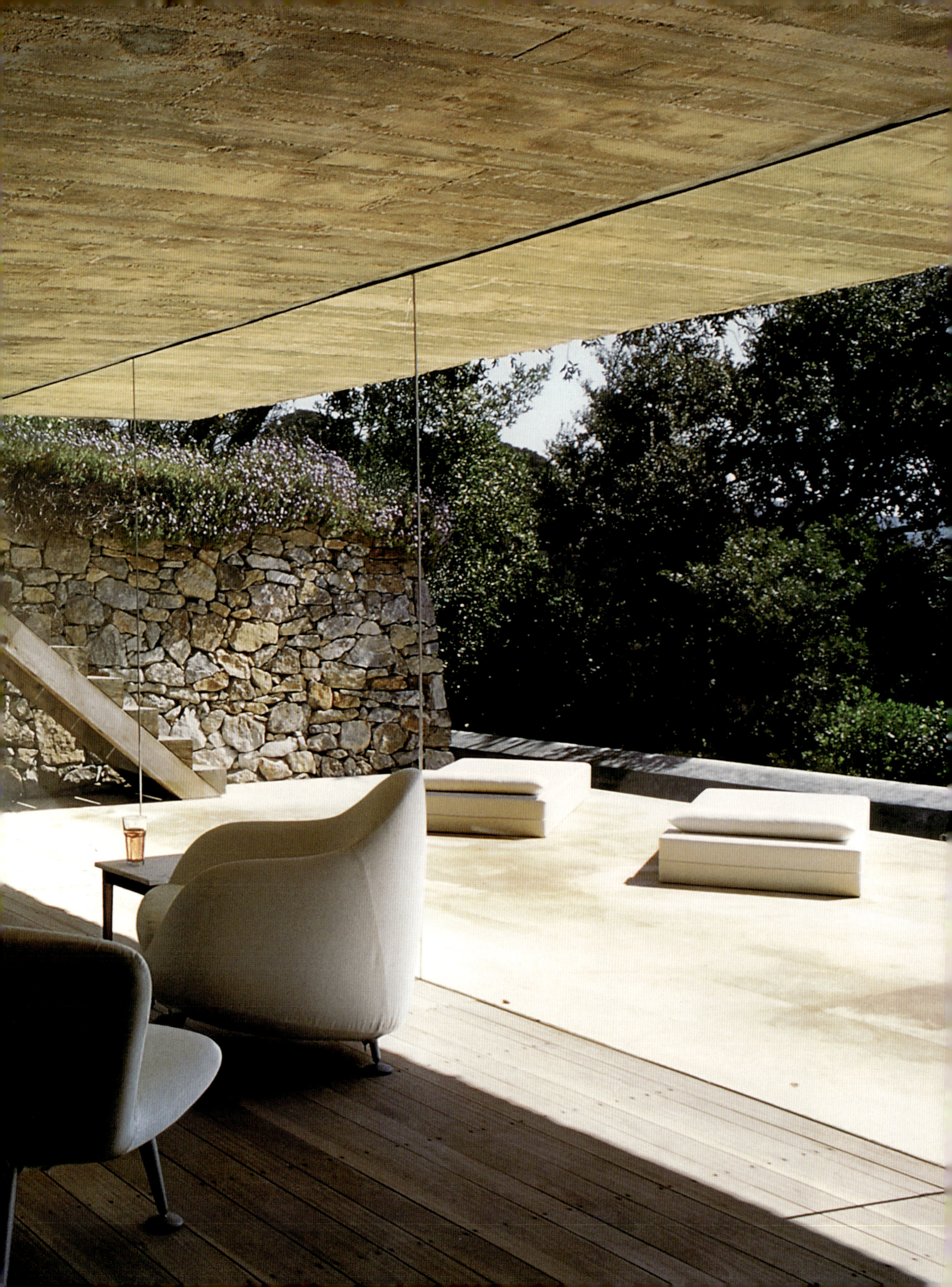

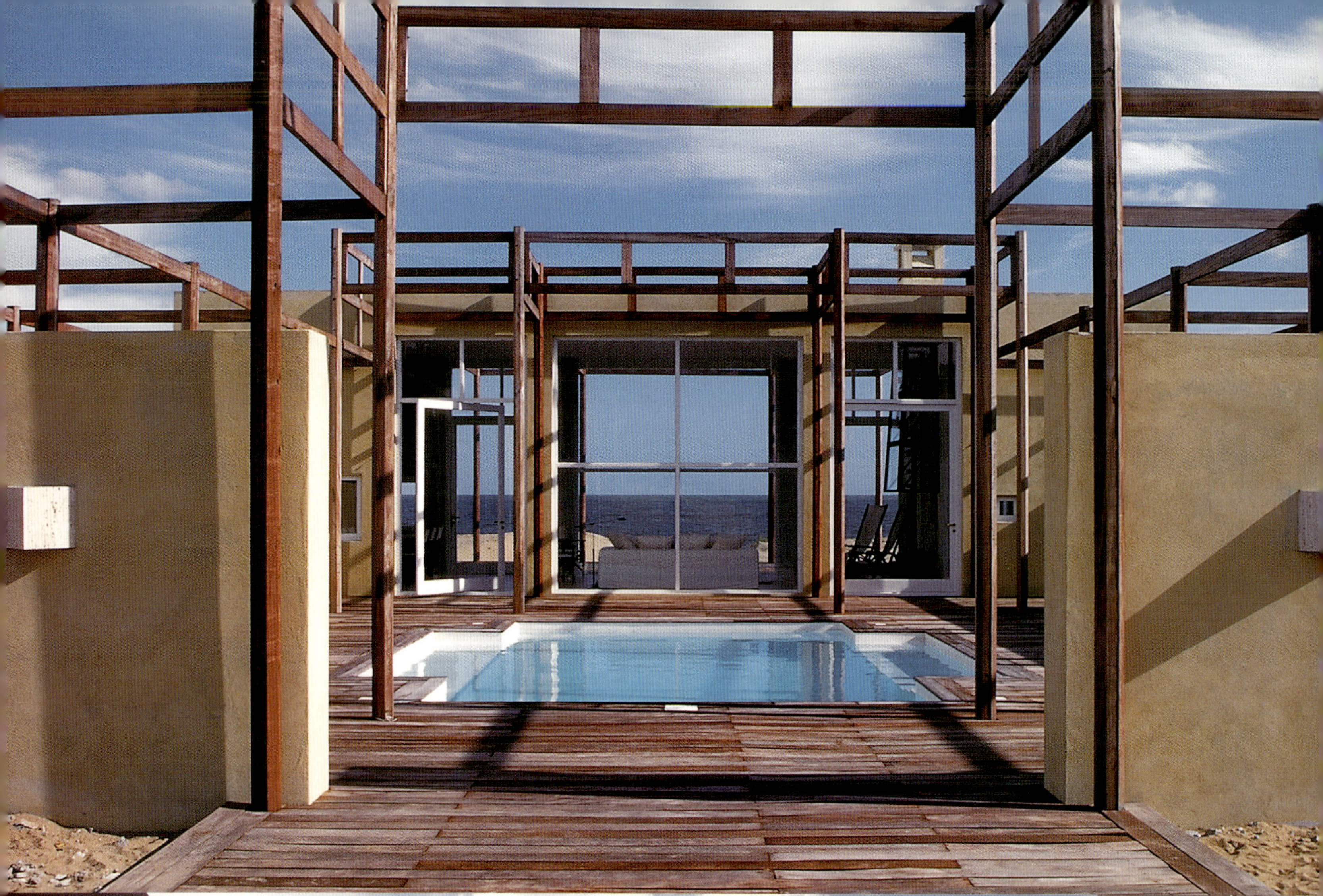
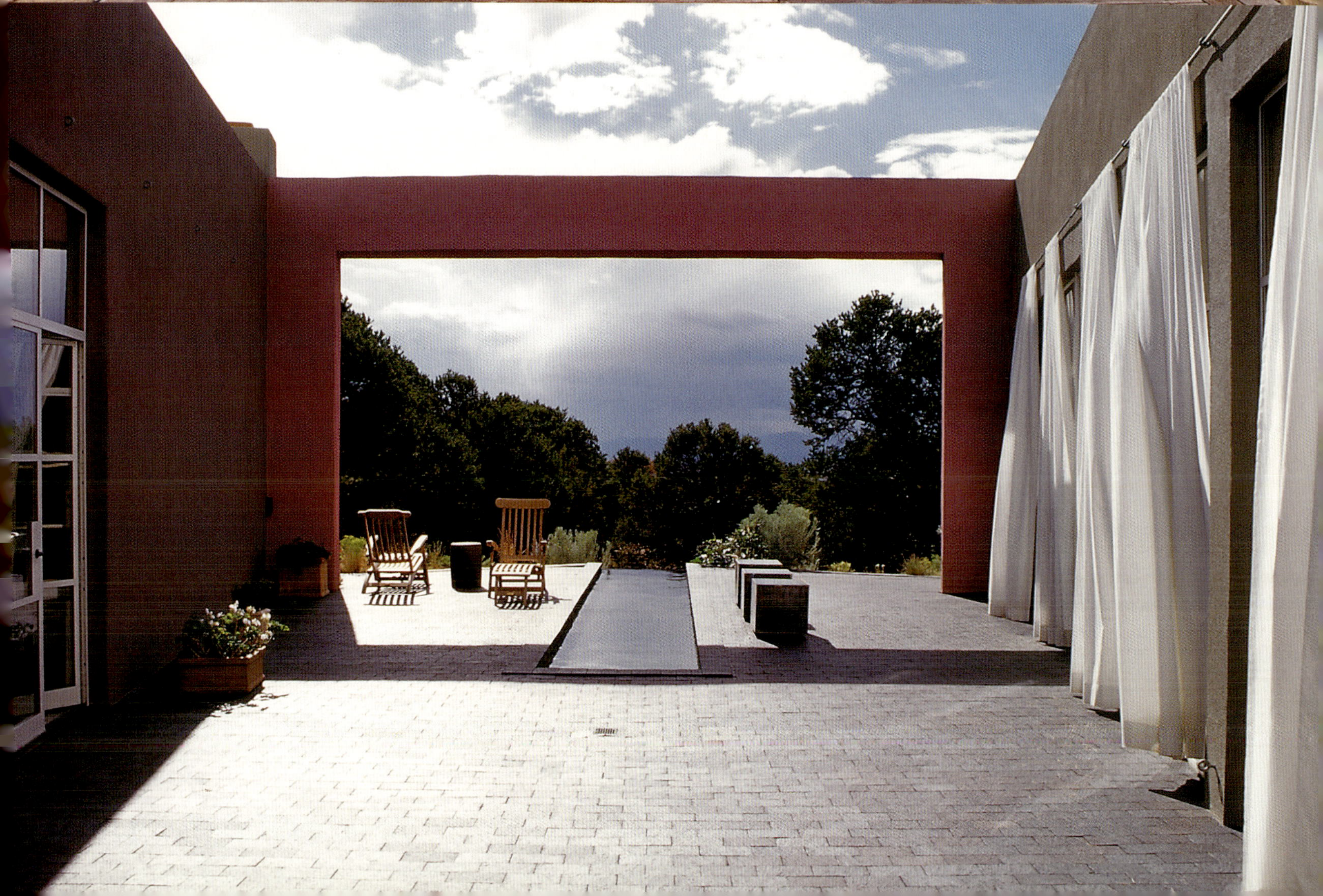

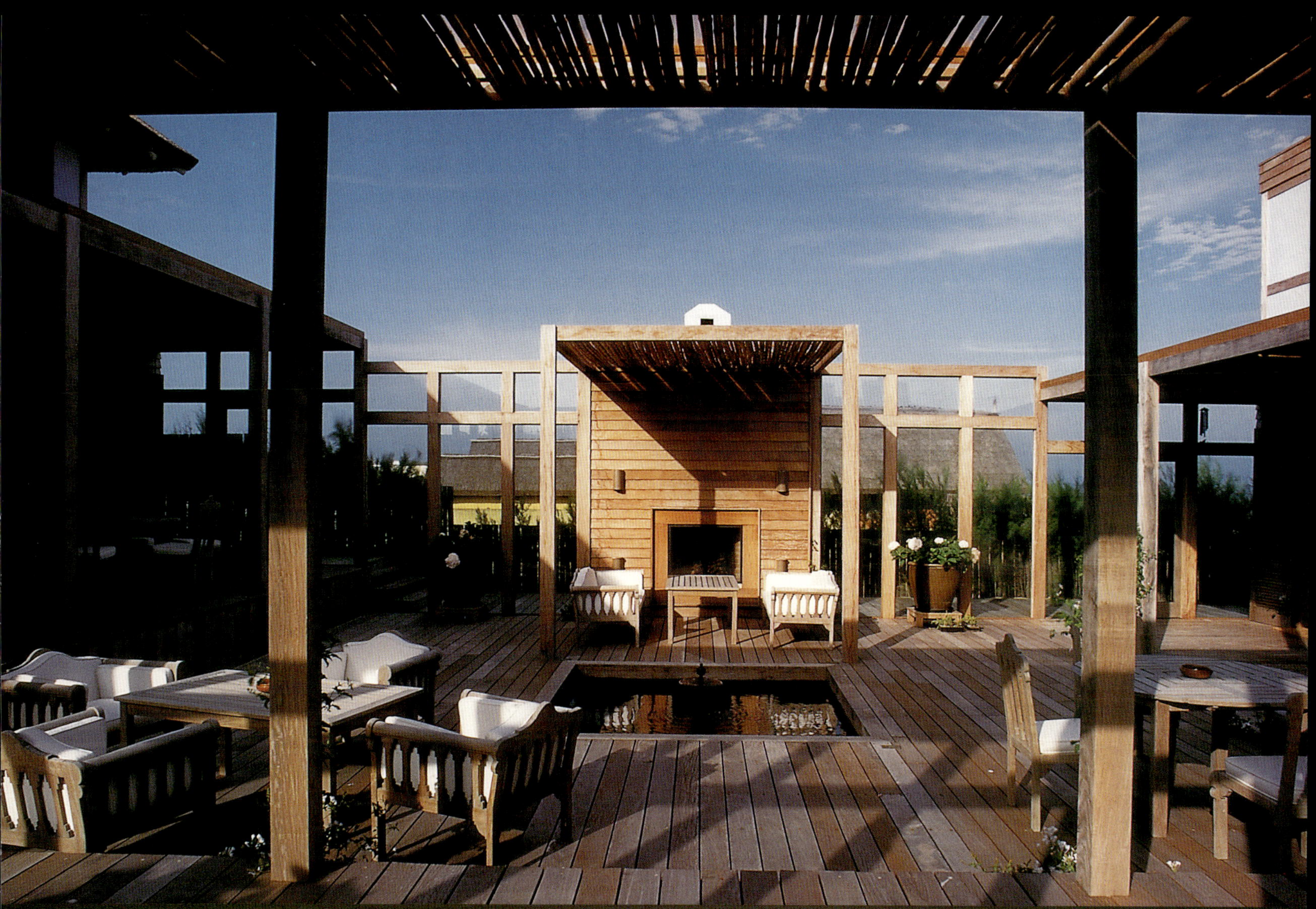
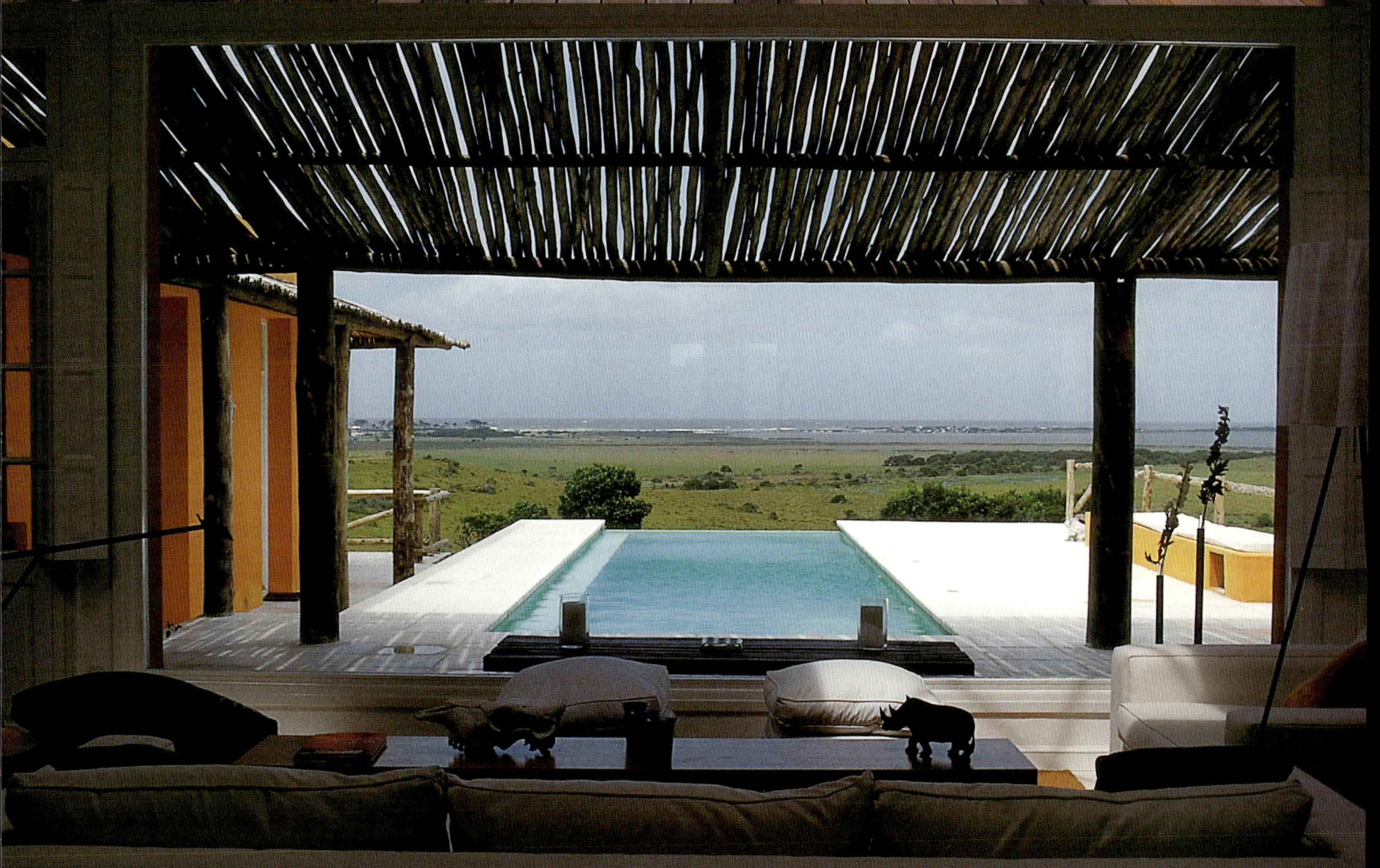

開放感

開放感

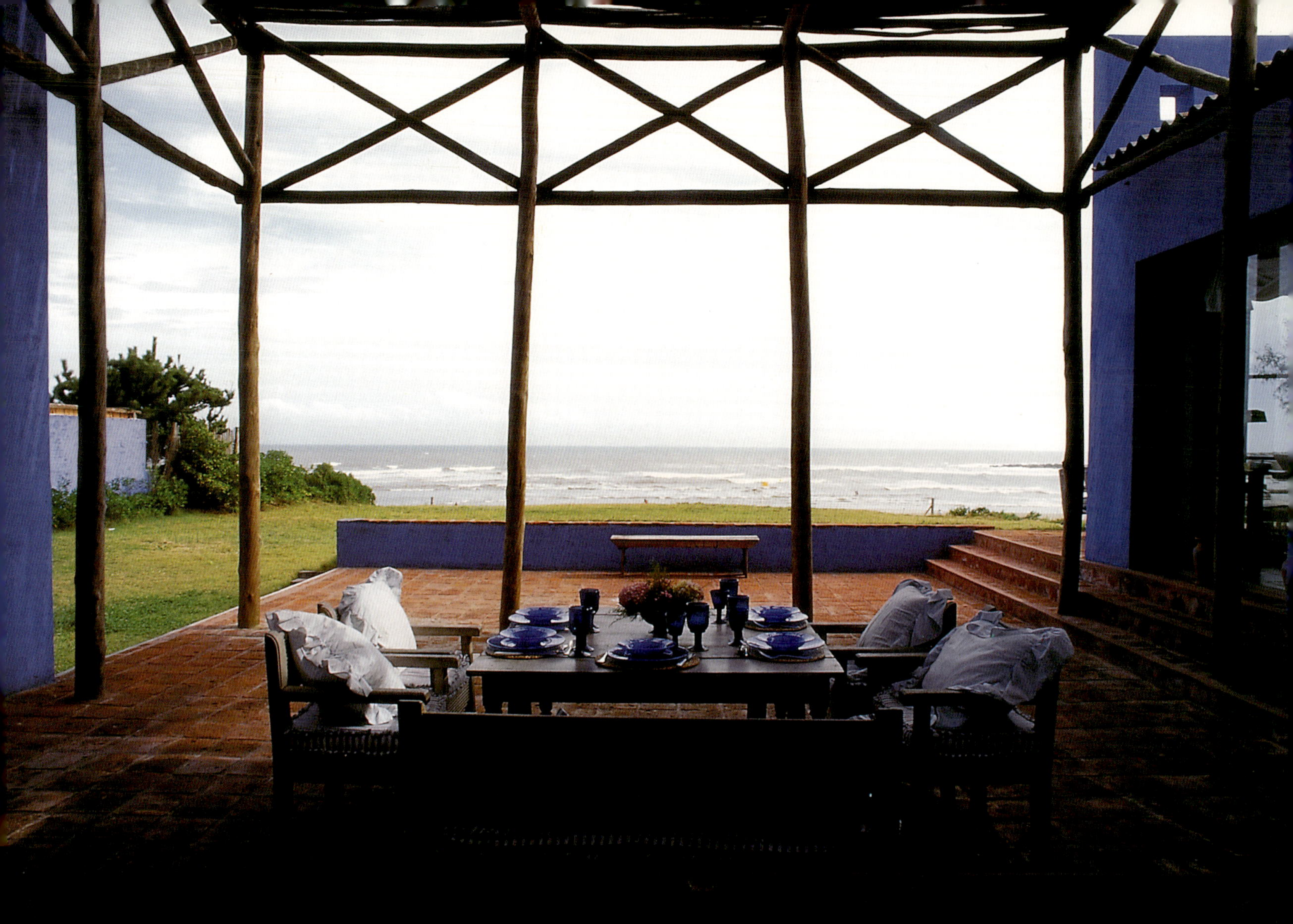
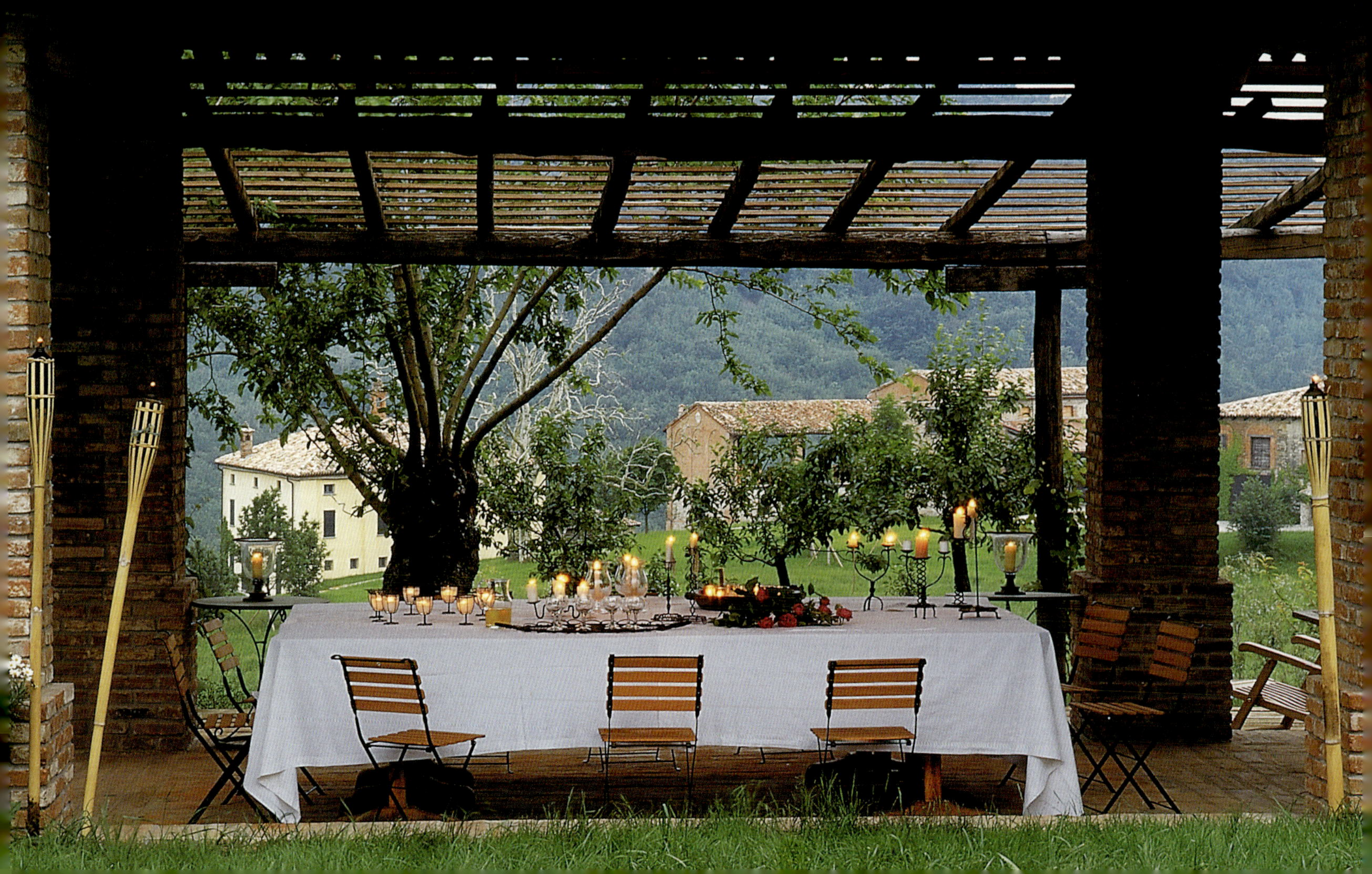

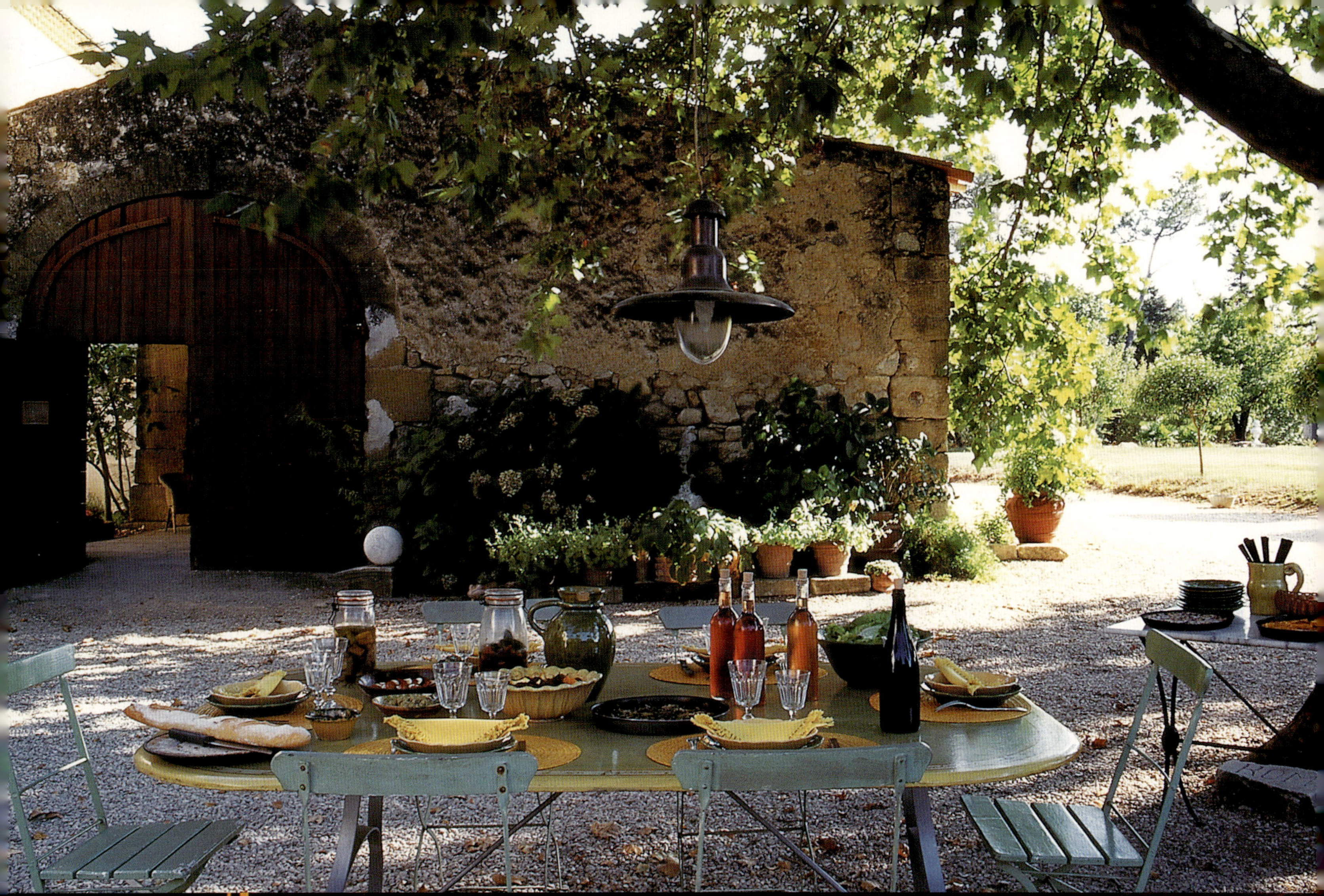

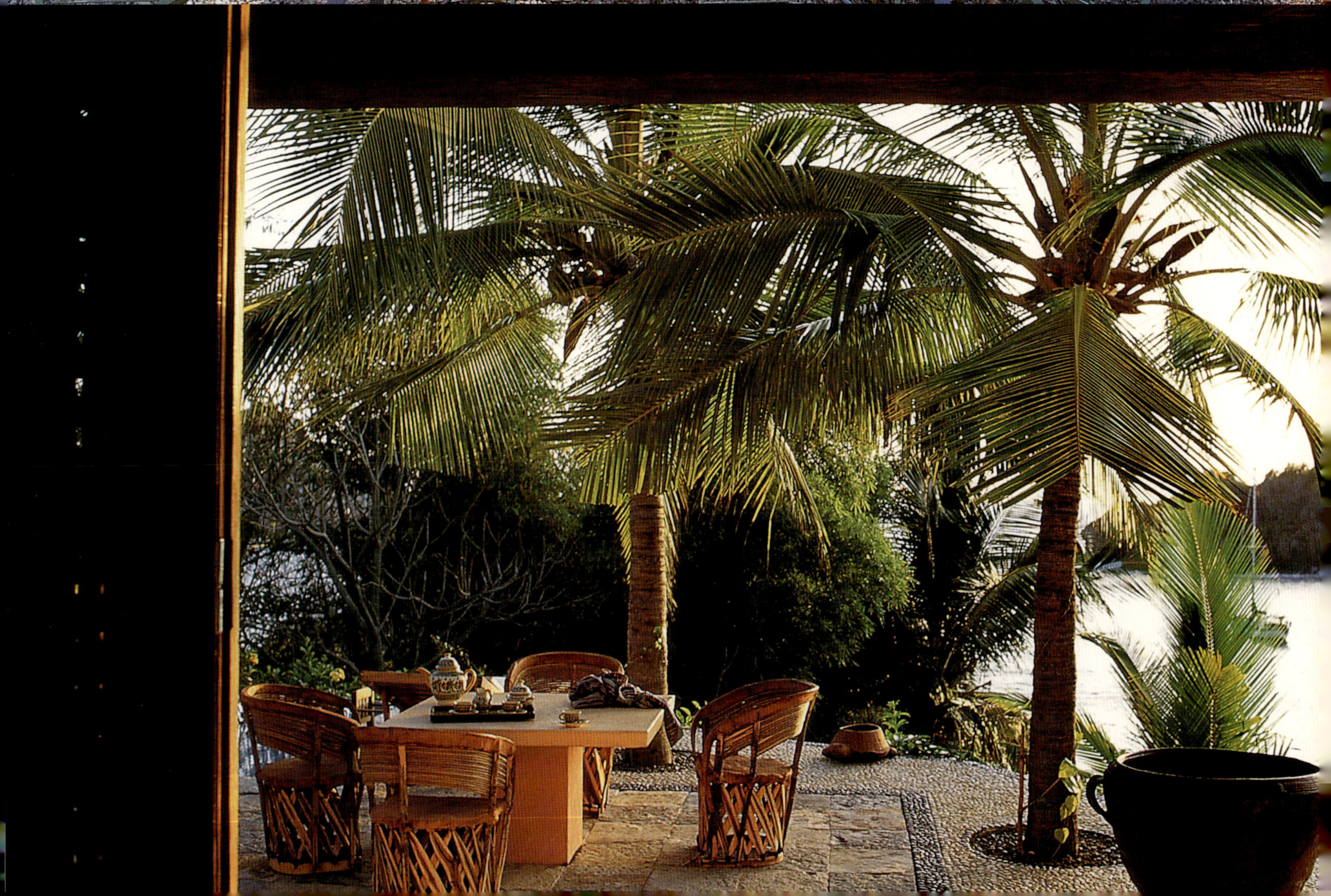

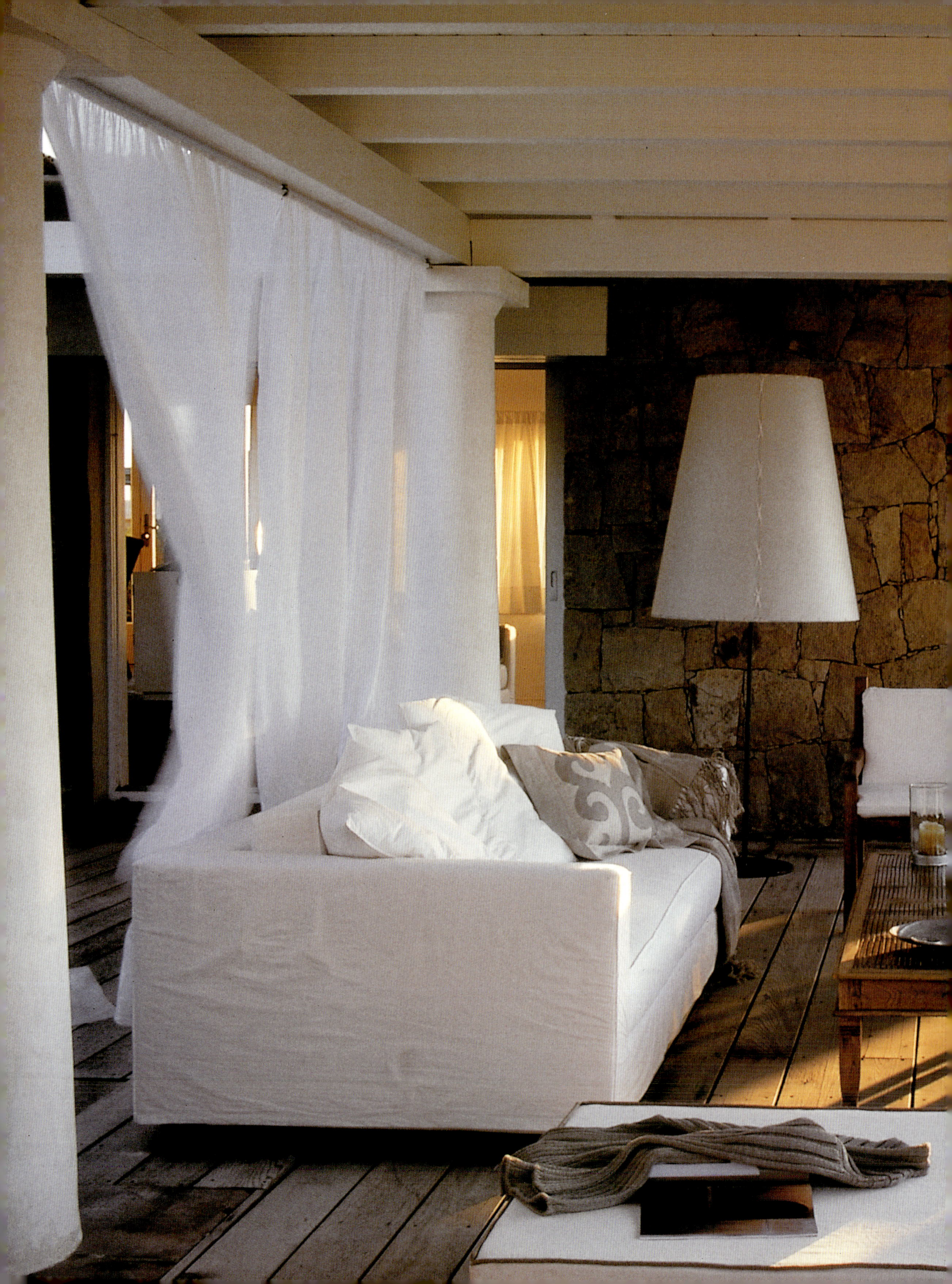

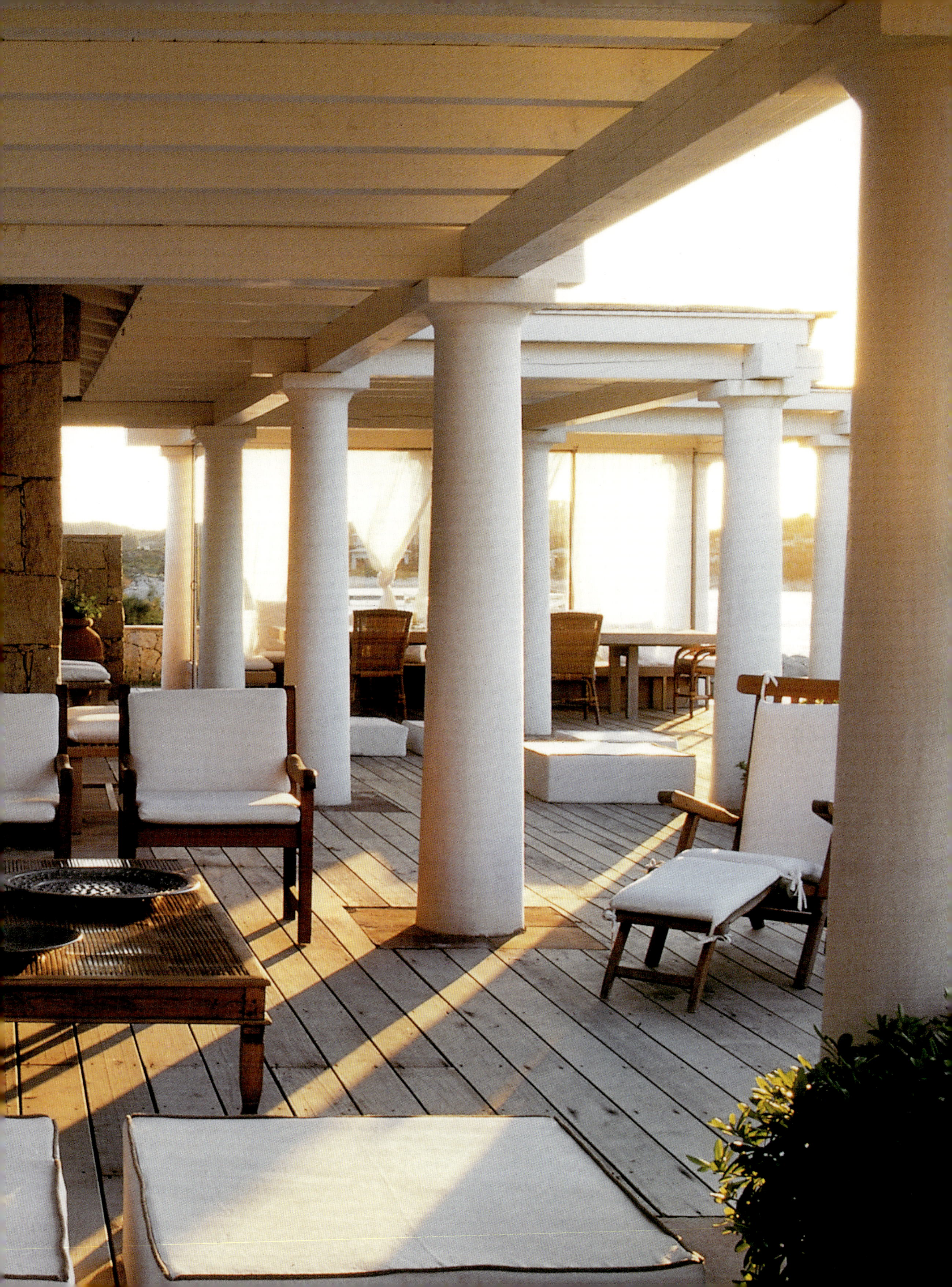

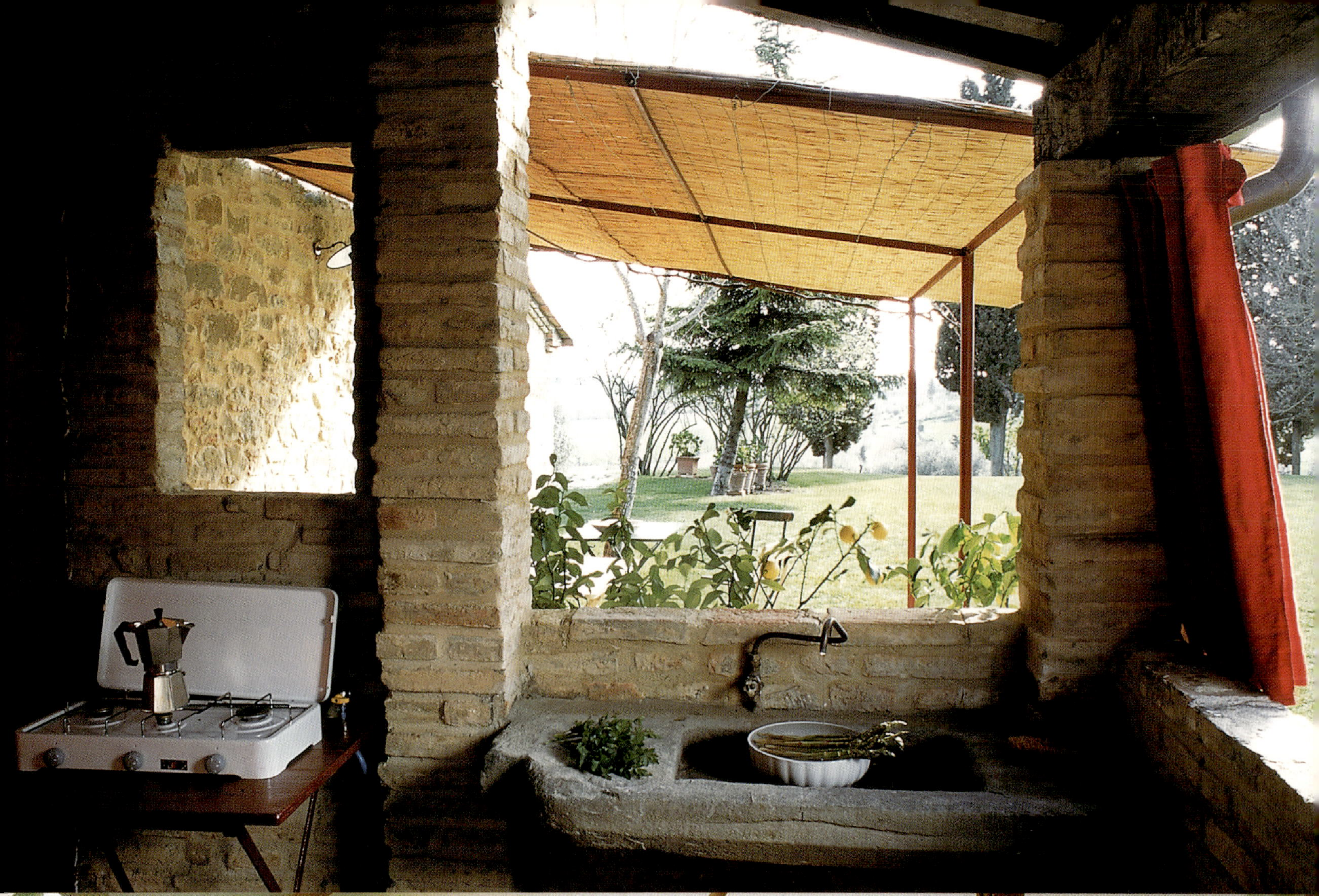

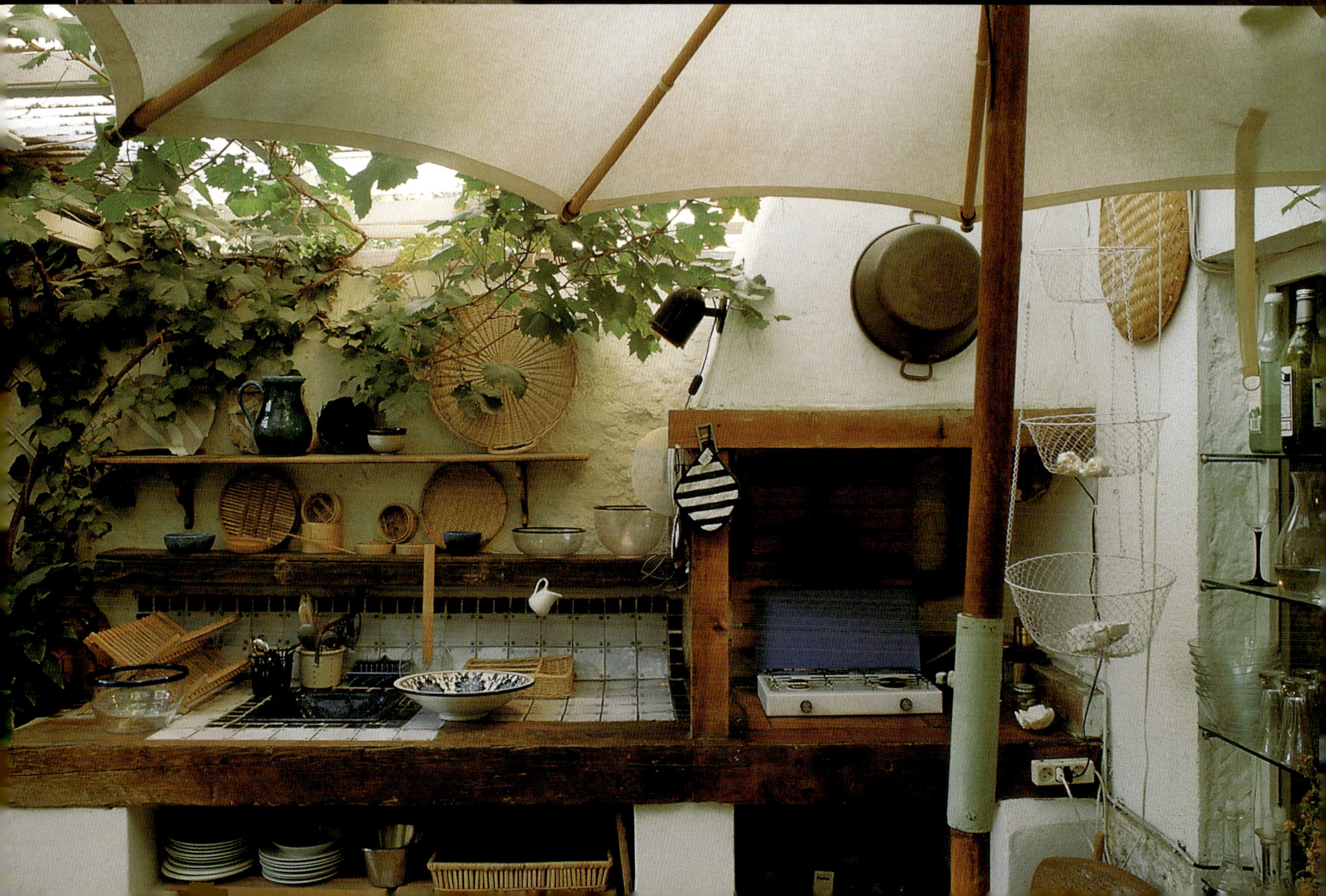

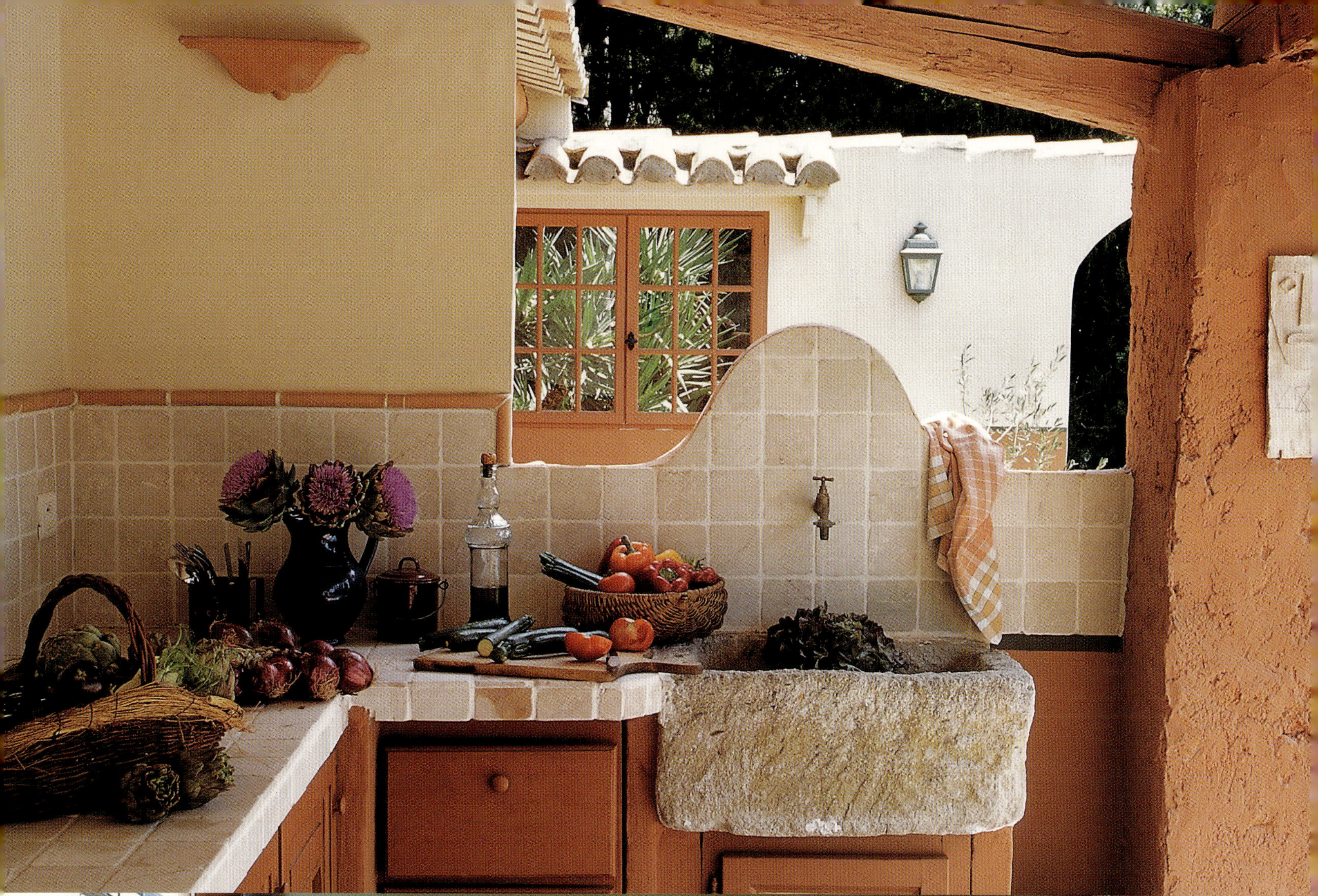
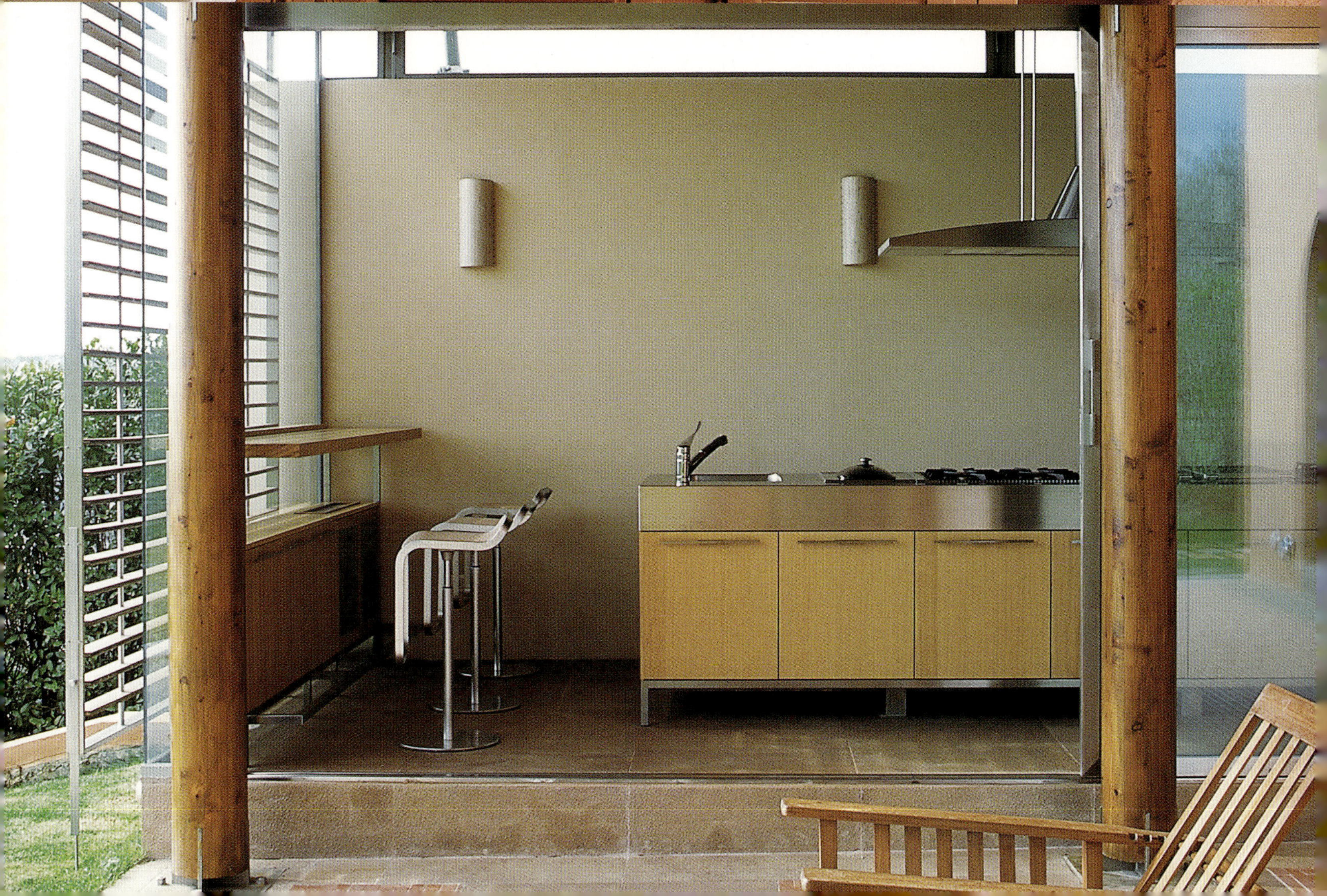

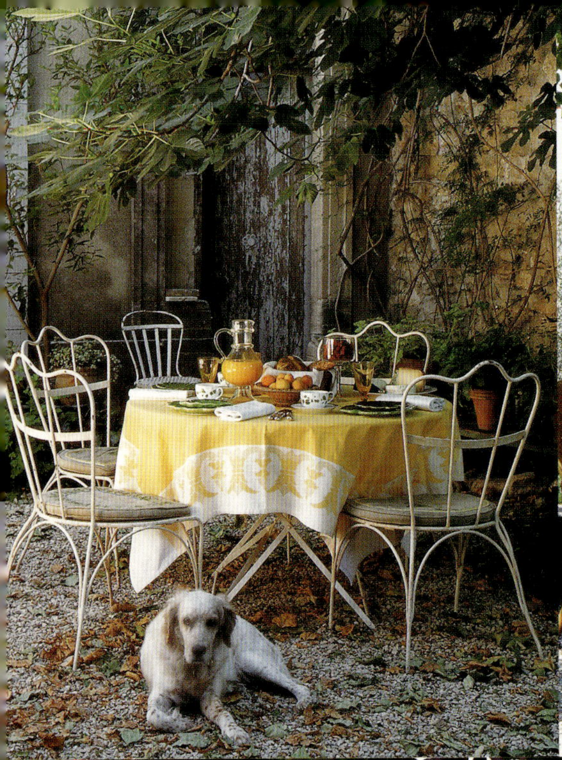
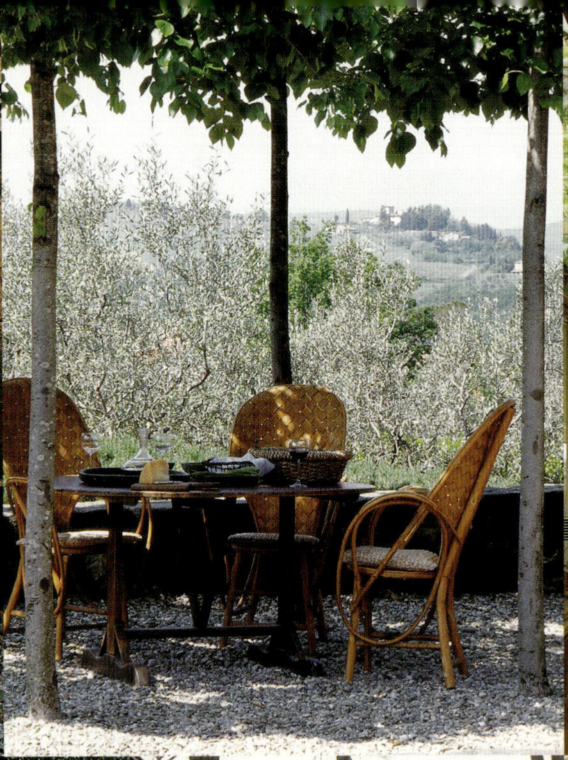
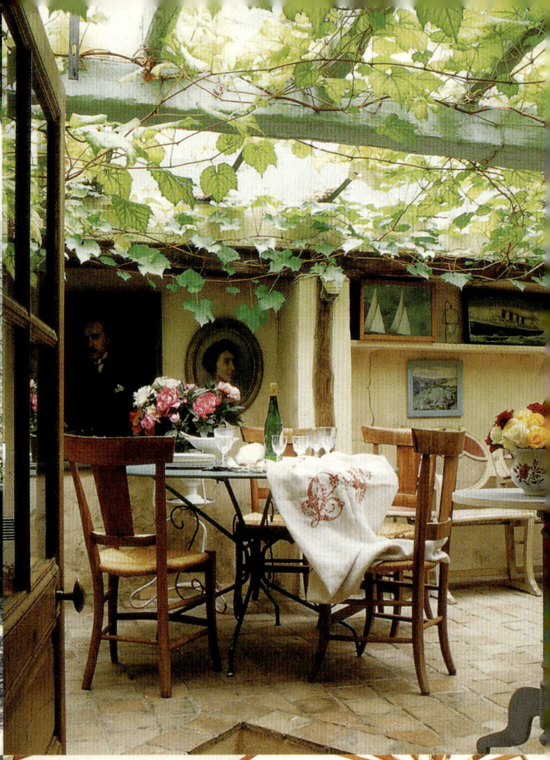
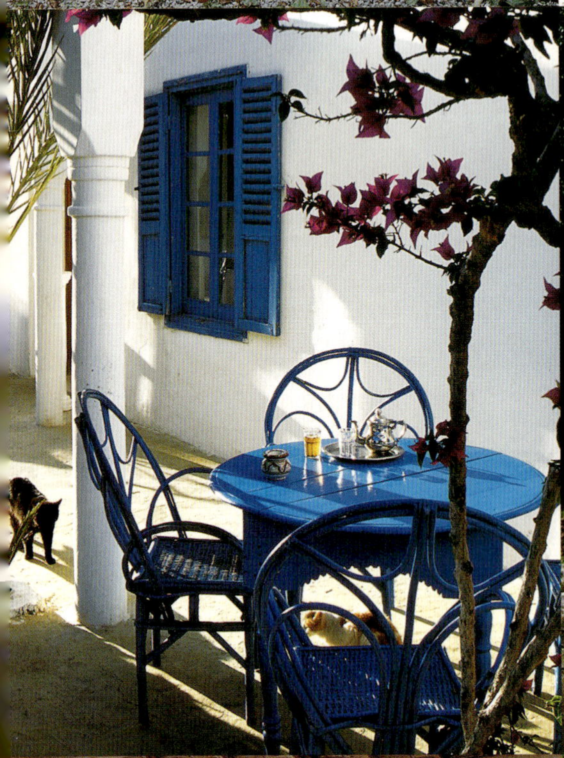
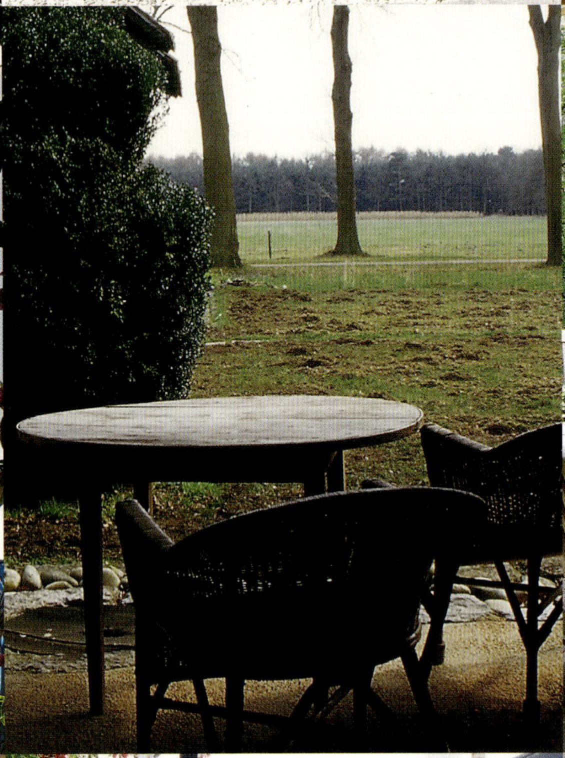
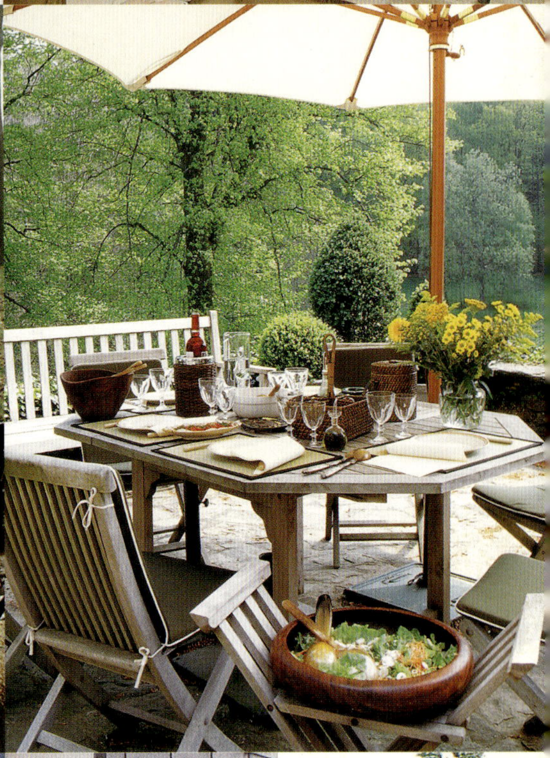
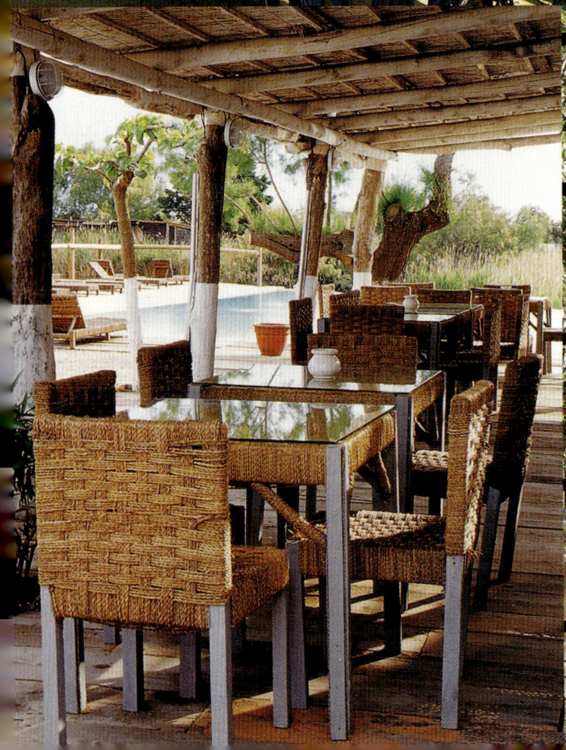
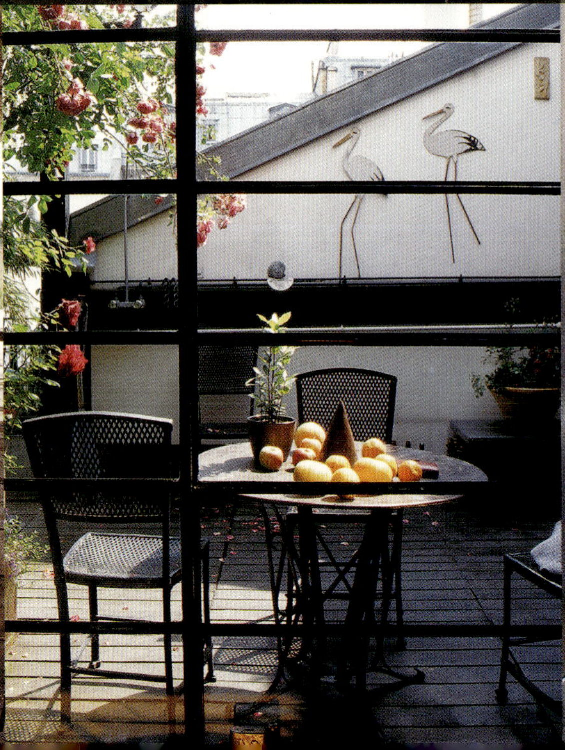
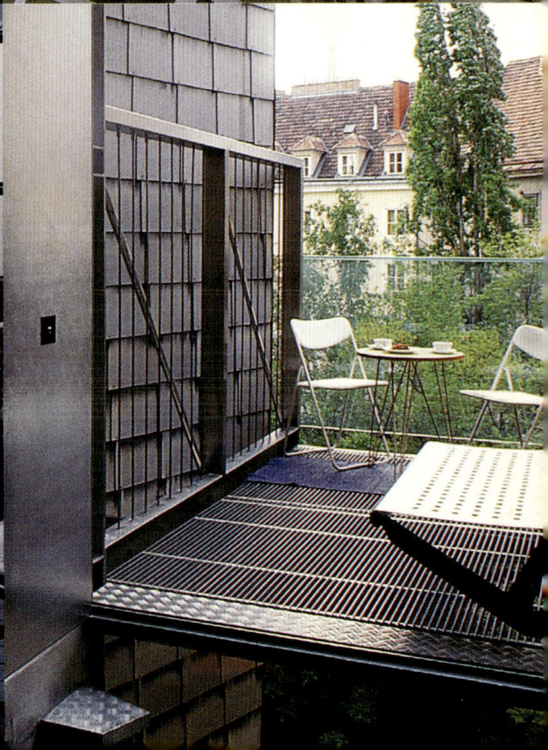

もうお分かりですね。住まいには、平凡も退屈もなく、そうである必要性もありません。自分の目を開き、可能性を見出すかどうかにかかっています。目を着けた場所が、新しい窓や、ガラスドア、古い戸棚、明るい色のラグなど、家のどの部分であろうと、アイデアはあらゆる所にありますし、家を持つ人には、できるだけ多くのアイデアが必要です。店や、ホテルやカントリーハウスを訪ねれば、すばらしいヒントが得られるでしょう。しかし、本や雑誌、テレビもまたヒントを与えてくれます。隣の家を訪ねただけで、アイデアを得ることだってあるはずです。

スタッフォード・クリフ
ロンドンにて

この本のページに登場する家は、どれも、世界中の多くの方が、愛情を込めて生み出した作品たちです。私は、過去20年の間に、ドアを開けて、私を自宅に招き入れてくださったすべての方々に感謝します。そのおかげで、私は、彼らの宝物を目にすることができたのです。また、すべての関係者にも心よりお礼を申し上げます。

クリスチャン・サラモン
パリにて

Page 16 top and bottom row, centre: Sunfold Systems make high-quality, high-security and highly insulating, sound-deadening aluminium panelled front doors. Design details are highlighted through the use of triple-glazed glass and stainless steel inlays. Their flush surfaces and clear aesthetic lines represent straightforward elegance in its purest form.
www.sunfold.com.

Page 17 (except for bottom right): Urban Front are specialist designers and manufacturers of unique, elegant and contemporary doors, made from hardwood and stainless steel. Each door has a reinforced steel core.
www.urbanfront.co.uk.

Page 154 fireplaces: top left, from Planika. A series of products that create real fire without any smoke. Incorporates an automatic, electronically controlled ethanol fuel feeding system.
www.planikafires.com.

Top right, from Smart Fire Ltd. The EcoSmart fire is an Australian innovation – an environmentally friendly open fireplace. Flueless, it does not require any installation or utility connection for fuel supply. Fuelled by methylated spirits,
it burns cleanly and is virtually maintenance free.
www.ecosmartfire.com.

Editorial Director　Jane O'Shea
Designer　Stafford Cliff
Photographer　Christian Sarramon
Design Assistant　Katherine Case
Editor　Laura Herring
Production　Vincent Smith,
Marina Asenjo

First published in 2008 by
Quadrille Publishing Limited
www.quadrille.co.uk

Design and layout © 2008
Quadrille Publishing Limited
Photography © 2008 Christian Sarramon
Text © 2008 Stafford Cliff

The rights of the author have been asserted.
All rights reserved. No part of this book may be reproduced, stored in a retrieval system or transmitted in any form or by any means, electronic, electrostatic, magnetic tape, mechanical, photocopying, recording or otherwise, without the prior permission in writing of the publisher.

1000 home ideas
ホームデザインブック

発　　　行　2010年 7月15日
発　行　者　平野　陽三
発　行　元　ガイアブックス
　　　　　　〒169-0074 東京都新宿区北新宿3-14-8
　　　　　　TEL.03(3366)1411　FAX.03(3366)3503
　　　　　　http://www.gaiajapan.co.jp
発　売　元　産調出版株式会社

Copyright SUNCHOH SHUPPAN INC. JAPAN2010
ISBN978-4-88282-749-8 C3052

落丁本・乱丁本はお取り替えいたします。
本書を許可なく複製することは、かたくお断わりします。
Printed in China

著　者：スタッフォード・クリフ（Stafford Cliff）
ロンドンを拠点にデザイン・コンサルタント、アート・ディレクターとして活動。長年、住宅関連のパンフレット、カタログ、雑誌の、デザインと執筆を行ってきた。テレンス・コンラン卿との、住宅カタログの制作を経て、1974年『The House Book』のデザインを担当。ロングセラーとなる。以降、デザイン、住宅関連書を60冊以上制作。主な作品に、世界中で行った住宅の調査結果を、480ページにまとめた、『The Way We live』、住まいに対する人々の意識をテーマに取り上げた草分け的な書、『Home』。近著に、『ダイニングキッチンブック』（産調出版）がある。

写　真：クリスチャン・サラモン（Christian Sarramon）
フランス人写真家。30年以上にわたって世界をめぐり、目を見張るようなアイデア豊富なキッチンを、カメラに収め続けている。

翻　訳：今井由美子（いまい　ゆみこ）
広島女学院大学英米文学科卒業。訳書に『自宅の緑化インテリア』『自宅の書棚』『ダイニングキッチンブック』（いずれも産調出版）など多数。